RAMESH SHASTRY
BELL—NORTHERN RESEARCH
OTTAWA, CANADA

PRACTICAL APPROACHES TO SPEECH CODING

**Prentice-Hall and Texas Instruments
Digital Signal Processors Series**

JONES/PARKS, *A Digital Signal Processing Laboratory Using the TMS32010* (1987)

PAPAMICHALIS, *Practical Approaches to Speech Coding* (1987)

TEXAS INSTRUMENTS, *Digital Signal Processing Applications with the TMS320 Family*, Volume 1 (1987)

TEXAS INSTRUMENTS, *First-Generation TMS320 User's Guide* (1987)

TEXAS INSTRUMENTS, *Second-Generation TMS320 User's Guide* (future)

TEXAS INSTRUMENTS, *Digital Signal Processing Applicants with the TMS320 Family Volume 2* (future)

PRACTICAL APPROACHES TO SPEECH CODING

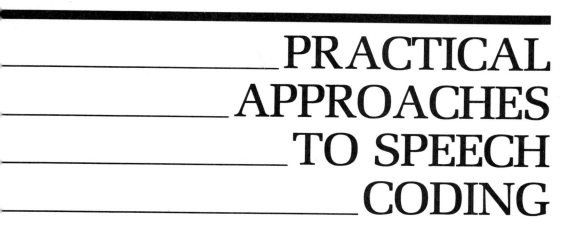

Panos E. Papamichalis
Texas Instruments, Inc.
Rice University

Prentice-Hall, Inc.
Englewood Cliffs, New Jersey

Prentice-Hall International, Inc., *London*
Prentice-Hall of Australia, Pty. Ltd., *Sydney*
Prentice-Hall Canada, Inc., *Toronto*
Prentice-Hall of India Private Ltd., *New Delhi*
Prentice-Hall of Japan, Inc., *Tokyo*
Prentice-Hall of Southeast Asia Pte. Ltd., *Singapore*
Editora Prentice-Hall do Brasil Ltda., *Rio de Janeiro*
Prentice-Hall Hispanoamericana, S.A., *Mexico*

© 1987 by

PRENTICE-HALL, INC.

Englewood Cliffs, N.J.

Library of Congress Cataloging-in-Publication Data

Papamichalis, Panos E.
　Practical approaches to speech coding.

　Bibliography: p.
　Includes index.
　1. Speech processing systems.　2. Vocoder.
I. Title.
TK7882.S65P36　1987　　006.5'4　　86-22525

ISBN　0-13-689019-8

Printed in the United States of America

Preface

Speech coding may be defined as a digital representation of the speech sound that provides efficient storage, transmission, recovery, and perceptually faithful reconstruction of the original speech. In other words, coding compresses the speech sound for digital storage and expands or decompresses the stored data to reconstruct the original sound without significant loss of quality. Digital storage also means the convenience of transmitting speech as a digital data file over any data network. From a transmission viewpoint, digital speech data transmission is relatively insensitive to noise, crosstalk, and distortion. However, we cannot expect to store, say, a second of speech in a very small amount of memory and reproduce speech that is of the same quality as the original.

Obviously, trade-offs exist and must be evaluated in integrating such technology with application systems. Such a task is very difficult and requires a clear understanding of all available speech coding methods and devices. The goal of this book is to provide the reader with this clear conceptual understanding along with some practical tools by exposing him to the various significant speech coding techniques in a logically organized manner.

Many examples of systems that integrate or utilize speech coding technology abound in the consumer and industrial market place. These systems have been made possible by the significant advances in semiconductor technology that has been a catalyst for the advancement of speech coding techniques. We can classify the many speech coder applications into two categories: Voice Response Systems, and Voice Store and Forward (VSF) Systems (which also include digital speech communication systems). Texas Instruments' Speak & Spell™ learning aid is an excellent example of a voice response system. Such systems have some fixed set of spoken material stored in a coded form and retrieved under command of the operator or a host computer or controller. The Speak & Spell learning aid pioneered the application of an advanced speech coding scheme called Linear Prediction Coding (LPC) to achieve very large data compression. A basic unit of Speak & Spell requires less than 1,200 bits of ROM for every second of speech. The simplest form of storing this vocabulary would be to digitize the speech waveform by means of an analog-to-digital converter (A/D), but would have required a ROM size of at least 64K bits for every second of speech. Examples of other voice response systems include talking copiers, cash registers, microwave ovens, and Chrysler's cars with speech warning systems instructing the driver to wear seat belts.

The Speech Command System (SCS) available on the Texas Instruments and the IBM PC includes another application of speech coding using the LPC technique. Real-time spoken input is stored as a coded digital file that can be forwarded to another person on a PC data network as a standard digital file. Upon reception he can listen to the digital file using his SCS on the PC. Such an application is popularly known as a Voice Store and Forward (VSF) system. Other VSF systems employing various speech coding techniques are provided by a number of companies like Wang, VMX, and so on.

Speech coders for another type of application are the digital speech communication systems, such as Marconi's Belgard vocoders and Time and Space Processing, Inc.'s TSP-100 vocoder. The main difference between digital speech communication and VSF is that the former is mainly a simultaneous real-time operation of coding and decoding, while in the latter, decoding takes place at a later point in time after coding. We note that many VSF systems are indeed capable of such real-time operation, but are not widely used as a real-time communication system. VSF is a typical office automation concept, where simultaneous real-time compression and expansion of speech are generally not required.

This book is written for the application engineer who has a need to integrate a speech subsystem in his product and needs to perform the quality vs. cost trade-off, do the complexity and reliability assessment, and other such tasks. It will also help him specify the requirements for his application in a meaningful and realistic manner. Another audience group is the home/personal/professional computer hobbyist with enough technical background who would like to incorporate some simple voice input-output capability on his machine. This book also provides that one place where many speech researchers and scientists can readily find a wealth of coding methods accompanied by a list of references. We are not interested in bogging the reader down in obscure mathematics, and chose to develop the various concepts and methods by means of simple reasoning, appeal of block diagrams, and using only the necessary mathematics, although exposure to systems concepts and digital signal processing would be very beneficial.

This book presents many practical approaches to speech coding. Various state-of-the-art techniques are grouped in a logical manner in the presentation to provide a clear understanding of the common principles involved. Chapter 1 introduces some tools of analysis and some basic material needed in developing and using speech coding systems. Chapter 2 describes how the statistical behavior of the amplitude and the temporal evolution (correlation) of the speech waveform can be used efficiently for coding. The use of the spectrum of the speech signal as an alternative means of waveform representation is discussed in Chapter 3. Then, Chapter 4 addresses the important methods of vocoding as an efficient way of representing the spectral information contained in the speech signal. The current state-of-the-art technique of Linear Prediction Coding (LPC) is developed in Chapter 5. A significant portion of the book is devoted to LPC because of the many practical systems that utilize the concept, and because a number of low-cost commercial devices are available. It is also the most practical and efficient way of obtaining a very high data compression without losing significant intelligibility.

The coding techniques described in Chapters 4 and 5 often require information about the speech source such as voicing and pitch. Chapter 6 focuses on the importance of such information and presents techniques of obtaining such information. Given that a number of coding techniques can adequately perform a speech representation task, how do we go about choosing the one that is superior? Unfortunately, a clear answer does not always exist. There are many measures of performance, none completely satisfactory, that can be used as guidelines. Such performance evaluation of speech coders is discussed in Chapter 7, where both objective and subjective measures are presented. In Chapter 8, we discuss some of the available speech and speech-related integrated circuit devices and their applications to practical systems, although pertinent applications are also discussed in the appropriate sections. Several systems are described in enough detail to bring out the way in which many techniques developed in the book are utilized.

Besides the aspects of automatic speech processing presented in this book, there are many other interesting aspects, such as voice recognition and speech enhancement, that are not discussed here. However, the analysis techniques we outline in the following chapters are common to all areas of speech processing, therefore giving the reader insight and background for venturing into other areas. With the practical information presented in the book, readers will be able to effectively use the speech coding techniques in their own applications. This will be my best reward.

Panos E. Papamichalis

___Acknowledgments

Many people contributed, directly or indirectly, to the creation of this book. The strongest influence came from Dr. P. K. (Raja) Rajasekaran, Senior Member of Technical Staff at Texas Instruments, who has been of constant moral support and inspiration. Our lengthy discussions on general and technical matters shaped my way of thinking and acting. Raja's friendship has been intellectually rewarding and a strong stimulus in the writing of this book.

Another strong influence has come from Dr. George R. Doddington, Chief Speech Scientist at Texas Instruments. I owe to him many of my technical abilities and insights into speech processing. He has always been an example of a dedicated researcher, and I am grateful for the support he provided during the writing of the book.

Mr. Gene Frantz and Dr. Kun Lin, both Senior Members of Technical Staff at TI, made particularly useful comments and suggestions on the manuscript. The careful review of the book by Dr. Joseph Picone and Messrs. J. Reimer, G. Troullinos, and A. Lovrich was very helpful in improving the presentation of many topics while Ms. Maridene Lemmon went carefully through the text to correct my many language errors. Finally, I acknowledge the permission of Texas Instruments Incorporated to include one of its applications reports as an appendix in this book.

Contents

2 STATIC AND DYNAMIC STRATEGIES FOR CODING THE SPEECH WAVEFORM *17*

3 EFFICIENT CODING USING THE SPEECH SPECTRUM *59*

4 EFFICIENT CODING USING ANALYSIS-SYNTHESIS *87*

Chapter 1

Speech Coding Tools: An Introduction

This chapter presents a general overview of the subject of speech coding in order to introduce you to this fascinating subject. Some general issues are addressed, and attention is focused on signal processing topics, such as sampling, and analog-to-digital and digital-to-analog conversion, which are common to all speech coding methods. Development tools for speech processing are also presented.

1.1 GENERAL CONSIDERATION OF SPEECH CODING

Speech has always been the main medium of communication between humans, and it has been extensively studied for its form and content. With the advent of the computer age, considerable interest was attracted on

- man–machine communication by voice, and
- effective communication between humans through a computer.

In the previous list, the key word is "effective." By computer manipulation of human speech, it is possible to

- compress it so that more conversations are carried over the same communications channel,
- enhance degraded speech to increase intelligibility, and
- encrypt the speech to ensure secure communication.

The man–machine communication by voice is a newer subject and has the objectives (as do all automation applications) of relieving human operators from boring tasks and reducing the operation costs by using a very undemanding mechanical "slave." There are also instances where response from a machine can be faster and more accurate than a human operator, as is the case in searching through large data bases for information and then supplying the answers. The environment where the man–machine communication by voice makes most sense is when the interaction takes place over the telephone, but it is also needed in "eyes-busy, hands-busy" applications.

The man–machine communication by voice has two aspects:

1. Speech input (i.e., speech and/or speaker recognition)
2. Speech output (i.e., speech coding/synthesis)

Speech input is a fascinating and challenging problem, and the subject of extensive current research. Considerable progress has been made, but until now the advances have not been sufficient to apply such technology in "real" applications where this functionality is really needed. An example of a desirable speech input application is speech recognition over a telephone line to be used in critical tasks, such as fund transfer. However, the subject of speech recognition has intrigued so many researchers that the fruits of all that effort may not be far away. Speech input is beyond the scope of this book but you can find useful information in the many excellent references found at the end of each chapter. (Bracketed numbers in text correspond to these references.)

Speech output from a machine is a better-understood subject and involves a more mature part of the speech technology. Of course, difficult problems still remain, like the treacherous subject of pitch tracking, but even with these limitations, speech output has found enough applications to demonstrate its utility.

Speech coding is a subject that includes not only the speech output from machines, but also the part of communication between humans that involves speech compression. Depending on the application, it is distinguished in

- voice response
- voice store-and-forward

The main difference between voice response and voice store-and-forward is the real-time requirement for speech analysis. In voice response, this is not necessary, and the speech material can be manually edited to achieve the desired level of bit rate and quality. In voice store-and-forward, on the other hand, both analysis and synthesis have to be done in real time, and correction of errors (for instance, of the pitch tracker) is not permitted.

Voice response supposes that speech has been analyzed and stored in the computer, and, when it is needed, it is synthesized and played back. Applications using these techniques are speaking toys with a well-defined vocabulary, warning systems in automobiles and trains, and so forth. In most cases, the whole data base of the needed speech material is processed and stored. However, if there is a need for a large or frequently varying vocabulary, this solution is not very practicable. It then becomes necessary to use constructive speech synthesis (also called synthesis-by-rule, or text-to-speech, or, simply, speech synthesis).

In constructive synthesis, we store the phonological elements of the language, which can be phonemes or allophones. When you are given a text to convert into speech, the text is first transcribed to a sequence of phonetic symbols. These phonetic symbols select the stored phonological elements to be concatenated and produce the synthetic speech. To convert the text into the phonetic symbols, extensive knowledge of the linguistic structure of the language and underlying rules is needed. Constructive synthesis depends heavily on the field of linguistics which is beyond the scope of this book. (Refer to [1–3] for more information on the subject.) In any case, the necessary information for analyzing and storing the phonological elements can be found in the coding methods of this book.

Under the subject of store-and-forward applications, we can classify not only man–machine communication, but also communication between humans where the speech signal is processed by the computer. The large store-and-forward systems, using mainframe computers and big storage capacities, belong to this category, but personal computers, equipped with appropriate hardware and telephone management capabilities, are also included. In the same category we include processing of speech signals to be transmitted over the digital transmission lines of the telephone companies.

Figure 1.1 shows a block diagram of the different speech processing applications, as described in this section. The rest of the book presents speech coding techniques to be used in the different applications, depending on the desired features of the application.

1.2 A ROAD MAP OF THE BOOK

The primary intent of the book is to be used as a reference of the different speech coding techniques that have been proved to work satisfactorily. Hence, the different chapters (and sections) can be read to a large extent independently of each other. The suggested way is to start from the section of interest, and read additional sections as the need arises. Figure 1.2 shows a possible map of dependencies between the different chapters. If you are interested in getting familiar with the whole field of speech coding, then a sequential reading of the book is recommended.

1.3 DIGITAL SPEECH: BIT RATE VERSUS QUALITY

In digital processing of speech signals, we have two conflicting requirements: First, we want to achieve the lowest possible bit rate. Second, we want to achieve this with minimum loss in speech quality. Satisfaction of these two requirements is the purpose of the

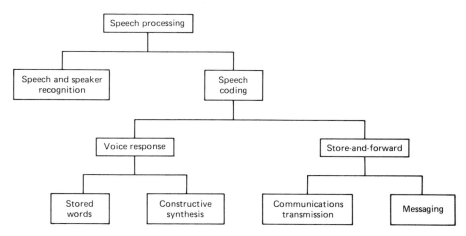

Figure 1.1 Block diagram of different types of speech processing.

ongoing research in speech coding, and the subject of all the speech algorithms in this book. Figure 1.3 shows the different bit rates in a one-dimensional scale, and an approximate designation of the speech quality that can be achieved at the different bit rates.

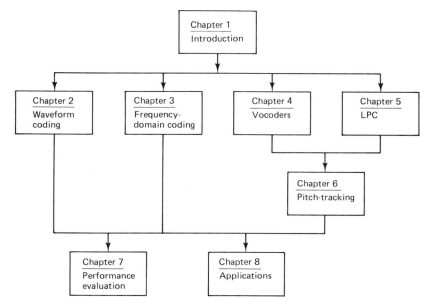

Figure 1.2 Suggested reading sequence of the book.

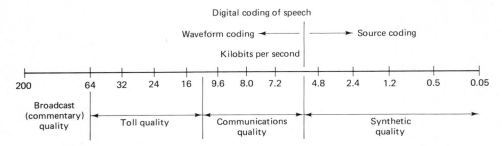

Figure 1.3 Spectrum of speech coding transmission rates in nonlinear scale and associated quality (after Flanagan et al. [4], © 1979 IEEE).

Figure 1.4 presents similar information in a two-dimensional diagram, where you can see how the best quality from the different speech coding techniques compares at each bit rate. Of course, the diagram is qualitative, but it still gives a rough idea of the speech quality expected from each system.

As you might expect, in order to achieve the best possible speech quality while reducing the bit rate, it becomes necessary to use more and more sophisticated algorithms. "Sophistication," in this context, implies longer computer programs, heavier computational load, and consequently, longer execution time. Table 1.1 shows a (qualitative) comparison of the complexity of several systems, some of which are discussed in later chapters.

The suggested trade-offs between bit rates, speech quality, and algorithm complexity are the concern of the system designer. Questions should be asked, such as:

- What level of speech quality loss is acceptable?
- What are the constraints on the storage or transmission capacity in bits per second (bits/s)?
- What are the real-time capabilities, required board area, and power consumption of the available hardware?
- What is an acceptable system cost?

For commercial applications, the last question is usually the determining factor in the final choice. In most cases there is no unique or unambiguous answer to these questions. The designer's experi-

TABLE 1.1 RELATIVE COMPLEXITY OF SPEECH CODING ALGORITHMS. THE COMPLEXITY IS ESSENTIALLY A RELATIVE COUNT OF LOGIC GATES. FOR COMPARISON, LOG PCM FALLS IN THE RANGE 1–5.

Relative Complexity		Coder
1	ADM:	adaptive delta modulator
1	ADPCM:	adaptive differential PCM
5	SUB-BAND:	sub-band coder (with CCD filters)
5	P-P ADPCM:	pitch-predictive ADPCM
50	APC:	adaptive predictive coder
50	ATC:	adaptive transform coder
50	ϕV:	phase vocoder
50	VEV:	voice-excited vocoder
100	LPC:	linear-predictive coefficient (vocoder)
100	CV:	channel vocoder
200	ORTHOG:	LPC vocoder with orthogonalized coefficients
500	FORMANT:	formant vocoder
1000	ARTICULATORY:	vocal-tract synthesizer; synthesis from printed English text.

(after Flanagan et al. [4], © 1979 IEEE).

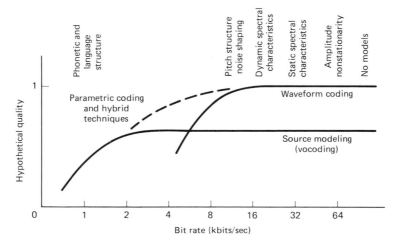

Figure 1.4 Quality vs. bit rate for speech coding techniques (after Crochiere and Flanagan [5], © 1983 IEEE).

ence and taste, as well as the application-dependent constraints, will suggest the solution.

1.4 SOME CONSIDERATIONS IN SPEECH DIGITIZATION

In the past, some of the speech coding techniques (for instance, the channel vocoder) were implemented with analog hardware. In recent years, as the computer and the VLSI technologies advance, practically all the speech coding methods have become digital. In this book, it is assumed that you start from a digital signal and then process it in order to achieve the desired results. Now let's examine briefly some aspects of speech digitization. (More information on digitization can be found in [6–8].)

Using a Fourier transform, any signal can be analyzed into a possibly infinite number of sinusoids, which, when added together, reconstruct the original signal. In the frequency domain, a sinusoid is represented by a single line, whose amplitude equals the amplitude of the sinusoid. Figure 1.5 shows the frequency spectrum of an idealized signal consisting of a finite number of sinusoids.

Each sinusoid, as the one in Figure 1.6a, can be completely represented by isolated samples, if these samples are taken frequently enough (Figure 1.6b). Actually, for a sinusoid it suffices to have two samples for every period, as shown in Figure 1.6c. In other words, a sinusoid can be reconstructed from its samples if the sampling rate is *at least* twice the frequency of the sinusoid. This sampling rate is a very important parameter, and it is called the *Nyquist rate*.

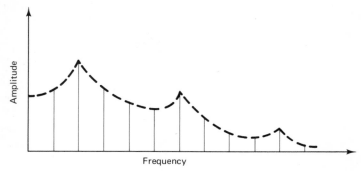

Figure 1.5   Frequency spectrum of a signal.

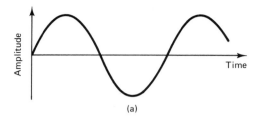

(a)

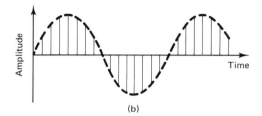

(b)

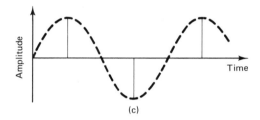

(c)

Figure 1.6 (a) Analog sinusoidal signal; (b) digital conversion of (a); (c) the signal of (a) is sampled at the Nyquist rate (after Lin and Frantz [9], © 1982 IEEE).

The Nyquist rate is sufficient for the reconstruction of a sinusoid, but what about a more complicated signal, like speech, comprising many sinusoids? In this case, the sampling rate must be high enough to represent accurately even the highest frequency sinusoid present in the signal. In other words, the sampling frequency of a signal has to be at least twice the highest frequency present in the signal. For instance, if you have a speech signal with frequency content between 0 and 4 kHz, the sampling frequency, F_s, has to be

$$F_s = 2 \times 4 \text{ kHz} = 8,000 \text{ samples/s}$$

or more. To save storage, you can usually sample the signals at this minimum rate (the Nyquist rate) necessary for the accurate reconstruction of the speech signal.

If the above sampling rule is violated, then you have the phenomenon of aliasing, which is shown in Figure 1.7. The sinusoid in solid line is sampled less frequently than twice its frequency. Then, if you try to reconstruct the signal from the samples, you actually get the sinusoid in broken line, which has a lower frequency. The result is that the higher frequency sinusoid is interpreted as a lower frequency one (i.e., it takes a different identity, hence the name aliasing), which causes audible distortion.

Viewing it another way, if the sampling rate is predetermined, you need to eliminate any frequencies above half the Nyquist frequency by filtering, in order to avoid aliasing. In most speech coding applications, the highest frequency and the sampling rate are determined from the characteristics of the telephone network. The bandwidth of the telephone lines is between 300 and 3,300 Hz, and therefore, the most often-used sampling rate is 8 kHz (8,000 samples/s).

The sampled signal needs to be quantized to a finite number of values so that it can be represented by a finite number of digits in a computer. The quantizer, discussed in Chapter 2, can be an 11–16 bit linear quantizer or a 7–11 bit nonlinear quantizer (codec, see also Chapter 8). The lowpass filtering, sampling, and quantization operations, shown in Figure 1.8, are usually grouped under the name of analog-to-digital (A/D) conversion. They are performed in the same device (with the possible exception of the filtering).

At the other end, when speech has been processed and you want to reconstruct the analog signal, you employ digital-to-analog (D/A) conversion. It consists of a sample-and-hold circuit followed by a lowpass filter, as shown in Figure 1.9.

The use of the appropriate A/D converter can be a very important factor in the performance of the speech coding algorithm, since a crude quantization or an aliased signal supply a distorted input. Of course, it would be desirable to have the best filtering and the

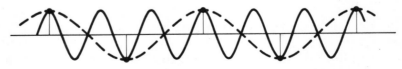

Figure 1.7 Aliasing when the sampling frequency is below the Nyquist rate.

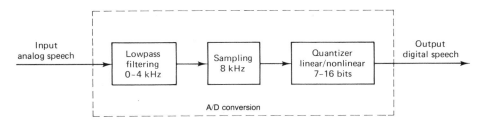

Figure 1.8 Block diagram of the analog-to-digital converter. The operations have been split into different blocks for conceptual simplification.

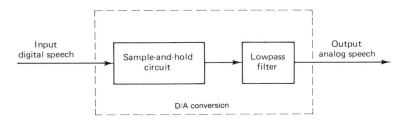

Figure 1.9 Block diagram of a digital-to-analog conversion.

highest possible precision in a linear quantizer, but economic considerations often force the designer to make compromises.

1.5 DEVELOPMENT TOOLS

In developing and implementing speech coding algorithms, it becomes necessary to evaluate the successive steps of development. Algorithmic deficiencies or programming bugs then can be identified and corrected. All the debugging tools for software development can be used here, but in addition, some tools that are pertinent to the processing of speech signals are required.

These tools are visual and audio. It is very important to be able to look at both the time and frequency behavior of the speech signal in order to identify any peculiar features that should be investigated further. Hence, a graphics capability is recommended. By examining the waveform (e.g., see Figure 1.10), among other things, you can get information about the periodicity of the signal that depends on its voiced or unvoiced nature. The corresponding spec-

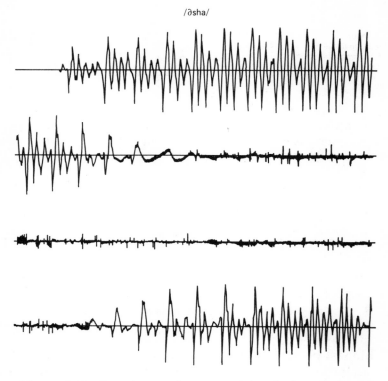

Figure 1.10 Speech waveform containing both voiced and unvoiced segments (word /əsha/) (L.R. Rabiner, R.W. Schafer [8], *Digital Processing of Speech Signals*, © 1978. Reprinted by permission of Prentice-Hall, Inc., Englewood Cliffs, NJ.).

trum (Figure 1.11) shows the frequency content of the speech signal. This information includes the resonances (formants) of the vocal tract and the possible harmonic content.

A very useful tool in speech processing is the spectrogram, described in more detail in Chapter 3. Figure 1.12 shows a spectrogram of a sentence. The abscissa of the plot is time, the ordinate is frequency, while the darkness indicates amplitude (higher amplitudes are represented by darker areas). The spectrogram gives very important information, since it displays the time dynamics of the frequency spectrum. The darker stripes show the movement of the natural frequencies of the human vocal tract (which are also called formants). These movements, together with the frequency content,

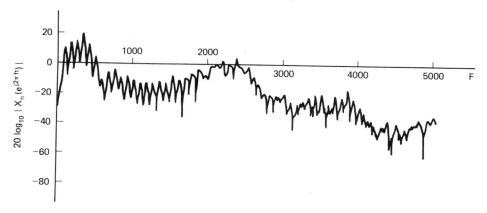

Figure 1.11   Log-spectrum of the voiced portion of a speech signal (L.R. Rabiner, R.W. Schafer [8], *Digital Processing of Speech Signals,* © 1978. Reprinted by permission of Prentice-Hall, Inc., Englewood Cliffs, NJ.).

are characteristic of the different elements of the language, such as vowels and consonants.

Audio tools are of paramount importance in speech coding development because what looks good does not always sound good! Despite considerable effort, as discussed in Chapter 7, no good objective measures have been found to assess the speech quality by applying some mathematical function to the signal. Instead, it is always necessary to listen to the speech processing results and, for an objective evaluation, even to conduct formal listening tests. In order to conduct formal or informal listening tests, it is required to have an interface to the analog world. In the past, this interface was implemented in house by the speech researchers. However, as the interest for speech processing spreads, appropriate interface systems are marketed by various companies. For instance, the Digital

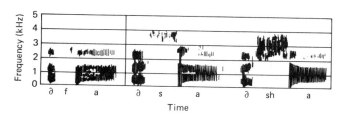

Figure 1.12   Spectrogram of the words /əfa/, /əsa/, /əsha/ (L.R. Rabiner, R.W. Schafer [8], *Digital Processing of Speech Signals,* © 1978. Reprinted by permission of Prentice-Hall, Inc., Englewood Cliffs, NJ.).

Sound Corp. (DSC) markets the DSC-200 audio data conversion system for speech input and output.

Other board-level products have been also introduced for personal computers, such as the ASPI (Atlanta Signal Processors, Inc.) board. These products are typically associated with some programmable digital signal processor (for instance, the ASPI board uses the Texas Instruments TMS32010 digital signal processor) and they can be used for development of algorithms targeted for that processor. If using such processors is the intention of the designer, these boards represent an excellent solution.

On the software level, whole packages are being developed to help the designer of speech systems with needed functions. This saves the designer the effort to develop all the software from scratch. One of the best known software packages is the Interactive Laboratory System (ILS) marketed by Signal Technology, Inc. The ILS consists of a large number of programs designed around a standardized set of speech files. The programs perform a number of functions applicable to speech analysis, synthesis, and recognition. The package was originally designed to be used with larger computers, but more recently versions have been developed for personal computers too. Another software package with very convenient features is the SPIRE system, developed at the Massachusetts Institute of Technology.

With all these tools, the developer of speech coding systems can develop, test, and implement a system with the minimum amount of trouble and in quite a short time.

1.6 FURTHER READING

This book assumes a working knowledge of digital signal processing. The two basic references that supply the necessary background information are the books by Oppenheim and Schafer [6], and by Rabiner and Gold [7]. Since the purpose of this book is to supply practical information about implementing speech algorithms, most of the theoretical and mathematical justification of the different techniques has been avoided. This kind of information can be found in the excellent books by Rabiner and Schafer [8], and by Jayant and Noll [10]. The book by Flanagan [11] contains very useful information but it is somewhat dated. The paper by Flanagan et al. [4] is also an excellent overview of the field of speech coding.

The IEEE Press collections of papers edited by Jayant [12] and by Schafer and Markel [13] contain very important contributions to the speech coding field, although at a theoretical level. Also at the theoretical level, the most current contributions can be found in the *IEEE Transactions on Acoustics, Speech, and Signal Processing (ASSP)*, and in the annual *Proceedings of the International Conference on ASSP (ICASSP)*. The magazines *Signal Processing* and *Speech Communication*, published by North Holland, contain information on the same level. On a more practical level, *Speech Technology* magazine (published by Media Dimensions, Inc.) contains interesting articles and information on speech businesses and products.

If you are interested in speech recognition, you will find pertinent information in the books by Dixon and Martin [14], and by Lea [15]. The books by Flanagan and Rabiner [1], Bristow [2], and Witten [3] contain extensive descriptions of constructive synthesis systems.

1.7 REFERENCES

1. Flanagan, J.L., and L.R. Rabiner, Eds. *Speech Synthesis*. Stroudsburg, PA: Dowden, Hutchinson & Ross, 1973.

2. Bristow, G., Ed. *Electronic Speech Synthesis*. New York: Granada, 1984.

3. Witten, I.H. *Principles of Computer Speech*. New York: Academic Press, 1982.

4. Flanagan, J.L., M.R. Schroeder, B.S. Atal, R.E. Crochiere, N.S. Jayant, and J.M. Tribolet. "Speech Coding." *IEEE Trans. on Comm.*, Vol. COM-27, No. 4 (April 1979): 710–737.

5. Crochiere, R.E., and J.L. Flanagan. "Current Perspectives in Digital Speech." *IEEE Comm. Magazine* (January 1983): 32–40.

6. Oppenheim, A.V., and R.W. Schafer. *Digital Signal Processing*. Englewood Cliffs, NJ: Prentice-Hall, 1975.

7. Rabiner, L.R., and B. Gold. *Theory and Applications of Digital Signal Processing*. Englewood Cliffs, NJ: Prentice-Hall, 1975.

8. Rabiner, L.R. and R. W. Schafer. *Digital Processing of Speech Signals.* Englewood Cliffs, NJ: Prentice-Hall, 1978.

9. Lin, K.S., and G.A. Frantz. "Speech Technology in Medicine." *Applications of Computers in Medicine,* IEEE publication No. TH0095-0 (1982): 2–16.

10. Jayant, N.S., and P. Noll. *Digital Coding of Waveforms.* Englewood Cliffs, NJ: Prentice-Hall, 1984.

11. Flanagan, J.L. *Speech Analysis Synthesis and Perception,* Second Ed. New York: Springer-Verlag, 1972.

12. Jayant, N.S., Ed. *Waveform Quantization and Coding.* New York: IEEE Press, 1976.

13. Schafer, R.W., and J.D. Markel. *Speech Analysis.* New York: IEEE Press, 1979.

14. Dixon, N.R., and T.B. Martin, Eds. *Automatic Speech and Speaker Recognition.* New York: IEEE Press, 1979.

15. Lea, W.A. *Trends in Speech Recognition.* Englewood Cliffs, NJ: Prentice-Hall, 1980.

Chapter 2

Static and Dynamic Strategies for Coding the Speech Waveform

When talking about encoding the speech signal, the simplest approach that comes to mind is to use the time waveform for the digital representation of speech. This chapter investigates different coding techniques based on the speech time waveform.

Since speech is represented digitally and only a finite number of symbols can be assigned to each sample, it follows that we need to sample the signal and then quantize it to a finite number of levels. Figure 2.1 shows the steps involved at the front end (transmitter) and the back end (receiver) of the system. After the signal has been sampled at a rate of F_s samples/s, which is at least twice the highest frequency of the signal, it is processed to achieve a digital representation. Then it is encoded and transmitted. The

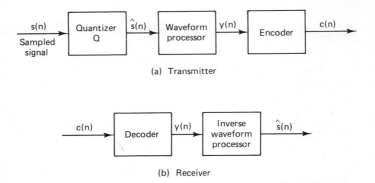

Figure 2.1   Waveform processing and coding; (a) transmitter (b) receiver.

encoder assigns labels (codewords) to the samples, so that the codewords rather than the actual values are transmitted. Very often, two or even all three stages of Figure 2.1 are implemented in one unit, but they are separated here for ease of presentation. Where necessary, they will be recombined in the presentation.

This chapter investigates methods of encoding the speech waveform efficiently. It starts with separate quantization of each speech sample and then proceeds to examine differential quantization. The differential quantization has the advantage of removing a large part of the redundancy that is inherent in the speech signal. In differential quantization, an estimate of the speech signal is subtracted from the actual signal and the resulting difference is quantized and transmitted. The computation of the signal estimate can be more accurate and complex or simpler and less accurate. One of the simplest implementations is the Delta Modulation, which is also studied in this chapter.

All these quantization techniques can be implemented either statically or dynamically. Static implementations remain fixed over time and do not try to adapt to the changing characteristics of the speech signal. On the other hand, dynamic strategies of waveform coding involve adaptation of the system based on the characteristics of the signal. As might be expected, adaptive methods give better performance. The price paid is an increased bit rate (because the adaptation must be conveyed to the receiver) and/or increased complexity of the system. Such techniques are the Adaptive Differential *PCM* (ADPCM) and the Adaptive Predictive Coding (APC).

Two more techniques examined in this chapter are the Mozer coding method and the *Time-Domain Harmonic Scaling* (TDHS). The Mozer coding method utilizes the knowledge that the signal being processed is speech, in order to reduce the required bit rate. The basic concepts used for that purpose are also encountered in analysis-synthesis methods (Chapters 4 and 5) but Mozer coding applies them in the time domain. The time-domain harmonic scaling uses the observation that, in voiced speech, the signal is periodic and the basic period is repeated several times with little variability. Data compression is then achieved by compressing two consecutive periods into one. Mozer coding and TDHS are smart techniques in the sense that they use information based on the nature of the signal.

2.1 QUANTIZATION

After the speech signal is sampled, it is quantized in order to be represented in digital form with a finite number of digits (bits). By increasing or decreasing the number of quantization bits, the bit rate and the speech quality are correspondingly increased or decreased. This section examines quantization methods that permit reduced bit rate without distorting the speech signal.

The uniform quantization, which is discussed first, is the most basic approach with a very simple implementation. Going one step further in sophistication, the logarithmic quantization is introduced. The logarithmic quantization reduces the necessary number of bits for the same speech quality, but it introduces nonlinearities. Finally, the Max algorithm and the maximum entropy quantization are presented. These two methods use the information on the statistical distribution of the signal to achieve bit-rate reduction.

2.1.1 UNIFORM QUANTIZATION

The simplest method of coding the speech waveform is to simply quantize it and transmit the quantized (and coded) samples. Quantization is used to represent the signal with only a finite number of amplitudes while coding is the assignment of labels to the quantization levels. This is known as *Pulse Code Modulation* (PCM). In this case, the waveform processor and inverse waveform processor do not perform any function and they can be removed, so that $y(n) = \hat{s}(n)$. Figure 2.2 shows the special case where Δ is the quantizer stepsize. Figure 2.3 describes the process of quantization: All the values of s between s_1 and s_2 are represented by (quantized to) $\hat{s}_2$, all values between s_2 and s_3 are quantized to $\hat{s}_3$, and so forth. In this example,

$$s_{i+1} - s_i = \Delta \qquad (2.1)$$

and

$$\hat{s}_{i+1} - \hat{s}_i = \Delta \qquad (2.2)$$

The quantization stepsize is Δ and the quantizer is called a *uniform quantizer*. Figure 2.4 shows an alternate representation for an eight-level quantizer. Notice that s is assumed to take values symmetrically around zero, and one of the quantization levels is chosen to be zero. This is called a midtread quantizer. Figure 2.5 shows another possibility, called the midriser quantizer, where the quantization levels do not include zero. Our discussion will consider

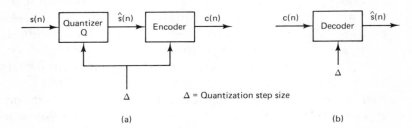

(a)   (b)

Figure 2.2   Quantization and coding; (a) coder (b) decoder.

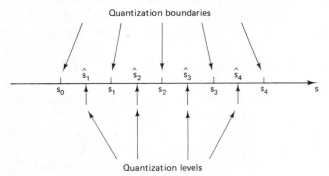

Figure 2.3   Four-level quantizer.

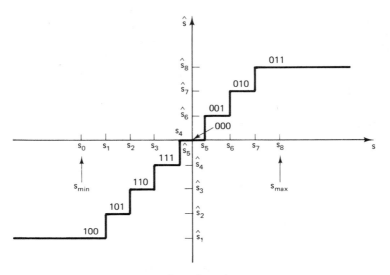

Figure 2.4 Midtread uniform quantizer.

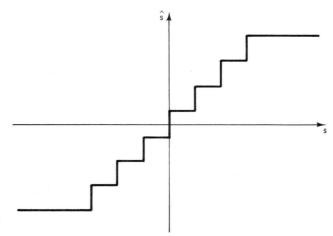

Figure 2.5 Midriser uniform
quantizer.

only the first case. Returning to Figure 2.4, notice that codewords with three bits represent the eight levels of the quantizer. The assignment of the codewords $c(n)$ to the quantization levels can be arbitrary. However, we have chosen to arrange them in a way that corresponds to two's-complement representation, so they can be processed by digital processors, most of which use this representation. Then, the decoder has a very simple structure given by

$$\hat{s}(n) = \Delta \times c(n) \qquad (2.3)$$

A figure of merit used very often to compare waveform coding systems is the Signal-to-quantization-Noise Ratio (SNR). The SNR is defined as the ratio of the AC signal energy to the AC noise energy, and is given by

$$SNR = \frac{\sum\limits_{n} s^2(n)}{\sum\limits_{n} e^2(n)} \qquad (2.4)$$

where the summation extends over the samples of a speech segment. The variable $e(n)$ is the quantization error defined by

$$e(n) = \hat{s}(n) - s(n) \qquad (2.5)$$

In the above expression for the SNR, we assume that the average value of both $s(n)$ and $e(n)$ over that speech segment is zero. If it is not, then we must subtract the mean values of s and e from $s(n)$ and $e(n)$ before the squaring and the summation.

Since we want to represent the quantization levels with codewords B bits long, we use quantizers with 2^B quantization levels. It can be shown [1] that under certain conditions, the SNR of a quantizer expressed in dB is given by

$$SNR \text{ (dB)} = 6B - 7.2 \qquad (2.6)$$

In other words, for every bit we add (which doubles the number of quantization levels), we gain 6 dB.

One of the conditions for the derivation of the formula of SNR is that we set the maximum value of the quantizer at $s_{max} = 4\sigma_s$ where σ_s^2 is the variance of the signal. You can estimate σ_s^2 by

$$\sigma_s^2 = \frac{1}{N} \sum_{n=1}^{N} (s(n) - \bar{s})^2 \qquad (2.7)$$

(usually we assume that the average value $\bar{s} = 0$). Another simplifying assumption is

$$s_{min} = -s_{max} \qquad (2.8)$$

Variables s_{min} and s_{max} correspond to s_0 and s_4 in Figure 2.3. Since we set $s_{max} = 4\sigma_s$, computation of the variance σ_s^2 over a long speech record can give us the value we need to design the quantizer.

2.1.2 LOGARITHMIC QUANTIZATION

A problem with the uniform quantizer is that the speech signal changes with time and the variance σ_s^2 can be quite different from one speech segment to another. If the quantizer is designed to accommodate strong signals with large σ_s^2 (like vowels), the quantization stepsize will be large and weaker signals (like consonants) will demonstrate a larger quantization error, which impacts the speech quality. To solve this problem, we abandon the uniform quantizer and design a quantizer whose stepsize increases with the signal amplitude. More precisely, the uniform quantizer now operates on the logarithm of the speech signal, which is a compressed version of the signal. Then, the signal is reconstructed at the receiver by expanding it. This process of compression-expansion is called *companding (COMpressing-exPANDING)*.

There are two widely used methods of companding: the μ-law and the A-law. The first one is used mostly in North America and the second one is used mostly in Europe in digital communications networks. Figure 2.6 shows a block diagram of the compressor and expander for quantization. The μ-law quantization is described by the operator M [2], which is given by

$$y(n) = M[s(n)] = s_{max} \frac{\log[1 + \mu \frac{|s(n)|}{s_{max}}]}{\log(1 + \mu)} \text{sgn}[s(n)] \qquad \textbf{(2.9)}$$

where

- s_{max} is the maximum absolute value of the signal
- $\text{sgn}[s(n)] = \pm 1$ when $s(n)$ is positive or negative
- $|s(n)|$ is the absolute value of $s(n)$
- μ is a parameter that determines the level of compression.

It has been found that $\mu = 255$ gives a quite good performance, and this is the value that is commonly used. At the decoder, the inverse process is described to be the inverse of the operator M

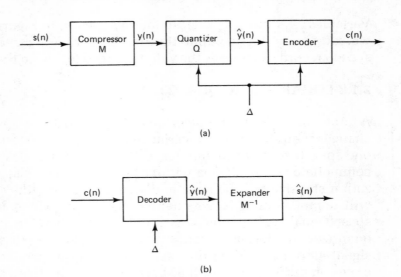

Figure 2.6 Quantization using companding (μ-law or A-law);
(a) transmitter (b) receiver.

$$\hat{s}(n) = M^{-1}[\hat{y}(n)] = \frac{S_{max}}{\mu}\left((1 + \mu)^{\frac{|\hat{y}(n)|}{S_{max}}} - 1\right)sgn[\hat{y}(n)] \qquad (2.10)$$

Instead of applying these equations on each speech sample, it is easier to use them once to compute the quantization boundaries and quantization levels of the quantizer, and then use the resulting nonuniform quantizer. Figure 2.7 shows an approximation of the μ-law transformation characteristic curve. This 15- or 16-segment approximation is used in practical systems for the implementation of the characteristic [9].

The A-law quantization is defined differently, but the end result is very close to the μ-law quantizer. The A-law compressor is specified by [4–5]

$$y(n) = M[s(n)] = \frac{A\ s(n)}{1 + \log A} \qquad \text{for } 0 \le |s(n)| \le \frac{s_{max}}{A}$$

$$y(n) = M[s(n)] = s_{max}\frac{1 + \log (A|s(n)|/s_{max})}{1 + \log A}sgn[s(n)] \qquad (2.11)$$

for

$$s_{max}/A < |s(n)| \le s_{max}$$

At the decoder, we have

$$\hat{s}(n) = M^{-1}[\hat{y}(n)] = \frac{1 + \log A}{A}\hat{y}(n) \quad \text{for } 0 \le |\hat{y}(n)| \le \frac{s_{max}}{1 + \log A}$$

(2.12)

$$\hat{s}(n) = M^{-1}[\hat{y}(n)] = \frac{s_{max}}{A} \exp[\frac{1 + \log A}{s_{max}} |\hat{y}(n)| - 1] \, sgn[\hat{y}(n)]$$

for

$$\frac{s_{max}}{1 + \log A} < |\hat{y}(n)| \le s_{max}$$

In the standard used for European telecommunications, a value of 87.56 has been chosen for A. Figure 2.8 shows a practical approximation of the input-output characteristic curve for A-law quantization [3].

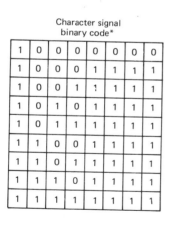

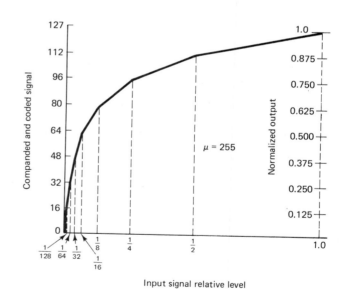

Input signal relative level

Figure 2.7 Companding curve of the μ-law compander. Each straight-line segment is divided into 16 smaller subsegments (after Fike and Friend [3], reprinted by permission of Texas Instruments Inc., © 1983).

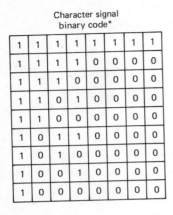

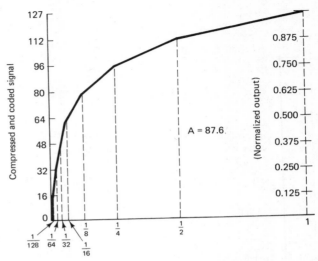

*For positive input values. The left-most bit is a 0 for negative input values. Even bits (beginning with 1 at the left) are inverted before transmission.

Figure 2.8 Companding curve of the A-law compander. Each straight-line segment is divided into 16 smaller subsegments. (after Fike and Friend [3], reprinted by permission of Texas Instruments Inc., © 1983).

The logarithmic quantization of speech has been shown to be very effective, and assigning 8 bits per sample in that method gives speech quality equivalent to 13 bits per sample for the uniform quantizer. Typically, the speech signal is sampled at 8 kHz for communications channels and, with 8 bits per sample, a bit rate of 64 kbits/s results. The quality of the resulting speech is very good. The logarithmic quantization has been widely implemented in integrated circuits. These circuits are known as CODECs (COders-DECoders) and are commercially available for a few dollars. Some of them even include antialiasing filters. The CODECs will be discussed again in Chapter 8.

2.1.3 OTHER TYPES OF NONUNIFORM QUANTIZATION

In the above quantization, no knowledge is assumed of the signal amplitude probability distribution. The next section describes methods that correct this weakness by dynamically changing the quantizer. The present section examines two methods of improving the quantizer performance by assuming that the probability distribution of the signal is known. This distribution does not change with time. The quantizers are designed with the quantization boundaries and quantization levels set in such a way as to optimize the performance of the quantizer. The two quantization schemes considered here are the

> Max quantization
> Maximum entropy quantization

Max quantization. If the input signal $s(n)$ is quantized to a value $\hat{s}_i$, the quantization error is

$$e(n) = \hat{s}_i - s(n) \tag{2.13}$$

In order to have an optimum quantizer with respect to a function of the error, we need to minimize the average value of that error function. Max [6] found that minimization of the average squared error, $e^2(n)$, gives quite interesting results:

- the quantization levels are the centroids of the probability between the corresponding quantization boundaries
- the quantization boundaries are equidistant from the quantization level between them (Figure 2.9)

In mathematical expressions, if $p(s)$ is the probability distribution of s, you have the following two conditions:

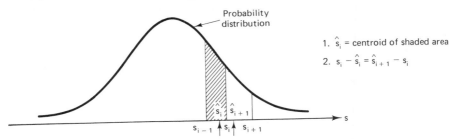

Figure 2.9 Relations between quantization boundaries and quantization levels in a Max quantizer.

$$\hat{s}_i = \int_{s_i}^{s_{i+1}} s \, p(s) \, ds \qquad \textbf{(2.14)}$$

$$s_i - \hat{s}_i = \hat{s}_{i+1} - s_i \qquad \textbf{(2.15)}$$

Based on these results, and with the assumption of a Gaussian distribution, Max derived tables of quantization boundaries and levels for quantizers of different sizes.

It has been demonstrated [7] that the speech signal amplitude follows a Gamma probability distribution rather than a Gaussian. Table 2.1 shows the corresponding quantization levels for Gamma distribution for several numbers of quantization levels. Note that only the positive quantization levels are shown, since the negative ones are their symmetrical equivalent around the origin. Note also that the tables are normalized for a signal with variance equal to 1. For a real signal, we should multiply the quantization boundaries and levels with the corresponding standard deviation.

In the case of a speech signal, instead of using the theoretical Gaussian or Gamma curves, we may want to use the actual distribution as computed by a histogram. It turns out, though, that the iterative procedure Max describes for computing the quantization boundaries and levels is very unwieldy and difficult to converge. The interested reader will find the technique described by Menez, Boeri, and Esteban [8] much easier to implement. Although the squared error function does not have any perceptual significance, it has been adopted widely because it is mathematically tractable and gives reasonable results.

Maximum Entropy Quantization. If the probability distribution of the signal amplitude is known either as a mathematical curve (like a Gaussian) or in the form of a histogram, we can use

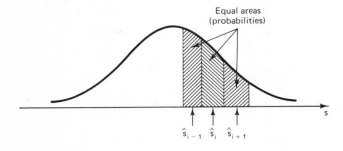

Figure 2.10 Maximum entropy quantization. The shaded areas are equal (equal probability). The corresponding quantization levels are located at the centroid of each area.

TABLE 2.1 QUANTIZATION BOUNDARIES AND QUANTIZATION LEVELS FOR GAMMA DENSITY DISTRIBUTION

Optimum Quantizers for Signals with Gamma Density ($\mu = 0$, $\sigma^2 = 1$)

N	2		4		8		16		32	
i	x_i	y_i	x_i	y_i	x_i	y_i	x_i	y_i	x_i	y_i
1	∞	0.577	1.205	0.302	0.504	0.149	0.229	0.072	0.101	0.033
2			∞	2.108	1.401	0.859	0.588	0.386	0.252	0.169
3					2.872	1.944	1.045	0.791	0.429	0.334
4					∞	3.799	1.623	1.300	0.630	0.523
5							2.372	1.945	0.857	0.737
6							3.407	2.798	1.111	0.976
7							5.050	4.015	1.397	1.245
8							∞	6.085	1.720	1.548
9									2.089	1.892
10									2.517	2.287
11									3.022	2.747
12									3.633	3.296
13									4.404	3.970
14									5.444	4.838
15									7.046	6.050
16									∞	8.043
MSE	0.6680		0.2326		0.0712		0.0196		0.0052	
SNR (dB)	1.77		6.33		11.47		17.07		22.83	

(after Paez and Glisson [7], © 1972, IEEE).

another intuitively appealing method of quantization: the maximum entropy quantization method (Figure 2.10). In the maximum entropy quantization, the quantization boundaries are set so that the probability of the signal s taking a value between any two consecutive boundaries is the same. In other words, the cross-hatched areas in Figure 2.10 are equal. Then, the quantization levels are set at the centroid of these areas. The quantization levels have equal probability of occurrence. This is a condition for maximizing the entropy of the quantizer and explains the name of the quantizer.

2.2 ADAPTIVE QUANTIZATION

As noted earlier, speech presents the problem of nonstationarity, with its statistical behavior changing over time. Therefore, in the case of companders, a quantizer designed around an s_{max} derived from a segment of speech will be inadequate for another segment where the speech signal has significantly increased or decreased in strength. A solution to that problem is to dynamically change the stepsize of the quantizer with time in order to adapt to the changing signal statistics. Alternatively, we can normalize the incoming signal in order to reduce its dynamic range. Both approaches result in a dynamically adaptive system, which is often called adaptive PCM (APCM).

The adaptation can be done at every sample or every few samples, in which case it is called *instantaneous adaptation*, or it can be done in longer intervals—e.g., 10–20 ms, in which case it is called *syllabic adaptation*.

Another classification of the adaptive quantizers is based on whether the adaptation is computed from the incoming signal into the encoder, or from the outgoing signal from the encoder into the channel. The first case is called *feedforward adaptation*, and the second one *feedback adaptation*. Figures 2.11 and 2.12 show the structures of adaptive quantizers, which are based on quantizer stepsize adaptation. Figure 2.11 represents feedforward adaptation and Figure 2.12 feedback adaptation.

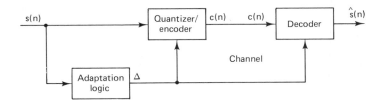

Figure 2.11   Feedforward adaptive quantizer.

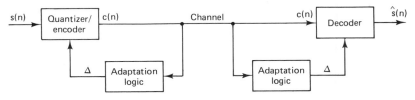

Figure 2.12   Feedback adaptive quantizer.

2.2.1 FEEDFORWARD ADAPTATION

In the case of feedforward stepsize adaptation, the stepsize at time n is given by

$$\Delta(n) = \Delta \times \sigma(n) \tag{2.16}$$

where $\sigma^2(n)$ is the variance of the signal, and Δ is the value chosen for unit variance. The variance of the signal can be computed from the segment of speech to be quantized:

$$\sigma^2(n) = \frac{1}{M} \sum_{m=n}^{n+M-1} s^2(m) \tag{2.17}$$

Alternatively, it can be computed recursively by

$$\sigma^2(n) = a\sigma^2(n-1) + s^2(n-1) \tag{2.18}$$

where $0 < a < 1$. The smaller the a, the faster the quantizer can track changes in the signal. A typical value of a is 0.9; $\Delta(n)$ is not allowed to assume any value, but is usually restricted to a range $\Delta_{min} \le \Delta(n) \le \Delta_{max}$. The ratio $\Delta_{max}/\Delta_{min}$ determines the dynamic range of the system. We usually take $\Delta_{max}/\Delta_{min} = 100$.

To have an accurate reconstruction of the signal, the decoder adaptation logic must be similar to the encoder. Since the decoder has no way of figuring out the adaptation from the quantized speech values, it is necessary to transmit information about $\Delta(n)$. This transmission increases the bit rate and, depending on the use of instantaneous or syllabic adaptation, the cost in increased bits/s can be higher (in instantaneous adaptation) or lower (in syllabic adaptation). The advantage of this approach is that it is possible to apply error protection on $\Delta(n)$ and avoid the deleterious effects of transmission errors.

2.2.2 FEEDBACK ADAPTATION

On the other hand, feedback stepsize adaptation has the advantage that no additional information needs to be transmitted besides the quantized speech signal. In that case the stepsize is adapted according to the rule [9]

$$\Delta(n) = P \, \Delta(n - 1) \tag{2.19}$$

The value of the multiplier P depends only on the value of $|c(n-1)|$, i.e., the magnitude of the codeword in the previous time instant. Table 2.2 gives typical values of P for midriser quantizers. As an example, if the quantizer was a 2-bit (4-level) quantizer and $c(n-1)$ corresponds to the (positive or negative) quantization level closest to zero, then $P = 0.6$. If $c(n-1)$ was the codeword corresponding to the (positive or negative) levels farthest away from zero, $P = 2.2$. The rationale behind this multiplication is that, for small $c(n-1)$,

TABLE 2.2 MULTIPLIERS P OF THE QUANTIZATION STEPSIZE FOR APCM AND FOR DIFFERENT QUANTIZER SIZES

Quantizer Bits	Multiplier P
2	0.6, 2.2
3	0.85, 1, 1, 1.5
4	0.8, 0.8, 0.8, 0.8
	1.2, 1.6, 2.0, 2.4
5	0.85, 0.85, 0.85, 0.85
	0.85, 0.85, 0.85, 0.85
	1.2, 1.4, 1.6, 1.8
	2.0, 2.2, 2.4, 2.6

the signal is small and we use $P < 1$ to diminish the stepsize and achieve a finer quantization. On the other hand, for large $c(n-1)$, $P > 1$ because the signal is "hitting the ceiling" and there is danger of clipping.

2.2.3 ADAPTIVE SIGNAL NORMALIZATION

As mentioned earlier, instead of varying the quantizer stepsize to match the changing statistics of the speech signal, we can normalize the incoming speech and keep the quantizer constant. Figures 2.13 and 2.14 show the two cases of feedforward and feedback adaptation using a variable normalizer (gain) for the speech signal. In both cases, the speech signal $s(n)$ is divided (normalized) by an adaptively estimated gain factor and then quantized by a fixed quantizer. At the receiver, the reconstructed signal is multiplied by the same factor to recover an estimate $\hat{s}(n)$ of the signal.

The gain factor is given by an expression

$$G(n) = G_0 \times \sigma(n) \qquad\qquad (2.20)$$

where the variance $\sigma^2(n)$ is computed in a manner analogous to the case of stepsize adaptation. For feedforward adaptation,

$$\sigma^2(n) = \frac{1}{M} \sum_{m=n}^{n+M-1} s^2(m) \qquad\qquad (2.21)$$

where the summation is applied over the buffered segment of speech to be transmitted. Since $\sigma(n)$ is computed from the input speech, $G(n)$ has to be transmitted to the receiver. On the other hand, for feedback adaptation (see Figure 2.14).

$$\sigma^2(n) = \frac{1}{M} \sum_{m=n-M}^{n-1} [\hat{x}(m) \times G(m)]^2 \qquad\qquad (2.22)$$

In this case, you do not need to transmit the gain factor to the receiver since $\sigma^2(n)$ can be computed from the transmitted signal. Note, though, that $\sigma^2(n)$ is now estimated from past speech samples only. The variable $\sigma^2(n)$ is a function of the past values of $\hat{x}(n)$ and the past values of $G(n)$.

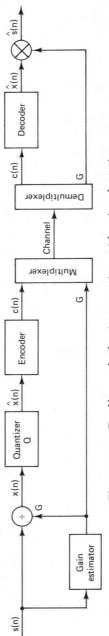

Figure 2.13 Feedforward adaptive quantizer with gain adaptation.

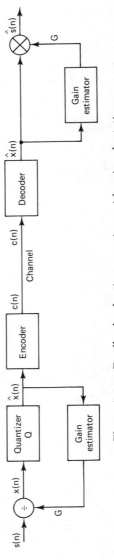

Figure 2.14 Feedback adaptive quantizer with gain adaptation.

34

In both cases of gain adaptation, limits are imposed on the size of the gain factor, as we did with the stepsize adaptation approach $G_{max} \leq G(n) \leq G_{min}$. The ratio G_{max}/G_{min} determines the dynamic range of the system. It has been found that $G_{max}/G_{min} = 100$ gives satisfactory performance.

2.3 DIFFERENTIAL QUANTIZATION

A closer examination of the speech signal, especially during voiced periods, reveals that there is a relatively smooth change from one speech sample to the next. In other words, there is considerable correlation between adjacent samples. As a result, it is expected that the difference of adjacent samples will have a smaller variance and dynamic range than the speech samples themselves, a fact that has been demonstrated in practice. Taking this idea one step further, instead of the speech signal $s(n)$, the input to the quantizer can be the difference $d(n) = s(n) - \tilde{s}(n)$, as shown in Figure 2.15; $\tilde{s}(n)$ is an estimate of $s(n)$.

By writing the equations around the adders of Figure 2.15, it can be shown that the quantization error $\hat{s}(n) - s(n)$ of the speech signal is equal to the quantization error $\hat{d}(n) - d(n)$ of the difference signal. The difference signal has a smaller variance, and so does the corresponding quantization error. With this approach we decrease the quantization error and we increase the SNR.

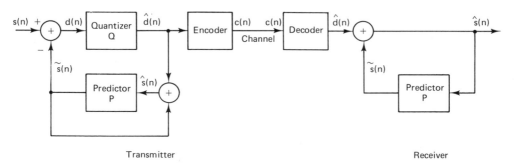

Figure 2.15   Transmitter and receiver of a differential quantization method.

2.3.1 FIXED DIFFERENTIAL QUANTIZATION

It is intuitively clear that the more accurate the estimate $\tilde{s}(n)$, the smaller the variance of $d(n)$, and the better the performance of the quantizer. The usual choice for the predictor P is a linear combination of past samples of $\hat{s}(n)$

$$\tilde{s}(n) = \sum_{k=1}^{P} a_k \hat{s}(n - k) \tag{2.23}$$

where p is called the order of the predictor. The coefficients a_k of the predictor are selected to minimize the prediction error

$$E = \sum_n [s(n) - \tilde{s}(n)]^2 \tag{2.24}$$

over a sufficiently long period of time. With some simplifying assumptions, it can be shown that the coefficients a_k are given by the matrix equation [1]

$$\begin{bmatrix} a_1 \\ a_2 \\ \cdot \\ \cdot \\ \cdot \\ a_p \end{bmatrix} = \begin{bmatrix} R(0) & R(1) & \cdots & R(p-1) \\ R(1) & R(2) & \cdots & R(p-2) \\ \cdot \\ \cdot \\ \cdot \\ R(p-1) & R(p-2) & \cdots & R(0) \end{bmatrix}^{-1} \begin{bmatrix} R(1) \\ R(2) \\ \cdot \\ \cdot \\ \cdot \\ R(p) \end{bmatrix} \tag{2.25}$$

$R(i)$ is the autocorrelation coefficient for the ith lag of the speech signal, and it is computed from $s(n)$ using the equation

$$R(i) = \sum_n s(n)s(n+i) \tag{2.26}$$

These equations will be examined in more detail in Chapter 5, in the context of Linear Predictive Coding. The system described above is called a differential PCM (DPCM) system. For DPCM systems, we typically choose $p = 4$.

2.3.2 ADAPTIVE DIFFERENTIAL QUANTIZATION

So far, the DPCM system has used a fixed predictor and a fixed quantizer. However, as it was observed in the case of quantization, much can be gained by adapting the system to track the time behavior of the input speech signal. The adaptation can be reformed on the quantizer, on the predictor, or on both. The resulting system is called *Adaptive Differential PCM* (ADPCM).

In quantizer adaptation we distinguish two cases, feedforward (Figure 2.16) and feedback adaptation (Figure 2.17). In the *feedforward adaptation*, the computation of the quantizer stepsize should be done on the input to the quantizer. However, for simplicity we choose the input signal. The adaptation algorithms are similar to the ones described for adaptive quantization. In this case it is necessary to transmit side information about the stepsize. For *feedback adaptation*, side information is not necessary since the computation is based on the coded signal. The advantages and the disadvantages of the two approaches are the same as those mentioned earlier: Feedback adaptation results in a lower bit rate while feedforward adaptation gives better protection against errors in the transmitted signal if we apply error correction coding on the transmitted stepsize.

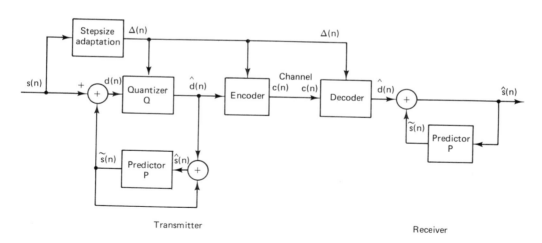

Figure 2.16   ADPCM with feedforward adaptation of the stepsize.

Besides the quantizer, another segment of the DPCM system that can be adapted to follow the changing behavior of the speech signal is the predictor. Figure 2.18 gives a block diagram for a feedforward adaptation. Of course, in addition to the predictor, the quantization stepsize could be adapted.

In the case of ADCPM with feedforward predictor adaptation, the predictor is still a linear combination of past samples, but now the coefficients of the linear combination are time dependent.

$$\tilde{s}(n) = \sum_{k=1}^{P} a_k(n)\hat{s}(n-k) \tag{2.27}$$

The coefficients $[a_k(n)]$ are computed and transmitted every 10–20 ms. The computation of the coefficients is done again using the matrix equation (2.25). However, in the present case the autocorrelation coefficients are not computed over the whole available speech, but only over a segment 20–30 ms long, where the speech signal remains relatively stationary. This segment is extracted by windowing the speech signal with a finite window 20–30 ms long. In windowing, the speech is multiplied by a signal that is nonzero over the interval we want to extract and zero everywhere else. The shape of the window is chosen to have good spectral properties. A popular choice is the Hamming window, which will be considered further in Chapter 3. Successive windowed segments are 10–20 ms apart, as shown in Figure 2.19.

For a windowed segment ending at sample i,

$$x_i(n) = s(n)w(i-n) \tag{2.28}$$

where $x_i(n) = 0$ outside the window. Then, the autocorrelation coefficients are estimated from

$$R(j) = \sum_n x_i(n) x_i(n+j) \tag{2.29}$$

The summation extends over the interval containing nonzero values of $x_i(n)$.

The solution of the matrix equation (2.25) to determine the $[a_k(n)]$, together with methods of quantization and representation of the $a_k(n)$, will be examined in more detail in Chapter 5.

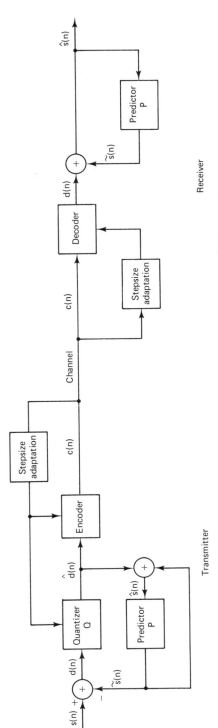

Figure 2.17 ADPCM with feedback adaptation of the stepsize.

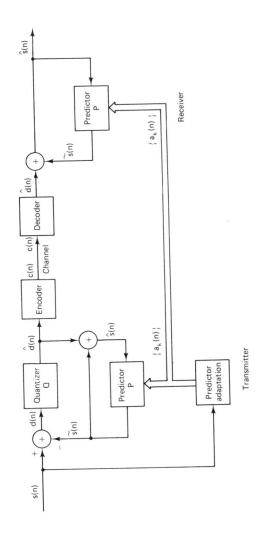

Figure 2.18 ADPCM with feedforward adaptation of the predictor.

For feedback adaptation of the predictor, you cannot use the same approach as in the feedforward method, because for the estimation of the predictor you need the output data, and to generate the output data you need the predictor. Therefore, for feedback adaptation, a gradient method is used where the predictor coefficients are updated every sampling instant. The new values are derived from the old values by adding a quantity proportional to the negative gradient of the prediction error. By using this adaptation, you are moving in a direction of reducing the error. The CCITT standard G.721 employs exactly this method for a 32 kbit/s coding scheme. A detailed description of the standard can be found in reference [10]. It is also outlined in Chapter 8 as an example of how speech coding has been applied.

2.5 ADAPTIVE PREDICTIVE CODING (APC)

The Adaptive Predictive Coding (APC) can be considered as an extension of the ADPCM. APC uses additional information about the speech signal in order to achieve effective coding at bit rates of 9.6–16 kbit/s. The additional information is based on the periodicity of the voiced speech. In ADPCM, the signal is predicted from the past p samples according to equation (2.23), repeated here for convenience.

$$\tilde{s}(n) = \sum_{k=1}^{P} a_k \hat{s}(n - k)$$

If the signal represents voiced speech, it is periodic with a period of T samples. In this case, it is reasonable to expect that the sample

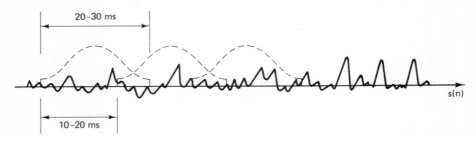

Figure 2.19   Speech signal with three consecutive windows.

$s(n - T)$ will be a good approximation of $s(n)$, and (2.23) can be rewritten as

$$\bar{s}(n) = \sum_{k=1}^{P} a_k \hat{s}(n - k) + b\,\hat{s}(n - T) \qquad \textbf{(2.30)}$$

The summation part of (2.30), which corresponds to (2.23), is called a spectral predictor. The remaining part is called a pitch predictor. For simplicity, (2.30) is implemented in two steps by considering the estimation of the spectral and the pitch predictors independently. The input to the pitch predictor is the output of the spectral predictor as shown in Figure 2.20. Figure 2.20 is a block diagram of both the transmitter and the receiver of an APC.

The spectral predictor is typically of order $p = 4$, and its coefficients are determined from the input speech signal as explained in the previous section on ADPCM. Chapter 5 on linear predictive coding also addresses this computation.

Besides the a_k, we need to determine the values of the coefficient b, the pitch period T, and the gain G. The gain G is estimated from the difference signal $s(n) - \bar{s}(n)$ using the methods discussed earlier in this chapter on adaptive quantization.

The determination of the pitch period T is a nontrivial task discussed extensively in Chapter 6. Pitch information is very essential in the implementation of vocoders. In the case of adaptive predictive coding, it is also very important but not critical. The method most often used for pitch tracking in APC is the Average Magnitude Difference Function (AMDF) described in Chapter 6. However, any other pitch tracker of similar performance could be used.

The pitch period information T is needed before the coefficient b is computed. For the determination of b, the spectral predictor is ignored and the input signal $s(n)$ is used. Minimization of the pitch predictor error leads to the equation

$$b = \frac{\sum_{n} s(n)s(n-T)}{\sum_{n} s^2(n)} \qquad \textbf{(2.4)}$$

which evaluates b.

At the receiver, the signal is denormalized by the gain, and

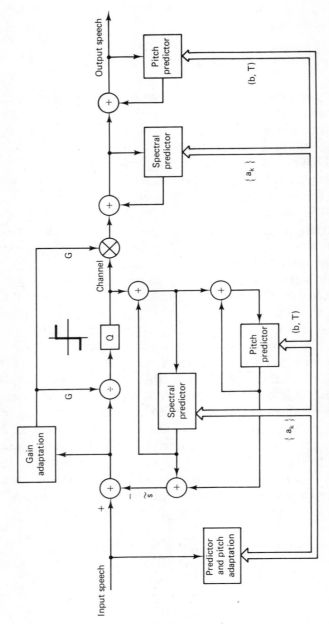

Figure 2.20 Block diagram of an APC system.

then is passed through the spectral predictor first, and the pitch predictor next to recover an approximation of the original signal.

APC has been used for coding speech at 9.6 and 16 kbits/s, and is an alternative to subband coding presented in the next chapter. Its main drawback is the computational load in the transmitter. This load is due to the need to estimate the pitch period of the signal in addition to the evaluation of the predictor coefficients.

Several forms of the adaptive predictive coder have been studied. A major variant of the technique includes noise shaping, where the noise of the quantizer is shaped appropriately. By shaping, the quantization noise is concentrated in areas of the spectrum where it is perceptually masked out by the energy of the main signal. References [11–13] discuss this technique further.

2.5 DELTA MODULATION

A special case of DPCM is the Delta Modulation (DM). In delta modulation (or coding), both the predictor and the quantizer assume a very special form. In particular, the predictor becomes a first-order predictor, so that

$$\bar{s}(n) = a\,\hat{s}(n-1) \qquad\qquad \textbf{(2.32)}$$

and the quantizer becomes a hard limiter, so that

$$
\begin{aligned}
\hat{d}(n) &= \Delta && \text{if } d(n) > 0 \\
&= -\Delta && \text{if } d(n) \le 0
\end{aligned}
\qquad\qquad \textbf{(2.33)}
$$

with Δ being the quantization stepsize.

2.5.1 LINEAR DELTA MODULATION

Figure 2.21 shows a block diagram of a delta modulation system. Based on the type of the quantizer, the codeword $c(n)$ is just one bit with value

$$
\begin{aligned}
c(n) &= 0 && \text{if } \hat{d}(n) = \ \ \Delta \\
c(n) &= 1 && \text{if } \hat{d}(n) = -\Delta
\end{aligned}
\qquad\qquad \textbf{(2.34)}
$$

Hence, the bit rate is equal to the sampling rate. To use this technique effectively, the signal must exhibit a high sample-to-sample

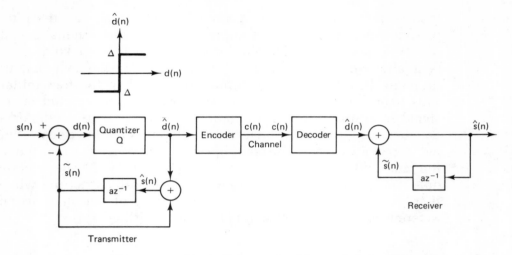

Figure 2.21   Block diagram of a delta modulation system.

correlation, so that one-bit coding is sufficient to represent the sample-to-sample differences (suggested by the one-tap predictor). The increased correlation is achieved by oversampling the speech signal, i.e., sampling it at rates considerably higher than the Nyquist rate. For the speech bandlimited to 4 kHz, you would have 24 or 32 kHz as sampling rate and a bit rate of 24 or 32 kbit/s, respectively.

Figure 2.22 shows an example of delta modulation, where the signals $s(n)$ and $\hat{s}(n)$ can be identified in Figure 2.21. In this case, we have set $a = 1$ in the predictor. (In general, a is chosen close to 1.) Since the reconstructed signal can increase at a maximum rate along a line of slope Δ/T, this type of coding is sometimes called *linear delta modulation*. As can be observed from Figure 2.22, if the slope of the signal is greater than Δ/T, which is the largest that the coder can accommodate, you have an error that worsens with increasing slope values. This condition is called slope overload. Also, you can see that in areas where the signal is relatively constant, the delta coder causes the reconstructed signal to jump at values around the actual signal. This introduces noise that is called granular noise. Granular noise is most noticeable during intervals of silence, where the signal coming in is only the background noise. Then, the background noise is accentuated by the granular noise.

The major attractiveness of the linear delta modulation is its

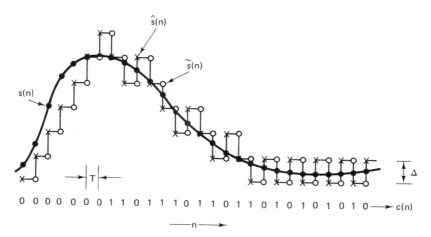

Figure 2.22   Example of delta modulation (linear delta modulation). T is the sampling period and Δ the quantizer stepsize.

simplicity of implementation with analog and digital integrated circuits. However, it also has drawbacks manifested by the slope overload and the granular noise conditions, which are caused by the time-varying nature of the speech signal. The above problems suggest investigating adaptive methods for delta coding that still preserve the simplicity of the original idea.

2.5.2 ADAPTIVE DELTA MODULATION

In Adaptive Delta Modulation (ADM), we usually employ feedback adaptation strategies on the quantizer stepsize, as shown in Figure 2.23.

One adaptation strategy that can be used is similar to the one discussed in the adaptive quantization section. In this approach, the quantization stepsize is derived from the stepsize in the previous sampling instant from the equation

$$\Delta(n) = M \, \Delta(n - 1) \qquad (2.35)$$

where $\Delta_{min} \leq \Delta(n) \leq \Delta_{max}$. The variable M can take the values P and Q where

$$
\begin{aligned}
M = P > 1 \qquad &\text{if } c(n) = c(n - 1) \\
M = Q < 1 \qquad &\text{otherwise}
\end{aligned}
\qquad (2.36)
$$

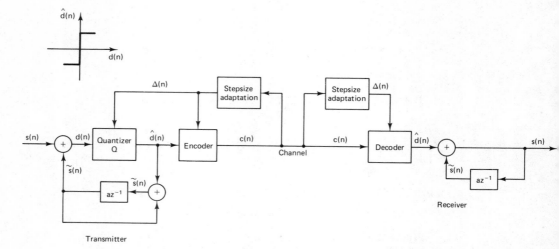

Figure 2.23 Adaptive Delta Modulation (ADM) with feedback adaptation of the quantizer stepsize.

Notice that the codeword for the present sample is used before the sample is actually quantized. This is permissible because $c(n)$ is determined only by the sign of the difference $\hat{d}(n) = s(n) - \tilde{s}(n)$. Figure 2.22 shows that you can determine if $s(n)$ is above or below $\tilde{s}(n)$ before the quantization of $\hat{d}(n)$, which makes $c(n)$ known in advance. Then, when $d(n)$ is computed, the estimated $\Delta(n)$ can be used.

Jayant [9] has determined that for stability, $PQ \leq 1$. Typical values for P are $1.25 < P < 2$. As an example, Figure 2.24 shows ADM with $P = 1.5$ and $Q = 0.6$.

2.5.3 CONTINUOUSLY VARIABLE SLOPE DELTA MODULATION (CVSD)

One drawback of this method of ADM is that transmission errors can cause degradation of the speech quality that can last for a long time. To recover from transmission errors, it is necessary to introduce some "leakage" in both the predictor and the adaptation strategy of the quantizer stepsize. One such method is the Continuously Variable Slope Delta modulation (CVSD).

In CVSD, the adaptation strategy depends on the present and

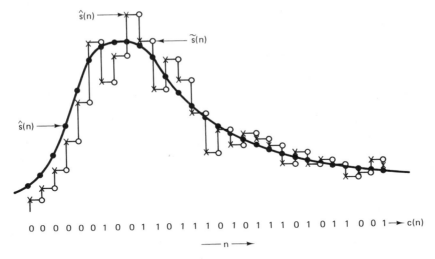

Figure 2.24 Example of adaptive delta modulation.

the past two values of $c(n)$, and is given by the relations

$$\Delta(n) = \beta \, \Delta(n - 1) + D_2 \quad \text{if } c(n) = c(n - 1) = c(n - 2)$$

$$\Delta(n) = \beta \, \Delta(n - 1) + D_1 \quad \text{otherwise}$$

(2.37)

where β is the "leakage," $0 < \beta < 1$, and $D_2 >> D_1 > 0$. Here it is unnecessary to impose upper and lower bounds on $\Delta(n)$ explicitly, because these bounds are implicit in the above equations and they are determined by β, D_1, and D_2. It can be shown that

$$\Delta_{max} = \frac{D_2}{1 - \beta}, \qquad \Delta_{min} = \frac{D_1}{1 - \beta} \qquad \text{(2.38)}$$

Equation (2.37) shows that $\Delta(n)$ increases during slope overload and otherwise decreases. For β close to 1, the rate of adaptation is slow, while for β approaching 0, the adaptation is faster. After choosing β, the parameters D_1 and D_2 are computed from the above equations by selecting Δ_{max} and Δ_{min}.

The CVSD method gives speech quality somewhat inferior to the other systems examined, but it has the important practical advantage of low sensitivity to channel errors. This low sensitivity is achieved not only by the factor β, but also by selecting $a < 1$ in the predictor.

2.6 MOZER CODING

A method of waveform coding that applies speech-specific ideas to reduce the transmitted bit rate is the Mozer coding (from the name of the inventor Forrest Mozer). It is also called time-domain synthesis [14, 15] to distinguish it from the frequency-domain synthesis techniques, described in Chapters 4 and 5, which use similar speech-specific information.

This method requires extensive processing of the input speech to estimate the signal that is coded and transmitted. Unlike the other waveform coding techniques described so far, no attempt is made to preserve the actual waveform shape. Instead, the estimated signal *sounds* like the original speech, although it does not look like it. Figure 2.25 compares the original waveform and the coded waveform for a segment of the word "zone." Because of the extensive processing required to generate the coded waveform, this technique is best suited for voice response systems, where the coded waveform is generated without any real-time restrictions and is stored to be played at a later time. The Mozer coding method gives good speech quality at rates down to 1,200–2,400 bits/s.

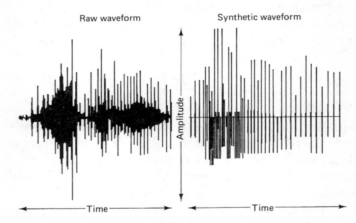

Figure 2.25 Original and synthetic waveforms of the word "zone" using Mozer coding (after Costello and Mozer [14]).

   The largest bit rate reduction in the Mozer coding technique is achieved by capitalizing upon the insensitivity of the human ear to the short-time phase. It has been demonstrated that for relatively short time intervals (less than about 20 ms), the ear perceives speech on the basis of the amplitude spectrum. Hence, the phase can be manipulated appropriately to achieve lower bit rates. In the Mozer coding method, the speech interval (analysis frame) selected for processing can be between 16 and 256 samples for a sampling rate of 8 kHz. Typically, it includes 128 samples. For voiced speech, the analysis frame is one period of the quasi-periodic waveform, while for unvoiced speech, where there is no periodicity, it is selected to be 10 ms long.

   First, let us examine the processing of voiced speech. Since the analysis frame is equal to one pitch period, it follows that pitch tracking is necessary to both determine the length of that period and separate voiced from unvoiced speech segments. The pitch information is stored and used for the reconstruction of the waveform. The pitch is necessary for the synthesis of the speech signal because all the analysis frames processed are represented by the same number of samples. Then, to reconstruct exact pitch periods, the stored waveform is padded with zeroes at the end, so that it attains the required length in samples. Careful examination of Figure 2.25 will show that, in the synthetic waveform, the distance between successive peaks varies to accommodate the prosody of the signal.

   Another consideration is the amplitude of the waveform. The varying intensity of the signal would require a larger number of quantization levels. This is avoided by normalizing the signal and storing an amplitude gain once for every period. This gain is quantized to 3 bits.

   The major gains of the method are attained by manipulating the phase. To accomplish this, a discrete Fourier transform of every period is taken and the amplitude of every transform coefficient is preserved while forcing the phase to be either 0 or π. For a 128-point analysis frame, you get 64 amplitudes and 64 phases. By assigning either of the two values to each phase, you have 2^{64} possible waveforms. All these waveforms sound the same, and they are all symmetrical about the center of each period. This symmetry helps reduce the bit rate by 50 percent, because you need store only half of the waveform. Figure 2.26 shows such an example.

Now, further reductions can be achieved by selecting the symmetric waveform that has two additional characteristics: First, it has very little energy in the first and the last quarter. In this case you can zero out these segments, as shown in Figure 2.26c, and store only one quarter of the waveform. Second, the amplitudes of the selected waveform concentrate roughly around 4 (or maybe 16) levels. This arrangement permits the use of 2 (or 4) bits for the representation of the samples. The problem with this approach is that it requires an exorbitant amount of computing time to do the search. However, there exist proprietary techniques that permit conducting the search in a reasonable time.

Additional savings in bit rate is achieved by recognizing that the shape of the pitch period varies relatively slowly over time. This observation suggests storing a pitch period together with a repetition factor, and then, at the synthesizer, repeating the pitch period the same number of times to generate the synthetic waveform. For example, if a pitch period is repeated three times, this corresponds to a reduction in bit rate (locally) roughly by three. A side benefit of the repetition is that the speech becomes smoother, since the phases of the speech components do not change every pitch period.

The above description applies to voiced sounds. For unvoiced analysis frames, there is no pitch period to consider, and the duration of the analysis frames is chosen to be 10 ms. Then, the phases of the discrete Fourier transform are varied until you get a waveform whose amplitudes concentrate around 4 or 16 levels, and they can be represented by 2 or 4 bits. Additional savings are obtained by repeating the analysis frame three to five times. However, such segment repetition introduces a very disturbing buzziness. This problem is rectified by quasi-random repetition of sections of the unvoiced analysis frame. For instance, if you have stored in the memory a 32-sample-long waveform, you can generate a satisfactory unvoiced output by playing back the sequence of samples from 1 up to 32, from 32 down to 1, 17 to 32, 1 to 16, 16 to 1, and 32 to 17.

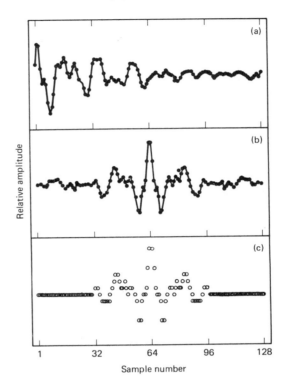

Figure 2.26 Processing of a pitch period in Mozer coding; (a) original pitch period; (b) phase modification to make it symmetrical; (c) symmetric phases chosen to minimize power in the first and last quarter of the pitch period (after Costello and Mozer [14]).

2.7 TIME-DOMAIN HARMONIC SCALING (TDHS)

The Time-Domain Harmonic Scaling (TDHS) method is a waveform coding technique that can be used to reduce the bit rate by a factor of 2. It can also be used to alter the scaling of the signal in the frequency domain in applications of speech processing to devices for the hearing-impaired.

The basic function of TDHS is to take two consecutive pitch periods at the transmitter and compress them into one. At the receiver, the signal is expanded to recover the missing pitch periods. It is clear from the above discussion that we need to extract pitch information from the signal in order to do TDHS processing. This is a drawback but there is some tolerance to pitch errors, especially pitch doubling. In TDHS, such errors are not as catastrophic as in the case of pitch-excited vocoders. Pitch detection methods are presented in Chapter 6.

Figure 2.27 shows a waveform coding system using TDHS. The output of the TDHS compression block is encoded for transmission using any of the waveform or frequency-domain methods, such as delta modulation, CVSD, subband coding, and so on. At the receiver, the inverse process is applied.

In the case of Figure 2.27, the pitch information is also encoded and transmitted to the receiver, since it is needed for the TDHS expansion. However, this increases the necessary bit rate and makes the system more sensitive to transmission errors. Another approach is shown in Figure 2.28, where the pitch information is not transmitted, but it is computed again at the synthesizer from the transmitted signal. Now the previous drawbacks are not present, but the performance of the pitch tracker at the synthesizer is degraded because it operates on a smaller number of pitch periods. Generally, the first method is preferred for better quality speech.

The implementation of the TDHS method is illustrated in Figure 2.29. It is assumed that the pitch period is P samples long, and we compress $2P$ consecutive samples into P samples. The compres-

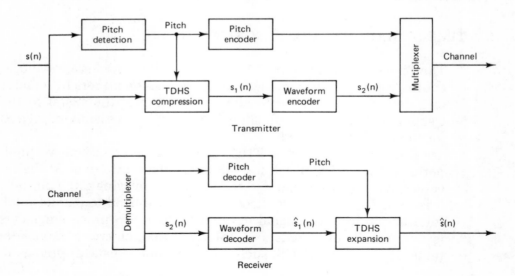

Figure 2.27   TDHS system with transmission of pitch information.

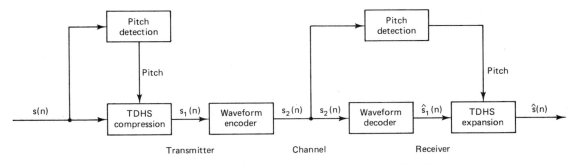

Figure 2.28 TDHS system without transmission of pitch information.

sion is done by windowing the first pitch period by a triangular window

$$w(n) = 1 - \frac{n}{P-1} \tag{2.39}$$

The second pitch period is windowed by $1 - w(n)$ as shown. Then, the two windowed periods are added together to generate the P

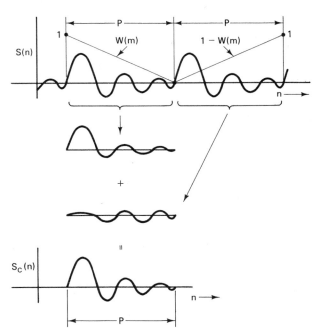

Figure 2.29 TDHS compression in the time domain (after Cox et al. [16], © 1982 IEEE).

samples of the compressed waveform. Because of the way that the compressed waveform was generated, the continuity with the speech signal before and after the 2P-samples segment is preserved.

At the receiver, the TDHS expansion is achieved as shown in Figure 2.30. The window $w(n)$ is applied to two consecutive periods of the compressed waveform, and the same is done with the window $1 - w(n)$. However, the two windows now overlap over the pitch period that we want to expand. The two windowed segments are then added together to generate the 2P samples of the expanded waveform. Again, the continuity with the preceding and the following signal is preserved.

The discussion so far has been centered around speech segments that exhibit periodicity, such as the voiced segments. But what about unvoiced segments? It turns out that the same approach can be applied, where the pitch period is chosen to be any number (within certain bounds). For instance, you can let the pitch tracker run all the time (without making voiced/unvoiced decisions) and

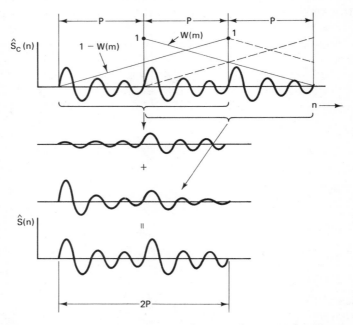

Figure 2.30 TDHS expansion in the time domain (after Cox et al. [16], © 1982 IEEE).

use the resulting output. Or, if you use the voiced/unvoiced decision, you can select some fixed number as the pitch period.

Using TDHS in conjunction with some other coding technique, such as CVSD or subband coding, you can obtain improved speech quality at bit rates around 9.6 kbits/s.

2.8 SUMMARY

This chapter discussed several waveform coding methods. The simplest method is quantization that operates separately on every sample. If the objective is to process the signal further, linear quantization is preferable because it does not introduce any nonlinearities. However, coarser quantization can lead to audible distortion. Usually, linear quantization is implemented with 12–16 bits per sample. Lower bit rate is achieved with logarithmic quantization (7–10 bits/sample) while preserving the speech quality. Logarithmic quantization devices (CODECs) are considerably cheaper than linear quantization devices (A/D and D/A converters) with the same speech quality. Max and maximum entropy quantization have not found many applications.

From the differential quantization techniques, the delta modulation (including CVSD) has been most widely used. There are integrated circuit implementations commercially available with typical bit rates of 24 to 32 kbits/s. In recent years, the adaptive techniques have become more and more popular. The ADPCM was chosen to implement a CCITT standard at 32 kbits/s, with speech quality approaching that of the 64 kbits/s log-PCM. Also, the adaptive predictive coding (APC), which utilizes a pitch predictor in addition to the spectral predictor, has been used for speech coding at 9.6 and 16 kbits/s.

Mozer coding has found commercial application in talking chips. It produces very good speech quality down to 2000 bits/s, but it imposes a heavy computational load. The method is a collection of ingenious tricks that achieve very high efficiency. However, the same fact is a limitation because the output cannot serve as input to further processing. The TDHS has not found many commercial applications yet, but it is extensively studied in both academic and industrial laboratories.

Overall, for less demanding applications, the logarithmic quantization can give a good solution, while for higher quality/lower bit rates, the ADPCM or some other adaptive approach may be best.

2.9 FURTHER READING

In waveform coding, the two most important sources of information are the books by Jayant and Noll [5], and by Jayant [17].

Jayant's book [17] contains extensive information about quantization, while Rabiner and Schafer [1] and Jayant and Noll [5] offer more unified treatments of the subject. The papers by Smith [2] and Max [6] discuss some important topics in quantization. In the books by Fike and Friend [3], and Bellamy [18], the reader can find a practical implementation of the μ-law and A-law companders.

The same sources, [5, 17], contain information on DPCM, ADPCM, Delta Modulation, and the other subjects discussed in this chapter. The CCITT recommendation [10] gives a detailed definition of the 32 kbits/s standard, while the report by Reimer et al. [19] presents an implementation of that standard.

The basic APC method is described in the paper by Atal and Schroeder [20]. The BBN report [11] discusses different kinds of implementations and provides an extensive study of that method. The papers [12, 13] describe the noise shaping method in APC. The book by Jayant and Noll [5] also contains information on the different APC systems.

The Mozer coding technique can be studied from the corresponding patent [15], from the articles by Costello and Mozer [14], and from the books by Bristow [21] and Kuecken [22].

The Time-Domain Harmonic Scaling (TDHS) is presented in detail in the papers by Malah [23], Malah et al. [24], and Cox et al. [16].

2.10 REFERENCES

1. Rabiner, L.R., and R.W. Schafer. *Digital Processing of Speech Signals.* Englewood Cliffs, NJ: Prentice-Hall, 1978.

2. Smith, B. "Instantaneous Companding of Quantized Signals," *Bell System Technical Journal*, Vol. 36, No. 3 (May 1957): 653–709.

3. Fike, J.L., and G.E. Friend. *Understanding Telephone Electronics*, Dallas, TX: Texas Instruments Incorporated, 1983.

4. Cattermale, K.W. *Principles of Pulse Coding Modulation*. London: Iliffe Books, 1969.

5. Jayant, N.S., and P. Noll. *Digital Coding of Waveforms*. Englewood Cliffs, NJ: Prentice-Hall, 1984.

6. Max, J. "Quantizing for Minimum Distortion." *IRE Trans. Inform. Theory*. Vol. IT-6 (March 1960): 7–12.

7. Paez, M.D., and T.H. Glisson. "Minimum Mean-Squared-Error Quantization in Speech PCM and DPCM Systems." *IEEE Trans. Commun.*, Vol. COM-20 (April 1972): 225–230.

8. Menez, J., F. Boeri, and D.J. Esteban. "Optimum Quantizer Algorithm for Real-Time Block Quantizing." *IEEE 1979 Intern. Conf. Acous., Speech and Signal Proc.* (April 1979): 980–984.

9. Jayant, N.S. "Adaptive Quantization With a One Word Memory," *Bell System Tech.* (September 1973): 1119–1144.

10. "32 Kbit/s Adaptive Differential Pulse Code Modulation (ADPCM)." *CCITT Recommendation G. 721* (October 1984).

11. Viswanathan, R., W. Russel, and A.W.F. Huggins. "Design and Real-Time Implementation of a Robust APC Coder for Speech Transmission over 16 Kbps Noisy Channels." BBN Rep. 4565, Bolt, Beranek and Newman Inc., December 1980.

12. Makhoul, J. and M. Berouti. "Adaptive Noise Spectral Shaping and Entropy Coding in Predictive Coding of Speech." *IEEE Trans. on Acous., Speech, and Signal Proc.*, Vol. ASSP-27, No. 1, (February 1979): 63–73.

13. Atal, B.S., and M.R. Schroeder. "Predictive Coding of Speech Signal and Subjective Error Criteria," *IEEE Trans. on Acous., Speech, and Signal Proc.*, Vol. ASSP-27, No. 3 (June 1979): 247–254.

14. Costello, J.B., and F.S. Mozer. "Time Domain Synthesis Gives Good-Quality Speech at Very Low Data Rates." *Speech Technology*, Vol. 1, No. 3 (September 1982): 62–68.

15. Mozer, F.S., and R.P. Standuhar. "Method and Apparatus for Speech Synthesizing." U.S. Patent 4,214,125, July 22, 1980.

16. Cox, R.V., R.E. Crochiere, and J.D. Johnston. "An Implementation of Time-Domain Harmonic Scaling with Application to Speech Coding." *IEEE 1982 Intern. Confer. on Commun.*, (1982): 4G.1.1–4.

17. Jayant, N.S., Ed. *Waveform Quantization and Coding*. New York: IEEE Press, 1976.

18. Bellamy, J.C. *Digital Telephony*. New York: John Wiley & Sons, 1982.

19. Reimer, J.B., M.L. McMahan, and M.M. Arjmand. "32-kbit/s ADPCM with the TMS32010." *Appl. Report*, Texas Instruments, Dallas TX, 1985 (see Appendix).

20. Atal, B.S., and M.R. Schroeder. "Adaptive Predictive Coding of Speech Signals." *Bell Sys. Tech. J.*, Vol. 49 (October 1970): 1973–1986.

21. Bristow, G., Ed. *Electronic Speech Synthesis*. New York: Granada, 1984.

22. Kuecken, J.A. *Talking Computers and Telecommunications*. New York: Van Nostrand Reinhold Co., 1983.

23. Malah, D. "Time-Domain Algorithms for Harmonic Bandwidth Reduction and Time Scaling of Speech Signals." *IEEE Trans. Acous., Speech, and Signal Proc.*, Vol. ASSP-27, No. 2 (April 1979): 121–133.

24. Malah, D., R.E. Crochiere, and R.V. Cox. "Performance of Transform and Subband Coding Systems Combined with Harmonic Scaling of Speech." *IEEE Trans. Acous., Speech, and Signal Proc.*, Vol. ASSP-29, No. 2 (April 1981): 273–283.

Chapter 3

Efficient Coding Using the Speech Spectrum

The frequency (or Fourier) representation of signals has been very fruitful in studying physical phenomena. It represents the signal as a superposition of sinusoids or complex exponentials, which makes the investigation of processing through linear systems very convenient. Even more important is the ability to look at another picture of the signal and determine features that are not obvious from the time-domain representation. This chapter presents methods of coding the speech signal in the frequency domain. These methods correspond to essentially the same representation as in the time domain, but they try to capitalize upon frequency-domain features of the speech signal. In Chapter 4, additional frequency-domain techniques will be studied, but these techniques differ from the

present ones since they use an explicit model for the speech excitation. In other words, here we use a nonparametric representation
of the speech signal, while in Chapter 4 the envelope of the speech
spectrum (corresponding to the vocal tract) is represented parametrically, along with information about the source of excitation.

Three coding methods are studied in this chapter: The short-
time Fourier analysis, the subband coding, and the adaptive transform coding. The short-time Fourier analysis discusses some very
important basic concepts of speech processing. With this opportu-
nity, the speech spectrogram, a very useful tool in speech system
development, is also explained.

The next method presented is subband coding, a very simple
and efficient way of achieving medium-band speech coding at
around 16 kbits/s. Subband coding is based on segmenting the
speech spectrum in subbands and encoding each one of them separately. The bit allocation is guided by the perceptual significance
of the subbands.

The adaptive transform coding (ATC) uses the discrete cosine
transform (related to the Fourier transform) to derive a set of parameters from the speech signal. These parameters can be used for
more effective encoding of the signal. Furthermore, ATC achieves
high-quality synthetic speech by dynamically allocating the available bits to each parameter from frame to frame.

3.1 SHORT-TIME FOURIER ANALYSIS

The short-time Fourier representation of the speech signal is considered in this section not so much for the coding efficiency that it
can give us, but for the understanding that it can supply on the
general frequency-domain methods. Also, it helps to introduce
concepts like windowing and tools like the spectrogram. Furthermore, short-time Fourier analysis forms the basis of many of the
vocoding techniques to be studied in the next chapter.

The short-time Fourier representation of the speech signal is
given by the equation (3.1).

$$X_n(e^{j\omega}) = \sum_{m=-\infty}^{\infty} w(n-m)\, x(m)\, e^{-j\omega m} \qquad (3.1)$$

The index n corresponds to the last time-sample considered, i.e., we have a time-frequency representation. However, most often we drop this index when we are talking about a particular segment (frame) of the speech signal. The variable $x(m)$ represents the digitized input signal at time mT (where T is the sampling period), and $w(m)$ is a real-valued "window" sequence. The window, $w(m)$, determines the portion of the signal that is to be processed by zeroing out the signal outside the region of interest. There are many possibilities for windows, but here we consider the two most popular choices: the rectangular window (equation (3.2), Figure 3.1)

$$
\begin{aligned}
w(m) &= 1 && \text{if } 0 \le m \le N - 1 \\
w(m) &= 0 && \text{otherwise}
\end{aligned}
\tag{3.2}
$$

and the Hamming window (equation (3.3), Figure 3.2).

$$
\begin{aligned}
w(m) &= 0.54 - 0.46 \cos(2\pi m/N) && \text{if } 0 \le m \le N - 1 \\
w(m) &= 0 && \text{otherwise}
\end{aligned}
\tag{3.3}
$$

For speech applications, the Hamming window is used more often because it has better spectral properties than the rectangular window. Figure 3.3 illustrates how the windowing is applied on a

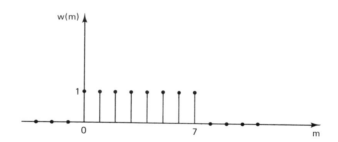

Figure 3.1   Rectangular window with length $N = 8$.

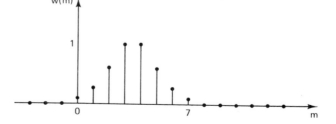

Figure 3.2   Hamming window with length $N = 8$.

speech signal to extract a frame, of which we can then find the Fourier transform.

Equation (3.1) gives the formal definition of the Fourier transform for discrete signals, but in the frequency domain we get a continuous function of the frequency ω. In practice, for efficient implementation of the Fourier transform, you can use the so-called Fast Fourier Transform (FFT). Equation (3.4) defines the forward and inverse Fourier transform. If N is a power of 2, this transform can be implemented as an FFT

$$X(k) = \sum_{m=0}^{N-1} x(m)\, e^{-j2\pi km/N} \qquad k = 0,1,..., N-1 \qquad \textbf{(3.4a)}$$

$$x(m) = \frac{1}{N} \sum_{k=0}^{N-1} X(k)\, e^{j2\pi km/N} \qquad m = 0,1,...,N-1 \qquad \textbf{(3.4b)}$$

where $X(k)$ are the Fourier transform values of the signal at frequencies $2\pi\, km/N$. Figure 3.4 shows an implementation of the FFT in FORTRAN. Note that this is only an example, and you may find other, more efficient implementations. For instance, the book by Burrus and Parks [1] contains many FFT programs both in FOR-TRAN and in the assembly language of the TMS32010 digital signal processor.

Use of the Fourier transform method for speech coding can offer some advantages and flexibility in applying modifications to

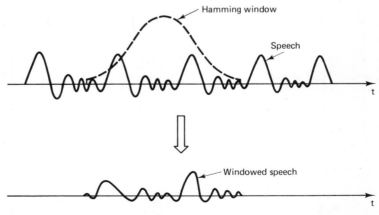

Figure 3.3   Application of Hamming window on a speech signal.

```
C
      A COOLEY–TUKEY RADIX-2, DIF FFT PROGRAM
C     COMPLEX INPUT DATA IN ARRAYS X AND Y
C
C         S. BURRUS, RICE UNIVERSITY, SEPT 1983
C- - - - - - - - - - - - - - - - - - - - - - - - - - - - - - - - - - - - - - -
C
C     SUBROUTINE FFT (X, Y, N, M)
      REAL X(1), Y(1)
C
C- - - - - - - - - - - - - - -MAIN FFT LOOPS - - - - - - - - - - - - - - - - -
C
      N2 = N
      DO 10 K = 1, M
         N1 = N2
         N2 = N2/2
         E = 6.283185307179586/N1
         A = 0
         DO 20 J = 1, N2
            C = COS (A)
            S = SIN (A)
            A = J*E
            DO 30 I = J, N, N1
               L = I + N2
               XT  = X(I)    − X(L)
               X(I) = X(I)   + X(L)
               YT  = Y(I)    − Y(L)
               Y(I) = Y(I)   + Y(L)
               X(L) = C*XT + S*YT
               Y(L) = C*YT − S*XT
30          CONTINUE
20       CONTINUE
10 CONTINUE
C
C- - - - - - - - - - - - - -DIGIT REVERSE COUNTER- - - - - - - - - - - - - - -
C
  100 J = 1
      N1 = N − 1
      DO 104 I = 1, N1
         IF (I.GE.J) GOXTO 101
         XT  = X(j)
         X(J) = X(I)
```

(*Figure 3.4 continues next page*)

Figure 3.4 An implementation of the FFT algorithm (after Burrus and Parks [1], reprinted by permission of Texas Instruments Inc., © 1985).

```
                 X(I) = XT
                 XT  = Y(J)
                 Y(J) = Y(I)
                 Y(I) = XT
      101        K = N/2
      102        IF (K.GE.J) GOTO 103
                     J = J - K
                     K = K/2
                     GOTO 102
      103      J = J + K
      104 CONTINUE
          RETURN
          END
```

Figure 3.4 An implementation of the FFT algorithm (*continued from previous page*).

the signal, since the operation is in the frequency domain. However, it is not one of the more effective schemes for reducing the bit rate. Figure 3.5 shows the block diagram of such a speech coding system. The D:1 decimation process, to be described in more detail in the section about subband coding, essentially means retaining 1 out of D consecutive speech samples. In most cases, all the decimators are the same. Interpolation is the opposite process, where the missing samples are restored. Decimation and interpolation can be applied without any loss of signal information only if the sampling frequency is at least $2D$ times the highest frequency of the signal. For example, a signal bandlimited to 4 kHz must be sampled at least at a rate of 16,000 samples/s in order to apply a 2:1 decimation.

An important consideration in the short-time Fourier transform representation is the sampling rate in both the time and frequency domains. The correct sampling rate in both domains is necessary for accurate reconstruction of the speech signal. Since windows of finite length N are typically used, the sampling frequency is given by the equations for the FFT. In other words, take N samples in the frequency domain. This is the minimum permissible number of samples. If we need more samples, we pad the sequence with the appropriate number of zeroes at the end before taking the FFT. However, this does not increase the resolution in the frequency domain. On the other hand, the fre-

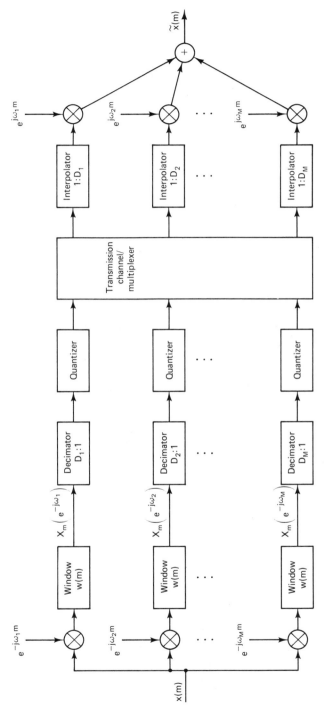

Figure 3.5 Block diagram of a speech coding system utilizing the short-time Fourier transform analysis with M channels. Variable $\tilde{x}(m)$ is the reconstructed signal. Each channel can be implemented as two subchannels and avoid the complex arithmetic (see [2,3]).

65

quency of taking FFTs in the time domain is determined by the type of the window and its length. The frequency of taking FFTs is the same concept as the frame rate, i.e., the number of frames considered per second of speech. The inverse of the frame rate is the frame period and equals the time interval between frames. It can be shown that equation (3.5) gives the frame rate for a rectangular window, while equation (3.6) is for a Hamming window.

$$R_{rect} = \frac{F_s}{N} \text{ frames/s} \tag{3.5}$$

$$R_{hamm} = \frac{2F_s}{N} \text{ frames/s} \tag{3.6}$$

F_s is the sampling rate of the speech signal, and N is the length of the window in samples. For example, for a window $N = 320$ points long and a sampling frequency of $F_s = 8,000$ Hz, the frame rate should be 25 frames/s (40 ms frame period) for the rectangular window and 50 frames/s (20 ms frame period) for the Hamming window. Figure 3.6 shows an example of positioning successive Hamming windows. In practice, the window has to be long enough so that the included points give an accurate description of the spectrum. On the other hand, the frames should be close enough to capture rapid variations of the speech signal. Combinations of these two requirements result in overlapping frames.

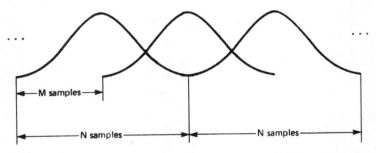

Figure 3.6 Positioning of successive Hamming windows for Fourier transform coding of speech. The window is N samples long. Successive windows are M samples apart.

The concept of the short-time Fourier transform has found an application for many years in the sound spectrograph. The sound spectrograph is a device used to generate a time-frequency representation of an utterance, called a spectrogram. The spectrogram, as shown in Figure 3.7, is a two-dimensional figure, where the abscissa is time and the ordinate is frequency. Each vertical slice of the plot corresponds to the magnitude (or sometimes, the log-magnitude) of the Fourier transform of the signal at that instant in time, with the amplitude of the plot being represented by the intensity of the gray-scale level. The spectrogram supplies a lot of information on the distribution of the energy in time and frequency, on the movement of the formants (i.e., the peaks of the spectrum), and on the voicing of the signal. If the length, N, of the window used is long, then you have good frequency resolution (but poor resolution along the time axis) and create a narrowband spectrogram. On the other hand, short windows result in wideband spectrograms with good time resolution and poor frequency resolution. Examples of such spectrograms (digitally generated) are given in Figure 3.7. Depending on the information sought, both extremes (i.e., narrowband and wideband spectrograms), and the whole range in between are useful.

The sound spectrograph is not used as widely any longer because, today, digitally generated spectrograms can be displayed on graphics terminals. To plot a spectrogram digitally, a FFT is computed as described above and the magnitude information is used to control the gray level of the display. Alternatively, the spectral envelope can be computed (e.g., by using the linear predictive model) and plotted. Spectrograms can even be plotted in color (e.g., see the cover of the September 1981 issue of *IEEE Spectrum*), which makes an impressive demonstration, although the amount of information is the same as in a black-and-white spectrogram with several gray-scale levels.

3.2 SUBBAND CODING (SBC)

An interesting method of speech coding that also falls into the waveform coding domain is subband coding (SBC) [4–7]. This method does not consider the waveform in a single band of fre-

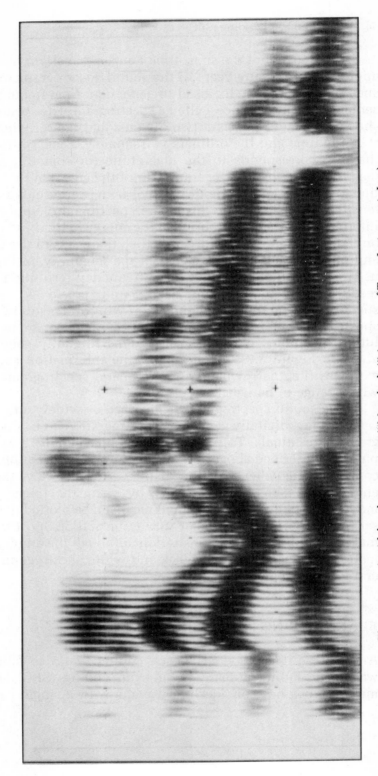

Figure 3.7a A wideband spectrogram ("Mary had a") (courtesy of Texas Instruments Inc.).

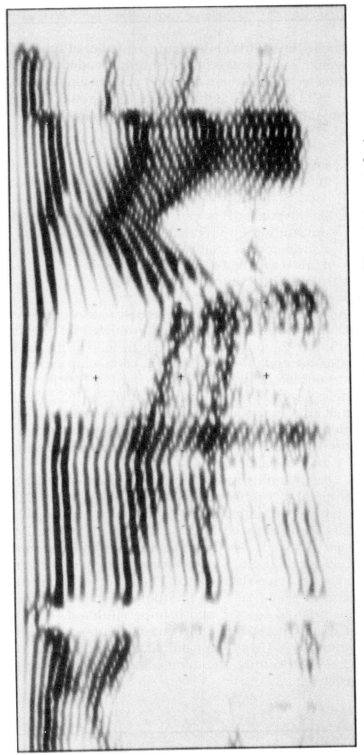

Figure 3.7b A narrowband spectrogram ("Mary had a") (courtesy of Texas Instruments Inc.).

69

quencies, but it first splits it into a number of subbands by bandpass filtering. Then, each subband output is coded using time waveform coding techniques such as adaptive delta modulation (ADM), adaptive PCM (APCM), and adaptive differential PCM (ADPCM) (see Chapter 2). There are two advantages obtained by quantizing the speech signal in subbands.

1. The quantization noise is localized in the corresponding frequency band, and no noise interference takes place from one band to the other.
2. The available bits can be distributed between the different subbands according to perceptual criteria, thus improving the overall speech quality as perceived by listeners, even though there may not be any improvement in the signal-to-quantization-noise ratio.

Figure 3.8 outlines the principles of operation of the Subband Coder. First, the input signal is filtered through a set of N bandpass filters that cover the portion of interest in the spectrum (e.g., 300–3,300 Hz for telephone speech). Then, each band is lowpass-translated and sampled at twice its bandwidth, or, if it is already in digital form as assumed here, it is decimated. For instance, if you filter the signal into two equal subbands, there will be a 2:1 decimation, which is accomplished very simply by throwing away every other speech sample. As we will see in the actual implementation, this is all that is necessary.

Each band is then quantized and coded using one of the several methods discussed in Chapter 2. However, since the sample-to-sample correlation of the bandpass-filtered signals is rather low, it has been proposed to use a simple adaptive PCM (APCM). The coded subbands are then multiplexed and transmitted to the receiver, or stored for later retrieval. At the receiver, the opposite sequence of steps takes place. The subbands are demultiplexed and decoded. Then, they are interpolated (possibly translated back to their original bands), and bandpass-filtered. The interpolation is performed by replacing the samples thrown away during the decimation by zeroes. The bandpass filters then sift the appropriate signal. The results are summed to give a replica of the original speech signal.

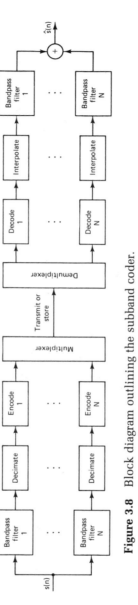

Figure 3.8 Block diagram outlining the subband coder.

71

Figure 3.9 gives an example of the decimation and interpolation processes in both the time and frequency domains for a low frequency signal. For D:1 decimation (in the figure, $D = 2$), you keep one out of every D consecutive samples, and throw away the rest. If you are interested in reconstructing exactly the signal, this decimation is permissible only if the sampling frequency is at least $2D$ times the highest frequency of the signal (see the example in Figure 3.9a–3.9b). To reconstruct the original signal from the decimated one, we apply interpolation, depicted in Figure 3.9c–3.9e: Between two samples of the decimated signal, place $D - 1$ zeros, and then lowpass-filter this signal. The result is the original signal. This explanation of decimation and interpolation is valid for baseband signals, but it can be extended to some bandpass signals, too.

A problem in the implementation of the subband coding is that after decimation there is danger of having considerable aliasing if the bandpass filters do not have sharp enough cutoffs. Esteban and Galand [8–9] solved this problem by using Quadrature Mirror Filters (QMF). The quadrature mirror filters operate in low-pass/highpass pairs as shown in Figure 3.10 where the highpass filter is a mirror image of the lowpass filter. Hence, only the lowpass filter needs to be specified. The QMF have to satisfy certain properties, e.g., the sum of the magnitudes of the lowpass and the highpass in the frequency domain have to be equal to 1, the FIR length has to be an even number, and so on. Table 3.1 shows an example of a quadrature mirror filter with 16 taps. Note that the filter coefficients given in Table 3.1 correspond to the lowpass filter. The highpass version of that is simply obtained by changing the sign of every other coefficient, starting from the second one. However, implementation of the highpass filter is not necessary. Figure 3.11 shows an example of bandsplitting and reconstruction by using a QMF with two taps where only the coefficients of the lowpass filter are used.

From the way the QMFs are constructed and operating, it is apparent that if we employ this method to implement the Subband Coding, then the number of subbands dividing the spectrum has to be a power of 2. In other words, we split the total band into two subbands, which are then decimated. Each of these two subbands can be split further into two equal subbands that are in turn decimated, and so on. Figure 3.12 shows an example of SBC imple-

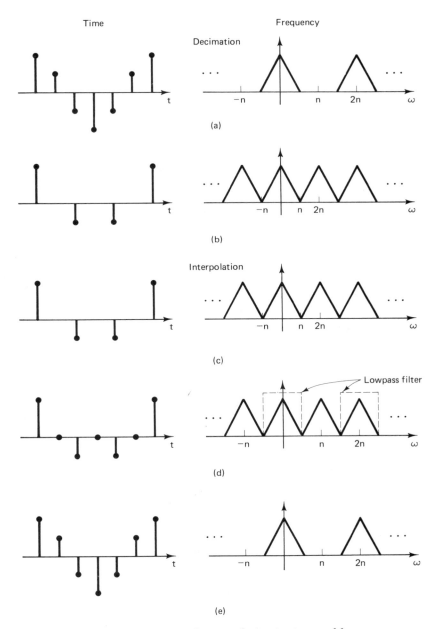

Figure 3.9 Decimation and interpolation in time and frequency;
(a) original signal; (b) signal decimation by removal of samples;
(c) original signal before interpolation; (d) signal with zeros at
the locations to be interpolated; (e) interpolated signal.

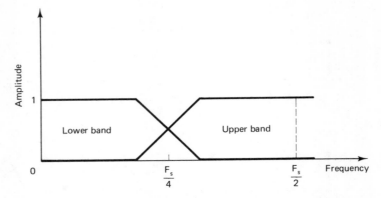

Figure 3.10 Spectral representation of the subbands where F_s is the sampling frequency.

mentation using QMF to split the whole band into four subbands. The quadrature mirror filters, which are enclosed in blocks, can be also implemented by using the method suggested by Figure 3.11.

In distributing the available bits, the lower bands have to get more bits because the signal is stronger in these regions. As an example, Table 3.2 shows the bit assignments for two-band SBC for

TABLE 3.1 QUADRATURE MIRROR FILTER WITH 16 TAPS

0.6525666	E-2
−0.2048751	E-1
0.1991150	E-2
0.4647684	E-1
−0.2627560	E-1
−0.9929550	E-1
0.1178666	
0.4721122	
0.4721122	
0.1178666	
−0.9929550	E-1
−0.2627560	E-1
0.4647684	E-1
0.1991150	E-2
−0.2048751	E-1
0.6525666	E-2

(after Johnston [10], © 1980 IEEE).

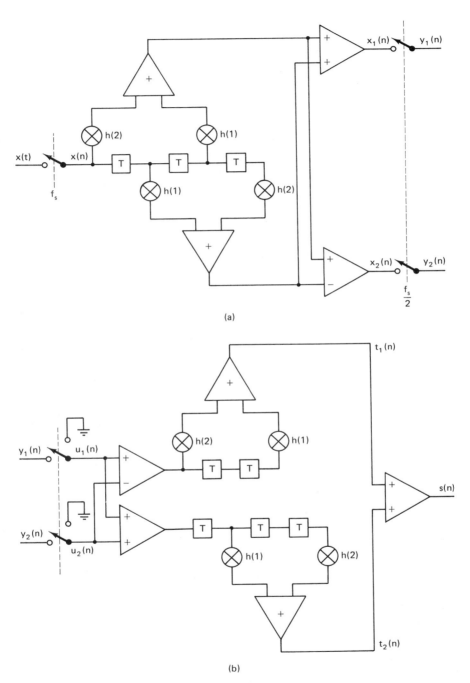

(a)

(b)

Figure 3.11 A Quadrature Mirror Filter with two taps; (a) quadrature channels splitting; (b) quadrature channels reconstruction (after Esteban and Galand [8], © 1977 IEEE).

TABLE 3.2 BIT ASSIGNMENTS FOR TWO-BOND SUBBAND
CODERS

	16 kbits/s	32 kbits/s
Low band:	3 bits (ADPCM)	5 bits (ADPCM)
High band:	1 bit (ADM)	3 bits (ADM)
Sampling frequency:	8 kHZ	

both 16 kbits/s and 32 kbits/s. It is indicated in parentheses what coding method is applied to the signal after passing through the QMFs.

The subband coding can be used for speech coding with bit rates between 9.6 and 32 kbits/s. In these bit rates, SBC compares favorably with other approaches such as ADPCM and ADM. However, the complexity of the method is also higher. Probably, 16 kbits/s could be considered a reasonable bit rate that still gives considerable advantages over the other methods. At that rate, subband coding has low complexity and gives good quality speech compared to other techniques, such as Adaptive Predictive Coding. When subband coding is teamed with time-domain harmonic scaling (TDHS, see Chapter 2), a good quality 9.6 kbits/s system results.

3.3 ADAPTIVE TRANSFORM CODING (ATC) AND THE DISCRETE COSINE TRANSFORM (DCT)

In Transform Coding systems, instead of coding the speech signal itself, we code a transformation of the signal. The objective is to use a transform that decorrelates the samples, and to achieve coding efficiency by assigning more bits to more important coefficients and fewer bits to less important coefficients. In transform coding, a block of speech samples is transformed into a set of transform coefficients. The transformation is implemented as a linear combination of the input samples $x(i)$ (see Figure 3.13), where the coefcients $a(i,j)$ are determined from the transformation selected. The operation can also be represented as a matrix multiplication (Figure 3.13) giving the coefficients $k(i)$ as a result. These transform coefficients are then quantized, coded, and transmitted. At the receiver, the coefficients are decoded and inversely transformed to

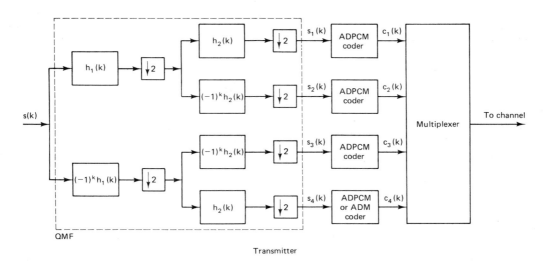

Transmitter

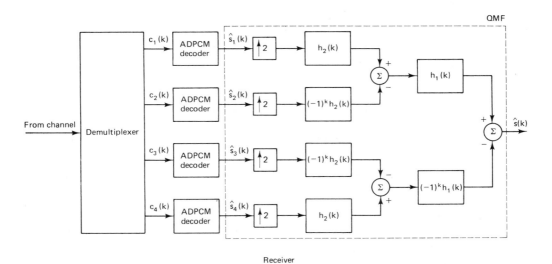

Receiver

Figure 3.12 Four-band subband coder. The QMFs at the transmitter and the receiver, which are enclosed with the broken line, can be also implemented using the scheme of Figure 3.10 (after Cox [11], reprinted with permission from *The Bell System Technical Journal*, © 1981).

$$k(1) = a(1,1) \cdot x(1) + a(2,1) \cdot x(2) + \cdots + a(n,1) \, x\,(n)$$
$$k(1) = a(1,2) \cdot x(1) + a(2,2) \cdot x(2) + \cdots + a(n,2) \, x\,(n)$$
.
.
.
$$k(n) = a(1,n) \cdot x(1) + a(2,n) \cdot x(2) + \cdots + a(n,n) \, x\,(n)$$

(a)

$$
\begin{bmatrix} k(1) \\ k(2) \\ \cdot \\ \cdot \\ \cdot \\ k(n) \end{bmatrix}
=
\begin{bmatrix} a(1,1) & a(2,1) & \ldots & a(n,1) \\ a(1,2) & a(2,2) & \ldots & a(n,2) \\ \cdot & & & \\ \cdot & & & \\ \cdot & & & \\ a(n,1) & a(n,2) & \ldots & a(n,n) \end{bmatrix}
\begin{bmatrix} x(1) \\ x(2) \\ \cdot \\ \cdot \\ \cdot \\ x(n) \end{bmatrix}
$$

Transform   Transformation matrix   Block to be
Coefficients   transformed

(b)

Figure 3.13 Transformation operation on a block of speech samples x(i). (a) equation form. (b) matrix form.

give an approximation of the original speech signal. The inverse transformation is performed by multiplying the vector of the coefficients by the inverse of the transformation matrix. In the applications we examine, the transformation matrices are unitary, i.e., their inverse is obtained simply by transposing the original matrix. For purposes of efficient coding of the speech signal, we consider only adaptive transform coding methods.

In Adaptive Transform Coding (ATC) [7, 12, 13], the distribution of the bits to the transform coefficients changes from frame to frame although the total number of bits remains the same for every frame of speech. The dynamic allocation of the bits is necessary in order to take into consideration the changing statistics of the speech signal. Since the speech signal is not stationary, it is necessary to also transmit some side information describing the changing statistics.

Several transformations can be used in transform coding, such as the Fourier Transform described earlier, the Karhunen-Loeve Transform (KLT), the Discrete Cosine Transform (DCT), and others.

It can be shown that the KLT is optimal and, theoretically, most desirable but difficulties in determining the statistical behavior of speech make it impractical. On the other hand, the DCT can be implemented easily and as efficiently as an FFT and at the same time has behavior closely tracking that of the KLT. For these reasons, the DCT is considered here.

The Discrete Cosine Transform (DCT) [14–17] is defined by the following relations:

$$V(k) = \sum_{n=0}^{N-1} v(n)\, c(k)\, \cos[(2n+1)\pi k/N] \qquad k = 0,1,..., N-1 \qquad (3.7a)$$

$$v(n) = \frac{1}{N} \sum_{k=0}^{N-1} V(k)\, c(k)\, \cos[(2n+1)\pi k/N] \qquad n = 0,1,..., N-1$$

$$(3.7b)$$

where

$$c(k) = 1 \text{ if } k = 0$$
$$c(k) = \sqrt{2} \text{ if } k = 1,2,..., N-1$$

The $v(n)$ represents the (windowed) input speech, $V(k)$ the transform coefficients, and N is the length of the buffer (number of samples in the block). Since the transformation is applied to a windowed signal, it is important to choose appropriate windows. It has been demonstrated that trapezoidal windows reduce block-end effects and improve the quality of the synthetic speech. Also, it is recommended that a small overlap of these windows (10 percent or less) be allowed in such a way so that the sum of the overlapped windows is always unity.

Figure 3.14 shows a block diagram of the ATC system. The buffer is needed to accumulate a block of speech samples to be used in the transformation. Typical block lengths are 128–256 samples. Each block is then transformed using the DCT.

The transform coefficients are the frequency representation of the input speech waveform. In other words, they represent the frequency-domain spectrum. This frequency-domain spectrum is also used for adapting the bit distribution to the changing speech statistics. If R is the number of the total available bits to be distributed to the transform coefficients, the best bit assignment is given by equation (3.8),

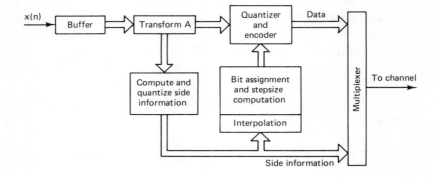

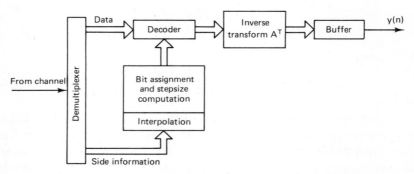

Figure 3.14 Block diagram of an adaptive transform coder. The side information (overhead bits) is used for bit allocation and quantizer stepsize (after Tribolet and Crochiere [7], © 1979 IEEE).

$$R(k) = \frac{R}{N} + \frac{1}{2} \left[\log_2(y^2(k)) \right.$$

$$\left. - \frac{1}{N} \sum_{k=0}^{N-1} \log_2(y^2(k)) \right] \text{ bits/sample}$$

(3.8)

where $y(k)$ is the variance of the kth transform coefficient, and N is the number of the transform coefficients (equal to the number of speech samples). Equation (3.8) can be interpreted as follows: The number of bits assigned to a transform coefficient $y(k)$ is the average bits per coefficient, incremented (or decremented) by an amount indicating how much stronger (or weaker) the energy of this coefficient is with respect to the average energy of all the transform coefficients.

In a practical implementation, we use an estimate of the $y(k)$ determined from the transform coefficients $V(k)$, as shown in Figure 3.15. The logarithm of the square of each coefficient is computed, and the thus-transformed coefficients are grouped in sets of N/L and averaged together. (Variable L represents the total number of points that we would like to transmit as side information. Typical values for L: 15–20.) These quantities represent the estimates of some of the $y(k)$, with the rest of the $y(k)$ computed from these values by interpolation, as shown in Figure 3.15c. Having the $y(k)$, it is easy to estimate the $R(k)$ from equation (3.8). Of course, the $R(k)$ has to be rounded to an integer number so that the sum of $R(k)$ is equal to R. If an $R(k)$ becomes negative, then it is set to zero. For the receiver to be able to determine the bit assignment and decode the transform coefficients, those of the quantities $\log(y^2(k))$ that were computed by averaging N/L consecutive $\log(V^2(k))$ are quantized and transmitted as side information, as indicated in Figure 3.14. The side information can be coded by using 2–5 bits per parameter. Differential coding of these parameters is also beneficial. Then, the transform coefficients $V(k)$ are encoded and transmitted using the bit allocation $R(k)$. Instead of coding and transmitting the transform coefficients $V(k)$, another possibility is to encode and transmit the differences $\log(V^2(k)) - \log(y^2(k))$.

It is also advantageous to assign the coding bits in a way that the quantization noise is masked by the signal. Studies indicate that if most of the noise energy is put in areas of high speech energy, then the effect of the noise is to a large extent masked. In the present method, this masking is achieved by writing (3.8) in the form of equation (3.9),

$$R(k) = \frac{R}{N} + \frac{1}{2} \left[\log_2(y^{2(1+c)}(k)) \right.$$

$$\left. - \frac{1}{N} \sum_{k=0}^{N-1} \log_2(y^2(k)) \right] \text{ bits/sample} \tag{3.9}$$

with the only difference being the coefficient $(1+c)$ in the exponent of $y(k)$. Variable c takes values between 0 and -1. For $c = 0$, equa-

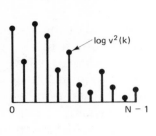

(a)

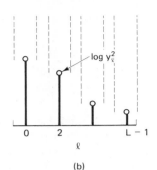

(b)

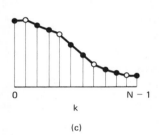

(c)

Figure 3.15 Adaptive bit allocation in transform coding of speech; (a) transform coefficients; (b) result of averaging N/L values in (a); (c) spectral envelope obtained by straight-line interpolation ($N=12$, $L=4$) (after Zelinski and Noll [12], © 1977 IEEE).

tion (3.9) reduces to equation (3.8), while for $c = -1$, all the transform coefficients are assigned the same number of bits. This last assignment leads to a quantization error that has exactly the shape of the speech spectrum. The best value of c should be determined experimentally for the desired bit rate. For example, it was found that for 16 kbits/s, $c = -0.125$ gave best results.

Adaptive transform coding is used to encode speech at bit rates between 9.6 and 20 kbits/s. However, for bit rates below 16 kbits/s, additional sophistication should be introduced (such as speech specific adaptation [7]) in order to preserve good speech quality. Note that the complexity of this system is higher than subband coding.

3.4 SUMMARY

This chapter examined three coding techniques involving the speech spectrum: the short-time Fourier analysis, the subband coding, and the adaptive transform coding. All three methods encode the same amount of information as the waveform coders, but they do it in the frequency domain.

The short-time Fourier transform is not a particularly efficient way of coding, but it is presented to explain some of the basic ideas involved in speech processing. The subband coding is a very simple and effective method for medium-band coding at 16 kbits/s. It can also be combined with time-domain harmonic scaling to achieve efficient coding at 9.6 kbits/s.

The adaptive transform coding is another effective method that also tracks the dynamic behavior of the speech signal and allocates the available bits appropriately. However, it has a higher complexity that may not be desirable in some applications.

3.5 FURTHER READING

Detailed explanation of the Fast Fourier Transform can be found in the books by Oppenheim and Schafer [18], Rabiner and Gold [19], and Brigham [20], while the IEEE Press book [21] and the book by Elliot and Rao [14] deal with efficient implementations of the FFT. The excellent book by Burrus and Parks [1] contains a detailed explanation of the DFT/FFT and many programs implementing the FFT. Besides the programs in FORTRAN, there are FFT programs written in the assembly language of the Texas Instruments TMS32010 digital signal processor. The first two references above [18,19], as well as the book by Rabiner and Schafer [2], discuss different kinds of windows. Implementation of the Fourier transform as a coding method is presented in [2,3], and the papers by Oppenheim [22] and Silverman and Dixon [23] present digital generation of spectrograms.

The basic subband coding method is described in the papers by Crochiere et al. [4], Crochiere [5,6], and Tribolet and Crochiere [7]. Esteban and Galand [8,9] outline the quadrature mirror filter implementation of subband coding, while Jayant and Noll [15], Esteban and Galand [8], and Crochiere and Rabiner [24] present the properties of QMFs. Crochiere and Rabiner [24], and Johnston [10] give examples of (the lowpass portion of) QMFs. A practical implementation of a subband coder using the TMS32010 digital signal processor is described by Barnwell et al. [25].

Jayant and Noll [15] discuss the Karhunen-Loeve, the discrete cosine, and other transforms in their book. More details of the Discrete Cosine Transform can be found in the book by Elliot and Rao [14], as well as in Ahmed et al. [16], Ahmed and Rao [17], and Zelinski and Noll [12], where efficient implementations of the DCT are also given. Zelinski and Noll [12,13] present the method of adaptive transform coding, while Tribolet and Crochiere [7] discuss some variations and improvements on ATC, such as the use of trapezoidal windows.

3.6 REFERENCES

1. Burrus, C.S., and T. Parks. *DFT/FFT and Convolution Algorithms.* New York: John Wiley & Sons, 1985.

2. Rabiner, L.R., and R.W. Schafer. *Digital Processing of Speech Signals.* Englewood Cliffs, NJ: Prentice-Hall, 1978.

3. Schafer, R.W., and L.R. Rabiner. "Design and Simulation of a Speech Analysis-Synthesis System Based on Short-Time Fourier Analysis." *IEEE Trans. on Audio and Electroacous.,* Vol. AU-21, No. 3 (June 1973): 165–174.

4. Crochiere, R.E., S.A. Webber, and J.L. Flanagan. "Digital Coding of Speech in Sub-bands." *Bell Syst. Tech. J.,* Vol. 55, (October 1976): 1069–1085.

5. Crochiere, R.E. "On the Design of Sub-band Coders for Low Bit-rate Speech Communication." *Bell Syst. Tech. J.,* Vol. 56, (May–June 1977): 747–770.

6. Crochiere, R.E. "Sub-band Coding." *Bell Syst. Tech. J.,* Vol. 60, (September 1981): 1633–1653.

7. Tribolet, J.M., and R.E. Crochiere. "Frequency-Domain Coding of Speech." *IEEE Trans. Acoustics, Speech, and Signal Proc.,* Vol. ASSP-27, No. 5, (October 1979): 512–530.

8. Esteban, D., and C. Galand. "Application of Quadrature Mirror Filters to Split Band Voice Coding Schemes." *Proc. 1977 IEEE Int. Conf. Acoustics, Speech, and Signal Proc.,* Hartford, CT (May 1977): 191–195.

9. Esteban, D., and C. Galand, "32 Kbps CCITT Compatible Split Band Coding Scheme," *Proc. 1978 IEEE Int. Conf. Acoustics, Speech, and Signal Proc.,* Tulsa, OK, 320–325, April 1978.

10. Johnston, J.D. "A Filter Family Designed for Use in Quadrature Mirror Filter Banks." *Proc. 1980 IEEE Int. Conf. Acoustics, Speech, and Signal Proc.,* Denver, CO (April 1980): 291–294.

11. Cox, R.V. "A Comparison of Three Speech Coders to Be Implemented on the Digital Signal Processor." *Bell Syst. Tech. J.,* Vol. 60 (September 1981): 1411–1421.

12. Zelinski, R., and P. Noll. "Adaptive Transform Coding of Speech Signals." *IEEE Trans. Acoustics, Speech, and Signal Proc.,* Vol. ASSP-25, No. 4, (August 1977): 299–309.

13. Zelinski, R., and P. Noll. "Approaches to Adaptive Transform Speech Coding at Low Bit Rates." *IEEE Trans. Acoustics, Speech, and Signal Proc.,* Vol. ASSP-27, No. 1, (February 1979): 89–95.

14. Elliot, D.F., and K.R. Rao. *Fast Transforms: Algorithms, Analyses, Applications.* New York: Academic Press, 1982.

15. Jayant, N.S., and P. Noll. *Digital Coding of Waveforms.* Englewood Cliffs, NJ: Prentice-Hall, 1984.

16. Ahmed, N., T. Natarajan, and K. Rao. "Discrete Cosine Transform." *IEEE Trans. on Computers,* Vol. C-23 (January 1974): 90–93.

17. Ahmed, N. and K.R. Rao. *Orthogonal Transforms for Digital Signal Processing,* New York: Springer-Verlag, 1975.

18. Oppenheim, A.V., and R.W. Schafer. *Digital Signal Processing.* Englewood Cliffs, NJ: Prentice-Hall, 1975.

19. Rabiner, L.R., and B. Gold. *Theory and Applications of Digital Signal Processing.* Englewood Cliffs, NJ: Prentice-Hall, 1975.

20. Brigham, E.O. *The Fast Fourier Transform.* Englewood Cliffs, NJ: Prentice-Hall, 1974.

21. Digital Signal Processing Committee. *Programs for Digital Signal Processing.* IEEE Acous., Speech, and Signal Proc. Soc., New York: IEEE Press, 1979.

22. Oppenheim, A.V. "Speech Spectrograms Using the Fast Fourier Transform." *IEEE Spectrum,* Vol. 7, (August 1970): 57–62.

23. Silverman, H.F., and N.R. Dixon. "A Parametrically Controlled Spectral Analysis System for Speech." *IEEE Trans. Acoustics, Speech, and Signal Proc.,* Vol. ASSP-22, No. 5, (October 1974): 362–381.

24. Crochiere, R.E., and L.R. Rabiner, *Multirate Digital Signal Processing,* Englewood Cliffs, NJ: Prentice-Hall, 1983.

25. Barnwell, T.P., III, R.W. Schafer, R.M. Mersereau, and D.L. Smith. "A Real-Time Speech Subband Coder Using the TMS32010." *IEEE Soutcon 1984,* paper 22/1.

Chapter 4

Efficient Coding Using Analysis-Synthesis

Analysis-synthesis methods use the spectral information contained in the speech signal for efficient coding. These methods try to identify the parameters that most effectively represent the speech signal (analysis), and then use these parameters at the receiver to reconstruct the speech signal (synthesis). Such techniques have become very popular because they can afford representation of the speech signal at low bit rates (2,400 to 9,600 bits/s) with good speech quality, while the methods described in the previous two chapters cannot preserve as good a quality at such low rates. Hence, for applications where bandwidth (or storage) conservation is of paramount importance, analysis-synthesis gives the best results. It should be noted, however, that analysis-synthesis modeling imposes an inherent upper bound to the speech quality. In other words, the speech quality cannot be improved beyond a certain level even if the data rate grows to the level of waveform coders.

The analysis-synthesis methods have also been traditionally called vocoders (for *VOice CODERS*). The reason is that they use an explicit model of the speech production, as depicted in Figure 4.1. In that model, the spectral envelope of the speech signal is separated from the fine structure that represents the excitation, and each of them is coded separately, leading to bit rate savings. Excitation and spectral envelope are assumed to be independent of each

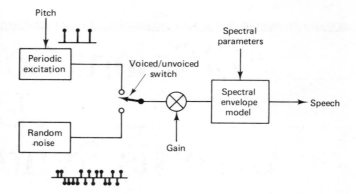

Figure 4.1   Speech production model for vocoders.

other. Figure 4.2 shows the Fourier transform of a 20 ms segment of speech, together with an envelope that could be fit on the spectrum. In the model of Figure 4.1, we select the periodic excitation or the random noise source when the speech is voiced or unvoiced, respectively. The most widely used vocoder is the *Linear Predictive Coder* (LPC) that has become so pervasive that we devote Chapter 5 to discuss it. In this section some other vocoders are considered.

The channel vocoder is examined first because it is the oldest and a very widely studied and applied method. It is linked to the short-time Fourier analysis. The parameters of the channel vocoder have been also used recently in speech recognition applications. The homomorphic vocoder uses a different parametrization of the vocal tract, based on the log-spectrum of the speech signal. It contains important concepts related to the separation of the excitation and the vocal tract information. The phase vocoder is more of a frequency-domain technique, where the spectral amplitude is coded like in the channel vocoder, while the phase is represented by its derivative. The formant vocoder is actually a class of vocoders that share the common feature of representing the vocal tract spectrum by the formants, i.e., the peaks of the smoothed spectrum. Other vocoders briefly mentioned are the phonetic vocoder, the voice-excited vocoder, and vector quantization.

4.1 THE CHANNEL VOCODER

One of the most popular, studied, and implemented vocoders is the Channel Vocoder. The basic idea was conceived by H. Dudley in

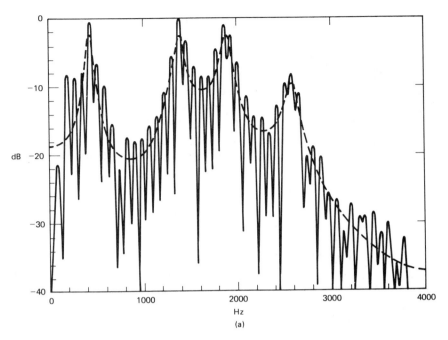

Figure 4.2a Fourier transform of a voiced speech segment.

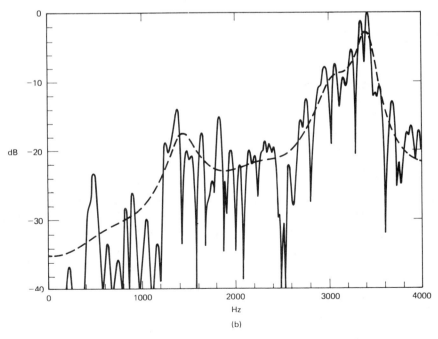

Figure 4.2b Fourier transform of an unvoiced speech segment.

the 1930s and it was demonstrated at the New York Fair in 1939. That was the first practical proof that speech could be presented by analysis-synthesis systems, where the vocal source and the vocal tract are separated and presented separately. The separation takes place at the analyzer (transmitter) and then the source and vocal tract information are coded and transmitted to the synthesizer (receiver). At the synthesizer, an approximation of the speech signal is reconstructed from the transmitted information. The determination of the excitation signal, i.e., if the speech is voiced or unvoiced and, if voiced, the pitch period, is a very important problem and it is treated separately in Chapter 6. Chapter 4 is primarily concerned with vocal tract representation.

The channel vocoder, like most vocoders, capitalizes on the properties of the human hearing mechanism rather than the method of production of the speech signal. In other words, we try to reconstruct a signal that *sounds* like the original speech, although the signal itself may not look very much like the original. This is the most important philosophical difference between the vocoders and the waveform coders described in Chapter 2. As a result, waveform-based objective quality measures, such as the signal-to-noise ratio, become meaningless when measuring the speech quality.

A property of the hearing mechanism we most often take advantage of is the relative insensitivity to the short-time phase. For short segments of speech (10–40 ms, corresponding to the length of the analysis window used) only the information contained in the magnitude of the spectrum needs be transmitted. At the synthesizer, this would include some appropriately selected phase substitutes for the correct one in reconstructing the signal. This property is used in the channel vocoder, where a bank of bandpass filters determines the amplitudes of the vocal tract spectrum in certain frequencies, and uses these parameters to represent the speech signal. Figure 4.3a shows the analyzer portion and Figure 4.3b shows the synthesizer portion of the channel vocoder.

As can be seen from Figure 4.3a, the speech signal is passed through a bank of bandpass filters covering the portion of the spectrum in which we are interested (usually 0–4 kHz). The more filters we use, the better the accuracy of the representation will be, but also, the higher the transmission bit rate since we need to transmit more information to the receiver. Typically, the number of channels is 16–19. Another consideration is the bandwidth of the bandpass filters. The simplest solution is to select all the filters

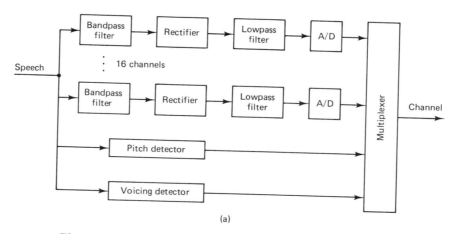

Figure 4.3a   Transmitter (analyzer) of the channel vocoder.

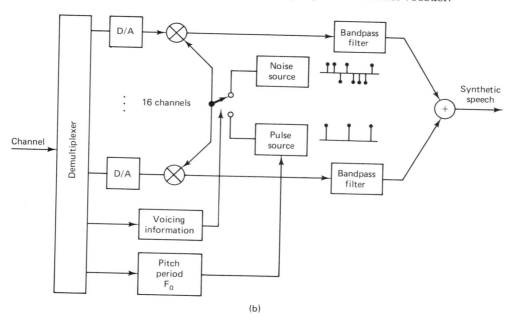

Figure 4.3b   Receiver (synthesizer) of the channel vocoder.

with the same bandwidth. However, since it has been demonstrated that the human ear responds linearly to a logarithmic scale of the frequencies, the bandwidths are chosen to increase proportionally with frequency. Figure 4.4 shows an example of such a choice of bandwidths for the case of four filters. Table 4.1 [2] shows a real-

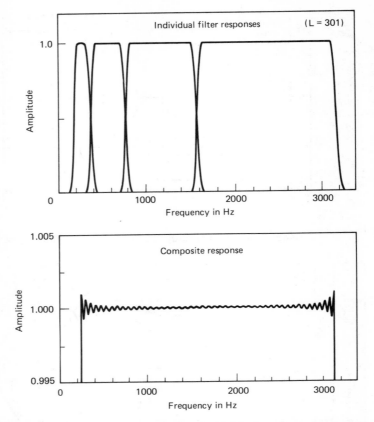

Figure 4.4 Frequency responses (individual and composite) of 4 bandpass filters with different bandwidths (after Schafer et al. [1], reprinted with permission from *The Bell System Technical Journal*, © 1975).

istic assignment of center frequencies and bandwidths for a channel vocoder with 19 filters. Note that the bandwidths used for synthesis are narrower than those used for analysis.

The output of each filter is rectified and lowpass-filtered in order to determine the envelope of the signal in that bandwidth. This envelope is then sampled at a lower rate, encoded, multiplexed with the outputs from the other filters, and transmitted to the receiver. The sampling is typically done around 50 times per second, corresponding to a frame period of 20 ms. The usual choices for frame period are 10–30 ms. At the receiver, the inverse process is taking place, as shown in Figure 4.3b, and a replica of the input speech is produced.

TABLE 4.1 FILTER FREQUENCIES FOR A CHANNEL VOCODER WITH 19 CHANNELS

Channel Number	Center Frequency (Hz)	Analysis Bandwidth (Hz)	Synthesis Bandwidth (Hz)
1	240	120	40
2	360	120	40
3	480	120	40
4	600	120	40
5	720	120	40
6	840	120	40
7	1000	150	40
8	1150	150	40
9	1300	150	40
10	1450	150	40
11	1600	150	40
12	1800	200	60
13	2000	200	60
14	2200	200	60
15	2400	200	60
16	2700	300	60
17	3000	300	60
18	3300	300	60
19 anal.	3750	500	—
19 synth.	3600	—	60
19a synth.	3750	—	500

(after Holmes [2]).

The first vocoders implemented used analog techniques for the bandpass filters and the other elements of the vocoder. However, our interest today focuses on digital implementations. This gives much flexibility both for processing of the signal and for encoding the output parameters. The different filters are implemented digitally as FIR filters with linear phase, and the coded parameters are quantized before multiplexing.

Experimentation has shown [3] that spectral signals more than 30 dB below the maximum signal can be zeroed out without noticeable difference. This suggests coding the maximum level in an absolute scale, and the rest of the filter bank outputs relative to that maximum. Another possibility is coding relative to the average signal. Yet another popular approach has been to encode the logarithmic differences between a channel and the previously coded channel. By "previous channel," it is meant the adjacent channel in frequency and not the same channel of the previous frame; that is, you take the difference within each frame.

The channel vocoder is the oldest of the vocoders and has gone through much refinement so that there are versions of the vocoder with very good quality speech. It has also been implemented in both analog and digital hardware [2]. The refinements have overcome the poorer quality of earlier versions, where the channels introduced an effect as though one were talking through a barrel. A typical bit rate for the channel vocoder is 2,400 bits/s.

4.2 THE HOMOMORPHIC VOCODER

The homomorphic vocoder represents another approach to separating the vocal tract spectrum from the excitation. It is based on the observation that the short-time spectrum of the speech signal is the product of the slow-varying vocal tract spectrum $V(e^{j\omega})$ and the fast-varying periodic excitation spectrum $P(e^{j\omega})$, as shown in Figure 4.5. The total spectrum is $P(e^{j\omega})V(e^{j\omega})$, where $V(e^{j\omega})$ behaves as the modulating signal for $P(e^{j\omega})$. If you consider the logarithm of the spectrum, the two components are combined with addition rather than multiplication. Since the human ear is relatively insensitive to the phase, the logarithm of the spectral magnitude is considered: $\log |P(e^{j\omega})| + \log |V(e^{j\omega})|$. In the additive form, the two components still retain their fast- and slow-varying behavior, respectively. If these components were some functions of time, one would correspond to low frequencies and the other to high frequencies in the frequency domain. However, you now have two functions of frequency. By taking the inverse transform of the log-spectrum, you move into a kind of "time" domain, called the cepstral domain, with the transform coefficients being the cepstral coefficients (Figure 4.5b). A properly chosen cutoff time in the cepstral domain can separate the portion corresponding to vocal tract from the portion corresponding to the excitation. Actually, the cepstrum has been used to estimate both the vocal tract spectrum and the excitation information (i.e., voicing and pitch).

Figures 4.6a and 4.6b show the analyzer and the synthesizer configuration of a homomorphic vocoder, respectively. The input speech is windowed using a Hamming window 20–40 ms long. Then the windowed speech is Fourier-transformed using an FFT. For instance, with a 40-ms window and 10 kHz sampling rate, a

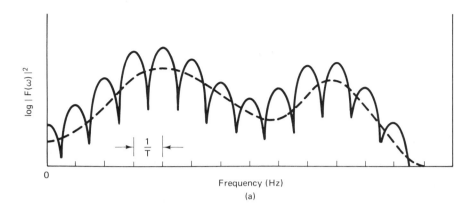

Frequency (Hz)

(a)

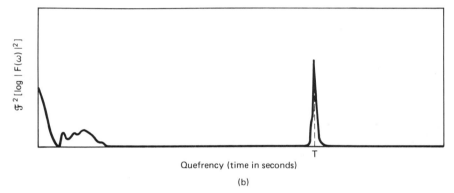

Quefrency (time in seconds)

(b)

Figure 4.5 (a) Short time spectrum of the speech signal. The spectral envelope corresponding to the vocal tract is superimposed and plotted with a broken line. (b) The corresponding cepstrum (after Noll [4]).

512-point FFT can be used. Successive windows can be placed 20 ms apart for a frame rate of 50 Hz. Possible choices for frame rate are 30–100 Hz. After the Fourier transformation, the logarithm of the magnitude is computed for each one of the points in frequency. These logarithms are then used in an inverse Fourier transform to determine the cepstral coefficients. When the cepstral coefficients become available, the question arises as to how to separate the portion corresponding to the vocal tract from the one corresponding to the excitation. A good rule of thumb is to select a cutoff time less than the smallest expected pitch period. For the above example where the sampling rate was 10 kHz, a reasonable choice is to assign the first 32 points to the vocal tract. (Often, the term

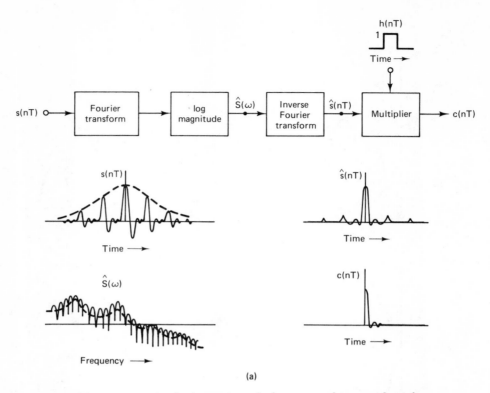

Figure 4.6a Analysis portion of a homomorphic vocoder (after Oppenheim [5]).

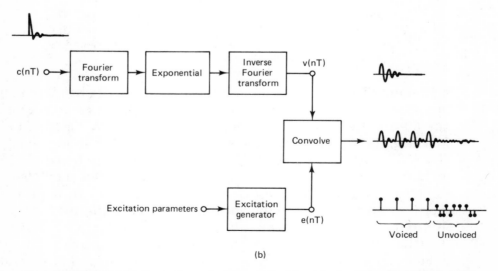

Figure 4.6b Synthesis portion of a homomorphic vocoder (after Oppenheim [5]).

"cepstrum" is reserved just for the portion corresponding to the vocal tract. Here, the term is used more loosely to mean either case, depending on the context.) The cepstral coefficients of the vocal tract are encoded and transmitted to the receiver together with the voicing and pitch information.

At the synthesizer (see Figure 4.6b), you take the Fourier transform of the vocal tract cepstral coefficients, and the resulting values are exponentiated. The inverse Fourier transform of these parameters gives the impulse response of the vocal tract. This impulse response is convolved with the excitation to produce the synthetic speech.

With the steps outlined above, the impulse response has zero phase. However, it has been observed that somewhat better speech is produced if you use speech-like phase instead, such as minimum phase. For zero phase, the vocal tract cepstrum is given by the equations

$$v(n) = v(-n) = c(n) \qquad 0 \le n \le N \qquad \textbf{(4.1a)}$$

$$v(n) = v(-n) = 0 \qquad N < n \qquad \textbf{(4.1b)}$$

where $c(n)$ are the cepstral coefficients and N is the number of coefficients for the vocal tract. In the above example, $N = 32$. For minimum phase,

$$v(n) = 2c(n) \qquad 0 < n \le N \qquad \textbf{(4.2a)}$$

$$v(n) = c(n) \qquad n = 0 \qquad \textbf{(4.2b)}$$

$$v(n) = 0 \qquad n < 0 \qquad \textbf{(4.2c)}$$

To improve the synthesizer performance, the impulse response of consecutive frames can be interpolated to produce approximations of the intermediate states of the vocal tract impulse response.

4.3 THE PHASE VOCODER

The phase vocoder is an analysis-synthesis system using the frequency-domain information of the speech signal. The present discussion is based on the presentation by Flanagan and Golden [6], who developed it. Despite the name vocoder, the system does not separate the vocal tract information from the excitation, but it encodes both the magnitude and the phase information in the frequency domain. Since the phase vocoder does not extract pitch information, it does not suffer from the problems of pitch tracking, but on the other hand it requires higher bit rates to transmit the parameters.

One half of the phase vocoder is identical to the channel vocoder, since it computes, encodes, and transmits the magnitude of the speech spectrum. The other half is the novel part, where the phase (more accurately, the phase derivative) is encoded and transmitted. As in the channel vocoder, the speech signal is passed through a bank of contiguous bandpass filters, the output of which, summed together, gives approximately the original signal. Figure 4.7 depicts this process of signal filtering and reconstruction. Here, however, it is assumed that the bandpass filters are generated from

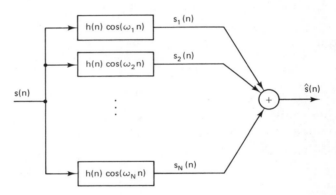

Figure 4.7 Filtering of speech by a bank of bandpass signals and reconstruction of the speech signal.

a lowpass–filter by modulating its impulse response to the desired center frequencies. It can be shown that the output of the ith filter is given by

$$s_i(n) = |S(\omega_i,n)| \cos[\omega_i n + \phi(\omega_i,n)] \qquad (4.3)$$

where $|S(\omega_i,n)|$ is the magnitude and $\phi(\omega_i,n)$ the phase of the speech spectrum. Variable ω_i is the center frequency of the ith filter. You can interpret this representation as a simultaneous amplitude and phase modulation of the carrier $\cos(\omega_i n)$.

The encoding of the magnitude is performed in a manner similar to the channel vocoder, and it will not be examined further. Instead, we concentrate on the representation of the phase. Since the phase varies in a relatively smooth way with time, it could be a candidate for quantization. Unfortunately, it is unbounded and, hence, unsuitable for encoding. Instead, the derivative of the phase with respect to time is used.

Let $a(\omega_i,n)$ and $b(\omega_i,n)$ be the real and imaginary parts of the speech spectrum:

$$S(\omega_i,n) = a(\omega_i,n) - j\, b(\omega_i,n) \qquad (4.4)$$

then

$$|S(\omega_i,n)|^2 = a^2(\omega_i,n) + b^2(\omega_i,n) \qquad (4.5)$$

It can be shown (by starting from the continuous-time domain) that an approximation of the phase derivative is given by

$$\dot{\phi}(\omega_i, n) = \frac{b(\omega_i,n)\,\Delta a - a(\omega_i,n)\,\Delta b}{a^2(\omega_i,n) + b^2(\omega_i,n)} \qquad (4.6)$$

where

$$\Delta a = a(\omega_i,n + 1) - a(\omega_i,n) \qquad (4.7a)$$

$$\Delta b = b(\omega_i,n + 1) - b(\omega_i,n) \qquad (4.7b)$$

Variables Δa and Δb are approximations to the derivatives of $a(\omega_i,t)$ and $b(\omega_i,t)$ with respect to time. Another way of computing them is to pass these two time signals through a differentiator filter. Figure 4.8 shows an example of such a filter.

The synthesis of the speech signal can be implemented through the equation

$$s_i(n) = |S(\omega_i,n)| \cdot \cos(\omega_i n + \sum_{k=0}^{n} \dot{\phi}(\omega_i,k)) \qquad (4.8)$$

Note that in this case zero initial phase is assumed. This assumption is a weakness of the approach, since it can introduce a reverberant quality when it is grossly in error. Figure 4.9 shows the analysis portion of the phase vocoder, and Figure 4.10 shows the synthesizer for a single channel. The differentiator in Figure 4.9 can be either a filter with frequency response as in Figure 4.8 or the simple difference equations outlined earlier. The integration in Figure 4.10 can be the simple addition implied in the synthesis equation of the phase vocoder. The interpolation is necessary to recover

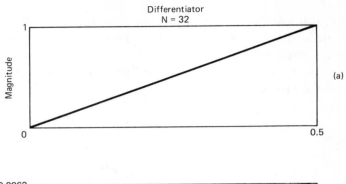

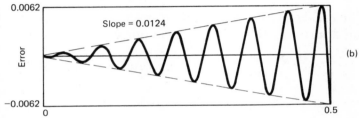

Figure 4.8 Frequency response and the corresponding error of a 32-point differentiator. (Lawrence R. Rabiner, Bernard Gold [7], *Theory and Application of Digital Signal Processing*, © 1975. Reprinted by permission of Prentice-Hall, Inc., Englewood Cliffs, NJ.)

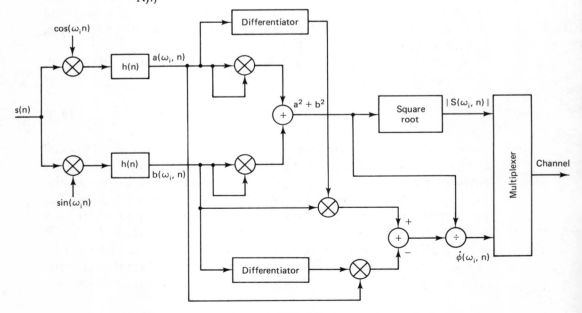

Figure 4.9 One channel of the phase vocoder analyzer.

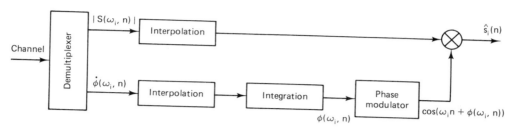

Figure 4.10   One channel of the phase vocoder synthesizer.

the original sample rate, and it can be performed by the interpolation approach outlined in Chapter 3.

Sometimes, the phase modulator is not very convenient to implement. Another kind of synthesizer is given by Figure 4.11, where the phase and magnitude are first converted to the real and imaginary parts and then used to reconstruct the speech signal.

Table 4.2 gives an example of parameter choice that results in a bit rate of 7.2 kbits/s. The phase can be quantized linearly. For the magnitude we can apply the methods of the channel vocoder.

The phase vocoder has not found very wide application in speech compression areas because of its limitations. However, its structure lends itself to manipulating the speech signal for purposes of speeding up or slowing down the speech without any alteration of the speech spectrum. This variation in speed can be done by multiplying (or dividing, respectively) the phase derivative and the center frequency ω_i by a factor of q and then playing

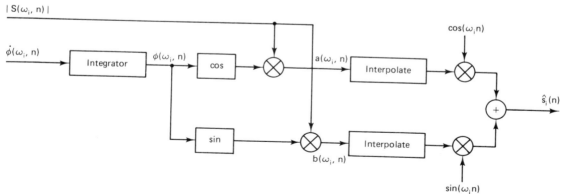

Figure 4.11   Alternative implementation of the phase vocoder synthesizer. (L.R. Rabiner, R.W. Schafer [8], *Digital Processing of Speech Signals*, © 1978. Reprinted by permission of Prentice-Hall, Inc.)

TABLE 4.2 AN EXAMPLE OF PARAMETER CHOICE FOR A PHASE VOCODER

		Magnitude	Phase
Number of channels:	28		
Spacing of channels:	100 Hz		
Phase and Magnitude sampling rate:	60 Hz		
Bit assignment			
Channels 1–18		2 bits	3 bits
Channels 19–28		1 bit	2 bits

back the speech q times faster (slower). Flanagan and Golden [6] give examples of spectrograms for such an application.

4.4 FORMANT VOCODERS

It has been demonstrated that, perceptually, the most important elements of the speech spectrum are the vocal tract resonances, which are also called formants. Figure 4.12 shows an example of a speech spectral envelope, where the formants have been marked. To describe accurately each formant, its center frequency F_i and its bandwidth B_i are needed. The formant can be realized as a second-order all-pole filter according to the equation

$$H_i(z) = \frac{1 - 2e^{-B_iT}\cos(2\pi F_iT) + e^{-B_iT}}{1 - 2e^{-B_iT}\cos(2\pi F_iT)\,z^{-1} + e^{-2B_iT}z^{-2}} \qquad (4.9)$$

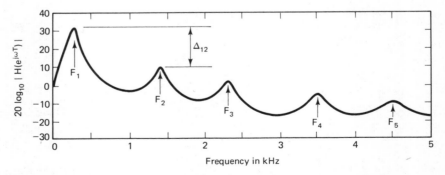

Figure 4.12 Example of speech spectral envelope with the formants F_i marked. (after Schafer and Rabiner [9].)

which has unity gain at zero frequency. Variable T is the sampling period for the speech signal. From the formant information, the speech can be synthesized as shown in Figure 4.13. In this example, we assume that four formants suffice to synthesize the speech signal. The assumption is based on the rule of thumb that there is one formant every 1,000 Hz and on the implicit condition that speech is lowpass-filtered at 4 kHz. Actually, for most practical purposes, just three formants give sufficiently intelligible speech and very often the fourth formant is fixed to a certain value to ensure that high frequencies have a proper spectral balance. Values suggested in [9] (when $T = 10^{-4}$s) are

$$B_1 = 60\pi$$
$$B_2 = 100\pi$$
$$B_3 = 120\pi$$
$$B_4 = 175\pi$$
$$F_4 = 4,000 \text{ Hz}$$

Note that formants are meaningful mostly for voiced sounds, and that's where they have been mostly used. However, the ideas can be extended to unvoiced areas, too.

For this extension the model of Figure 4.13 can be used again. In this case the unvoiced speech is synthesized by passing scaled

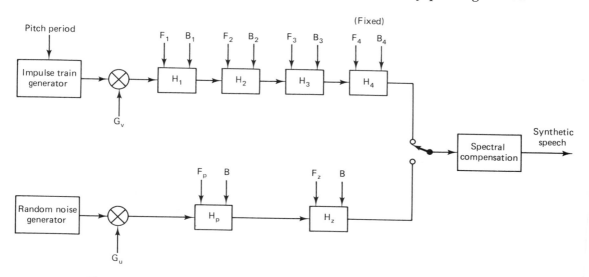

Figure 4.13 Speech production model using a formant synthesizer.

random noise through a system that consists of a complex pole and a complex zero.

$$H_p = \frac{1 - 2e^{-BT}\cos(2\pi F_p T) + e^{-2BT}}{1 - 2e^{-BT}\cos(2\pi F_p T)\, z^{-1} + e^{-2BT}z^{-2}} \qquad (4.10)$$

$$H_z = \frac{1 - 2e^{-BT}\cos(2\pi F_z T)\, z^{-1} + e^{-2BT}z^{-2}}{1 - 2e^{-BT}\cos(2\pi F_z T) + e^{-2BT}} \qquad (4.11)$$

Typical values chosen:

$B = 200\pi$

F_p = Greatest peak of the smoothed log spectrum above 1,000 Hz.

$F_z \cong (0.0065\, F_p + 4.5 - \Delta)(0.014\, F_p + 28) \qquad (4.12)$
(empirical formula)

In the above equations, $\Delta = 20\log_{10}(\ |\ H(e^{-j2\pi F_p})/H(e^{-j0})\ |\ )$ where H represents the smooth spectrum. In other words, Δ gives the amplitude (in dB) of the greatest peak above the DC value of the smooth spectrum.

Alternatively, the formant vocoder can be used in voiced segments, while some other method of coding, such as Linear Predictive Coding (LPC), can be applied to unvoiced segments.

The spectral compensation in Figure 4.13 approximates the contributions of the glottal pulse and the lip radiation to the speech spectrum. Its transfer function is given by

$$S(z) = \frac{(1 - e^{-aT})(1 + e^{-bT})}{(1 - e^{-aT}z^{-1})(1 + e^{-bT}z^{-1})} \qquad (4.13)$$

with representative values for a and b being

$a = 400\pi$

$b = 5,000\pi$

The formant synthesizer is usually represented in the form of Figure 4.13, where the resonators are cascaded. This is not, however, the only solution. The resonators can also be combined in parallel with their outputs summed together as depicted in Figure 4.14. In that case the gain of each resonator should be selected carefully because zeros are introduced in the transfer function in

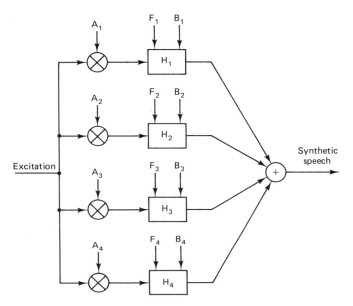

Figure 4.14 Parallel combination of the resonators of a formant synthesizer.

addition to the poles. The references [10,11] give a detailed comparison and implementation of the two methods.

Keep in mind, though, that these implementations have been inspired by voice synthesis applications (where the speech is synthesized from text according to certain rules), rather than analysis-synthesis applications.

The hardest problem in the formant vocoder, which has hindered its popularity despite its other advantages, is the determination of the formant values. The two most often used methods are cepstral analysis and linear predictive coding. We are going to examine the first approach here, while the second one will be examined in Chapter 5, after the LPC method has been explained.

As discussed earlier in this chapter, cepstral analysis gives an estimate of the short-time spectral envelope of the speech signal. Then the desired formant frequencies can be identified by picking the peaks of that envelope (see Schafer and Rabiner [9]). In [9], probable regions of the formants are specified (Figure 4.15). Then, the formants are determined essentially by finding the highest peak of the smoothed spectrum in each region.

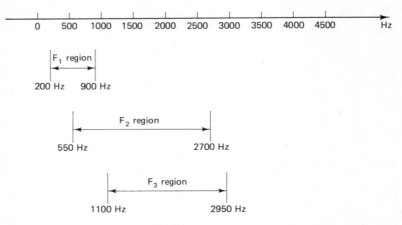

Figure 4.15 Empirical frequency ranges for the first three formants for male speakers. (After Schafer and Rabiner [9].)

One of the difficulties of this method is that, occasionally, two formants will get so close together that it is difficult to discriminate between the two peaks. If this is the case (and the algorithm in [9] specifies criteria detecting that case), you can use the Chirp Z-Transform (CZT) to enhance the resolution between the two peaks. The CZT is a Fourier transform evaluated not on the unit circle, but on a circle with a smaller radius, which still encloses all the poles. Figure 4.16 gives an example of the effectiveness of the CZT for a system with two poles.

Some typical values of bit assignments for the formant vocoder parameters for voiced speech are:

Pitch	6 bits
F1	3 bits
F2	4 bits
F3	3 bits
$\log(Gv)$	2 bits

The bandwidth of F_4 is fixed.

The formant vocoder is believed to be one of the most efficient ways of encoding speech at very low bit rates (below 1,000 bits/sec). Yet, it has met with only limited application because of the difficulties of automatically extracting the formants. It still holds con-

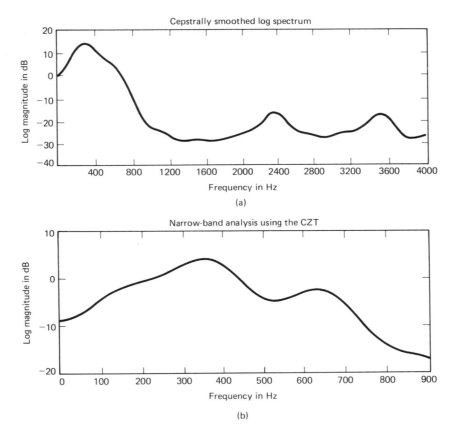

Figure 4.16 (a) Spectral envelope in which F_1 and F_2 are too close to be resolved; (b) application of CZT over a narrow band (0-900 Hz) and on a contour inside the unit circle. (after Schafer and Rabiner [9].)

siderable promise for effective speech coding since the formants are the most important parameters perceptually.

4.5 OTHER ANALYSIS-SYNTHESIS SYSTEMS

In this section we mention some more analysis-synthesis systems that have been proposed. For two of them (Vector Quantization and voice-excited vocoders), there will be a more detailed discussion in Chapter 5. The rest represent attempts to describe the vocal tract system by different sets of parameters.

Vector Quantization. In vector quantization, the speech signal is segmented into frames, and each frame is described by a set of parameters (e.g., cepstral coefficients, channel-bank outputs, LPC parameters) that are considered as a vector. Then, instead of encoding each parameter separately, the vector is encoded as one unit. This is done by having a codebook of vectors available to both the analyzer and the synthesizer. At the analyzer, the codebook vector "closest" to the input vector is found and its label is transmitted to the synthesizer. The synthesizer then uses the selected codebook vector to synthesize the speech.

Two of the most important considerations in vector quantization are the selection of the vocal tract parameters and the choice of the distance metric, which will determine the "closeness" of the vectors. A simple choice for the distance can be a Euclidean distance (sum of squares of the differences). However, in many instances the preference is the LPC parameters and the Itakura log-likelihood ratio associated with them. The vector quantization has been demonstrated to give good speech quality down to 800 bits/s and is expected to go even lower. These bit rates seem to be sufficient for most applications demanding low bit rates.

Phonetic Vocoders: An ideal solution for very low bit rate coding is to identify the phonemes spoken in the speech signal and transmit that information. This method is called a phonetic vocoder. Since there are very few phonemes (about 50 for the English language), and in a normal rate we pronounce about 10 per second, quite low bit rates would result (about 60 bits/s). Of course, one problem associated with the approach is that the speaker's identity is lost. However, even if we are willing to accept this loss, the problem of phonetic vocoding remains extremely difficult. Its difficulty stems from the fact that in order to identify the spoken phonemes we need speech recognition techniques. Unfortunately, the existing speech recognition techniques do not have acceptable performance for this application. So, until some breakthroughs come about, the phonetic vocoders will not find much application.

Voice-excited Vocoders: The major problem that most analysis-synthesis systems have is the separation of voiced from unvoiced speech and the determination of the fundamental frequency (the pitch) when the speech is voiced. Early on, it was observed that the speech signal itself contains that kind of information and it could become the basis for an excitation. In voice-excited vocoders, instead of detecting, encoding, and transmitting the pitch, a low-frequency segment (the baseband) of the speech signal is encoded and transmitted. At the synthesizer, the baseband is spread to cover the whole spectrum through the use of some nonlinearity, and then it is used as the excitation signal. The method can give good results by using the speech signal as the excitation, but for practical purposes, a variant of that is used in connection with the LPC method. In this case (which will be considered in more detail in Chapter 5), the excitation signal is based on the residual signal remaining after the LPC analysis. This signal contains information about voicing and pitch and it can give quite robust quality of synthetic speech at the expense of bit rate.

4.6 SUMMARY

This chapter investigated some vocoders, the most important of which is the channel vocoder. The channel vocoder, based on a channel bank approach, has been studied extensively since its introduction in 1939, and has been implemented in both analog and digital hardware. Together with linear predictive coding, it is one of the standard choices for a 2,400 bits/s system. The other vocoders presented have not found as many practical applications because they lack the robustness of the channel vocoder.

The homomorphic vocoder uses the logarithm of the spectrum to separate the excitation from the vocal tract. Then, the inverse Fourier transform of the log-spectrum generates the parameters that represent the vocal tract. The phase vocoder uses the phase derivative as a means of encoding the spectral phase, while the magnitude is encoded as in the channel vocoder. The formant vocoders attempt to describe the vocal tract spectrum in terms of its resonances (formants). This last vocoder can lead to bit rates below 1,000 bits/s, but the formant tracking is a very difficult problem.

The next chapter is devoted to another vocoder, the linear predictive method (LPC). LPC has become the most popular way of vocoding for low bit rates around 2,400 bits/s. Furthermore, the resulting parametric representation of speech has found applications in other areas of speech processing, such as speech recognition.

4.7 FURTHER READING

The books by J.L. Flanagan [12] and, especially, by L.R. Rabiner and R.W. Schafer [8], present a very good discussion of the different analysis-synthesis systems presented here.

The popular channel vocoder is the subject of the papers by Holmes [2] and Gold and Rader [3], and is also the subject of references [13–15]. The paper by Dudley [13] reports the first attempt in that direction and has mostly historical value.

The homomorphic vocoder is described by Oppenheim [5]. Weinstein and Oppenheim [16], and Patisaul and Hammett [17] give some variations and advances in the basic homomorphic system. A detailed presentation of the phase vocoder with some examples of its application can be found in the paper by Flanagan and Golden [6], while Portnoff [18] outlines the theoretical basis for an implementation of the phase vocoder using DFTs.

The subject of formant vocoders has been investigated in the context of different types of speech processing. The present discussion was based on the paper by Schafer and Rabiner [9], but other approaches can be found in the collection of papers by Schafer and Markel [19]. The approach that is based on LPC will be presented in Chapter 5. The papers by Klatt [10] and Holmes [11] discuss implementations of formant synthesizer in cascade or in parallel for speech synthesis applications.

4.8 REFERENCES

1. Schafer, R.W., L.R. Rabiner, and O. Hermann. "FIR Digital Filter Banks for Speech Analysis." *Bell Sys. Tech. J.*, Vol. 54, No. 3 (March 1975): 531–544.
2. Holmes, J.N. "The JSRU Channel Vocoder." *IEE Proceedings*, Vol. 127, Pt. F, No. 1 (February 1980): 53–60.
3. Gold, B., and C.M. Rader. "The Channel Vocoder." *IEEE Trans. Audio Electroacous.*, Vol. AU-15 (December 1967): 148–161.
4. Noll, A.M. "Cepstrum Pitch Determination." *J. Acous. Soc. Am.*, Vol. 41 (February 1967): 293–309.

5. Oppenheim, A.V. "Analysis-Synthesis by Homomorphic Filtering." *J. Acous. Soc. Am.*, Vol. 45 (February 1969): 458–465.

6. Flanagan, J.L., and R.M. Golden. "Phase Vocoder." *Bell Sys. Tech. J.*, Vol. 45 (November 1966): 1493–1509.

7. Rabiner, L.R., and B. Gold. *Theory and Applications of Digital Signal Processing.* Englewood Cliffs, NJ: Prentice-Hall, 1975.

8. Rabiner, L.R., and R.W. Schafer. *Digital Processing of Speech Signals.* Englewood Cliffs, NJ: Prentice-Hall, 1978.

9. Schafer, R.W., and L.R. Rabiner. "System for Automatic Formant Analysis of Voiced Speech." *J. Acous. Soc. Am.*, Vol. 47 (February 1970): 634–648.

10. Klatt, D.H. "Software for a Cascade/Parallel Formant Synthesizer." *J. Acous. Soc. Am.*, Vol. 67, No. 3 (March 1980): 971–995.

11. Holmes, J.N. "Formant Synthesizers: Cascade or Parallel?" *Speech Communication*, North Holland, Vol. 2, No. 4 (December 1983): 251–273.

12. Flanagan, J. L. *Speech Analysis Synthesis and Perception*, Second Ed. New York: Springer-Verlag, 1972.

13. Dudley, H. "The Vocoder." *Bell Labs Record*, Vol. 17 (1939): 122–126.

14. Schroder, M.R. "Vocoders: Analysis and Synthesis of Speech." *Proc. IEEE*, Vol. 54 (May 1966): 720–734.

15. Gold, B., and C.M. Rader. "Systems for Compressing the Bandwidth of Speech." *IEEE Trans. Audio and Electroacous.*, Vol. Au-15, No. 3 (September 1967): 131–135.

16. Weinstein, C.J., and A.V. Oppenheim. "Predictive Coding in a Homomorphic Vocoder." *IEEE Trans. on Audio and Electroacous.*, Vol. AU-19, No. 3 (September 1971): 243–248.

17. Patisaul, C.R., and J.C. Hammett. "Time-Frequency Resolution Experiment in Speech Analysis and Synthesis." *J. Acous. Soc. Am.*, Vol. 58, No. 6 (December 1975): 1296–1307.

18. Portnoff, M.R. "Implementation of the Digital Phase Vocoder Using the Fast Fourier Transform." *IEEE Trans. Acous., Speech, and Signal Proc.*, Vol. ASSP-24 (June 1976): 243–248.

19. Schafer, R.W., and J.D. Markel, Eds. *Speech Analysis.* New York: IEEE Press, 1979.

Chapter 5

Linear Predictive Coding: A Parametric Description of Speech

The *Linear Predictive Coding* (LPC) method is one of the most popular approaches for processing speech. Since it has been so widely studied and applied, an entire chapter is devoted to it, although it could have been classified as one of the vocoding methods in the previous chapter.

The chapter begins with a discussion of two issues, windowing and preemphasis, which are important in the accurate determination of the speech parameters. Then, the computation of the LPC parameters is explained, with the LeRoux-Gueguen method of LPC parameter determination particularly well suited for fixed-point arithmetic. Such arithmetic is used in the currently available digital signal processors that can be used to implement linear predictive coding of speech.

Besides the reflection coefficients, which are the most often used LPC parameters, there are other sets of parameters carrying exactly the same information. These alternative parameter sets have different quantization and interpolation properties. They are derived from the reflection coefficients and are used in cases where their properties can lead to better speech quality.

From the basic LPC method, additional techniques have been developed to achieve good speech quality at different bit rates. Such methods, examined in this chapter, are residual-excited linear predictive vocoder (RELP), the formant vocoders, the vector quantization, the multipulse excitation, and the line spectrum pairs (LSP).

The popularity of LPC stems from the fact that it employs a model of speech production that works amazingly well. The parametric representation of speech through LPC also facilitates the use of very low bit rates for speech coding, down to about 2.4 kbits/s. Another very important characteristic of the LPC parameters is that they preserve essentially all the intelligibility information of the speech signal, and so they can be (and have been) used for speech recognition. In this way, since the same parameters can be used for coding or recognition, the task of building a system with both functions becomes somewhat easier.

The linear predictive coding method is based on the same speech production model as the other vocoders. This model is repeated in Figure 5.1. For the application of the model, it is nec-

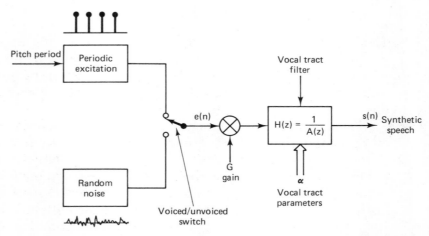

Figure 5.1   Speech production model for Linear Predictive Coding (LPC).

essary to determine if the signal is voiced or unvoiced and, if voiced, to compute the pitch period. The main difference between LPC and the other vocoders is in the modeling of the vocal tract filter (and secondarily, the computation of the gain, G). In LPC, the vocal tract is modeled as an all-pole digital filter, i.e., as a filter that only has poles and no zeroes. Incorporating the gain, G, into that filter, we can express it as

$$H(z) \; = \; \frac{G}{1 \, + \, a_1 z^{-1} \, + \, \ldots \, + \, a_p z^{-p}} \; = \; \frac{S(z)}{E(z)} \qquad \textbf{(5.1)}$$

where p is the order of the model. If $s(n)$ is the speech output of the model, and $e(n)$ is the excitation input, the equation above can be written in the time domain as

$$s(n) \; = \; G \, e(n) - a_1 s(n \, - \, 1) \, - \, \ldots \, - a_p s \, (n \, - \, p) \qquad \textbf{(5.2)}$$

In other words, every speech sample is computed as a linear combination of the previous speech samples with a contribution from the excitation. This formulation is also the reason for calling the method Linear Predictive Coding.

5.1 WINDOWING OF THE SPEECH SIGNAL

The LPC method is accurate when it is applied to stationary signals, i.e., to signals whose behavior does not change with time. However, this is not the case with speech. To be able to apply the LPC method, we segment the speech signal into small segments, called *frames*, which are quasi-stationary. Figure 5.2 shows an example of speech segmentation. The segmentation is done by multiplying the speech signal, $s(n)$, by a window signal, $w(n)$, which is

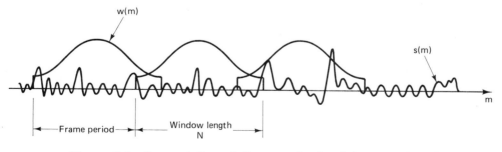

Figure 5.2 Segmentation of the speech signal into quasi-stationary frames by windowing. The frames are overlapping.

zero outside the interval we want to extract. Although it is a possibility, we generally avoid extracting the signal by simply zeroing out everything outside the region of interest, because this would smear the signal in the frequency domain. The windowing is necessary in the autocorrelation method of LPC analysis, which will be presented later, while it is not necessary in the covariance and Burg methods.

The most popular choice is the Hamming window, discussed in Chapter 3. The Hamming window is given by

$$w(n) = 0.54 - 0.46 \cos \frac{2\pi n}{N}, \ 0 \le n \le N - 1$$

$$w(n) = 0 \qquad\qquad\qquad \text{otherwise}$$

$$(5.3)$$

Here, N is the desired window length in samples and is generally chosen in the range of 20–40 ms, with 30 ms being a typical value. If you consider speech sampled at 8 kHz (8,000 samples/s), the typical window length is $N = 240$ samples. Usually, the successive windows are chosen to overlap, and the distance between successive windows is called the *frame period*. The frame period is expressed also in milliseconds (or in samples if the sampling frequency is known). Typical values of frame period are 10–30 ms. The choice will depend on the final desired bit rate: the more often we transmit speech frames, the higher the bit rate will be. Another factor influencing the selection of the frame period is the desired speech quality: the smaller the frame period, the better the quality, because we are better able to capture transitions of the speech signal. The inverse of the frame period is the frame rate, expressed in frames/s. For instance, a frame period of 20 ms corresponds to a frame rate of 50 frames/s (or Hz).

5.2 PREEMPHASIS OF THE SIGNAL

Figure 5.3 shows a typical spectral envelope of the speech signal for a voiced sound. Note how the spectrum rolls off in high frequencies. If this is permitted to happen, the LPC model will satisfactorily approximate the low frequencies, but it will do a poor job in high frequencies. To prevent this, we pass the speech signal through a filter with transfer function $1 - az^{-1}$, called a *preemphasis filter*, which emphasizes the high frequencies before pro-

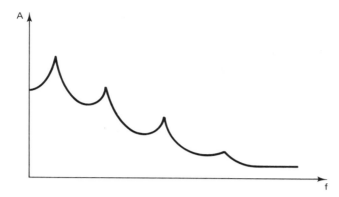

Figure 5.3 Typical spectral envelope of a voiced sound.

cessing. Viewing it another way, the spectral rolloff is caused by the radiation effects of the sound from the mouth, and we use the preemphasis filter to remove these effects. Typical values of coefficient a are around 0.9, with a usual choice $a = {}^{15}\!/_{16} = 0.9375$. Then, if $s(n)$ is the input signal, the preemphasized signal $s'(n)$ is

$$s'(n) = s(n) - 0.9375\ s(n - 1)$$

After processing at the synthesizer, the signal is deemphasized by using

$$s(n) = s'(n) + 0.9375\ s(n - 1)$$

5.3 ESTIMATION OF THE LPC PARAMETERS

For a complete representation of the LPC model, the vocal tract filter parameters (i.e., the filter coefficients a_i, and the gain G) must be determined. To do that, we set

$$\hat{s}(n) = -a_1 s(n - 1) - \ldots - a_p s(n - p) \qquad \textbf{(5.4)}$$

to be the estimate of $s(n)$ from the previous samples, and we determine the coefficients a_i, so that the error

$$\sum_n (s(n) - \hat{s}(n))^2$$

is minimized over all the available samples. Minimization of the total squared error with respect to a_i leads to the following set of linear equations:

$$
\begin{aligned}
a_1 r(0) + a_2 r(1) + \ldots + a_p r(p-1) &= -r(1) \\
a_1 r(1) + a_2 r(0) + \ldots + a_p r(p-2) &= -r(2)
\end{aligned}
\tag{5.5}
$$

$$
\cdot
$$
$$
\cdot
$$
$$
\cdot
$$

$$
a_1 r(p-1) + a_2 r(p-2) + \ldots + a_p r(0) = -r(p)
$$

Or in matrix form,

$$
R \cdot \mathbf{a} = -\mathbf{r}
\tag{5.6}
$$

where

$$
\mathbf{r}^T = [\ r(1)\ r(2)\ \ldots\ r(p)\ ]
\tag{5.7}
$$

$$
\mathbf{a}^T = [\ a_1\ a_2\ \ldots\ a_p\ ]
\tag{5.8}
$$

$$
R = \begin{Bmatrix}
r(0) & r(1) & r(2) & \ldots & r(p-1) \\
r(1) & r(0) & r(1) & \ldots & r(p-2) \\
r(2) & r(1) & r(0) & \ldots & r(p-3) \\
\cdot & \cdot & \cdot & & \\
\cdot & \cdot & \cdot & & \\
\cdot & \cdot & \cdot & & \\
r(p-1) & r(p-2) & r(p-3) & \ldots & r(0)
\end{Bmatrix}
\tag{5.9}
$$

In the above equations we have defined

$$
r(i) = r(-i) = \sum_{n=0}^{N-i-1} s(n)\, s(n+i)
\tag{5.10}
$$

to be the ith autocorrelation. In this formulation, the signal s(n) is windowed (for instance, with a Hamming window of length N) so that $s(n) = 0$ for $n < 0$ and $n \geq N$. Then, the ith autocorrelation is computed by shifting the signal by i samples, multiplying it by the unshifted version and summing up the nonzero products, as shown in Figure 5.4. Figure 5.5 shows a FORTRAN subroutine that computes the autocorrelation of a speech signal that has already been windowed.

This formulation is called the *autocorrelation method* and produces a matrix R that is a Toeplitz matrix. A Toeplitz matrix is one whose diagonals are composed of identical elements. Such a matrix is nonsingular and it can always be inverted. Hence, we can always find a solution

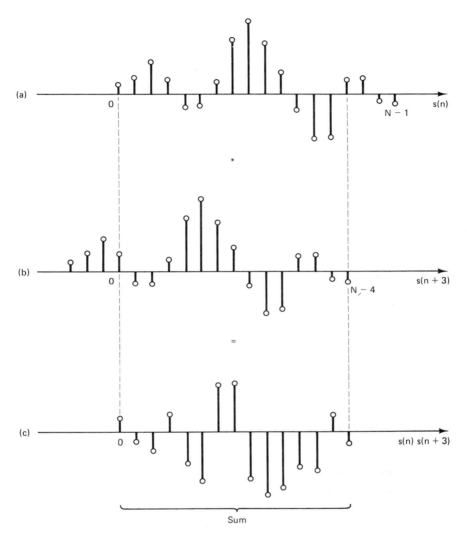

Figure 5.4 Computation of the autocorrelation coefficient $r(3)$. (a) signal $s(n)$; (b) shifted signal $s(n + 3)$; (c) product $s(n) . s(n + 3)$ to be summed in order to compute $r(3)$.

$$\mathbf{a} = -R^{-1}\,\mathbf{r} \qquad\qquad (5.11)$$

Besides the autocorrelation method, another possibility is to use the *covariance method*. In the covariance method, the speech signal, $s(n)$, is not windowed and instead of the autocorrelations $r(i)$, you compute the covariances $r(i,j)$ for the (i,j) element of the matrix R. The covariance $r(i,j)$ is computed from

```
      SUBROUTINE AUTOC (S, LEN, N, R)
C
C     THIS ROUTINE COMPUTES THE AUTOCORRELATION TERMS R(1) – R(N + 1)
C     OF AN INPUT SEQUENCE S(1)–S(LEN).
C
      DIMENSION R(1), S(1)
C
      DO 100 I = 1, N + 1
          R(I) = 0.
          DO 100 J = 1, LEN–I + 1
              R(I) = R(I) + S(J) * S(J + I – 1)
100   CONTINUE
      RETURN
      END
```

Figure 5.5   FORTRAN program to compute autocorrelations.

$$r(i,j) = \sum_n s(n+i)\, s(n+j) \qquad\qquad (5.12)$$

Now the matrix R is not guaranteed to be invertible. It is possible that the above system of equations does not have a solution, in which case the LPC filter is unstable. For that reason, we are not going to examine the covariance method further, but we will concentrate on the autocorrelation method, which happens to be the most popular.

A third approach to LPC speech analysis is the Burg method. The Burg method combines the advantage of the covariance method of not using a window, with the advantage of the autocorrelation method of guaranteeing the stability of the resulting filter. This method uses the lattice structure of the all-pole filter to generate the reflection coefficients. Although Burg's method demonstrates some advantages in other fields, such as spectral estimation, it does not seem to perform any better than the autocorrelation method in speech processing. The interested reader can find more information on this subject in references [1,2].

The solution to the previous set of equations (5.5) and (5.6) can be found by using one of the classical methods of numerical analysis, such as Gauss elimination. This process gives the filter coefficients a_i

$$\mathbf{a} = -R^{-1}\,\mathbf{r}$$

However, since R is a Toeplitz matrix, we have a very efficient way of obtaining the solution to that equation by Durbin's recursive

method. In Durbin's method, start with the autocorrelation coefficients $r(i)$, $i = 0, \ldots, p$ and compute recursively the filter coefficients, a_i, from the following relations:

$$E(0) = r(0) \tag{5.13}$$

$$K_i = -\frac{r(i) + a_1^{(i-1)}r(i-1) + \ldots + a_{i-1}^{(i-1)} r(1)}{E(i-1)} \text{ for } i = 1, \ldots, p \tag{5.14}$$

$$a_i^{(i)} = K_i \tag{5.15}$$

$$a_j^{(i)} = a_j^{(i-1)} + K_i a_{i-j}^{(i-1)} \qquad j = 1, \ldots, i-1 \tag{5.16}$$

$$E(i) = (1 - K_i^2) E(i-1) \tag{5.17}$$

The coefficients $a_j^{(i)}$, $j = 1, \ldots, i$ are the filter coefficients of an ith-
order model. Hence, the coefficients of the desired pth-order model
are:

$$a_j = a_j^{(p)}, \quad j = 1, \ldots, p \tag{5.18}$$

Example: Assume that you want to estimate a second-order model,
$p = 2$, with autocorrelation coefficients $r(0)$, $r(1)$, and $r(2)$. Then,

$$E(0) = r(0) \tag{5.19a}$$

$$K_1 = -\frac{r(1)}{E(0)} = -\frac{r(1)}{r(0)} \tag{5.19b}$$

$$a_1^{(1)} = K_1 \tag{5.19c}$$

$$E(1) = (1 - K_1^2) E(0) = (1 - K_1^2) r(0) \tag{5.19d}$$

$$K_2 = -\frac{r(2) + a_1^{(1)} r(1)}{E(1)} \tag{5.19e}$$

$$a_2^{(2)} = K_2 \tag{5.19f}$$

$$a_1^{(2)} = a_1^{(1)} + K_2 a_1^{(1)} = K_1 (1 + K_2) \tag{5.19g}$$

$$E(2) = (1 - K_2^2) E(1) = (1 - K_1^2) (1 - K_2^2) r(0) \tag{5.19h}$$

Since a second-order model is being considered,

$$a_1 = a_1^{(2)} \tag{5.19i}$$

$$a_2 = a_2^{(2)} \tag{5.19j}$$

In the above series of equations, all the results can be expressed in terms of the autocorrelations r(i) by making the appropriate substitutions.

Durbin's solution gives the parameters K_i, $i = 1, \ldots, p$, and $E(p)$ as a side product. These are very important parameters. First, $E(p)$ is the square of the gain G needed in the synthesis model:

$$G^2 = E(p) \tag{5.20}$$

This quantity can be encoded as one of the necessary parameters for synthesis. However, since

$$E(p) = (1 - K_1^2)(1 - K_2^2) \ldots (1 - K_p^2)\, r(0) \tag{5.21}$$

instead of $E(p)$, you can encode and transmit r(0), which is the energy of the speech frame analyzed. Then, G is recovered by multiplying r(0) by $(1 - K_1^2) \ldots (1 - K_p^2)$ during synthesis. This is preferable, because the synthesis model is less sensitive to the

```
       SUBROUTINE DURBIN (R, N, K, A)
C
C      THIS ROUTINE USES THE DURBIN ALGORITHM TO
C      TRANSFORM THE AUTOCORRELATION COEFFICIENTS R(1)–R(N+1)
C      TO THE REFLECTION COEFFICIENTS K(1)–K(N) AND TO THE FILTER
C      COEFFICIENTS A(1)–A(N+1) (A(1) = 1).
C
       REAL    K(1), R(1), A(1)
C
       A(1) = 1
       K(1) = - R(2) / R(1)
       ALPHA = R(1)   *   (1 - K(1)**2)
       A(2) = K(1)
       DO 200 I = 2, N
             ERROR = 0.
             DO 100 J = 1, I
                   ERROR = ERROR + A(J)    R(I+2-J)
100          CONTINUE
             K(I) = - ERROR / ALPHA
             ALPHA = ALPHA * (1 - K(I)**2)
             A(I+1) = K(I)
             DO 200 J = 2, I
                   A(J) = A(J) + K(I)   * A(I+2-J)
200    CONTINUE
       RETURN
       END
```

Figure 5.6   FORTRAN program to compute the filter coefficients and the reflection coefficients using Durbin's algorithm.

quantization noise of $r(0)$ than that of G. Figure 5.6 shows a FOR-
TRAN program that computes both the filter coefficients and the
reflection coefficients from the autocorrelations using Durbin's
method.

The set of parameters K_i, $i = 1, \ldots, p$ are called *reflection
coefficients* or *PARCOR* (*PAR*tial *COR*relation) *coefficients*, and
play a central role in the LPC method. They have the following
properties:

1. They are equivalent to the filter coefficients, a_i. In other words,
   you can derive the K's from the a's and vice-versa according to
   the relations:

   K's to a's:

   $$a_i^{(i)} = K_i \tag{5.22}$$

   $$a_j^{(i)} = a_j^{(i-1)} + K_i\, a_{i-j}^{(i-1)} \qquad \begin{aligned} i &= 1, \ldots, p \\ j &= 1, \ldots, i-1 \end{aligned} \tag{5.23}$$

   a's to k's:

   $$K_i = a_i^{(i)} \tag{5.24}$$

   $$a_j^{(i-1)} = \frac{a_j^{(i)} - a_i^{(i)}\, a_{i-j}^{(i)}}{1 - K_i^2} \qquad \begin{aligned} i &= p, \ldots, 1 \\ j &= 1, \ldots, i-1 \end{aligned} \tag{5.25}$$

   Figures 5.7 and 5.8 contain FORTRAN programs that implement the conversions between the k's and the a's.

2. For a stable filter, i.e., an LPC filter with all the poles inside the
   unit circle,

   $$-1 < K_i < 1 \qquad i = 1, \ldots, p \tag{5.26}$$

   This is a very important condition because, by making sure
   that the K_i are between -1 and $+1$ even after quantization, we
   guarantee the stability of the filter. Also, the well-defined range
   of values that the K_i can take, (-1 to $+1$), makes the quantization easier. On the other hand, the a_i do not have any property to guarantee the stability of the filter, and the quantization
   of the a_i's can actually lead to instabilities. Primarily for this
   reason, the reflection coefficients (instead of the filter coefficients) are selected to represent the vocal tract filter.

3. In order to implement the vocal tract filter $H(z)$ in Figure 5.1,
   it is not necessary to convert the K's to a's and then use a direct-

```
          SUBROUTINE ATOK (A, N, K)
C
C
C         SUBROUTINE TO CONVERT THE N+1 FILTER COEFFICIENTS A(1)−A(N+1)
C         TO THE CORRESPONDING N REFLECTION COEFFICIENTS K(1)−K(N).
C         THE INVERSE FILTER IS OF THE FORM
C
C                   1 + SUM [A(I) Z⁻¹]
C
          REAL K(1)
          DIMENSION A(1), B(21), BB(21)
C
          DO 100 I = 1, N+1
100       B(I) = A(I)
C
          DO 300 I = N+1, 2, −1
              K(I−1) = B(I)
              SQK = 1. − B(I)**2
              DO 200 J = 1, I
                  BB(I) = B(I)
200           CONTINUE
              DO 300 J = 1, I−1
                  B(J) = (BB(J) − K(I)*BB(I−J+1) ) / SQK
300       CONTINUE
          RETURN
          END
```

Figure 5.7   FORTRAN program to convert filter coefficients to reflection coefficients.

```
          SUBROUTINE KTOA (K, N, A)
C
C         SUBROUTINE TO CONVERT THE N REFLECTION COEFFICIENTS K(1)−K(N)
C         TO THE CORRESPONDING N+1 FILTER COEFFICIENTS A(1)−A(N+1).
C         THE INVERSE FILTER IS OF THE FORM
C
C                   1 + SUM [A(I) Z⁻¹]
C
          REAL K(1), A(1)
C
          A(1) = 1
          DO 50 I = 2, N+1
50        A(I) = 0.
C
          DO 100 I = 1, N
              DO 100 J = 2, I+1
                  A(J) = A(J) + K(I) * A(I−J+2)
100       CONTINUE
          RETURN
          END
```

Figure 5.8   FORTRAN program to convert reflection coefficients to filter coefficients.

form implementation of the filter. Instead, it is possible to implement the filter in *lattice form* using the reflection coefficients, K_i, directly. Figure 5.9 shows the lattice implementation of the vocal tract filter. The equations implementing the lattice filter are:

$$f^{(i-1)}(n) = f^{(i)}(n) - K_i b^{(i-1)}(n-1) \tag{5.27}$$

$$b^{(i)}(n) = K_i f^{(i-1)}(n) + b^{(i-1)}(n-1) \tag{5.28}$$

with

$$f^{(p)}(n) = G\,u(n) \tag{5.29}$$

and $u(n)$ being the excitation. The superscript indicates the stage in the lattice filter, while the argument is the time index. The output is then

$$s(n) = f^{(0)}(n) \tag{5.30}$$

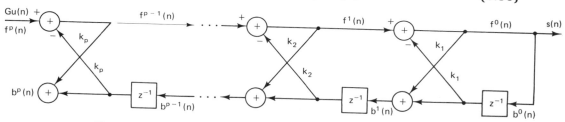

Figure 5.9 Lattice filter to synthesize speech from the excitation $G\,u(n)$ and the reflection coefficients, k_i.

The above equations introduce the quantities $f^{(i)}(n)$ and $b^{(i)}(n)$, which are called forward error and backward error, respectively. If these equations are written in the form

$$f^{(i)}(n) = f^{(i-1)}(n) + K_i b^{(i-1)}(n-1) \tag{5.31}$$

$$b^{(i)}(n) = b^{(i-1)}(n-1) + K_i f^{(i-1)}(n) \tag{5.32}$$

they represent the inverse filter $A(z)$ in Figure 5.1. When the input to the above filter is the input signal $s(n)$, the output is the *residual error signal* $e(n)$. This filter is implemented as shown in Figure 5.10 with

$$f^{(0)}(n) = s(n) \tag{5.33a}$$

$$b^{(0)}(n) = s(n) \tag{5.33b}$$

and output

$$e(n) = f^{(p)}(n) \tag{5.34}$$

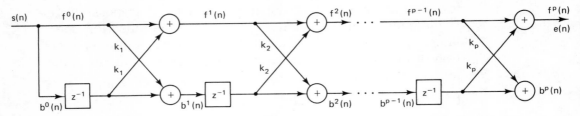

Figure 5.10 Lattice implementation of the LPC inverse filter. The input is the speech signal; the output is the residual error.

Note that if the residual error signal, $e(n)$, is fed into the synthesis filter of Figure 5.9, the output will be the exact input speech, $s(n)$. In other words, you can use the residual error signal, $e(n)$, as excitation for the vocal tract filter. This method is actually implemented in the residual-excited linear predictive (RELP) vocoder, which will be examined later.

5.4 LEROUX-GUEGUEN ANALYSIS METHOD

Durbin's method gives an efficient way to determine the LPC parameters, but if our objective is to compute the reflection coefficients, K_i, we are forced to also compute the filter coefficients, a_i, as intermediate quantities. The filter coefficients have a large dynamic range, and the whole computation becomes awkward in a fixed-point device, such as the currently available digital signal processors. LeRoux and Gueguen [3] solved that problem by introducing the quantities

$$e^j(i) = r(i) + a_1^{(j)} r(i-1) + \ldots + a_j^{(j)} r(i-j) \qquad (5.35)$$

where $r(i)$ are the autocorrelation coefficients. Then, the reflection coefficients can be computed from the relations

$$K_j = \frac{-e^{j-1}(j)}{e^{j-1}(0)} \qquad\qquad j = 1, \ldots, p \qquad (5.36)$$

$$e^j(i) = e^{j-1}(i) + K_{j-1}e^{j-1}(j-i) \qquad i = -p+j, \ldots, p \qquad (5.37)$$

with initial condition

$$e^0(i) = r(i) \qquad\qquad i = -p, \ldots, p \qquad (5.38)$$

where $r(-i) = r(i)$. Also, the residual energy is

$$E(i) = e^i(0) \qquad (5.39)$$

In equation (5.37), the values of $e^j(i)$, $i = 1, \ldots, j$, turn out to be zero, so they need not be computed. The flowchart of Figure 5.11 gives the above procedure in a pictorial way while Figure 5.12 gives a FORTRAN program that implements this method.

One important result of this formulation is that if the auto-correlation sequence is normalized, i.e., $r(i) \leq 1$, then all the quantities $e^j(i)$ lie between -1 and $+1$. Consequently, we can implement the computation of the K_is using fixed-point arithmetic only.

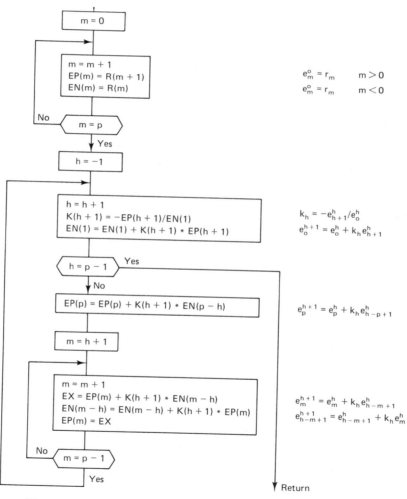

Figure 5.11   Flowchart of the LeRoux-Gueguen method to compute the reflection coefficients (after LeRoux and Gueguen [3], © 1977 IEEE).

```
       SUBROUTINE LERGUE (R, N, K)
C
C      THIS ROUTINE USES THE LEROUX-GUEGUEN METHOD TO
C      TRANSFORM THE AUTOCORRELATION COEFFICIENTS R(1) – R(N + 1)
C      TO THE REFLECTION COEFFICIENTS K(1) – K(N).
C
       REAL           K(1), R(1)
       DIMENSION      EP(25), EN(25)
C
       DO 100 I = 1, N
             EP(I) = R(I + 1)
             EN(I) = R(I)
100    CONTINUE
       EN(N) = R(N + 1)
C
       DO 200 J = 1, N
             K(J) = – EP(J) / EN(1)
             DO 200 I = J, N
                   TEMP = EP(I) + K(J) * EN(I – J + 1)
                   EN(I – J + 1) = EN(I – J + 1) + K(J) * EP(I)
                   EP(I) = TEMP
200    CONTINUE
       RETURN
       END
```

Figure 5.12   FORTRAN program to compute the reflection coefficients using the LeRoux-Gueguen method.

5.5 DIFFERENT FORMS OF LPC PARAMETERS

We noted earlier that the vocal tract filter can be represented either by the filter coefficients or by the reflection (or PARCOR) coefficients. The two representations are equivalent and equations (5.22)–(5.25) show how we can convert one set of parameters to another. Also, these two sets of parameters are equivalent to the set of the autocorrelation coefficients, $r(i)$, from which they are both derived. Depending on the application, one form of the LPC parameters may be preferred over another, but they are all equivalent.

In addition to the above sets of LPC parameters, there are several other types of LPC parameters that are equivalent to the above. These parameters are the LPC poles, the cepstral coefficients, the log-area ratios (LAR), and the inverse sine transforms of the K's. The following paragraphs provide a brief description of each of these parametric representations.

The poles of the LPC filter are the zeros of the denominator polynomial in equation (5.1). The sharpest of these poles correspond to the peaks of the frequency spectrum of speech. These peaks, also called formants, have been shown to be very important perceptually. Actually, the formant vocoders (see Chapter 4) encode these peaks exactly and very economically. Therefore, the LPC poles could, in principle, be used for formant vocoders. Since the denominator polynomial in equation (5.1) can be expressed as a product of terms $(1 - z_i z^{-1})$, where z_i is a pole of the LPC filter, the set of poles is equivalent to the filter coefficients and, consequently, to all other LPC parameters. Encoding of the LPC poles also guarantees the stability of the filter by making sure they lie inside the unit circle. However, the poles have the disadvantage of not being an ordered set of parameters, like the K's, and it is not easy to develop statistics that could lead to efficient encoding. Another drawback is that, to compute the poles, additional computation is needed on top of the computation of the filter coefficients. This computational overhead makes the use of the LPC poles for coding unsuitable for many applications.

In Chapter 4 we discussed the homomorphic vocoder, where the speech spectrum is represented by the cepstral coefficients. We can use the same set of parameters here to describe the LPC vocal tract. The cepstral coefficients, C_i, describing the LPC vocal tract filter, are related to the filter coefficients, a_i, according to the equations

$$C_0 = E(0) = r(0) \tag{5.40}$$

$$C_1 = -a_1 \tag{5.41}$$

$$C_i = -a_i - \sum_{k=1}^{i-1} \frac{i-k}{i} C_{i-k} a_k \qquad i = 2, \dots, p \tag{5.42a}$$

$$C_i = -\sum_{R=1}^{p} \frac{i-k}{i} C_{i-k} a_k \qquad i = p+1, \dots \tag{5.42b}$$

From the equations (5.41) and (5.42a), you can see that the set of the first p cepstral coefficients is equivalent to the LPC filter coefficients, and they uniquely determine all the cepstral coefficients. Variable C_0 is the energy of the frame. Figures 5.13 and 5.14 contain FORTRAN programs that do the conversion between the filter coefficients and the cepstral coefficients.

```
      SUBROUTINE ATOC (A, NLPC, C, NC)
C
C     THIS SUBROUTINE COMPUTES THE CEPSTRAL COEFFICIENTS C(1)-C(NC)
C     FROM THE PREDICTOR COEFFICIENTS A(1)-A(NLPC+1). NLPC IS THE
C     ORDER OF THE LPC MODEL, AND NC IS GREATER THAN OR EQUAL TO NLPC.
C     THE CEPSTRAL COEFFICIENT C(O) MUST BE OBTAINED FROM THE GAIN G.
C
      INTEGER   NLPC,NC
      REAL      A(1), C(1)
C
      C(1) = - A(2)
      DO 100 J = 2, NLPC
           C(J) = - FLOAT(J) * A(J+1)
           DO 100 K = 1, J-1
                C(J) = C(J) - C(K) * A(J-K+1)
100   CONTINUE
C
      IF (NC.GT.NLPC) THEN
           DO 200 J = NLPC+1, NC
                C(J) = 0.
                DO 200 K = 1, NLPC
                     C(J) = C(J) - C(J-K) * A(K+1)
200        CONTINUE
      END IF
C
      DO 300 J = 1, NC
300   C(J) = C(J) / FLOAT(J)
      RETURN
      END
```

Figure 5.13   FORTRAN program to convert filter coefficients to cepstral coefficients.

The cepstral coefficients can be used for coding, but they are less preferable than the reflection coefficients because they demonstrate the same sensitivity to quantization errors as the a's. However, they provide an efficient computation of the log-spectral distance between two frames. It turns out that the quantity

$$d^2 = \sum_{k=-\infty}^{\infty} (C_k - C'_k)^2 \tag{5.43}$$

is the square of the log-spectral distance between two frames whose LPC filters have cepstral coefficients C_k and C'_k. Since $C_{-k} = C_k$, (5.43) can also be written as

$$d^2 = (C_0 - C'_0)^2 + 2 \sum_{K=1}^{\infty} (C_k - C'_k)^2 \tag{5.44}$$

```
C        SUBROUTINE CTOA (C, NLPC, A)
C
C        THIS SUBROUTINE COMPUTES THE PREDICTOR COEFFICIENTS A(1) –
C        A(NLPC + 1) FROM THE CEPSTRAL COEFFICIENTS C(1) – C (NLPC).
C        THE CEPSTRAL COEFFICIENT C(O) IS RELATED TO THE GAIN.
C
C        DIMENSION A(1), C(1)
C
         A(1) = 1.0
         A(2) = – C(1)
         DO 200 J = 2, NLPC
              A(J + 1) = FLOAT(J) * C(J)
              DO 100 K = 1, J – 1
                   A(J + 1) = A(J + 1) + FLOAT(K) * C(K) * A(J – K + 1)
100           CONTINUE
              A(J + 1) = – A(J + 1) / FLOAT(J)
200      CONTINUE
         RETURN
         END
```

Figure 5.14 FORTRAN program to convert cepstral coefficients to filter coefficients.

For practical computations, you can truncate the sum to the first 30 terms.

Using the LPC method, you encode speech by preserving the shape of the LPC spectrum. As noted earlier, the reflection coefficients are the most preferable parameters for such encoding, since they guarantee the stability of the filter as long as they lie between -1 and $+1$. However, experimentation has shown that when a reflection coefficient takes values close to the boundaries -1 or $+1$, the LPC spectrum becomes very sensitive to quantization error. Viswanathan and Makhoul [4], and Gray and Markel [5], derived two transformations of the reflection coefficients that make the sensitivity of the spectrum uniform for all values. These transformations are the log area ratios, LAR_i, and the inverse sine transforms, g_i, respectively. The transformations warp the scale of the parameters, and a uniform quantization of the transformation corresponds to a nonuniform quantization of the reflection coefficients, K_i.

The log-area ratios are defined by the equations

$$LAR_i = \log \frac{1 + K_i}{1 - K_i} \qquad i = 1, \ldots, p \tag{5.45}$$

and, conversely, the reflection coefficients can be recovered from the LAR by the equations

$$K_i = \frac{e^{LAR_i} - 1}{e^{LAR_i} + 1} \qquad i = 1, \ldots, p \qquad \text{(5.46)}$$

The log-area ratios have been widely used because of their excellent performance. They are probably the best choice for LPC parameters.

The inverse sine transforms are defined by

$$g_i = \arcsin(K_i), \qquad i = 1, \ldots, p \qquad \text{(5.47)}$$

with the inverse transform

$$K_i = \sin(g_i), \qquad i = 1, \ldots, p \qquad \text{(5.48)}$$

The g_i's have the additional attractive feature that they are bounded between $-\pi/2$ and $\pi/2$, while the LAR's are unbounded (theoretically). However, the LAR's still remain most popular, although there is little difference in actual performance between LAR and g_i.

5.6 SYNTHESIS CONSIDERATIONS

For LPC systems, the analysis window is typically 30 ms long, and the frame period is 10–25 ms. Longer frame periods correspond to lower frame rate and, consequently, to lower bit rate if the same number of bits per frame is used. If, however, we update the filter parameters once every frame, the spectral transitions from one frame to the next become abrupt and the speech quality suffers. Therefore, it is recommended to interpolate the parameters so that there is a new set of parameters, say, every 5 ms. The best set of LPC parameters for interpolation are the LPC poles, but since they are not readily available, you can use the reflection coefficients, K_i, or the log-area ratios, LAR_i. With this adjustment, the quality of the synthetic speech improves.

Selection of the excitation has very significant impact on the speech quality. It is generally accepted that the most important defect of the LPC and the other pitch-excited vocoders is erroneous determination of pitch. At present, though, we are only concerned with the effect of the excitation on synthesis.

For voiced sounds, the excitation is usually a sequence of samples of amplitude A that are t samples apart. The distance t is determined by the pitch period expressed in samples, while A is determined from the gain G so that the total energy of the excitation in the frame is G^2. For unvoiced sounds we use a random number generator to determine the sign of each sample, while the amplitude A of the samples is again determined so that the total energy of the excitation in the frame is G^2.

The above selection of the unvoiced excitation is pretty much standard, but for voiced excitation, there can be many choices. One possibility is to use the government-furnished excitation given in Table 5.1. In this case, we do not have an impulse for every pitch period, but we do have a carefully selected waveform to resemble a glottal pulse.

TABLE 5.1 EXCITATION SIGNAL FOR
VOICED SOUNDS SUGGESTED IN THE
DOD STANDARD LPC-10 ALGORITHM

Index	Amplitude
1	249
2	− 262
3	363
4	− 362
5	100
6	367
7	79
8	78
9	10
10	− 277
11	− 82
12	376
13	288
14	− 65
15	− 20
16	138
17	− 62
18	− 315
19	− 247
20	− 78
21	− 82
22	− 123
23	− 39
24	65
25	64
26	19
27	16
28	32
29	18
30	− 15
31	− 29
32	− 21
33	− 18
34	− 27
35	− 31
36	− 22
37	− 12
38	− 10
39	− 10
40	− 4

(after [6]).

5.7 MULTIPULSE EXCITATION

Despite all the caution taken to have carefully determined excitations, the quality of the synthesized speech is perceived as having a mechanical sound, which has been attributed to the simplistic model of the excitation. More recently the *multipulse excitation* [7] has attempted to rectify this problem. In multipulse excitation, you do not separate voiced and unvoiced frames but you instead try to determine a number of impulses for each frame (usually 8–10 impulses), so that the end result of the synthesis is as close to the original speech as possible. The algorithm determines the position and the amplitude of these impulses sequentially. When one impulse is computed, its effect is subtracted from the speech signal and the procedure is repeated.

In multipulse excitation, the location and amplitude of a pulse is determined so that the synthetic speech waveform is as close to the original waveform as possible. If $s(n)$ is the original signal and $s'(n)$ the synthetic waveform, it is desired to minimize the energy of the error signal

$$e(n) = [s(n) - s'(n)] * w(n) \qquad (5.49)$$

where $w(n)$ is a weighting function, and the asterisk denotes convolution. In the frequency domain,

$$E(z) = [S(z) - S'(z)] W(z) \qquad (5.50)$$

If $H(z)$ is the LPC vocal tract filter, a usual choice for the weighting function is

$$W(z) = \frac{H(bz)}{H(z)} \qquad (5.51)$$

where

$$H(bz) = \frac{G}{[1 + a_1 b^{-1} z^{-1} + \ldots + a_p b^{-P_z - P}]}$$

b is a number between 0 and 1. The spectrum $H(bz)$ has the same shape like $H(z)$ but the formant peaks are less sharp. Experimentation has shown that $b = 0.8$ gives good quality speech.

Notice that $S(z)/H(z)$ is the residual signal and $S'(z)/H(z)$ is the excitation of the synthetic speech. This excitation in our case is the pulse to be determined. Let this pulse have amplitude A_m, with m

indicating its position. Both m and A_m must be determined. Also, let $h(n)$ be the impulse response of $H(bz)$. With these substitutions in equation (5.50), the error energy to be minimized is given by

$$\sum_n e^2(n) = \sum_n [d(n) - A_m h(n - m)]^2 \tag{5.52}$$

where $d(n)$ is the result of filtering the residual signal $r(n)$ through $H(bz)$, as shown in Figure 5.15. Minimization of (5.52) is achieved when

$$A_m = \frac{\sum_n d(n)\, h(n-m)}{\sum_n h^2\,(n-m)} = \frac{C_m}{\phi} \tag{5.53}$$

where $C_m = \Sigma\, d(n)\, h(n - m)$ is the cross-correlation between $h(n)$ and $d(n)$, and $\phi = \Sigma\, h^2(n - m)$ is the energy of $h(n)$. The corresponding minimum energy is

$$E = (\Sigma\, d^2\,(n)) - \left(\frac{C_m^2}{\phi}\right) \tag{5.54}$$

In (5.54), C_m is the only quantity depending on m. Hence, for minimization, the position m of the pulse is selected so that the absolute value of the cross-correlation C_m is maximized. Then, the amplitude of the pulse is determined by (5.53). Once this pulse is

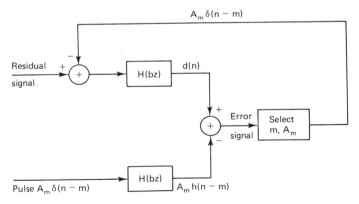

Figure 5.15 Block diagram of the pulse-amplitude and position determination in multipulse excitation.

determined, it is subtracted from the residual signal. This is equivalent to subtracting the resulting synthetic waveform from the original waveform. To determine the next pulse, the same procedure is repeated using this last computed difference as the residual signal.

The effect of adding such pulses in the excitation is demonstrated in Figure 5.16. The resulting synthetic signal approximates the original signal. In the limit, the multipulse excitation will produce one impulse for every sampling interval, and it will almost coincide with the residual signal.

The impulses thus computed are used for the excitation of the synthesizer. Multipulse LPC is used for bit rates around 9,600 bits/s.

5.8 THE RELP VOCODER

As mentioned earlier, if the speech signal $s(n)$ is passed through the inverse filter $A(z)$, you get the residual error signal, $e(n)$. Passing this error signal through the LPC filter regenerates the original speech signal. This procedure is depicted in Figure 5.17. From this arrangement, it becomes apparent that if you could code and transmit efficiently the residual signal, $e(n)$, you could have very good quality reconstructed speech. This approach is taken in the Residual-Excited Linear Prediction (RELP) vocoder.

The residual signal has the property of its spectrum being relatively flat. This is a consequence of our effort to estimate the LPC parameters so that the LPC spectrum is the envelope of the speech spectrum. However, the spectrum of the residual signal preserves all the excitation information (and whatever information the LPC model did not manage to pick up) and this information is more or less uniform over the different frequencies. As a result, the necessary coding and transmission efficiency can be achieved by encoding and transmitting only a small portion of the residual spectrum, e.g., between 0–1,000 Hz. At the synthesizer, this baseband is repeated to generate the higher frequencies in a copy-up procedure. Then, the reconstructed residual signal is used as the excitation of the LPC filter.

Usually, the encoding of the residual signal is performed in the frequency domain. An FFT of the residual signal is computed and we extract the frequencies 0–1,000 Hz. These samples are encoded as magnitude and phase, and transmitted. At the receiver, an inverse FFT is performed to recover the baseband residual from the transmitted information.

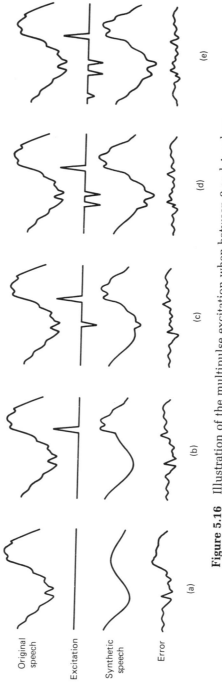

Original
speech

Excitation

Synthetic
speech

Error

(a)   (b)   (c)   (d)   (e)

Figure 5.16 Illustration of the multipulse excitation when between 0 and 4 pulses are used. With 0 pulses, the filter has as initial conditions the last outputs of the previous speech frame (after Atal and Remde [7], © 1982 IEEE).

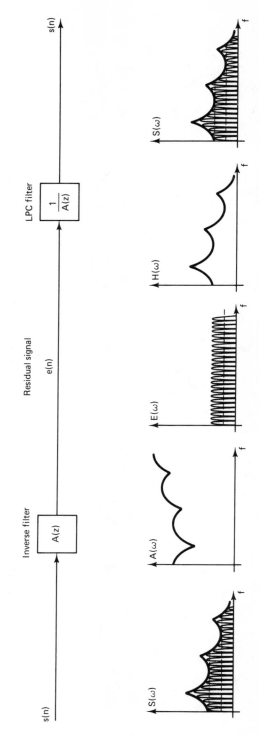

Figure 5.17 Effect of inverse filtering of the speech signal, followed by an LPC filter.

138

One problem of the copy-up procedure during voiced speech is that the harmonics around 1,000 Hz, 2,000 Hz, and so forth, will not be properly spaced because it is very improbable to have the last harmonic of the baseband exactly on 1,000 Hz. The problem can be alleviated if we go ahead and extract pitch information. Then, instead of selecting the transmitted baseband to be exactly 1,000 Hz wide, its width can be made variable, so that when it is copied up, the harmonics are properly spaced. Of course, in this case you also need to transmit the pitch information so that the receiver knows the width of the baseband. This increases the bit rate to some extent, but it can also be used to your advantage in the following way. Since the pitch information is now available all the time, if the transmission channel becomes very loaded, you can switch to a significantly lower bit rate by not transmitting the residual signal and using only the rest of the information. In other words, you can switch from a RELP vocoder to a pitch-excited vocoder, thus creating a multirate system.

The RELP Vocoder is typically used for bit rates around 9,600 bits/s.

5.9 FORMANT VOCODERS

In Chapter 4 we mentioned that the formant vocoders can potentially lead to very low bit rates. However, the formants are elusive quantities and their determination is hard. In the most often used approaches, the formants are determined as the peaks of the envelope of the speech spectrum. For this application, the LPC model offers some advantages in determining the speech formants.

First, the LPC spectrum represents a smooth envelope of the actual speech spectrum, and it can be used with the regular peak-picking techniques to determine the formants. In addition to that, the LPC model has the advantage of being described by an analytic expression, the all-pole digital filter. The poles of the LPC model can then be used for the determination of the speech formants.

Use of the LPC poles to determine the speech formants can yield good results, but there are still issues to be addressed, such as what pole corresponds to what formant, and what to do with the nonformant poles. Despite these difficulties, there is reason to believe that encoding the LPC poles will yield good speech quality at very low bit rates.

5.10 VECTOR QUANTIZATION

The method of vector quantization is not tied only to the LPC modeling (for instance, it has also been used with waveform coders). However, it is discussed here since it is often used with the LPC model to achieve low bit rate coding.

When we use the LPC parameters to represent a speech frame, we essentially pick one point in the p-dimensional spectral space, where p is the order of the LPC model. In other words, we treat the set of p LPC parameters as a p-dimensional vector lying in a p-dimensional space. In the regular coding method (called scalar quantization to contrast it with vector quantization), each parameter is coded separately. The coding levels divide the p-dimensional space into a uniform grid, as shown in Figure 5.18 for the case

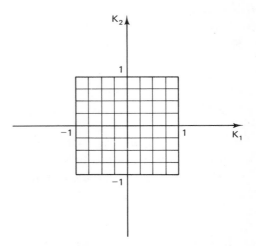

Figure 5.18 Example of a two-dimensional space with scalar quantization.

$p = 2$. If we used a second-order LPC model, the quantized parameters in one of the squares of the grid would represent the spectrum of the speech frame under consideration. However, it turns out that this representation is quite wasteful since it expects the speech frames to more or less occur uniformly throughout the two-dimensional grid.

A more realistic distribution of the speech spectrum is shown in Figure 5.19, where each dot represents a frame. This representation suggests that instead of wasting bits to represent areas where

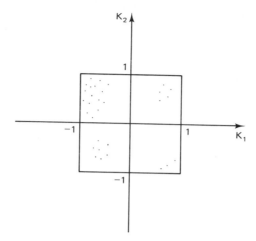

Figure 5.19 Distribution of speech frames that are represented by a second-order LPC model.

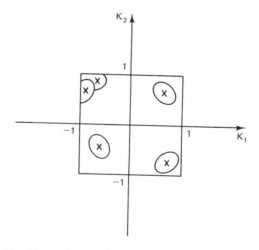

Figure 5.20 Clustering of the speech frames to generate the codebook quantization vectors for vector quantization (two-dimensional example).

speech frames do not occur, you can concentrate on the areas of actual occurrence. For instance, you could partition the example of Figure 5.19 as shown in Figure 5.20, where each x represents a K-parameter vector to which all the vectors in that cluster will be quantized. This idea can be generalized for the p-dimensional space.

The vector quantization method is implemented by first computing a codebook of quantization vectors, and then using these vectors to encode speech. To generate a dependable codebook, we need a large set of training vectors. These vectors are then grouped together in a predetermined number of clusters, and each cluster i is represented by its centroid y_i. The determination of the clustering and of the centroid is based on a distance measure, $d(V_1, V_2)$, between vectors V_1 and V_2, which will be discussed later.

Once the codebook is determined, it is stored at both the transmitter and the receiver. The quantization of an input speech vector, x_i, is then done as follows. By comparing the distances $d(x_i, y_i)$ between x_i and all the vectors y_i of the codebook, you select the vector y_m for which the distance d is minimum. This selected vector y_m will represent x_i. You then transmit the index m to the receiver, from which the vector y_m is selected as the representation of x_i.

The selection of the distance metric $d(V_1, V_2)$ is very important, because it should be perceptually significant. You want to make sure that when you say that x is "closer" to y_1 than to y_2, you mean that x sounds more like y_1 than like y_2. Unfortunately, none of the existing distance measures correlates 100 percent with human perception. The measures usually selected are analytically tractable and have been shown to work acceptably well. One possible choice is the Euclidean distance

$$d^2 (V_1, V_2) = \| V_1 - V_2 \|^2 \qquad (5.55)$$

which is the sum of the squared differences of the elements of the vectors. This distance metric is preferable if the vector elements correspond to formants or to the channel bank outputs of a channel vocoder.

A more popular choice in the case of the LPC model is Itakura's likelihood ratio. This metric can be determined as follows: Let a_1, R_1, a_2, R_2 be the coefficient vectors and the autocorrelation matrices corresponding to vectors V_1 and V_2, as defined from the equations (5.6)–(5.9). Then, Itakura's likelihood ratio is defined by

$$d(V_1, V_2) = \frac{a_1^T R_1 a_1}{a_2^T R_1 a_2} \qquad (5.56)$$

Since this distance is nonsymmetric, sometimes we use $1/2[d(V_1, V_2) + d(V_2, V_1)]$.

The vector quantization method has been shown to give the lowest currently available bit rates with reasonable quality of speech. Systems with 400–800 bits/s have been demonstrated successfully. The main problems with vector quantization are the large storage required for the codebook vectors and the difficulty in computing a good codebook. So far, the systems that have been implemented tend to be speaker-dependent in order to achieve a good performance. Finally, the computational requirements during encoding can be significant if the size of the codebook is large. However, there are techniques to alleviate this last problem.

Despite these shortcomings of vector quantization, it seems that it is a very good method for encoding speech below 1,000 bits/s. In addition to low bit rate parametric coders, it has also found application in waveform coders and in speech recognition.

5.11 LINE SPECTRUM PAIRS (LSP)

A representation of the LPC parameters that has been gaining interest is the Line Spectrum Pairs (LSP). The LSPs are related to the poles of the LPC filter $H(z)$ (or the zeros of the inverse filter $A(z)$). They are derived from $A(z)$ as follows:

Assuming for concreteness a tenth-order model, the inverse LPC filter is given in the z-domain by

$$A(z) = 1 + a_1 z^{-1} + \ldots + a_{10} z^{-10} \qquad (5.57)$$

From (5.57), we compute the polynomials $P(z)$ and $Q(z)$:

$$
\begin{aligned}
P(z) &= A(z) + z^{-11} A(z^{-1}) \\
&= 1 + (a_1 + a_{10}) z^{-1} + (a_2 + a_9) z^{-2} + \ldots + \\
&\quad (a_{10} + a_1) z^{-10} + z^{-11}
\end{aligned}
\qquad (5.58)
$$

$$
\begin{aligned}
Q(z) &= A(z) - z^{-11} A(z^{-1}) \\
&= 1 + (a_1 - a_{10}) z^{-1} + (a_2 - a_9) z^{-2} + \ldots + \\
&\quad (a_{10} - a_1) z^{-10} - z^{-11}
\end{aligned}
\qquad (5.59)
$$

$A(z)$ can be recovered from $P(z)$ and $Q(z)$ by

$$A(z) = \frac{[P(z) + Q(z)]}{2} \qquad (5.60)$$

The polynomial $P(z)$ has a real root at $z = -1$ and all the other roots complex. Similarly, $Q(z)$ has one real root at $z = 1$ and all the other roots are complex. These complex roots of $P(z)$ and $Q(z)$ have the following properties:

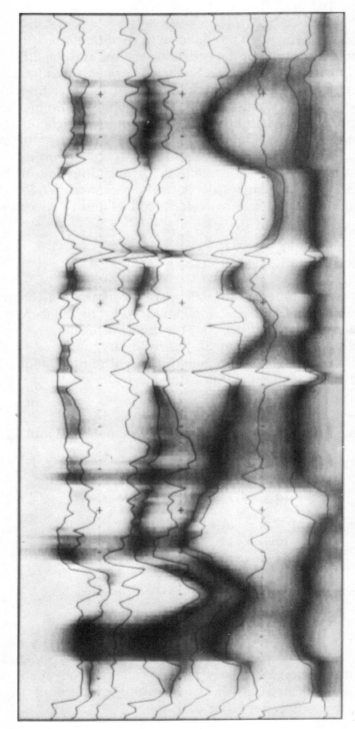

Figure 5.21 Line spectrum pairs superimposed on a spectrogram.

144

1. All the roots lie on the unit circle. Hence, each polynomial can be represented by the angles of the five roots on the upper half of the unit circle. The other five are their complex conjugates, and have angles that are the negatives of the first ones.
2. The roots of $P(z)$ and $Q(z)$ alternate on the unit circle. This is a necessary and sufficient condition for the stability of $A(z)$, and it should be carefully observed in the quantization of the roots.

Since the roots are on the unit circle, they can be expressed as $e^{j\omega}$. The angles ω are the line spectrum pairs. If one uses the second-order sections of the complex conjugate pairs to implement the synthesis filter, it is possible to encode either the LSPs themselves or their cosines.

Figure 5.21 shows the LSPs superimposed on a spectrogram. It is easy to see that the LSPs are related to the formants and they carry a significant amount of information. As synthesis parameters, they have excellent properties since they are best suited for interpolation at synthesis time. Their drawbacks are the heavy computational load in evaluating the roots of $P(z)$ and $Q(z)$, and their sensitivity to quantization when successive roots of $P(z)$ and $Q(z)$ are very close to each other.

The line spectrum pairs have been used to achieve bit rates around 2,400 bits/s. Their primary application has been voice response systems, but they hold considerable promise for low bit-rate, high-quality speech coding.

5.12 SUMMARY

This chapter described the linear predictive method of speech coding (LPC) and some derivative methods. LPC is based on a speech production model that requires both determination of the excitation and parametric description of the vocal tract.

The LPC parameters are computed from the incoming signal that has been subjected to windowing and preemphasis. These parameters represent an all-pole digital filter, and they are determined so that the energy of the error between the original and the synthetic signal is minimized. Such a minimization leads to a set of linear equations from which the coefficients of the all-pole filter are computed.

Besides the filter coefficients, other equivalent representations of the LPC parameters are the reflection coefficients and the log-area ratios. The log-area ratios have much lower sensitivity to quantization errors and are usually preferred for the representation of the LPC model. The reflection coefficients can be computed effectively by the LeRoux-Gueguen method.

There are several interesting derivatives of the basic LPC method. The multipulse excitation uses the LPC model to systematically generate a set of pulses to be used as the excitation. The residual-excited LPC (RELP) vocoder uses a compressed version of the residual signal that is generated by passing the original speech signal through the inverse LPC filter as an excitation. For illustration purposes, the excitation of the LPC filter by the residual can be thought of as a limiting case of the multipulse excitation, where a pulse is computed at every sample.

In vector quantization, instead of quantizing every parameter separately, the whole vector of LPC parameters is quantized in a multidimensional space, thus leading to bit-rate savings. This method is used for speech coding at rates below 1,000 bits/s. Vector quantization does not have to use the LPC parameters but since this is the usual choice, it is examined here.

Finally, the line spectrum pairs (LSP) represent a way of encoding the poles of the LPC model. They have considerable advantages in preserving good speech quality at low bit rates around 2,400 bits/s. However, they also impose a computational burden since they require solution of high-order equations with complex roots.

5.13 FURTHER READING

The linear predictive method has been one of the most popular approaches for speech coding in recent years. This has resulted in an extensive volume of literature on that subject. The book by Rabiner and Schafer [8] gives an excellent introduction to the subject, while the collection of papers by Schafer and Markel [9] contains some basic contributions to the LPC field. The paper by Makhoul [10] is the most often referenced tutorial on LPC, while the book by Markel and Gray [11], although somewhat difficult to read, is a very important monograph covering in depth most aspects of LPC. The classical papers by Atal and Hanauer [12], and by Itakura and Saito [13] are considered to be the founders of LPC.

The lattice implementation of the linear prediction filter is discussed in Makhoul's paper [1]. LeRoux and Gueguen [3] and Rajasekaran and Hansen [14] examine the subject of fixed-point implementation of the LPC analysis. The different forms of LPC parameters are studied by Viswanathan and Makhoul [4], and are presented in the book by Rabiner and Schafer [8].

The multipulse excitation was introduced by Atal and Remde [7] in 1982, and since then there have been several papers every year in the proceedings of the International Conference on ASSP (ICASSP), such as the ones in References [15–17]. For the residual-excited LPC vocoder, a very detailed implementation is described in the NRL report [18] by Kang et al.

Another coding method that has gained much popularity in recent years is the vector quantization. The basic approach is described by Linde et al. [19], while Gray [20] gives a very good overview of this field. The papers by Buzo et al. [21] and Wong et al. [22] contain interesting discussions of the subject. Vector quantization has been applied to many domains of speech processing, such as waveform coding and speech recognition. The interested reader is directed to look at the proceedings of the ICASSP in recent years for more information.

The line spectrum pairs (LSP) method [23–26] has been mostly developed in the Japanese literature. The paper by Soong and Juang [25] contains an interesting development of the method, while Crosmer and Barnwell [26] describe an effective quantization scheme.

5.14 REFERENCES

1. Makhoul, J. "Stable and Efficient Lattice Methods for Linear Prediction." *IEEE Trans. Acous., Speech, and Signal Proc.*, Vol. ASSP-25, No. 5 (October 1977): 423–428.

2. Gray, A. H., Jr., and D. Y. Wong. "The Burg Algorithm for LPC Speech Analysis/Synthesis." *IEEE Trans. Acous., Speech, and Signal Proc.*, Vol. ASSP-28, No. 6 (December 1980): 609–615.

3. Le Roux, J., and C. Gueguen. "A Fixed Point Computation of Partial Correlation Coefficients." *IEEE Trans. Acous., Speech and Signal Proc.*, Vol. ASSP-25 (June 1977): 257–259.

4. Viswanathan, R., and J. Makhoul. "Quantization Properties of Transmission Parameters in Linear Predictive Systems." *IEEE Trans. Acous., Speech and Signal Proc.,* Vol. ASSP-23 (June 1975): 309–321.

5. Gray, A. H., Jr., and J. D. Markel. "Quantization and Bit Allocation in Speech Processing." *IEEE Trans. Acous. Speech and Signal Proc.,* Vol. ASSP-24 (December 1976): 459–473.

6. Documentation of the Government Standard LPC-10 Algorithm.

7. Atal, B. S., and J. R. Remde. "A New Model of LPC Excitation Producing Natural-Sounding Speech at Low Bit Rates." *Proc. 1982 IEEE Int. Conf. Acous., Speech, and Signal Proc.* (May 1982): 614–617.

8. Rabiner, L. R., and R. W. Schafer. *Digital Processing of Speech Signals.* Englewood Cliffs, NJ: Prentice-Hall, 1978.

9. Schafer, R. W., and J. D. Markel, Eds., *Speech Analysis.* New York: IEEE Press, 1979.

10. Makhoul, J., "Linear Prediction: A Tutorial Review." *Proc. IEEE,* Vol. 63 (April 1975): 561–580.

11. Markel, J. D., and A. H. Gray, Jr. *Linear Prediction of Speech.* New York: Springer-Verlag, 1976.

12. Atal, B. S., and S. L. Hanauer. "Speech Analysis and Synthesis by Linear Prediction of the Speech Wave." *J. Acous. Soc. Am.,* Vol. 50, No. 2 (1971): 637–655.

13. Itakura, F., and S. Saito. "Analysis Synthesis Telephony based on the Maximum Likelihood Method." *Proc. of 6th Int. Congress on Acoustics,* Tokyo (August 1968): C17–20.

14. Rajasekaran, P. K., and J. C. Hansen. "Finite Word Length Effects of the LeRoux-Gueguen Algorithm in Computing Reflection Coefficients." *Proc 1982 IEEE Int. Conf. Acous., Speech, and Signal Proc.* (May 1982): 1286–1290.

15. Singhal, S., and B. S. Atal. "Improving Performance of Multi-Pulse LPC Coders at Low Bit Rates." *Proc. 1984 IEEE Int. Conf. Acous., Speech, and Signal Proc.* (March 1984): 1.3.1-4.

16. Berouti, M., H. Garten, P. Kabal, and P. Mermelstein. "Efficient Computation and Encoding of the Multipulse Excitation of LPC." *Proc. 1984 IEEE Int. Conf. on Acous., Speech, and Signal Proc.* (March 1984): 10.1.1-10.1.4.

17. Senensieb, G. A., A. J. Milbourn, A. H. Lloyd, and I. M. Warrington. "A Non-Iterative Algorithm for Obtaining Multi-Pulse Excitation for Linear-Predictive Speech Coders." *Proc. 1984 IEEE Int. Conf. on Acous., Speech, and Signal Proc.* (March 1984): 10.2.1-10.2.4.

18. Kang, G. S., L. Fransen, and E. L. Kline. "Multirate Processor (MRP)." *NRL Report,* September 1978.

19. Linde, Y., A. Buzo, and R.M. Gray. "An Algorithm for Vector Quantizer Design." *IEEE Trans. on Comm.*, Vol. COM-28 (January 1980): 84–95.

20. Gray, R. M. "Vector Quantization." *IEEE ASSP Magazine*, Vol. 1, No. 2 (April 1984): 4–29.

21. Buzo, A., A. H. Gray, Jr., R. M. Gray, and J. D. Markel. "Speech Coding Based upon Vector Quantization." *IEEE Trans. Acous., Speech, and Signal Proc.*, Vol. ASSP-28 (October 1980): 562–574.

22. Wong, D., B. H. Juang, and A. H. Gray, Jr. "An 800 bit/s Vector Quantization LPC Vocoder." *IEEE Trans. Acous., Speech, and Signal Proc.*, Vol. ASSP-30 (October 1982): 770–779.

23. Itakura, F. "Line Spectrum Representation of Linear Predictive Coefficients of Speech Signals." *J. Acous. Soc. Am.*, 57, 535(A), 1975.

24. Sugamura, N., and F. Itakura. "Speech Data Compression by LSP Analysis-Synthesis Technique." *Trans. IECE '81/8*, Vol. J 64-A, No. 8: 599–606.

25. Soong, F. K., and B.-H. Juang. "Line Spectrum Pair (LSP) and Speech Data Compression." *Proc. 1984 IEEE Int. Conf. on Acous., Speech, and Signal Proc.* (March 1984): 1.10.1–1.10.4.

26. Crosmer, J. R., and T. P. Barnwell. "A Low Bit Rate Segment Vocoder Based on Line Spectrum Pairs." *Proc. 1985 IEEE Int. Conf. on Acous., Speech, and Signal Proc.* (March 1985): 240–243.

Chapter 6

Pitch Detection and Its Importance in Speech Coding

The determination of the periodicity in a speech segment is very important in many speech coding algorithms. This periodicity determines if the speech segment is voiced or unvoiced and, if voiced, what is the fundamental period. Accurate answers to these questions not only play a critical role in the speech quality of the vocoders, but also have serious impact on other coding schemes that utilize this information.

The fundamental frequency of the speech signal is sometimes designated as F_0 and it is usually called pitch frequency. More correctly, the term "pitch" is defined as a subjective quality of the speech signal related to F_0. For the purposes of the present discussion, and following the accepted terminology, we will use all these terms interchangeably. The inverse of the pitch frequency

$$\tau = \frac{1}{F_0}$$

(6.1)

is the pitch period and it is usually expressed in milliseconds or, if the sampling frequency is understood, in samples. Expression of the pitch period in samples is the most often used quantity for coding purposes.

The determination of the pitch has two stages. In the first stage, you must determine if the speech segment is voiced or unvoiced. If it is voiced, the actual pitch period is estimated in the second stage. The two stages are not always distinct, and there are algorithms that interleave them.

The pitch estimation has remained the most vulnerable part of pitch-excited vocoding systems, and this fact has stimulated the development of numerous pitch detection algorithms. The book by Hess [1] is an impressive compilation of different algorithms. However, the problem remains to a large extent unsolved. Voiced segments with clear periodicity and unvoiced segments with clear lack of any periodicity can easily be identified by any reasonable pitch tracking algorithm. The identification of in-between segments, though, becomes difficult and no algorithm has been found that performs robustly in all cases in accordance with human perception.

In this chapter we will describe five of the better-known pitch detection and estimation algorithms, which have been shown to perform reasonably well under most circumstances. The first algorithm presented has been developed by Gold and Rabiner, and it uses time-domain information to extract the pitch period. On the other hand, the homomorphic pitch tracker uses the cepstrum as a means of separation of the vocal tract and the excitation. The autocorrelation pitch tracker relies on the properties of the autocorrelation to extract pitch information. Related to the autocorrelation method is the average magnitude difference function (AMDF) method. The AMDF has been used in the LPC vocoder standard established by the US Government. Finally, the SIFT algorithm for pitch tracking is based on the LPC model.

Besides these methods of pitch determination, there are post-processing techniques to improve the accuracy of the estimate and recover from possible gross errors. The post-processing techniques can be combined with any one of the pitch tracking algorithms.

6.1 GOLD-RABINER PITCH TRACKER

The pitch tracking algorithm that has been used most widely is the Gold-Rabiner pitch tracker. The Cold-Rabiner pitch tracker is a time-domain processing technique that computes six sets of parameters from the time waveform. Each of these sets is processed separately to generate a pitch period estimate, and the resulting estimates are compared with each other to generate the final decision after some rather sophisticated processing, which is described below. Since the above six sets of parameters can be processed independently, we can apply parallel processing techniques to reduce the time required for computation.

Figure 6.1 outlines the steps of the Gold-Rabiner pitch tracking algorithm. The speech signal is first filtered by a 100–900 Hz bandpass filter. The filtering can be done with analog circuits before digitization or digitally after the A/D converter. The objective of the filtering is to render a smooth waveform, and also to cut off the 60 Hz hum. Of course, if the speech is coming from the telephone circuits or if it is the digitized output of a codec, we only need to lowpass-filter it since the frequencies below 100 Hz are already eliminated.

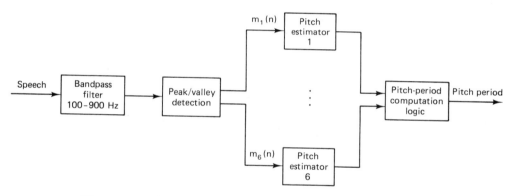

Figure 6.1   Block diagram of the Gold-Rabiner pitch tracking algorithm.

The filtered speech, $s(n)$, is then used to generate the six waveforms, $m_1(n) - m_6(n)$, which are the six sets of parameters mentioned earlier. Figure 6.2 describes how these quantities are computed. For every peak of the speech signal, the quantities $m_1(n)$, $m_2(n)$, and $m_3(n)$ are computed; for every valley, we compute $m_4(n)$, $m_5(n)$, and $m_6(n)$.

- $m_1(n)$ is the magnitude of the peak.
- $m_2(n)$ is the distance of a peak from the previous valley.
- $m_3(n)$ is the distance of a peak from the previous peak. If $m_3(n)$ < 0, we set $m_3(n) = 0$.
- $m_4(n)$ is the magnitude of the valley.

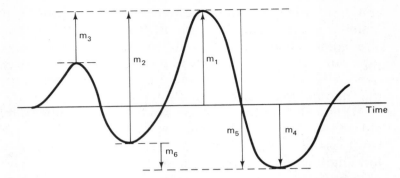

Figure 6.2 Basic measurements made on the filtered speech for the Gold-Rabiner pitch tracker. These measurements are input to the six estimators (after Gold and Rabiner [2]).

- $m_5(n)$ is the distance of the valley from the previous peak.
- $m_6(n)$ is the distance of a valley from the previous valley. Again, if $m_6(n) < 0$, we set $m_6(n) = 0$.

All the m_i's are represented as positive pulse trains by taking the absolute value. Figure 6.3 shows an example of the computation of $m_1(n) - m_6(n)$ for a sample signal. Note that the pitch period derived from $m_3(n)$ and $m_6(n)$ is correct, while the one derived from the rest of the measurements is incorrect.

    After the six sets of parameters have been estimated, each one of them is passed through the corresponding pitch estimator of Figure 6.1. The operation of each pitch estimator is illustrated by the example of Figure 6.4. When a pulse is detected, a blanking interval is imposed during which no pulses are detected. After the blanking interval, the envelope decays exponentially until a pulse is found whose value exceeds the envelope. Then, the value of the envelope is reset to the new pulse, and the procedure is repeated. The distance P_{new} between two detected pulses is the current pitch period estimate in milliseconds. To determine the blanking period t and the rundown constant b of the exponential, we use a smoothed estimate P_{av} of the pitch period. The current value $P_{av}(n)$ is computed from the previous value $P_{av}(n-1)$ and the current pitch estimate P_{new}.

$$P_{av}(n) = \frac{P_{av}(n-1) + P_{new}}{2} \tag{6.2}$$

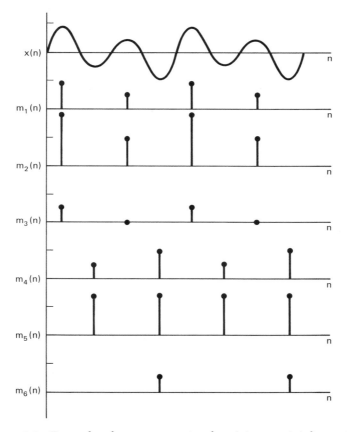

Figure 6.3 Example of measurements of $m_1(n)$ − $m_6(n)$ for a simple waveform with a strong second harmonic. The pitch measurements from $m_3(n)$ and $m_6(n)$ are correct, while the measurements from $m_1(n)$ and $m_2(n)$, $m_4(n)$ and $m_5(n)$ are incorrect. (L. R. Rabiner, R. W. Schafer [3], DIGITAL PROCESSING OF SPEECH SIGNALS, © 1978. Reprinted by permission of Prentice-Hall, Inc., Englewood Cliffs, NJ.)

Variable P_{av} is not permitted to go below 4 ms (250 Hz) or above 10 ms (100 Hz) (pitch period).

Then, the P_{av} is used to determine the blanking period, t, from the equation

$$t = 0.4P_{av} \tag{6.3}$$

and the rundown time constant, b, from

$$b = \frac{P_{av}}{0.695} \tag{6.4}$$

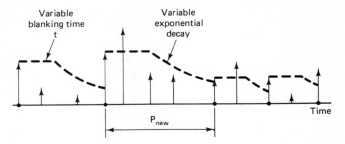

Figure 6.4 Operation taking place in each pitch estimator in Figure 6.1 (after Gold and Rabiner [2]).

The constants in the above equations have been estimated experimentally.

After the computation of the six pitch estimates, the final determination of the pitch period is done in the block labeled "Pitch Period Computation Logic" in Figure 6.1. To determine the final pitch period, we generate six pitch candidates from each of the pitch estimators. These candidates are shown in Figure 6.5 for the ith pitch estimator, and consist of the present and the previous two pitch estimates for that estimator, p_{i1}, p_{i2}, and p_{i3}. From these values we compute three more pitch estimates

$$P_{i4} = P_{i1} + P_{i2} \tag{6.5}$$

$$P_{i5} = P_{i2} + P_{i3} \tag{6.6}$$

$$P_{i6} = P_{i1} + P_{i2} + P_{i3} \tag{6.7}$$

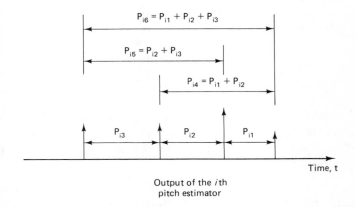

Figure 6.5 Determination of pitch candidates from the output of the ith pitch estimator. P_{i1} is the present pitch estimate of that estimator.

to take into account that the original estimates of the pitch period
may correspond to the second or third harmonic. With these candidates from the six pitch estimators we generate a 6 × 6 matrix, as
shown in Figure 6.6.

This matrix is used for the computation of the pitch period.
Each of the entries is compared with every other entry, and the
number of entries that are "close enough" to it are counted. The
entry with the highest number of "close-enough" values is selected
as the pitch period estimate. The computation of the matrix and the
determination of the pitch is repeated every 5 ms.

As a final step, we need to define more precisely what is meant
by "close enough." The table of Figure 6.7 gives four tolerances for
a certain value of pitch. For instance, assume that an entry p_{ij} of the
table with the candidate pitch periods has a value of 5.25 ms. We
want to compare this entry with the other 35 values of the table of
Figure 6.6. The value 5.25 lies in the range of the second row of
Figure 6.7, which has tolerances 200, 400, 600, and 800 μs.

PITCH ESTIMATOR NUMBER

		1	2	3	4	5	6
PITCH PERIOD	1	p_{11}	p_{21}	p_{31}	p_{41}	p_{51}	p_{61}
CANDIDATE	2	p_{12}	p_{22}	p_{32}	p_{42}	p_{52}	p_{62}
	3	p_{13}	p_{23}	p_{33}	p_{43}	p_{53}	p_{63}
	4	p_{14}	p_{24}	p_{34}	p_{44}	p_{54}	p_{64}
	5	p_{15}	p_{25}	p_{35}	p_{45}	p_{55}	p_{65}
	6	p_{16}	p_{26}	p_{36}	p_{46}	p_{56}	p_{66}

(a)

PITCH ESTIMATOR NUMBER

		1	2	3	4	5	6
PITCH PERIOD	1	5.25	5.80	5.25	6.10	5.54	6.10
CANDIDATE	2	1.50	5.95	11.73	5.54	6.10	5.54
	3	4.00	6.80	21.30	7.50	5.54	27.20
	4	6.75	11.75	16.98	11.64	11.08	11.64
	5	5.50	12.75	33.03	13.04	11.64	32.74
	6	10.75	18.55	38.78	19.14	16.62	38.84

(b)

Figure 6.6 (a) 6 × 6 matrix of all the candidate pitch periods. Two
entries coincide if they are within the distances specified by the table of
Figure 6.7. (b) An example of the matrix with pitch periods in ms (after
Gold [4]).

We compare P_{ij} with the other entries four times. The first time, all the values that are within the range 5.25 ± 0.2 ms are considered "close enough." The other three times, the close-enough values are within the ranges 5.25 ± 0.4, 5.25 ± 0.6, and 5.25 ± 0.8 ms.

Since the number of coincidences increases with the tolerance, a compensatory penalty is introduced. For tolerances of the first column of the table in Figure 6.7, the number of counted coincidences is reduced by 1, for the second column, the number is reduced by 2, for the third by 5, and for the fourth by 7. These biased counts are then used for the final decision.

One remaining issue in the Gold-Rabiner pitch tracker is the voiced/unvoiced decision. The voiced/unvoiced decision is based again on the table of Figure 6.6, and is explained in [4]. To make a voiced/unvoiced decision, consider only the six most recent estimates, i.e., only the first row of the table in Figure 6.6. For each one of them, compute four sets of coincidences, as described above, using also the table of Figure 6.7. Then, take the differences of these counts from four experimentally determined thresholds [4]. Repeat the same procedure with all the entries of the first row of Figure 6.6, and keep the difference with the largest absolute value. If this difference is positive, the speech segment is declared voiced; otherwise, it is declared unvoiced.

Figure 6.7 Coincidence window width in hundreds of microseconds. Two pitch periods coincide if their distance in hundreds of microseconds is less than the corresponding table entry. The pitch period range determines which row will be used for each pitch period candidate. The bias is the number by which the number of coincidences is reduced (after Gold and Rabiner [2]).

		BIAS			
		1	2	5	7
PITCH PERIOD	1.6– 3.1	1	2	3	4
RANGE (MS)	3.1– 6.3	2	4	6	8
	6.3–12.7	4	8	12	16
	12.7–25.5	8	16	24	32

6.2 HOMOMORPHIC PITCH TRACKER

In Chapter 4 the homomorphic vocoder is described as a method of encoding the speech spectrum. The homomorphic vocoder is based on the cepstrum, which is the inverse Fourier transformation of the logarithm of the speech spectrum magnitude. The cepstrum properties make possible the voiced/unvoiced decision on the speech signal and, if voiced, the determination of the pitch period. Let us revisit the speech cepstrum to see how this can be accomplished.

A voiced speech segment has a spectrum like the one shown with the solid line in Figure 6.8. This spectrum can be considered as containing a smooth-varying portion, which is shown in a broken line, and a rapidly-varying fine structure. The smooth portion is the envelope of the spectrum and corresponds to the vocal tract, while the fine structure corresponds to the periodic excitation of the speech signal, i.e., the pitch harmonics.

If we represent the spectrum as the product of the vocal tract

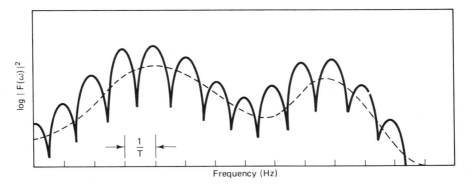

Figure 6.8 Example of log spectrum of a voiced second. The broken line shows the envelope; the continuous line is the fine structure (after Noll [5]).

envelope $V(e^{j\omega})$ and the pitch harmonics $P(e^{j\omega})$, then the cepstrum is computed as the inverse Fourier transform of the logarithm of the spectral magnitude:

$$c(n) = F^{-1}[\log | V(e^{j\omega})P(e^{j\omega}) |]$$
$$= F^{-1}[\log | V(e^{j\omega}) |] + F^{-1}[\log | P(e^{j\omega}) |] \tag{6.8}$$

Since the vocal tract envelope varies smoothly, it contains low "frequency" components, while the fine structure varies more rapidly and contains high "frequency" components. Of course, after the transformation (6.8), the low- and high-frequency components correspond to low time and high time, as shown in Figure 6.9. Note that the periodic pitch component is transformed to a high-time peak. This is a typical picture of a speech cepstrum and suggests the following way of determining the pitch period:

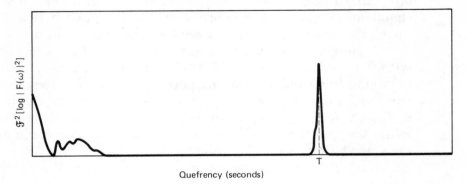

Figure 6.9 Cepstrum of the signal with spectrum that of Figure 6.8 (after Noll [5]).

- Find the cepstrum of the speech signal.
- Search for the largest peak beyond a certain time.
- If that peak is smaller than a preset threshold, declare the speech segment unvoiced and proceed to the next speech frame.
- If the peak is greater than the threshold, declare the speech segment voiced and select as pitch period the time T where this peak occurs (within some constraints, to be described).

A detailed description of the pitch tracking algorithm using the speech cepstrum is given in reference [5]. Here we present some of the highlights and the issues in that algorithm.

Each speech segment whose pitch period you seek to determine is first windowed by a Hamming window. The window can be about 30 ms long, and successive speech segments are placed 10–20 ms apart. Then, an FFT computes the discrete Fourier transform of the speech frame, and after taking the logarithm of the absolute value, an inverse FFT gives the speech cepstrum.

The cepstrum is weighted linearly between 1 and 15 ms with weight 1 at 1 ms and weight 5 at 15 ms. In this way the decreasing amplitude of the cepstrum is compensated for over time. Then, search for the maximum peak between 1 and 15 ms, and compare that peak with a threshold. This threshold is computed experimentally and is used to determine if the speech segment is voiced or unvoiced. The threshold can be estimated by manually establishing the voiced and unvoiced segments of a sufficiently large data base, and then computing statistics on the highest peak of the corresponding cepstra.

Since the cepstral peaks tend to decrease in amplitude at the end of the voiced-speech segments, you need to compensate for the possibility that the maximum peak may erroneously fall below the threshold. The compensation is done by reducing the threshold by a factor of 2 in the range of ± 1 ms of the immediately preceding pitch period estimate. Hence, you need to have the previous pitch estimate stored. This compensation is applied only if you have a string of voiced frames.

For each frame i, besides the pitch estimate of the previous frame $i - 1$, you need a preliminary estimate of the pitch for the following frame $i + 1$. In this way, if you detect that frame i is voiced while frames $i - 1$ and $i + 1$ are unvoiced, you can disregard that result and declare the frame i also unvoiced. Another reason you need the pitch estimate of frame $i + 1$ is pitch doubling, i.e., estimating a pitch period twice the actual value.

Pitch doubling is avoided as follows:

- After having detected a cepstral peak above the threshold, determine if this value is located at time ≥ 1.6 times the pitch period estimate of the previous frame.
- If yes, there is a possibility of pitch doubling. Find the maximum peak in a range ± 0.5 ms around one-half the time of the present peak.
- If this half-time peak falls in the range ± 1 ms of the previous frame's pitch, reduce the threshold in half.
- If the half-time peak exceeds the (possibly modified) threshold, then its time occurrence is chosen as the pitch period.

Figure 6.10 shows an example of successive cepstra and the corresponding log-spectra for a female speaker. Notice how the pitch period doubles before the speech becomes unvoiced. This pitch doubling, however, is the correct solution to the pitch tracking question in this example.

The amplitude of the peak at the pitch period in the cepstrum is an important factor in the accurate determination of pitch. This amplitude is sensitive to the type of window chosen and to its

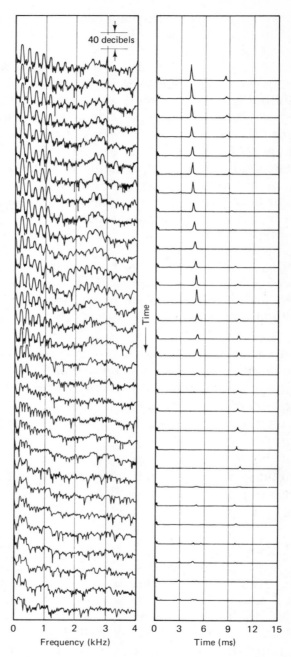

Figure 6.10   Series of log spectra and cepstra for a female speaker (after Noll [5]).

placement. Hamming windows that are 30–40 ms long are sufficient for male speakers, and they can be shortened for female
speakers. One possibility is to let the estimated pitch guide the
window length selection.

Since the pitch determination can be very unreliable, compensation algorithms must be incorporated to obtain satisfactory results. For example, you can improve the performance of the pitch
tracker by forcing the pitch to vary smoothly. You can also improve
the performance by using additional information, such as zero
crossing and energy.

6.3   AUTOCORRELATION PITCH TRACKER

A very popular method of pitch tracking is to use the autocorrelation function. Let $s(n)$ be a segment of the speech signal starting at
$n = 0$ and having a length of N samples. We also assume that $s(n)$
has been windowed. Then the autocorrelation function is defined
by the equation

$$R(k) = \sum_{n=0}^{N-1} s(n)\, s(n+k) \qquad k = 0,1,2,\dots \qquad \textbf{(6.9)}$$

Figure 6.11 shows examples of the autocorrelation function for
voiced and unvoiced speech. Variable k is the time index, which in
this case is called a lag. Notice that the voiced speech, which demonstrates periodicity, has sharper peaks at the lags corresponding
to the pitch period, while unvoiced speech does not demonstrate
such peaks. Those observations suggest that the autocorrelation
function can be used both for the voiced/unvoiced decision, and, if
voiced, for the computation of the pitch period.

Observe from Figure 6.11a that the autocorrelation function
contains the information you need, but it also contains information
associated with the vocal tract. This additional information can
lead to confusion and erroneous decisions. To improve the representation of the pitch information only, process the speech signal
by center clipping. Center clipping suppresses the signal between
certain levels, and what is not suppressed starts from the zero level.
Figure 6.12 shows the characteristic of the center clipper, which
can be written in equation form as follows:

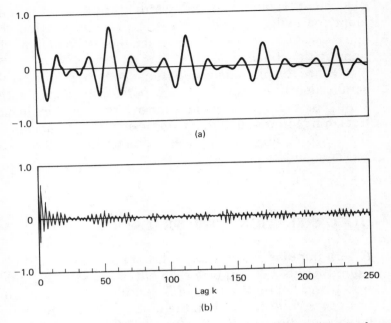

Figure 6.11 Examples of autocorrelation functions; (a) voiced speech; (b) unvoiced speech. (L. R. Rabiner, R. W. Schafer [3], DIGITAL PROCESSING OF SPEECH SIGNALS, © 1978. Reprinted by permission of Prentice-Hall, Inc., Englewood Cliffs, NJ.)

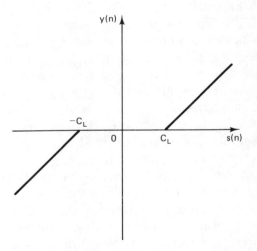

Figure 6.12 Characteristic of a center clipper.

$$y(n) = s(n) - C_L \qquad \text{if } s(n) \geq C_L$$
$$y(n) = s(n) + C_L \qquad \text{if } s(n) \leq -C_L \qquad \textbf{(6.10)}$$
$$y(n) = 0 \qquad\qquad \text{otherwise}$$

Figure 6.13 is an example of a waveform before and after center clipping. The effect of center clipping is to destroy the formant information and retain only the information on periodicity. The threshold level C_L is computed for every speech segment as a percentage of the maximum signal value, A_{max}. A typical value can be

$$C_L = 0.3\, A_{max} \qquad\qquad \textbf{(6.11)}$$

Note that the higher the clipping level the clearer the indication of periodicity. So, why not use a higher level than (6.11)? The danger arises when the amplitude of the signal varies considerably during the speech segment, and a high threshold would cause much of the signal to be lost. To avoid this problem and use higher percentages of the peak signal for center clipping, do the following:

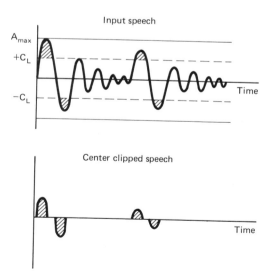

Figure 6.13   Example of application of center clipping to a speech waveform (after Sondhi [6], © 1968 IEEE).

- Find the maximum amplitude A_1 in the first third of the speech segment, and the maximum amplitude A_2 in the last third.
- Set the threshold at the following level:

$$C_L = K \min [A_1, A_2], \qquad K = 0.6\text{--}0.8 \qquad \textbf{(6.12)}$$

In the past, one of the main concerns in the autocorrelation method was the computation burden because of the required number of multiplications. Now, with the availability of DSP chips with fast hardware multipliers, this is not much of a problem. However, if there is still concern, the multiplication load can be reduced by using a 3-level clipping, which is a special form of center clipping. The 3-level clipping is described by the equation

$$
\begin{aligned}
y(n) &= 1 & \text{if } s(n) \geq C_L \\
y(n) &= -1 & \text{if } s(n) \leq -C_L \\
y(n) &= 0 & \text{otherwise}
\end{aligned}
\qquad \textbf{(6.13)}
$$

In this way, the products to be summed for the autocorrelation are 1, -1, or 0.

Description of a hardware implementation of an autocorrelation pitch tracker can be found in reference [7]. Besides the conditions mentioned above, some additional considerations for the implementation of such a pitch tracker are the following:

- The speech signal is lowpass-filtered with a cutoff at 900 Hz to eliminate extraneous harmonics and high frequency noise.
- Typical window lengths are 30 ms, and successive windows are placed 10 ms apart (20 ms overlap).
- The largest peak of the autocorrelation function is located and compared to a threshold equal to 0.3 R(0). If it falls below the threshold, the segment is declared unvoiced. Otherwise, it is declared voiced with pitch period equal to the lag of the largest peak.
- The voicing decision is influenced by the voicing of the previous frame and a preliminary voicing decision of the following frame: A voiced frame between two unvoiced frames is declared unvoiced and, conversely, an unvoiced frame between two voiced frames is declared voiced. There are also other post-processing techniques, which will be discussed in a later section.

A variation of the autocorrelation method is the *cross-corre-lation method*. In the cross-correlation method, we consider the correlation between a speech segment of length N and a subsection N' of that segment. The cross correlation function is computed from the relation:

$$R(k) = \frac{1}{N'} \sum_{n=0}^{N'-1} s'(n)\, s(n+k) \qquad k = 0,1,2,\ldots \qquad \textbf{(6.14)}$$

For instance, we can select N = 36 ms and N' = 20 ms, although values as low as N = 23 ms and N' = 8 ms can be used. The advantage of the cross-correlation method is that the correlation peaks tend to remain constant as a function of delay, and this can improve the detection of the pitch period location.

6.4 AMDF PITCH TRACKER

The autocorrelation pitch tracker is quite attractive but it requires a heavy computational load of multiplications and additions. With the advent of fast digital signal processors in recent years, such as the Texas Instruments TMS320, this problem has been greatly alleviated. These DSPs can do a single-cycle multiplication, which makes the autocorrelation computation no more burdensome than any other approach. However, the multiplications were of much concern earlier, and if it is still desirable to avoid them (for instance, in order to control the dynamic range of the result), the Average Magnitude Difference Function (AMDF) can be used.

The AMDF was developed as the "poor man's autocorrelation function." For a windowed signal $s(n)$, which is nonzero between $n = 0$ and $N - 1$, the AMDF is defined by

$$D(k) = \sum_{n=0}^{N-1} |\, s(n) - s(n+k)\, | \qquad k = 0,1,2,\ldots \qquad \textbf{(6.15)}$$

From this definition we observe that at the pitch period, when $s(n)$ and $s(n + k)$ have approximately the same amplitudes, $D(k)$ will demonstrate a valley where the autocorrelation function would have a peak. Other than this reversal in interpretation, the use of the AMDF is analogous to the autocorrelation.

Figure 6.14 shows examples of the AMDF for voiced and unvoiced speech, corresponding to the same material as in Figure 6.11. A detailed algorithm for the implementation of the AMDF algorithm is given in [8]. This method of pitch tracking is the one chosen for the NSA-developed Government Standard LPC-10 algorithm.

The algorithm for determining the pitch period from the AMDF is analogous to the one described earlier in the autocorrelation method and is not repeated here. It should be emphasized again, though, that with the currently available DSPs there is no need to avoid the multiplications. Actually, in some more recent generations of the DSP devices, it may be more economical to do the multiply-add function repeatedly than to take the absolute value of differences.

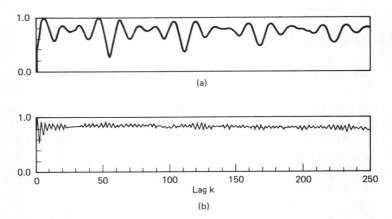

Figure 6.14   Examples of the AMDF for the same speech segments as in Figure 6.11. (L. R. Rabiner, R. W. Schafer [3], DIGITAL PROCESSING OF SPEECH SIGNALS, © 1978. Reprinted by permission of Prentice-Hall, Inc., Englewood Cliffs, NJ.)

6.5 THE SIFT ALGORITHM FOR PITCH EXTRACTION

In Chapter 5, when discussing the linear predictive method (LPC) of speech analysis, it was pointed out that the residual error signal contains much information about the excitation of the speech signal, including pitch information. The residual error is obtained from the speech signal by inverse filtering, as shown in Figure 6.15. The inverse filter $A(z)$ is given by the equation

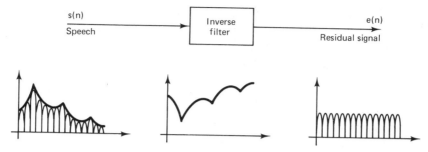

Figure 6.15 When the input speech passes through the inverse filter, the output residual signal has a flat spectrum.

$$A(z) = 1 + a_1 z^{-1} + \ldots + a_p z^{-p} \qquad (6.17)$$

or in the time domain,

$$e(n) = s(n) + a_1 s(n-1) + \ldots + a_p s(n-p) \qquad (6.18)$$

The coefficients a_i are computed using the methods of LPC analysis described in Chapter 5. Figure 6.16 gives an example of speech waveforms and the corresponding LPC residual error signal. In this example, the pitch information is evident and $e(n)$ could be used for pitch estimation in an autocorrelation method approach. Use of the residual signal $e(n)$ is preferred to the original speech signal $s(n)$ because the vocal tract information has been removed by the inverse filtering. The Simplified Inverse Filter Tracking (SIFT) algorithm was developed by Markel [10] to implement this approach.

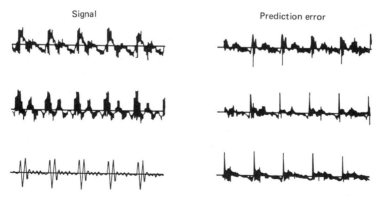

Figure 6.16 Examples of LPC residual signal (prediction error) for the vowels "i," "e," and "a" (after Strube [9]).

Figure 6.17 describes the SIFT algorithm in block diagram form. The input signal is first lowpass-filtered with a cutoff frequency of 800 Hz, and then downsampled at 2 kHz. For instance, if the original speech was sampled at 10 kHz, you obtain the downsampled signal by retaining one out of every five consecutive samples. By working on the downsampled signal, you reduce the amount of computation significantly. Markel [10] gives the detailed specifications of a 3-pole Chebyshev filter to be used for the lowpass filter.

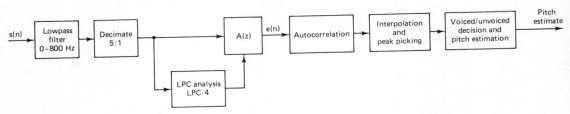

Figure 6.17   Block diagram of the SIFT algorithm.

Since the inverse filter is to be applied to the lowpass-filtered and downsampled signal, it is sufficient to use a 4th-order LPC model ($p = 4$ in equation (6.18)). The reason that LPC-4 is satisfactory is that we have 2 formants at most in the frequency region 0–1 kHz. The LPC analysis is applied to segments of 64 points, which correspond to 32 ms of speech. In such an interval, we expect to have approximately three pitch periods for a typical male voice.

Next, we compute the autocorrelation $r(n)$ of the residual error signal $e(n)$. Use of the autocorrelation is recommended over using just the $e(n)$ for the pitch determination. If P is the pitch period of the previous frame, we look for the largest peak of the autocorrelation function in a region ± 7 lags around P. This peak determines the current pitch estimate. In the case of an unvoiced frame, the previous frame's pitch estimate is reset to some initial value.

When looking for the peak of the autocorrelation function, the successive autocorrelation lags are 0.5 ms apart, corresponding to the sampling rate of 2 kHz. This means, for instance, that for an actual pitch period of 6 ms, the maximum pitch estimation error can be 7.0 Hz, which is quite large. To improve the accuracy of the pitch period estimation, we interpolate the autocorrelation function, so that the peak of the autocorrelation is determined more precisely. Reference [10] gives a detailed description of an efficient way to do the interpolation.

To decide if the frame is voiced or unvoiced, the largest peak of the autocorrelation function is compared to a threshold. This threshold is set to be 0.378 $r(0)$–0.400 $r(0)$. If the detected peak is greater than the threshold, the speech segment is declared voiced and the pitch period is equal to the time lag of the peak. Otherwise, the speech segment is unvoiced. In order to avoid errors caused by small values of the autocorrelation peaks, if an unvoiced frame is found between two voiced frames, it is redefined to be voiced. Its pitch period is equal to the mean of the pitch periods of the two surrounding frames.

The SIFT algorithm is typically applied to speech segments at 16 ms intervals using a 32 ms sliding window. The peak of the residual signal's autocorrelation function is expected to be found in the range 2–16 ms, and this is the range searched.

6.6 POST-PROCESSING TECHNIQUES FOR PITCH DETECTION

The pitch detection methods described in this chapter give reasonable results most of the time. Unfortunately, none of them gives reliable results all the time. Depending on the speaker, the noise level in the environment, the section in the speech material, and so on, we end up with wrong voicing decisions and wrong pitch estimates. Such failures of the pitch tracker make the synthetic speech very objectionable no matter how well the vocal tract information is preserved and represented. That's why considerable effort has been applied to devising new pitch tracking algorithms and improving the reliability of the acquired estimates. In this section, we deal with the last question, i.e., how we can process the raw estimates of pitch to eliminate possible errors.

An assumption used previously is that it is not possible to have a single voiced frame between two unvoiced frames, or an unvoiced frame between two voiced frames. In this case, the middle frame is converted to the type of the two end frames. If the result is voiced, the middle frame is typically assigned a pitch period that is the average of the pitch periods of the two end frames.

Another post-processing technique very widely used is median smoothing. For smoothing out the raw pitch estimates, it is not advisable to use a linear smoother (i.e., a linear filter) because it would fail to correct the errors, and at the same time, would introduce distortion. For pitch track smoothing we need a nonlinear smoother, such as a median filter.

A median filter of length N works as follows:

- Consider the samples $s(n)$, $s(n-1)$, . . . , $s(n-N+1)$ of the pitch track.
- Find the median of these samples, i.e., find the value s^* which is greater than or equal to half of the samples and less than or equal to the other half. This is accomplished simply by ordering the values by amplitude and selecting the one that is in the middle.
- Set the nth sample in the filtered sequence equal to s^*.

In this way, gross voiced/unvoiced errors are corrected and pitch estimation errors are smoothed out. Typical lengths of median filters are 3 and 5. Figure 6.18 shows an example of pitch contour smoothing using a median filter. For the example in this figure, besides the median smoothing, linear smoothing has also been applied. The linear FIR filter used has length 3 and is defined by its impulse response, $h(n)$:

$$h(0) = \frac{1}{4}, \qquad h(1) = \frac{1}{2}, \qquad h(2) = \frac{1}{4} \qquad \textbf{(6.19)}$$

Figure 6.19 shows a possible way of connecting a median smoother and a linear filter for best results. The delays are necessary to account for the delays introduced by the two filters. The median filter of length N has a delay $(N-1)/2$, and the linear filter has a delay corresponding to the length of the impulse response.

One remaining question is what assumptions to make at the beginning and the end of the sentence when applying the median filter. The suggested solution is to extrapolate the pitch track backward and forward, respectively, by assuming that the signal remains constant.

Dynamic programming can be also applied to improve the pitch estimate. Several pitch candidates are retained for each speech frame, and the best paths from the previous frame are selected to

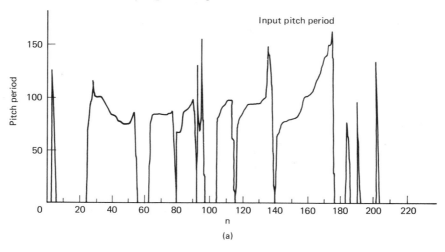

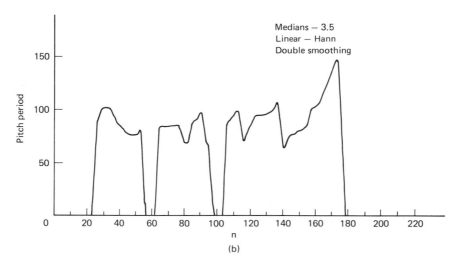

Figure 6.18 Example of nonlinear smoothing of a pitch contour (after Rabiner et al. [11], © 1975 IEEE).

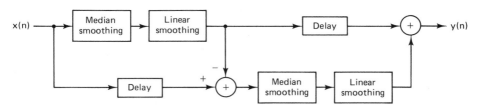

Figure 6.19 Nonlinear smoothing system with delay compensation (after Rabiner et al. [11], © 1975 IEEE).

minimize a chosen distortion criterion. In this way the robustness of the pitch estimates increases significantly in the difficult cases, but the computational load also increases. Secrest and Doddington [12] outline such a post-processing technique using dynamic programming.

Rabiner et al. [13] have investigated several of the pitch tracking algorithms and present a comparison of the strengths and weaknesses of these algorithms.

6.7 SUMMARY

The subject of pitch tracking has occupied many researchers who have produced many algorithms to solve the problem. Unfortunately, no single algorithm has been shown to perform satisfactorily in all cases. In this chapter, five of the better-known and applied methods were presented.

The first method was developed by Gold and Rabiner, and uses time-domain information. A set of six waveforms is generated from measurements on the peaks and valleys of the incoming speech signal. Each of these waveforms generates a pitch candidate, and the final choice is made essentially by a majority vote.

The homomorphic pitch tracker relies on the cepstrum to separate the vocal tract shape from the faster varying fine structure that corresponds to the excitation. The pitch information is extracted by sifting the high-time components of the cepstrum.

The autocorrelation and the AMDF (average magnitude difference function) methods are related in the sense that they both determine the pitch period by comparing the speech signal with itself. In the autocorrelation technique, this is done by estimating the autocorrelation of the signal and determining the lag that gives the first peak. In the AMDF technique, instead of computing the autocorrelation (which is the sum of the products of the values), we compute the AMDF (which is the sum of the absolute values of the differences). The AMDF was developed to avoid the computational load of autocorrelations, which involve a lot of multiplications. However, with the availability of digital signal processors equipped with hardware multipliers, this is no longer a consideration.

Finally, the SIFT algorithm is similar to the autocorrelation method but, instead of starting with the speech signal, it starts with the LPC residual. The LPC residual is the output of the LPC inverse filter when the input is the original speech.

To improve the raw pitch-estimates, post-processing techniques, such as median smoothing and dynamic programming, are applied. In this way, gross errors are avoided and the level of confidence in the final pitch estimate is increased.

6.8 FURTHER READING

The subject of pitch tracking has attracted many efforts over the years but it still remains elusive. The book by Hess [1] is the most exhaustive listing of the different pitch tracking algorithms (over 90 pages of references!). In terms of the better-known and applied algorithms, though, the collection of papers by Schafer and Markel [14] is a very useful source. In that book one can find the references [2,5,6,8,10,13] covering the kinds of pitch tracking we talked about in this chapter.

6.9 REFERENCES

1. Hess, W. *Pitch Determination of Speech Signals*. New York: Springer-Verlag, 1983.
2. Gold, B., and L. Rabiner. "Parallel Processing Techniques for Estimating Pitch Periods of Speech in the Time Domain." *J. Acous. Soc. Am.*, Vol. 46 (August 1969): 442–448.
3. Rabiner, L. R., and R. W. Schafer. *Digital Processing of Speech Signals*. Englewood Cliffs, NJ: Prentice-Hall, 1978.
4. Gold, B. "Note on Buzz-Hiss Detection." *J. Acous. Soc. Am.*, Vol. 36 (September 1964): 1659–1661.
5. Noll, A. M. "Cepstrum Pitch Determination." *J. Acous. Soc. Am.*, Vol. 41 (February 1967): 293–309.
6. Sondhi, M. M. "New Methods of Pitch Extraction." *IEEE Trans. Audio Electroacous.*, Vol. AU-16 (June 1968): 262–266.
7. Dubnowski, J. J., R. W. Schafer, and L. R. Rabiner. "Real-Time Digital Hardware Pitch Detector." *IEEE Trans. Acous., Speech, and Signal Proc.*, Vol. ASSP-24, No. 1 (February 1976): 2–8.
8. Ross, M. J., H. L. Shaffer, A. Cohen, R. Freudberg, and H. J. Manley. "Average Magnitude Difference Function Pitch Extractor." *IEEE Trans. Acous., Speech, and Signal Proc.*, Vol. ASSP-22 (October 1974): 353–362.

9. Strube, H. "Determination of the Instant of Glottal Closure from the Speech Wave." *J. Acous. Soc. Am.*, Vol. 56, No. 5 (November 1974): 1625–1629.

10. Markel, J. D. "The SIFT Algorithm for Fundamental Frequency Estimation." *IEEE Trans. Audio Elecroacous.*, Vol. AU-20 (December 1972): 367–377.

11. Rabiner, L. R., M. R. Sambur, and C. E. Schmidt. "Applications of a Nonlinear Smoothing Algorithm to Speech Processing." *IEEE Trans. Acous., Speech, and Signal Proc.*, Vol. ASSP-23, No. 6 (December 1975): 552–557.

12. Secrest, B. G., and G. R. Doddington. "An Integrated Pitch Tracking Algorithm for Speech Systems." *Proc. of 1983 IEEE Int. Conf. on Acous., Speech, and Signal Proc.* (April 1983): 1352–1355.

13. Rabiner, L. R., M. J. Cheng, A. E. Rosenberg, and C. A. McGonegal. "A Comparative Performance Study of Several Pitch Detection Algorithms." *IEEE Trans. Acous., Speech, and Signal Proc.*, Vol. ASSP-24 (October 1976): 399–417.

14. Schafer, R. W., and J. D. Markel. *Speech Analysis*. New York: IEEE Press, 1979.

Chapter 7

Measurement of Performance: How Good Is a Speech Coder?

One of the most difficult subjects in speech coding is the assessment of the relative performance of the different systems. The major problem is that it has not been possible to quantify in a mathematical expression what is meant by the words "speech quality." This is because it is not completely understood how the human ear and the brain process the speech signal. Furthermore, there is no unambiguous definition of what consists of "good speech quality." For instance, with two systems having similar performance but introducing different types of distortion, one listener may prefer system A, while another listener may prefer system B. Also, the adaptability of the human ear/brain has a "training" effect. This effect can make acceptable, after repeated hearing, speech that was originally thought to be unacceptable. Despite these limitations, you still need to have an assessment of the speech quality.

It is generally agreed that listening to coded speech can give a much better evaluation of the quality than any objective measurement using mathematical expressions. However, to do the subjective testing correctly requires appropriate facilities and, usually, trained crews of listeners. This makes the subjective testing quite expensive and suggests that objective measures could be used to aid the comparison.

The suggested approach to speech evaluation consists of three phases, as shown in Figure 7.1. While the system is being developed, an appropriate objective measure will roughly determine how well the system performs, especially if it is compared with a system of known performance. Also, informal subjective listening can give valuable information. The stages (1) and (2) in Figure 7.1 are not separate, but are usually interweaved. After it has been decided

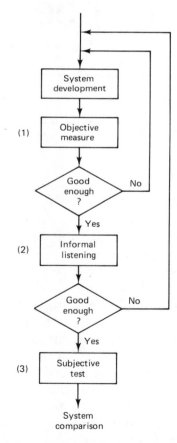

Figure 7.1 Stages in the development of a speech coding system using objective and subjective quality measurements.

that a good system has been developed, it is necessary to formalize the quality assessment by a subjective test, preferably in a fashion permitting comparison with other known systems.

Since both objective and subjective measures and tests of the speech quality are needed, we will describe both kinds in this chapter, indicating the advantages and the limitations of each method.

7.1 OBJECTIVE MEASURES OF SPEECH QUALITY

The term "objective measures" refers to mathematical expressions that are used to determine the speech quality. In speech coding, we distinguish two classes of coders. The first one, called waveform coders, tries to preserve the shape of the speech time waveform, while the second one, usually called vocoders, is not concerned with the exact shape of the time waveform as long as the resulting waveform sounds like the original. In accordance with this distinction we use two types of objective measures. The SNR-related (SNR = Signal to Noise Ratio) measures are better suited for waveform coders, while spectral distance measures better describe the vocoders. Let us start with the SNR-related measures.

7.1.1 SIGNAL-TO-NOISE-RATIO (SNR)

The most widely used objective measure in waveform coders is the Signal-to-Noise Ratio (SNR), which is defined as follows. Let $s(n)$ be the original speech signal at time n, and $\hat{s}(n)$ the corresponding processed signal. The error signal is then given by

$$e(n) = s(n) - \hat{s}(n) \qquad (7.1)$$

To find the SNR for a record of N samples, we compute the energy (AC energy) of the original signal

$$E_s^2 = \frac{1}{N} \sum_{n=1}^{N} s^2(n) - \left(\frac{1}{N} \sum_{n=1}^{N} s(n) \right)^2 \qquad (7.2)$$

and the error energy

$$E_e^2 = \frac{1}{N} \sum_{n=1}^{N} e^2(n) - \left(\frac{1}{N} \sum_{n=1}^{N} e(n) \right)^2 \qquad (7.3)$$

The SNR is defined by

$$SNR = \frac{E_s^2}{E_e^2} \tag{7.4}$$

If the signal $s(n)$ and the error $e(n)$ have a zero mean, then the second terms of (7.2) and (7.3) are zero and can be omitted. Very often the SNR is expressed in dB as follows:

$$SNR(dB) = 10 \log_{10}(SNR) \tag{7.5}$$

The SNR is selected as a distance measure primarily for its mathematical simplicity. It is not necessarily correlated with any subjective attribute of the speech quality, and that's why when we need better performance measures, we try to incorporate more information into the SNR.

One of the characteristics of the speech signal is its time-varying nature, which results in some speech segments with high energy and other segments with low energy. If the error energy E_e^2 is more or less constant, the resulting SNR is deceptively high, because the perceptual effects of the noise in the regions of lower E_s^2 are more severe. To take this effect into consideration, the *segmental SNR* is used, denoted as SNRSEG.

To compute the SNRSEG, we divide the speech signal of interest into segments 15–20 ms long (typically 16 ms), and we compute the SNR(m)(dB), $m = 1, \ldots, M$, for each one of them. The index m now indicates segment number. The segmental SNR is defined by

$$SNRSEG = \frac{1}{M} \sum_{m=1}^{M} SNR(m)(dB) \tag{7.6}$$

and is also expressed in dB. In this way the SNRs of the different segments are averaged together, and the strong portions of the signal do not overwhelm the SNR.

When the SNR(m)(dB) gets to very high or to very low values, its perceptual contribution is not proportional to its numerical contribution and we should take steps to limit such effects. For instance, values of SNR(dB) above approximately 35 dB do not represent greatly perceptible differences, and in equation (7.6) all values of SNR(dB) greater than 35 dB can be replaced with 35 dB. On the other hand, during silence periods, the SNR(dB) can attain very low negative values that are not representative of the perceptual contributions of this type of signal. This can be rectified in either of two ways: You can detect silence segments and eliminate them from the computation of the SNRSEG, or, more simply, you can set a low threshold T (for instance, 0 dB $\geq T \geq -20$ dB), and if the SNR (dB) falls below T, you replace it with T.

7.1.2 ARTICULATION INDEX

The properties of the speech signal can be used by incorporating frequency information into the computation of SNR. This is done in the determination of the *articulation index (AI)*. The articulation index, originally used with analog signals, is a method of assessing the speech quality. To compute the AI, the signal is bandpass filtered into 20 bands, shown in Table 7.1. For each band m, we compute the signal-to-noise ratio $SNR(m)(dB)$, and from that the articulation index

$$AI = \frac{1}{20} \sum_{m=1}^{20} \frac{min\ (SNR(m)(dB),30)}{30} \qquad (7.7)$$

As can be seen from this equation, the SNR is limited to a maximum allowable 30 dB. The articulation index is analogous to

TABLE 7.1 FREQUENCY BANDS (IN Hz) OF EQUAL CONTRIBUTION TO THE ARTICULATION INDEX.

Number	Limits	Mean	Number	Limits	Mean
1	200 to 330	270	11	1660 to 1830	1740
2	330 to 430	380	12	1830 to 2020	1920
3	430 to 560	490	13	2020 to 2240	2130
4	560 to 700	630	14	2240 to 2500	2370
5	700 to 840	770	15	2500 to 2820	2660
6	840 to 1000	920	16	2820 to 3200	3000
7	1000 to 1150	1070	17	3200 to 3650	3400
8	1150 to 1310	1230	18	3650 to 4250	3950
9	1310 to 1480	1400	19	4250 to 5050	4650
10	1480 to 1660	1570	20	5050 to 6100	5600

(N. S. Jayant, Peter Noll [1] *Digital Coding of Waveforms: Principles and Applications to Speech and Video,* © 1984. Reprinted by permission of Prentice-Hall, Inc., Englewood Cliffs, NJ.)

SNRSEG, except that the segmentation takes place in the frequency domain instead of the time domain. Note also from Table 7.1 that the bandwidth of the bandpass filters increases with frequency. A drawback of the AI is the increased computational requirements because, in addition to the computation of SNR, the signal has to be bandpass filtered.

7.1.3 LOG SPECTRAL DISTANCE

When encoding the speech signal, in the case of vocoders, only the magnitude of the spectrum is usually preserved according to the hypothesis that the human ear is not very sensitive to the (short-term) phase. As a result, the synthetic waveform can be quite different from the original speech, and still sound the same. It is then obvious that the signal-to-noise ratio is no longer a meaningful measure of reproduction fidelity. Instead, we have to use distance metrics that are sensitive to spectral differences. One such metric is the log-spectral distance.

In the log-spectral distance, as well as Itakura's likelihood ratio and the Euclidean distances presented next, the distance metric is not between the original and the synthetic speech. Rather, it is between two synthetic signals represented parametrically. One of the signals is assumed to be closest to the original speech and the other is the one under test. The reason for this approach is that these distance metrics use the parameters of speech models and, once the speech is parametrized, we no longer have the original signal exactly.

Since the distance measures for vocoders are most often used in the context of the LPC method, we concentrate our attention on that method. In LPC, the spectral envelope representing the vocal tract is given by the expression

$$H(e^{j\omega}) = \frac{G}{A(e^{j\omega})} \tag{7.8}$$

where the inverse filter A(z) is given by

$$A(z) = 1 + a_1 z^{-1} + \ldots + a_p z^{-p} \tag{7.9}$$

Usually, $p = 10$. The log-spectral distance between two LPC models $H_1(e^{j\omega})$ and $H_2(e^{j\omega})$ is defined by

$$d = \left[\int_{-\pi}^{\pi} \mid \ln \mid H_1(e^{j\omega}) \mid^2 - \ln \mid H_2(e^{j\omega}) \mid^2 \mid^2 \frac{d\theta}{2\pi} \right]^{1/2} \qquad (7.10)$$

or, using (7.8),

$$d = \left[\int \mid \ln \frac{G_1}{G_2} + \ln \mid A_2(e^{j\omega}) \mid^2 - \ln \mid A_1(e^{j\omega}) \mid^2 \mid^2 \frac{d\theta}{2\pi} \right]^{1/2} \qquad (7.11)$$

In equation (7.11), the gains G_i and the coefficients a_i of the inverse filter are known from the LPC modeling. Then, (7.11) can be computed by taking an FFT of $A_1(e^{j\omega})$ and $A_2(e^{j\omega})$ with enough points to have an accurate conversion of the integral in equation (7.11) into a summation. However, there is a better way of computing the log-spectral distance through the cepstral coefficients.

The cepstral coefficients, c_i, are computed from the filter coefficients, a_i, by the equations

$$c_1 = -a_1 \qquad (7.12)$$

$$c_i = -a_i - \sum_{k=1}^{i-1} \frac{i-k}{i} c_{i-k} a_k \qquad for \ i = 2, \ldots, p \qquad (7.13a)$$

$$c_i = - \sum_{k=1}^{p} \frac{i-k}{i} c_{i-k} a_k \qquad for \ i = p+1, \ldots \qquad (7.13b)$$

Additionally, c_0 is equal to the energy of the signal, which is given by the zero-lag autocorrelation. The log-spectral distance can be computed from

$$d_{LS} = \left[(c_0 - c_0{}')^2 + 2 \sum_{k=1}^{\infty} (c_k - c_k{}')^2 \right]^{1/2} \qquad (7.14)$$

where c_i and $c_i{}'$ are the cepstral coefficients of H_1 and H_2, respectively. Since the computation of the infinite summation is not practicable, it is usually truncated to an appropriate length depending on the desired level of accuracy. It has been found that retaining only the first 30 terms gives satisfactory results. The log-spectral distance is usually expressed in dB by multiplying d_{LS} by $10/ln(10) \cong 4.34$.

The log-spectral distance is a reasonable measure to use for the determination of quality if we assume that one of the spectra H_1 and H_2 is the true representation of the speech signal, while the other is an approximation whose goodness we are testing. For instance, H_1 can be the model computed with the full precision of a large computer, while H_2 is the processed version after quantization, which is used to reduce the bit rate. This kind of distance metric also finds wide application in speech recognition systems.

7.1.4 ITAKURA'S LIKELIHOOD RATIO

An even more popular distance metric is Itakura's likelihood and log-likelihood ratios. These ratios are defined as follows. Let

$$\mathbf{a}_1 = [\ 1\ a_{11}\ \dots\ a_{1p}\ ]^T \tag{7.15}$$

$$
R = \begin{Bmatrix}
r_1(0) & r_1(1) & \dots & r_1(p-1) \\
r_1(1) & r_1(0) & \dots & r_1(p-2) \\
\cdot & \cdot & & \cdot \\
\cdot & \cdot & & \cdot \\
\cdot & \cdot & & \cdot \\
r_1(p-1) & r_1(p-2) & \dots & r_1(0)
\end{Bmatrix} \tag{7.16}
$$

be the coefficient vector and the autocorrelation matrix for the LPC vocal tract model H_1. Also, let $\mathbf{a}_2$, R_2 be the corresponding quantities for H_2. Then, define the likelihood ratio either as

$$d_{LR1} = \frac{\mathbf{a}_2{}^T R_1 \mathbf{a}_2}{\mathbf{a}_1{}^T R_1 \mathbf{a}_1} \tag{7.17}$$

or as

$$d_{LR2} = \frac{\mathbf{a}_1{}^T R_2 \mathbf{a}_1}{\mathbf{a}_2{}^T R_2 \mathbf{a}_2} \tag{7.18}$$

The log-likelihood ratios are the logarithms of these expressions:

$$d_{LLR} = 10 \log_{10}(d_{LR}) \tag{7.19}$$

and they are expressed in dB. The metrics of (7.17) and (7.18) are nonsymmetric, while we often want a symmetric measure. In this case we can use the quantity

$$d_{LRS} = \frac{(d_{LR1} + d_{LR2})}{2} - 1 \qquad \textbf{(7.20)}$$

which has the desired property of symmetry.

The expression $\mathbf{a}_i{}^T R_i \mathbf{a}_i$ is the energy of the residual signal after LPC modeling. The filter coefficients a_j are computed from the autocorrelation coefficients $r(j)$ in such a way as to minimize this energy. Hence, if we replace $\mathbf{a}_i$ with any other nonzero vector of coefficients, this expression increases. This means that $d_{LR} \geq 1$ always. It has been found that

$$d_{LR} = 1.4$$

is a threshold above which the difference between H_1 and H_2 becomes increasingly perceptible.

Often, it is necessary to compute the expressions of the equations (7.17) and (7.18) repeatedly with different filters. Then, instead of performing the indicated matrix multiplications, it is computationally more convenient to use the autocorrelation sequence $r(i)$ of the speech signal, and the autocorrelation sequence $r_a(i)$ of the filter coefficients. The autocorrelation sequence $r_a(i)$ is defined by

$$r_a(i) = \sum_{k=i}^{p} a_k a_{k-i} \qquad i = 0, \ldots, p \qquad \textbf{(7.21)}$$

with

$$a_0 = 1 \qquad \textbf{(7.22)}$$

Then, $\mathbf{a}^T R \mathbf{a}$ is computed from

$$\mathbf{a}^T R \mathbf{a} = r_a(0)\, r(0) + 2 \sum_{i=1}^{p} r_a(i)\, r(i) \qquad \textbf{(7.23)}$$

With the appropriate choice of $\mathbf{a}$ and R, the numerators and denominators of (7.17) and (7.18) can be computed very efficiently, and from them, the likelihood or log-likelihood distance measures.

7.1.5 EUCLIDEAN DISTANCE

Another possibility for a distance metric is to use a Euclidean distance of a set of LPC parameters. The set of LPC parameters used could be the reflection coefficients K_i, the autocorrelation coefficients $r(i)$, or any other equivalent set of parameters. In practice, it has been shown that the best choice are the log-area ratios, LAR_i, which are derived from the reflection coefficients according to the relations

$$LAR_i = ln \frac{1+K_i}{1-K_i} \qquad \textbf{(7.24)}$$

Then, if LAR_{1i} and LAR_{2i} are the sets of log-area ratios corresponding to H_1 and H_2, we define their Euclidean distance metric to be

$$d_{LAR} = \left[\sum_{i=1}^{p} (LAR_{1i} - LAR_{2i})^2 \right]^{1/2} \qquad \textbf{(7.25)}$$

The performance of d_{LAR} has been shown to be quite close to the performance of d_{LR}. However, the likelihood ratio remains the most popular distance metric.

7.2 SUBJECTIVE MEASURES

Objective distortion measures provide some indication about the speech quality of a system. However, if you want a real assessment of the quality, you need to conduct subjective tests. During the development stages of a system, informal listening is sufficient, but after the development has been completed, some type of formal listening test is necessary to establish the performance of that system. Following are descriptions of the most often used subjective tests for speech systems.

The subjective tests can be divided into two basic categories: the ones testing intelligibility and the ones testing quality. The two classes are not disjoint, of course, and good quality implies good intelligibility while the converse is not necessarily true. From the intelligibility tests, we will discuss the *Diagnostic Rhyme Test* (DRT) and the *Modified Rhyme Test* (MRT), while from the quality tests we will consider the *Diagnostic Acceptability Measure* (DAM), the paired comparisons, and the *Mean Opinion Score* (MOS).

7.2.1 INTELLIGIBILITY TESTS

The intelligibility tests are based on the ability of listeners to distinguish phonemes with common attributes. That is, the listener is presented with one word from a pair and is asked to determine what word was spoken. The alternate choice is a word differing from the presented word only in one phoneme, usually a consonant.

The most popular and widely used of the intelligibility tests is the Diagnostic Rhyme Test (DRT). Although the DRT can be designed for in-house use, most developers of speech systems employ the services of an independent company (i.e., Dynastat, in Austin, Texas), which also developed the method. The advantages are the objectivity of a third party, and the use of trained crews, which yields highly accurate and repeatable results.

The DRT works as follows: It uses a corpus of 192 words in 96 rhyming pairs, shown in Table 7.2. In a given instance, one word of

TABLE 7.2   WORD PAIRS USED IN THE DIAGNOSTIC RHYME TEST (DRT)

VEAL-FEEL	BEAN-PEEN	ZOO-SUE	DUNE-TUNE
MEAT-BEAT	NEED-DEED	MOOT-BOOT	NEWS-DUES
VEE-BEE	SHEET-CHEAT	FOO-POOH	SHOES-CHOOSE
ZEE-THEE	CHEEP-KEEP	JUICE-GOOSE	CHEW-CHOO
WEED-REED	PEAK-TEAK	MOON-NOON	POOL-TOOL
YIELD-WIELD	KEY-TEA	COOP-POOP	YOU-RUE
GIN-CHIN	DINT-TINT	VOLE-FOAL	GOAT-COAT
MITT-BIT	NIP-DIP	MOAN-BONE	NOTE-DOTE
VILL-BILL	THICK-TICK	THOSE-DOZE	THOUGH-DOUGH
JILT-GILT	SING-THING	JOE-GO	SOLE-THOLE
BID-DID	FIN-THIN	BOWL-DOLE	FORE-THOR
HIT-FIT	GILL-DILL	GHOST-BOAST	SHOW-SO
ZED-SAID	DENSE-TENSE	VAULT-FAULT	DAUNT-TAUNT
MEND-BEND	NECK-DECK	MOSS-BOSS	GNAW-DAW
THEN-DEN	FENCE-PENCE	THONG-TONG	SHAW-CHAW
JEST-GUEST	CHAIR-CARE	JAWS-GAUZE	SAW-THAW
MET-NET	PENT-TENT	FOUGHT-THOUGHT	BONG-DONG
KEG-PEG	YEN-WREN	YAWL-WALL	CAUGHT-TAUGHT
VAST-FAST	GAFF-CALF	JOCK-CHOCK	BOND-POND
MAD-BAD	NAB-DAB	MOM-BOMB	KNOCK-DOCK
THAN-DAN	SHAD-CHAD	VON-BON	VOX-BOX
JAB-GAB	SANK-THANK	JOT-GOT	CHOP-COP
BANK-DANK	FAD-THAD	WAD-ROD	POT-TOT
GAT-BAT	SHAG-SAG	HOP-FOP	GOT-DOT

(Courtesy of Dynastat, Inc.).

the pair is presented and the listener is asked to determine which word was spoken. The two words of each pair, for instance "zeal"-"seal," differ only in one attribute of the first consonant (in this example, voicing). So, a correct response from the listener indicates that the speech coding system under examination preserves that attribute. There are six elementary phonemic attributes that are tested: voicing, nasality, sustention, sibilation, graveness, and compactness. Table 7.3 gives a classification of the 23 tested consonants with respect to these attributes. The symbol "+" means the attribute is present, "−" means it is absent, and "0" means neutral. The importance of the breakdown in terms of these attributes lies in the accurate determination of the intelligibility, and also in the diagnostic capability provided. By knowing where the system fails, the designer can determine what features of the speech are not preserved well enough.

The final score of the DRT is given in percent correct responses P as follows:

$$P = \frac{R - W}{T} 100 \qquad (7.26)$$

where

R = number of right answers

W = number of wrong answers

T = total number of items involved

Typical values of DRT range between 75 and 95. A "good" system would have a DRT score of about 90. Figure 7.2 shows the format in which Dynastat presents the results. A more detailed breakdown can also be obtained.

One of the issues in the DRT is the number and the sex of the speakers. The number of speakers is important since the speech processing method may have different effects on different speakers because of vocal tract and pitch characteristics. The sex of a speaker is important because for many processing systems, female voices score consistently lower than male voices (for reasons unclear at the present). Of course, there is an economic consideration since the testing expense increases with the number of speakers. Experience has shown that three male and three female speakers are sufficient for reliable results.

TABLE 7.3 CLASSIFICATION OF THE CONSONANTS WITH RESPECT TO THE DRT ATTRIBUTES. NO SPECIFIC WORD-PAIRS TEST THE PRESENCE OR ABSENCE OF THE "VOWEL-LIKE" ATTRIBUTE

	/m/	/n/	/v/	/ð/	/z/	/ʒ/	/ʒ̂/	/b/	/d/	/g/	/w/	/r/	/l/	/j/	/f/	/θ/	/s/	/ʃ/	/ʃ̂/	/p/	/t/	/k/	/h/
Voicing	+	+	+	+	+	+	+	+	+	+	+	+	+	+	-	-	-	-	-	-	-	-	-
Nasality	+	+	-	-	-	-	-	-	-	-	-	-	-	-	-	-	-	-	-	-	-	-	-
Sustention	-	-	+	+	+	+	-	-	-	-	+	+	+	+	+	+	+	+	-	-	-	-	+
Sibilation	-	-	-	-	+	+	+	-	-	-	-	-	-	-	-	-	+	+	+	-	-	-	-
Graveness	+	-	+	-	-	0	0	+	-	0	+	-	0	0	+	-	-	0	0	+	-	0	0
Compactness	-	-	-	-	-	+	+	-	-	+	-	-	0	+	-	-	-	+	+	-	-	+	+
Vowel-like	-	-	-	-	-	-	-	-	-	-	+	+	+	+	-	-	-	-	-	-	-	-	-

(courtesy of Dynastat, Inc.).

Contractor:			Test Condition: EZA-QUIET-ALTEC				Date Tested: 11/11/74	
	Present	S.E.*	Absent	S.E.*	Bias	S.E.*	Total	S.E.*
VOICING	99.0	1.04	98.4	1.10	0.5	1.66	98.7	0.67
FRICTIONAL	97.9	2.08	96.9	2.19	1.0	3.32	97.4	1.35
NONFRICTIONAL	100.0	0.00	100.0	0.00	0.0	0.00	100.0	0.00
NASALITY	100.0	0.00	99.5	0.52	0.5	0.52	99.7	0.26
GRAVE	100.0	0.00	100.0	0.00	0.0	0.00	100.0	0.00
ACUTE	100.0	0.00	99.0	1.04	1.0	1.04	99.5	0.52
SUSTENTION	99.5	0.52	96.9	1.52	2.6	1.35	98.2	0.92
VOICED	100.0	0.00	96.9	2.19	3.1	2.19	98.4	1.10
UNVOICED	99.0	1.04	96.9	2.19	2.1	1.36	97.9	1.57
SIBILATION	99.0	0.68	100.0	0.00	-1.0	0.68	99.5	0.34
VOICED	99.0	1.04	100.0	0.00	-1.0	1.04	99.5	0.52
UNVOICED	99.0	1.04	100.0	0.00	-1.0	1.04	99.5	0.52
GRAVENESS	89.1	1.35	94.3	2.22	-5.2	3.22	91.7	0.88
VOICED	99.0	1.04	96.9	2.19	2.1	2.61	97.9	1.11
UNVOICED	79.2	2.23	91.7	4.17	-12.5	6.10	85.4	1.36
PLOSIVE	97.9	1.36	96.9	1.52	1.0	2.46	97.4	0.76
NONPLOSIVE	80.2	2.70	91.7	4.45	-11.5	6.67	85.9	1.56
COMPACTNESS	99.0	0.68	100.0	0.00	-1.0	0.68	99.5	0.34
VOICED	97.9	1.36	100.0	0.00	-2.1	1.36	99.0	0.68
UNVOICED	100.0	0.00	100.0	0.00	0.0	0.00	100.0	0.00
SUSTAINED	99.0	1.04	100.0	0.00	-1.0	1.04	99.5	0.52
INTERRUPTED	99.0	1.04	100.0	0.00	-1.0	1.04	99.5	0.52
BK/MD	99.0	1.04	100.0	0.00	-1.0	1.04	99.5	0.52
BK/FR	99.0	1.04	100.0	0.00	-1.0	1.04	99.5	0.52
EXPERIMENTAL**	100.0	0.00	100.0	0.00	0.0	0.00	100.0	0.00

SPEAKER	LL	CH	RH
LIST #	302B	307A	310B
DRT SCORE	98.2	97.1	98.3
S.E.*	0.43	0.55	0.52

8 LISTENERS, CREW (2), 576 TOTAL WORDS
3 SPEAKER(S), 192 WORDS PER SPEAKER
STANDARD ERROR FOR SPEAKERS = 0.37
TOTAL VOICED SCORE = 98.7
TOTAL UNVOICED SCORE = 95.7
* STANDARD ERRORS BASED ON LISTENER MEANS.
** EXPERIMENTAL ITEMS ARE NOT INCLUDED IN ANY SUMMARY SCORES.

```
XXXXXXXXXXXXXXXXXXXXXXXXXXXXXXXXXXXXXXX
X  TOTAL DRT SCORE  = 97.9          X
X  STANDARD ERROR*  = 0.33          X
XXXXXXXXXXXXXXXXXXXXXXXXXXXXXXXXXXXXXXX
```

Figure 7.2 Format in which the DRT Results Are Presented. (courtesy of Dynastat Inc.).

The diagnostic rhyme test gives very reliable results, which have been used mainly on a comparative basis against the typical range of values mentioned earlier. However, DRT is based on differences of initial consonants only, and the listener is asked to select among pairs of words. The Modified Rhyme Test (MRT) is another intelligibility test that is based on the same philosophy of testing differences between consonants, but it has relaxed the above two restrictions of DRT.

In MRT, the listener is presented with one word, and is asked to select his answer from a list of six words. Table 7.4 shows the groups of the words presented to a listener. Note that from the 50 sets of six words, the first 25 differ in the ending consonant, while the last 25 differ in the beginning consonant.

The modified rhyme test has not become as popular as the DRT and, to the author's knowledge, it has been used only internally by developers of speech systems.

7.2.2 QUALITY TESTS

The intelligibility tests, and especially the DRT, are widely accepted because they measure something that is well defined, and their results are accurate (small standard deviations) and repeatable (not time varying). However, when we ask "How good is this system?" we equate it with the question "How good is the resulting speech quality?" The answer is extremely difficult because the space of speech distortion is multidimensional. Suppose that we compare two systems, one that produces speech with a little warbling and another that produces speech with a lot of warbling of the same kind. It is reasonable to expect that the decision on which system is better would be unanimous and unvarying, and it might even be quantified by the amount of warbliness. Unfortunately, different speech systems introduce different types of distortion, and different people have different preferences. It is even probable that these preferences change over time. The end result is that the very important question of speech quality remains largely unanswered, and this limitation should be kept in mind when considering the different kinds of quality tests.

A very systematic approach to determining the speech quality quantitatively has been taken also by Dynastat, and it is applied in the Diagnostic Acceptability Measure (DAM). One of the main

TABLE 7.4 GROUPS OF WORDS USED IN THE MODIFIED RHYME TEST

			WORD LIST			
	A	B	C	D	E	F
Part 1						
1	BAT	BAD	BACK	BASS	BAN	BATH
2	TAB	TAN	TAM	TANG	TACK	TAP
3	PUN	PUFF	PUP	PUCK	PUS	PUB
4	TEACH	TEAR	TEASE	TEAL	TEAM	TEAK
5	HEAR	HEATH	HEAL	HEAVE	HEAT	HEAP
6	CUT	CUB	CUFF	CUP	CUD	CUSS
7	FILL	FIG	FIN	FIZZ	FIB	FIT
8	BUN	BUS	BUT	BUFF	BUCK	BUG
9	RAVE	RAKE	RACE	RATE	RAZE	RAY
10	PEACE	PEAS	PEAK	PEAL	PEAT	PEACH
11	DIG	DIP	DID	DIM	DILL	DIN
12	SING	SIT	SIN	SIP	SICK	SILL
13	MAP	MAT	MATH	MAN	MASS	MAD
14	KICK	KING	KID	KIT	KIN	KILL
15	SAD	SASS	SAG	SACK	SAP	SAT
16	SUD	SUM	SUB	SUN	SUP	SUNG
17	CAME	CAPE	CANE	CAKE	CAVE	CASE
18	SAKE	SALE	SAVE	SANE	SAFE	SAME
19	PASS	PAT	PACK	PAD	PATH	PAN
20	SEEP	SEEN	SEETHE	SEED	SEEM	SEEK
21	LATE	LAKE	LAY	LACE	LANE	LAME
22	PILL	PICK	PIP	PIG	PIN	PIT
23	DUCK	DUD	DUNG	DUB	DUG	DUN
24	PAGE	PANE	PACE	PAY	PALE	PAVE
25	BEAN	BEACH	BEAT	BEAM	BEAD	BEAK
Part 2						
26	LED	SHED	RED	BED	FED	WED
27	RAW	PAW	LAW	JAW	THAW	SAW
28	SIP	RIP	TIP	DIP	HIP	LIP
29	WAY	MAY	SAY	GAY	DAY	PAY
30	WILL	HILL	KILL	TILL	FILL	BILL
31	BOOK	TOOK	SHOOK	COOK	HOOK	LOOK
32	PEEL	REEL	FEEL	HEEL	KEEL	EEL
33	DIG	WIG	BIG	RIG	PIG	FIG
34	TOP	HOP	POP	COP	MOP	SHOP
35	RANG	FANG	GANG	BANG	SANG	HANG
36	HARK	DARK	MARK	LARK	PARK	BARK
37	NEST	VEST	WEST	TEST	BEST	REST
38	TEN	PEN	DEN	HEN	THEN	MEN
39	FOIL	COIL	BOIL	OIL	TOIL	SOIL
40	KIT	BIT	FIT	SIT	WIT	HIT
41	BUST	JUST	RUST	MUST	GUST	DUST
42	KICK	LICK	SICK	PICK	WICK	TICK
43	MEAT	FEAT	HEAT	SEAT	BEAT	NEAT
44	SUN	NUN	GUN	FUN	BUN	RUN
45	HOT	GOT	NOT	POT	LOT	TOT
46	FAME	SAME	CAME	NAME	TAME	GAME
47	TENT	BENT	WENT	DENT	RENT	SENT
48	GALE	MALE	TALE	BALE	SALE	PALE
49	PIN	SIN	TIN	WIN	DIN	FIN
50	SOLD	TOLD	HOLD	FOLD	GOLD	COLD

(after House et al. [2]).

characteristics of the diagnostic acceptability measure is that it needs listener crews who are highly trained and are constantly calibrated in order to determine any drift in the individual performance.

In DAM, the listener is presented with sentences taken from the Harvard list of phonetically balanced sentences (e.g., "Add the sum to the product of these three."), and is asked to rate the speech quality both in terms of overall acceptability and in terms of the individual characteristics (parametrically). In the parametric characterization of the speech, the listener is asked to rate qualities referring to the background, to the speech signal itself, and to the total effect. Table 7.5 gives the different characteristics evaluated by DAM. For each characteristic, the listener is asked to give a

TABLE 7.5   SYSTEM CHARACTERISTICS EVALUATED BY THE DIAGNOSTIC ACCEPTABILITY MEASURE

SIGNAL QUALITIES

Diagnostic Scale	Typical Descriptor	Exemplar
SF	Fluttering	Interrupted or Amplitude Modulated Speech
SH	Thin	High Pass Speech
SD	Rasping	Peak Clipped Speech
SL	Muffled	Low Pass Speech
SI	Interrupted	Packetized Speech with "Glitches"
SN	Nasal	2.4K bps Systems

BACKGROUND QUALITIES

Diagnostic Scale	Typical Descriptor	Exemplar
BN	Hissing	Noise-Masked Speech
BB	Buzzing	Tandemed Digital Systems
BF	Babbling	Narrow Band Systems with Errors
BR	Rumbling	Low-Frequency Noise-Masked Speech

TOTAL EFFECT

Scale

Intelligibility
Pleasantness
Acceptability

(courtesy of Dynastat, Inc.)

grade between 0 and 100. Figure 7.3 shows some examples of the DAM system rating form.

The results of these ratings are then processed, placing a different weight on each parameter, depending on its impact on speech quality. The ratings are used in a multiple, nonlinear regression equation to give a parametric estimate of the acceptability of the system. The results are further modified to adjust variations in listener performance. Figure 7.4 shows an example of the format in which the DAM results are reported.

Regarding the number of speakers to be used for testing, the comments on the DRT apply here, too. Again, it is recommended to use three male and three female speakers. Typical values of DAM scores range between 40 and 55 percent with a "good" system having a score of about 50 percent.

DAM can be a good indication of the speech quality, but it entails expenses that the designer may not want to incur until he is certain of the performance of his system. Meanwhile, other subjective tests may be used in-house to determine the speech quality. The simplest such test is the paired comparisons.

TYPICAL SIGNAL RATING SCALE

| 0 | 10 | 20 | 30 | 40 | 50 | 60 | 70 | 80 | 90 | 100 |

FLUTTERING

Negligible   TWITTERING PULSATING   Extreme

TYPICAL BACKGROUND RATING SCALE

| 0 | 10 | 20 | 30 | 40 | 50 | 60 | 70 | 80 | 90 | 100 |

HISSING

Negligible   SIMMERING FIZZING   Extreme

TYPICAL TOTAL EFFECT RATING SCALE

| 0 | 10 | 20 | 30 | 40 | 50 | 60 | 70 | 80 | 90 | 100 |

INTELLIGIBLE

Negligible   UNDERSTANDABLE MEANINGFUL   Extreme

Figure 7.3   Examples of the rating forms for the Diagnostic Acceptability Measure (courtesy of Dynastat, Inc.).

DIAGNOSTIC ACCEPTABILITY MEASURE RESULTS

CUSTOMER: DYNASTAT, INC. CONDITION: SYSTEM CONDITION A DATE RUN; 01 DEC 1976 NO. LISTENERS: 14

SIGNAL QUALITY SCORES

FACTOR	DESCRIPTOR	EXEMPLAR	MEAN	SE
SF	FLUTTERING	INTERRUPTED SPEECH	68.6	2.4
SH	THIN	HIGH PASS SPEECH	83.4	1.2
SD	HARSH	PEAK CLIPPED SPEECH	85.6	.7
SL	MUFFLED	LOW PASS SPEECH	82.1	1.2
SI	INTERRUPTED	PACKETIZED SPEECH WITH GLITCHES	83.3	1.8
SN	NASAL	2.4K BPS SYSTEMS	72.5	3.9
TOTAL SIGNAL QUALITY			57.1	1.6

BACKGROUND QUALITY SCORES

FACTOR	DESCRIPTOR	EXEMPLAR	MEAN	SE
BN	HISSING	NOISE MASKED SPEECH	87.5	.6
BB	BUZZING	TANDEMED DIGITAL SYSTEMS	83.9	1.4
BF	BABBLING	NARROW BAND SYSTEMS WITH ERRORS	80.0	1.8
BR	RUMBLING	LOW FREQUENCY MASKING NOISE	84.3	1.0
TOTAL BACKGROUND QUALITY			77.9	1.7

TOTAL EFFECT SCORES

RATING DIMENSION	ISOMETRIC SCORES MEAN	SE	PARAMETRIC ACCEPTABILITY MEAN	SE	COMPOSITE ACCEPTABILITY? MEAN	SE	EQUIVALENT SCORES MEAN	SE
INTELLIGIBILITY	59.1	1.5	48.4	1.8			(DRT) 87.1	1.3
							[SE ESTIMATE=4.8]	
PLEASANTNESS	36.6	1.9	45.4	2.6				
ACCEPTABILITY	47.1	1.8	47.9	1.5	47.2	1.6	(PARM) 52.8	2.0
							[SE ESTIMATE=3.4]	

SPEAKER(S): CH LL

PREDICTED PERCENT USER ACCEPTANCE = 76.5

COMPOSITE ACCEPTABILITY SCORE BASED ON COMBINATION OF PARAMETRIC SCORES FOR INTELLIGIBILITY, PLEASANTNESS AND ACCEPTABILITY, AND ISOMETRIC SCORE FOR ACCEPTABILITY.

Figure 7.4 Example of a DAM Report (courtesy of Dynastat, Inc.).

195

Paired comparisons involve two different systems. Each sentence is processed by both systems and the pair of sentences are presented to the listener in a randomized order. The listener decides if he likes sentence A or sentence B better. For purposes of completeness, and in order to verify the reliability of the listener, each system can be compared against itself and against the original. The results can be presented in the form of a preference matrix, as shown in Figure 7.5. Each number represents the percentage of times that the system of the row was preferred over the system of the column. If we permit a "no preference" vote for the listener, we then split that vote between the two systems. Figure 7.5 is a synthetic example where we conveniently chose system A to be preferred over C, C over B, and B over D. Unfortunately, in real testing the results do not always come out so clean and there may be cases where A is preferred over B, B over C, and C over A. In that case, an interpretation of results is called for.

Figure 7.5 Example of a preference matrix in paired comparisons. Each number represents the percentage of times that the system of the row was preferred over the system of the column.

	A	B	C	D
A	49	66	53	88
B		50	41	62
C			48	74
D				51

It seems that every speech system designer has his own personal preference in combining and presenting the results of the paired comparisons, and the preceding way is only one of them. However, the mere fact that several listeners take the test introduces an element of objectivity and removes the natural bias that the designer has in favor of his own system. So, formal subjective testing is recommended even if it is less than perfect.

Mean Opinion Scores (MOS). The paired comparisons involve a binary decision that may be easier for the listener, but makes rank ordering of systems very difficult. Also, they require a reference system whose performance and acceptability is well understood. To alleviate these problems, researchers have used the Mean Opinion Score (MOS). In MOS, the listener is asked to rate a system on an absolute scale, usually ranging between 1 and 5. Typical meaning of the grades are:

5. excellent
4. good

3. fair

2. poor

1. bad

The quality scale ranges from imperceptible degradation for grade 5, to very annoying and objectional for grade 1. New listeners may have problems assessing the quality, especially for the first few sentences. In this case, it may be helpful to present some examples of good and bad speech before the test in order to anchor the listeners.

A typical value for extremely high-quality, unimpaired speech is between 4 and 5 since listeners sometimes give a conservative grade of 4 to speech that is actually 5. Because of the ill-defined nature of speech quality, testing the same speech material at two different points in time may give different results. So, to have a more reliable assessment of the quality, it is advisable to consider the standard deviation in addition to the MOS. As an example, a test on a 64 kbps PCM system gave an MOS of 4.53 with a standard deviation of 0.57.

7.3 SUMMARY

To evaluate a speech-coding system, it is necessary to determine the quality of the resulting synthetic speech. This chapter investigated two types of quality measures: objective and subjective.

The objective measures are mathematical expressions that give an indication of the speech quality. The higher the correlation of an objective measure to the human perception, the more accurate the speech quality determination will be. There are different objective measures for different coding techniques. For the waveform coders, the signal-to-noise ratio (SNR) with its derivatives, and the articulation index can be used. For vocoders, distance metrics, such as the log-spectral distance, Itakura's likelihood ratio, and Euclidean distance between speech parameters are more appropriate.

Since the objective measures do not always give accurate results, subjective testing is necessary. Some subjective tests, like the Diagnostic Rhyme Test (DRT) and the Modified Rhyme Test (MRT), measure intelligibility. Other tests, such as the Diagnostic Acceptability Measure (DAM), the paired comparisons, and the Mean Opinion Score (MOS), measure the overall quality. Informal subjective tests are also recommended for a gross calibration of the speech system.

7.4 FURTHER READING

The field of subjective and objective evaluation of speech quality has not been very well documented. The pertinent information is found scattered in several papers and reports. The paper by Kitawaki et al. [3] gives a brief overview of the different objective and subjective measures. The two papers by Voiers [4,5] discuss the DAM and the DRT tests, while the report by Meister [6] describes in detail an implementation of the DRT. The CCITT recommendations on transmission quality are discussed in [7]. Regarding the objective quality measures, Barnwell [8] examines several kinds of objective measures and their correlation with the results from subjective evaluation.

7.5 REFERENCES

1. Jayant, N.S., and P. Noll. *Digital Coding of Waveforms*, Englewood Cliffs, NJ: Prentice-Hall, 1984.
2. House, A.H., C.E. Williams, M.H.L. Hecker, and K.D. Kryter. "Articulation-Testing Methods: Consonantal Differentiation with a Closed-Response Set." *J. Acous. Soc. Am.*, Vol. 37, No. 1 (January 1965): 158–166.
3. Kitawaki, N., M. Honda, and K. Itoh. "Speech-Quality Assessment Methods for Speech-Coding Systems." *IEEE Comm. Magazine*, Vol. 22, No. 10 (October 1984): 26–33.
4. Voiers, W.D. "Diagnostic Acceptability Measure for Speech Communication Systems." *Proc. IEEE 1977 Int. Conf. Acous., Speech, and Signal Proc.* (1977): 204–207.
5. Voiers, W.D. "Diagnostic Evaluation of Speech Intelligibility." in *Speech Intelligibility and Recognition*, M. E. Hawley, Ed. Stroudsburg, PA: Dowden, Hutchinson and Ross, 1977.
6. Meister, S. "The Diagnostic Rhyme Test (DRT): An Air Force Implementation." RADC report RADC-TR-78-129, May 1978.
7. CCITT-Yellow Book, Vol. V. "Telephone Transmission Quality." 12 & 41, VIIth Plenary Assembly, Geneva, SZ: 1981.
8. Barnwell, T.P., III. "Objective Fidelity Measures for Speech Coding Systems." *J. Acous. Soc. Am.*, Vol. 65, No. 6, December 1979.

Chapter 8

How to Apply Speech Coding: Some Examples

The previous chapters have presented several methods of speech coding. In this chapter you will be looking at some actual implementations of the speech coding algorithms, and some hardware devices used for implementing speech coding. The hardware devices range from simple waveform coders, such as codecs, to sophisticated waveform and parametric coders. On the other hand, the devices range from dedicated devices to more general-purpose digital signal processors. The algorithms whose implementations are presented here are well-defined standards. In particular, we discuss the NSA algorithm for a 2,400 bits/s system using the LPC-10 approach (i.e., the LPC method with a 10th-order model), and the 32 kbits/s ADPCM algorithm that has been standardized by the CCITT (International Telegraph and Telephone Consultative Committee).

Until the mid 1970s, almost all of the speech coding methods were implemented either in large computers in laboratories or on special-purpose hardware. With the recent advances in VLSI technology, speech coding has proliferated considerably in the commercial market, and it becomes more and more widespread. Yet, there is always a trade-off between implementation of a speech algorithm on a large computer system or on hardware dedicated to this purpose. Even if one plans to build a hardware board to realize a speech coding algorithm, it is always advisable to implement the algorithm on a large computer first. In a general-purpose computer, the debugging tools available are more powerful and the performance of the algorithm can be checked more effectively. On the other hand, there are applications, such as large store-and-forward systems, where implementation of the algorithm on a large computer is the only solution. The choice depends on the economics and the particular application.

Another question that arises in the design of a speech coding system is the use of programmable versus dedicated devices. For hardware implementations, if the volume of the application is high enough, it is worthwhile to consider an integrated circuit devoted entirely to that function. However, in most cases falling within the scope of this book, we are interested in off-the-shelf dedicated or programmable devices. The advantages of the dedicated over the programmable devices are that they are cost-effective and usually faster. On the other hand, their major disadvantage is their inflexibility. With a programmable device it is possible to incorporate later improvements of the speech algorithm, or even to change the algorithm entirely without affecting the hardware configuration. Naturally, the application again dictates the choice. The use of programmable devices is very attractive to technologists, but it may be an overkill in some situations. However, if the application is a borderline case, the programmable devices are recommended.

The speech coding applications can be divided roughly into two classes: voice response and communications applications. The main distinction between the two classes is the need for real-time operation at the transmitter.

In voice response systems, the requirements of speech synthesis are well defined, and the speech is prestored and played back at the time of synthesis (Figure 8.1). Such systems have the advantage that they can apply very sophisticated analysis algorithms, without any real-time constraints, in order to achieve the highest quality with the maximum data compression. Hand editing of the speech to be stored is, in principle, possible, and this has been the case with the available speech synthesis chips. Such examples have been the "talking cars" that use verbal warnings to alert the driver to possible safety hazards (door open, seat belts unbuckled) or to the status of the car (oil, fuel, and so on).

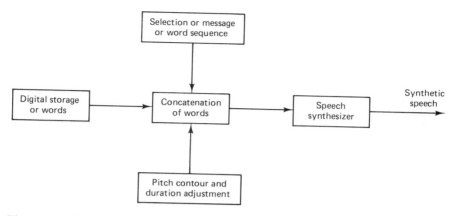

Figure 8.1 Conceptual block diagram of a voice-response system. Besides storing whole messages, it is possible to string together individual words to form messages. In this case it may be necessary to adjust the pitch contour and the duration of the words to form a coherent sentence.

When the vocabulary is limited and does not change frequently, the above solution is quite acceptable and it has been used in such diverse applications as learning aids, cars, clocks, and cameras. If, however, there is a need for a large and varying vocabulary, such as having a computer to supply information over the telephone about a subject whose content is changing over time, the above approach is impractical. A better solution to this voice-response scenario is a text-to-speech system.

The text-to-speech systems are a large subject by themselves and they are not considered in this book. The interested reader can find more information in other sources, such as [1–3] and their references. Basically, in a text-to-speech system (Figure 8.2, also referred to as a synthesis-by-rule system), information about the elements of the language (phonemes, allophones) is stored and, during synthesis, these elements are strung together according to certain rules to produce the output speech. The speech quality is not as good as when we store the actual words, but the added flexibility makes the method very attractive. Today, there are a number of commercially available text-to-speech systems in the form of stand-alone boxes, boards, or software that can be bought or licensed.

In the class of communications systems, we include the speech coding systems that are used to convert the speech into digital form

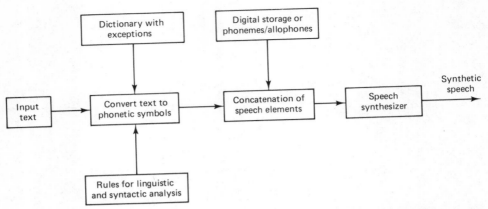

Figure 8.2   Block diagram of a text-to-speech system. Besides using phonemes or allophones, the synthetic speech can be generated from the phonetic symbols by using a dynamic model of the vocal tract.

in order to be transmitted from one end point (e.g., telephone) to another. This application has a great potential for using the advantages of digital transmission and also conserving bandwidth. We will examine the ADPCM standard developed for that purpose.

In the same class we also include the store-and-forward systems. In a store-and-forward system, the received voice message is recorded digitally in a computer memory and it can be played back at a later point in time. The principle of this type of system is very similar to the regular answering machines that use analog tapes, but with some very important differences. With a store-and-forward system, it is possible to:

- Have a centralized storage system of very large capacity.
- Listen to messages selectively.
- Delete or store the messages selectively.
- Use special features, such as edit, speed-up, etc.
- Forward the message to other interested parties.
- Call up the central system and listen to the messages over the phone.

Wang, VMX, and other companies. have such large systems commercially available. On a smaller physical scale, this functionality is available in board-level products from various companies, such as Texas Instruments, for personal computers.

In this chapter some examples of systems and hardware that are used for speech coding are presented. The examples can be classified into three groups:

1. Standardized speech coding algorithms to be used by the government and for telecommunications. The examples considered are
   - the NSA LPC-10 algorithm
   - the 32 kbit/s ADPCM algorithm defined by the CCITT
2. Implementation of a speech coding algorithm in hardware. The example presented is
   - the JRSU channel vocoder
3. Devices used for speech coding. In this category we include
   - codecs
   - speech synthesis chips
   - programmable digital signal processors
   - board and system level applications

The list of examples is by no means exhaustive, and it is only intended to illustrate how the methods presented in the previous chapters have been or can be implemented.

8.1 THE GOVERNMENT STANDARD LPC-10 ALGORITHM

In 1976, the US Government defined a standard algorithm for speech transmission at 2,400 bits/s, and companies, such as ITT, RCA, TRW, and E-Systems, have been developing special hardware for its implementation. The algorithm is sometimes referred to as the NSA (or the DoD standard) LPC-10 algorithm.

Table 8.1 summarizes the main features of the algorithm while the bit distribution with some comments is given in Table 8.2. More details on the algorithm can be found in reference [4].

The Government standard algorithm uses the Linear Predictive Coding (LPC) method with a 10th-order model. The speech frame period is 22.5 ms and, since we use 54 bits/frame for encoding, a final bit rate of 2,400 bits/s results. To generate the LPC parameters for each frame, we segment the speech signal in frames of 22.5 ms (180 samples for the sampling rate of 8 kHz), and we apply the LPC covariance analysis to a segment 130 samples long

TABLE 8.1 MAIN FEATURES OF THE GOVERNMENT STANDARD LPC-10 ALGORITHM

Sampling rate:	8 kHz
LPC predictor order	10 for voiced speech
	4 for unvoiced speech
Data rate	2,400 bits/s
Frame length	22.5 ms
Assigned bits/frame	54
Pitch	AMDF method
	Range: 51.3–400 Hz
	Coding: Semilog, 60 values
Gain	RMS value
	Coding: Semilog, 32 values
LPC analysis	Semi-pitch-synchronous
Analysis method	Covariance
LPC parameter coding	Log-area ratios for K_1-K_2
—	Linear for K_3-K_{10}
Synthesis	Pitch synchronous
Excitation	Stored waveform for voiced frame

TABLE 8.2 BIT ASSIGNMENT FOR THE LPC-10 GOVERNMENT STANDARD

Parameter	Voiced	Unvoiced	Comments
Pitch	7	7	6 bits pitch, 1 voicing
			60 values, semilog
Energy	5	5	32 values, semilog
K1	5	5	LAR
K2	5	5	LAR
K3	5	5	Linear
K4	5	5	Linear
K5	4	—	Linear
K6	4	—	Linear
K7	4	—	Linear
K8	4	—	Linear
K9	3	—	Linear
K10	2	—	Linear
Synchron.	1	1	Alternating 1s and 0s
Error protect.	—	21	
TOTAL	54	54	

within the frame. The location of the segment is determined in such a way as to achieve the pitch synchronous analysis. Figure 8.3 shows an example of consecutive frames and the positioning of the analysis windows. Notice that, since we are using the covariance method, we do not need any special window (such as a Hamming window), but simply use the actual sample values within the window (i.e., we are essentially using a rectangular window).

As can be seen from Table 8.2, we use a 10th-order LPC model for voiced frames, but only a 4th-order model for unvoiced frames. The reason is that the speech spectrum of unvoiced sounds is described sufficiently well by the lower-order model. The remaining bits are used for error protection of the bit stream.

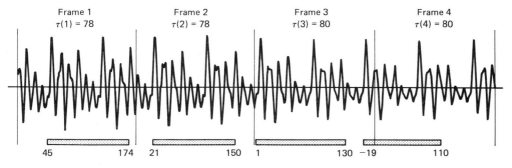

Figure 8.3 Examples of the positioning of the analysis window in consecutive figures for the LPC-10 DOD standard (after [5]).

For pitch tracking, the *Average Magnitude Difference Function* (AMDF) method is used. For the voicing decision, the algorithm uses

- the low-band energy
- the AMDF maximum to AMDF minimum ratio
- the zero-crossing count

The pitch and voicing results are further corrected by the use of a dynamic programming algorithm.

Figures 8.4 and 8.5 show the transmitter and the receiver portions of the LPC-10 algorithm. To establish the quality of the synthetic speech from LPC-10, the system was submitted to the subjective tests described in Chapter 7. Performance evaluation of the LPC-10 gave the following results:

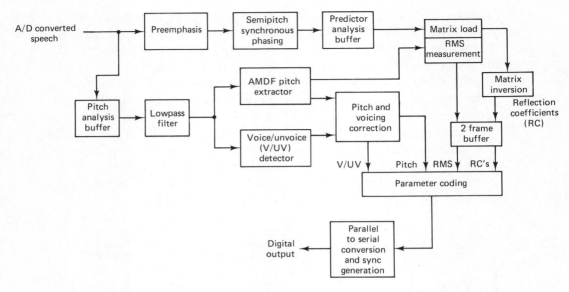

Figure 8.4 Transmitter of the LPC-10 algorithm (after [5]).

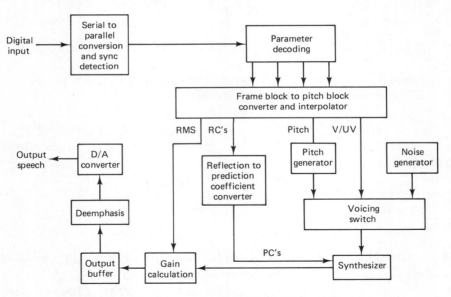

Figure 8.5 Receiver of the LPC-10 algorithm (after [5]).

DRT 90%

DAM 48%

These values (although only for male speakers) indicate that the system is of sufficiently high quality.

Note that the U.S. Department of Defense makes available the software implementation of the LPC-10 to American companies for a nominal licensing fee [4]. The software implementation is on a Philco-Ford signal processor (PFSP) and on the PDP-11 computer.

8.2 THE CCITT STANDARD 32 KBIT/S ADPCM ALGORITHM

The CCITT (International Telegraph and Telephone Consultative Committee) is an international organization that sets telecommunications standards. It started as a mainly European organization, but it progressively becomes more and more global as the international telecommunications network expands. CCITT publishes its standards in the form of Recommendations.

CCITT has established a standard for PCM coded digital speech at 64 kbit/s to be used in digital transmission. This standard defines the A-law companding method (described in Chapter 2, and used primarily by European telephone companies), and the µ-law companding, used by the American (and the Japanese) telephone companies. As the digital telephone network expands, the need arises for other bit rates. In response to this need, it was decided to establish standards for bit rates that are submultiples of the 64 kbit/s rate. The systems implementing these standards will start from the 64 kbit/s companded signal and transform it to the other bit rates. Such bit rate converters are called transcoders. The first transcoder standard established is the 32 kbit/s ADPCM.

With the progressive integration of telecommunications and the computer, a major concern of the telephone companies has been the digital transmission not only of voice, but also of data. Therefore, in establishing the 32 kbit/s standard, both voice and data transmission were considered. Here we present an outline of this standard, which is described in detail in the CCITT Recommendation G.721 [6].

Figures 8.6 and 8.7 show the encoder and the decoder portion of the ADPCM system. The input to the encoder is 64 kbit/s PCM which has been either A-law or μ-law companded. In other words, the new standard takes into consideration both the European and the American standards for PCM.

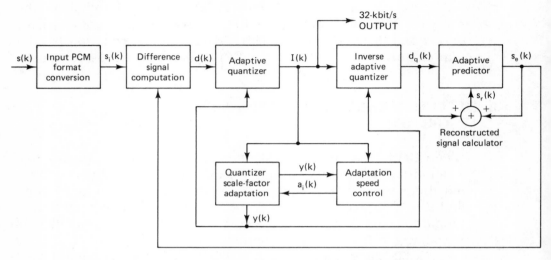

Figure 8.6 ADPCM encoder block diagram (after [6]).

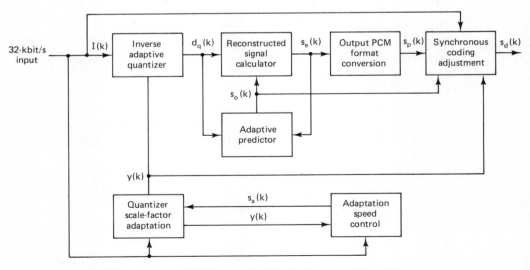

Figure 8.7 ADPCM decoder block diagram (after [6]).

- The input signal to the encoder is converted from log-PCM to linear before processing. Then, the output of the decoder is converted back to log-PCM.

- For the quantization of the difference signal and its representation by codewords, a 4-bit (16-level) adaptive quantizer is used. An inverse quantizer reconstructs the quantized values from the codewords to be used in the predictor.

- A signal estimate, computed from the previous estimates and the difference signals through an adaptive predictor, is subtracted from the linearized input PCM signal.

- The decoder includes a structure identical to the feedback portion of the encoder.

- The block of synchronous coding adjustment at the decoder, prevents cumulative distortion from tandem codings. Tandem coding is the successive PCM-ADPCM-PCM-ADPCM conversions that may occur several times as the signal travels through the telecommunications network.

- The adaptation used is of the feedback type, i.e., the transmitted signal is used for the adaptation. This has the advantage that no side information needs to be transmitted, and both the encoder and the decoder have all the information they require for the adaptation from the transmitted signal.

Since the standard is to be used for interfacing different networks, there is a strong need to guarantee the compatibility of the different implementations. A set of input test vectors and the corresponding output vectors have been defined to test the accuracy of the transcoding. Each vector consists of a sequence of 1s and 0s, and a successful implementation is expected to produce results that are bit-by-bit identical with the output vectors.

The standard was defined with the intention of being implemented on special-purpose integrated circuits to achieve the necessary speed and cost. However, a report has been published on the implementation of the algorithm on TI's programmable digital signal processor, the TMS32010 [7]. Such implementations demonstrate the power of the programmable digital signal processors. This report is included in the appendix as a detailed example of a practical implementation of a speech coding system.

8.3 THE JSRU CHANNEL VOCODER

As was mentioned in Chapter 4, one of the oldest methods of speech coding is the channel vocoder. By 1966, the Joint Speech Research Unit (JSRU) of the British Government had developed a channel vocoder that was then contracted to the industry (Marconi Space and Defense Systems) to develop a hardware implementation. This first model was given the code name Belgard, which is still occasionally used for this family of channel vocoders. Here the term JSRU is used for the channel vocoder. Holmes [8] gives a detailed description of the JRSU channel vocoder.

Besides the original implementation, Marconi developed other variants of the channel vocoder, all of which had the common feature of using analog channel filters. In more recent years, Marconi developed an all-digital implementation of the vocoder [9] under the commercial name Growler, which is described here.

Figure 8.8 shows the analysis part of this channel vocoder, and Figure 8.9 shows the synthesis part. Table 8.3 shows the different parameters used in the implementation of the vocoder, and the distribution of the quantization bits. The actual bit rate is 1,800 bits/s, but it is increased to 2,400 bits/s if 12 bits/frame are added for error protection. Error protection is necessary for reliable communication in noisy communications channels. Pitch extraction is done by the Gold-Rabiner pitch tracker, which is followed by a 3-point median smoother (see Section 6.1).

The vocoder uses 19 bandpass channels that cover the fre-

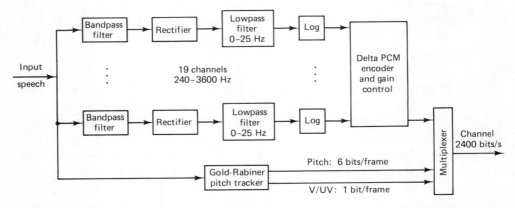

Figure 8.8   Analysis part of the Marconi channel vocoder (after Kingsbury and Amos [9], © 1980 IEEE).

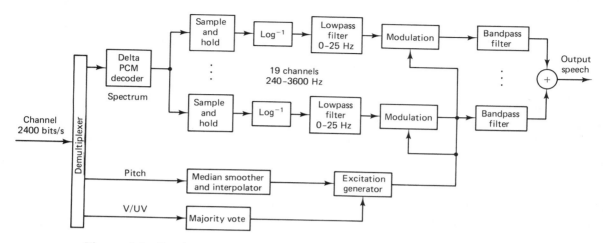

Figure 8.9 Synthesis part of the Marconi channel vocoder (after Kingsbury and Amos [9], © 1980 IEEE).

TABLE 8.3 PARAMETERS AND BIT ALLOCATION FOR THE MARCONI CHANNEL VOCODER.

Frame rate	50 frames/s (20 ms frame period)
Number of channels	19
Bit distribution	
Pitch	6 bits
V/UV	1 bit
Channel 1	3 bits (6 dB step)
Channel 2–9	2 bits each, delta coding (± 3, ± 9 dB)
Channel 10–19	1 bit each, delta coding (± 6 dB)
Error protection	12 bits (optional)
Total number of bits	48
Pitch extractor	Gold-Rabiner
Sampling rate	10 kHz

quency range 240–3,600 Hz. The output of the channels is sampled 50 times/s and the logarithm of the amplitude is coded. Actually, only the first channel's amplitude is coded that way. For the rest channels, instead of applying PCM on the log value, you code the delta-PCM. In other words, you take the difference of the log value from the previous channel and encode this difference. The spectrum encoder applies automatic gain control to achieve maximum efficiency in encoding the first channel. (The other channels are coded relative to the first one.)

This channel vocoder has been implemented using an Intel 8085 microprocessor. It is available either as a stand-alone half-duplex board pack or within a 3.5-inch high, 19-inch rack-mounted variant originally developed for the British Royal Navy [10].

8.4 CODECS

With the proliferation of digital telephony, which uses 64 kbit/s log-PCM coded speech, many semiconductor companies have developed custom chips to perform the digitization of the analog signal at the transmitter, and the conversion of the digital signal to analog at the receiver. These chips are called codecs for COders-DECoders. (Typically, when we talk about codecs we imply log-PCM coding, while A/D and D/A converters imply linear PCM.)

Codecs have been developed for μ-law and A-law PCM waveform coding. Also, in recent years, integrated circuits have been developed for Adaptive Delta Modulation (ADM), Continuously Variable Slope Delta (CVSD) coding, and Adaptive Differential PCM (ADPCM). Here we are going to consider two examples of log-PCM and CVSD chips.

The Texas Instruments chip TCM2913 (and TCM2914) is a combination of a PCM codec and filter. Table 8.4 summarizes the features of this codec. Figure 8.10 shows a block diagram of the transmitter and receiver sections of the chip. Note that it is possible to use this integrated circuit for either μ-law or A-law PCM. Table 8.5 gives an indicative list of companies manufacturing codecs and of the part numbers of some of their codecs.

TABLE 8.4 FEATURES OF THE TEXAS INSTRUMENTS PCM CODEC AND FILTER TCM2913 / TCM2914.

---

* Compatible with CCITT recommendations G.711 and G.712.
* TCM2913 operates with synchronous clocks only.
* TCM2914 offers:
    * Loopback test capability.
    * 8th bit signaling capability with AT&T D-type channel banks.
    * Asynchronous clocks.
* Pin-selectable μ-law or A-law PCM.
* Clock rates:
    * Variable mode: 64-4,096 kHz.
    * Fixed mode: 1.536, 1.544, 2.048 MHz.
* NMOS process technology.

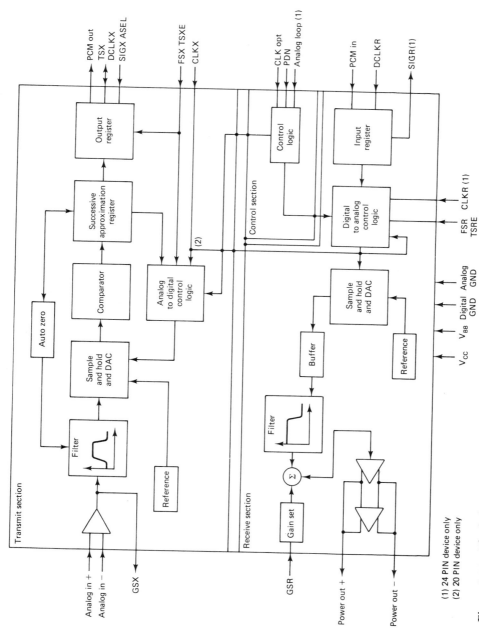

Figure 8.10 Block diagram of the transmit and receive sections of the Texas Instruments TCM2913/TCM2914 Codecs (reprinted by permission of Texas Instruments Inc., © 1982).

213

TABLE 8.5 PARTIAL LIST OF SEMICONDUCTOR
COMPANIES AND THEIR CODECS

Company	Part Number
AMI	S3500 series
HITACHI	MD44211
INTEL	2910 series
MOSTEK	MK5100 series
MOTOROLA	MC14400 series
NATIONAL	TP3000 and TP5100 series
SIGNETICS	ST100
TEXAS INSTRUMENTS	TCM2900 series

The Motorola chips in the MC3517/18 series provide Continuously Variable Slope Delta (CVSD) modulation. Table 8.6 summarizes their features, and Figures 8.11 through 8.13 show respectively the receive and transmit sections block diagrams, and an example of a CVSD waveform.

The available devices to convert analog to digital speech and vice versa can be viewed as waveform coders but most often are treated just as interface devices. The concept of waveform coders is typically applied to more sophisticated devices that take the output of the codecs as their input. Such devices can be the programmable digital signal processors discussed in a later section.

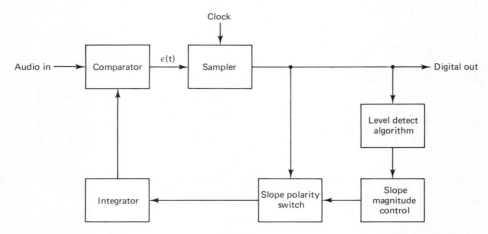

Figure 8.11 Block diagram of the CVSD encoder (courtesy of Motorola Inc.).

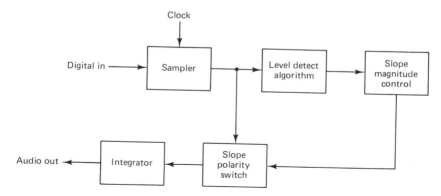

Figure 8.12 Block diagram of the CVSD decoder (courtesy of Motorola Inc.).

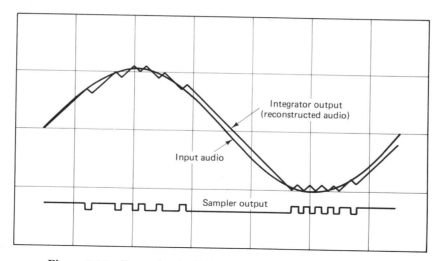

Figure 8.13 Example of a CVSD waveform (courtesy of Motorola Inc.).

TABLE 8.6 FEATURES OF THE MOTOROLA CVSD CHIP SERIES MC3517/18

* Encoding and decoding on the same chip with a digital input for selection.
* Selectable digital input threshold.
* I^2L process technology.
* CMOS or TTL compatible output.
* MC3517 has a 3-bit algorithm (general communications).
* MC3518 has a 4-bit algorithm (commercial telephone).

8.5 SPEECH SYNTHESIS CHIPS

In 1978, Texas Instruments introduced the "Speak & Spell"™ learning aid, a product designed to teach spelling by speaking a word and asking the user to input the spelling. This application started a revolution in speech processing by machines. Until then, the implementation of the speech coding algorithms was associated either with large general-purpose computers or with bulky dedicated hardware. Now, a new approach was introduced: speech coding in an integrated circuit. Since the introduction of the "Speak & Spell"™ learning aid, even larger strides have been made, to be described in the next section.

Speech synthesis chips are typically used in voice-response applications. The speech is analyzed and stored in read-only memory (ROM) using a waveform or parametric coding method. Then, at synthesis time, the stored information is supplied into the synthesis chip that produces the synthetic speech output. Table 8.7 is an indicative list of speech synthesis chip vendors with the corresponding part number, year of introduction, silicon processing method, and speech coding technique [11].

Taking as an example the speech synthesis chip used in the "Speak & Spell" learning aid, some more details of both the technique applied and the hardware configuration are presented. The synthesis chip in the "Speak & Spell" learning aid uses the LPC coding method. The model order for voiced speech is 10, while for unvoiced speech it's 4. Consecutive speech frames are examined for similarity and, if the speech signal has not changed much, the LPC parameters of the previous frame are repeated. This is signaled by a repeat bit. Silent frames are also signaled by zero energy level, and no more information is transmitted. With all these techniques it was possible to reduce the bit rate to an average of 1,200 bits/s.

Figure 8.14 is a block diagram of the chip operation [3], while Figure 8.15 shows the hardware configurations of the speech synthesis products [11]. The basic synthesis chips are designated as TMS5100 and TMS5200. Table 8.8 summarizes the bit distribution to the different LPC parameters, and Figure 8.16 shows an example of the stored code for the word HELP.

The speech synthesis chips have been used extensively in low-cost voice response applications, from automobiles to talking clocks. However, they are limited in their flexibility because they do not support analysis of the speech signal, and they also need

TABLE 8.7 LIST OF VENDORS OF SPEECH SYNTHESIS ICS

Vendor	Dev name	Intro	Proc	Technique
TI	TMS 5100	1978	P MOS	LPC-10
	TMS 5200	1979	P MOS	LPC-10
G.I.	SP-250	1980	N MOS	LPC-12
	SP-256*	1980	N MOS	LPC-12
Hitachi	HD38880	1980	P MOS	LPC-10
	HD61885*	1980	C MOS	LPC-10
Matsushita	MN6401	1980	N MOS	LPC-10
	MN1261	1980	C MOS	LPC-10
M.B.	1 chip	1980	N MOS	LPC-12
National	SPC	1980	N MOS	Mozer
Sharp	LR-3680	1980	C MOS	Delta-Mod.
Votrax	SC-01	1980	C MOS	Formant/ Phoneme
AMI	S-3610*	1981	C MOS	LPC-10
Fujitsu	MB8760	1981	N MOS	LPC
Mitsubishi	M58817	1981	P MOS	LPC
Motorola	DSP	1981	C MOS	LPC-10
NEC	UPD7751	1981	N MOS	ADPCM
Sanyo	VSY-100	1981	N MOS	LPC
TSI	PDSP	1981	N MOS	LPC-10

(after Lin and Frantz [11], © 1982 IEEE).

*Synthesizer ROM

editing to achieve the desired data compression. Because of these limitations, and in order to expand speech processing hardware in other domains, such as speech recognition, programmable digital signal processors have been introduced in recent years.

8.6 PROGRAMMABLE DIGITAL SIGNAL PROCESSORS

The programmable Digital Signal Processors (DSP) can be considered as a special form of a microprocessor. They demonstrate the programmability of the microprocessors, but their instruction sets are tailored for DSP applications. On the other hand, they are faster than the microprocessors, and have special features and architectural arrangements that match the needs of digital signal processing applications. Such a feature is, for instance, a hardware multiplier for single-cycle multiplication.

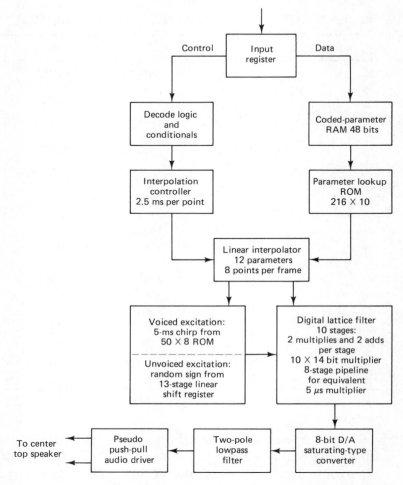

Figure 8.14   Block diagram of the operation of the "Speak and Spell" chip (after Morgan [3]).

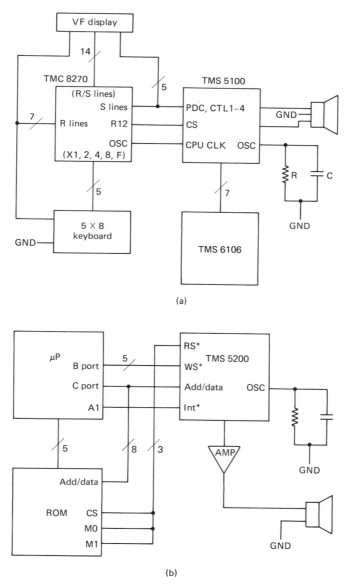

Figure 8.15 Hardware configurations of speech synthesis products. (a) System using TMS5100; (b) System using TMS5200 (after Lin and Frantz [11], © 1982 IEEE).

TABLE 8.8 BIT ALLOCATION IN THE "SPEAK & SPELL" CHIP. ENERGY CODED TO THE FIRST LEVEL, 0000, SIGNALS SILENCE. ENERGY CODED TO THE LAST LEVEL, 1,111, SIGNALS END-OF-WORD. PITCH CODED TO THE FIRST LEVEL, 00000, SIGNALS AN UNVOICED FRAME

Parameter	Voiced frame	Unvoiced frame	Repeat frame	Silence of end-or-word
Energy	4	4	4	4
Pitch	5	5	5	—
Repeat	1	1	1	—
K_1	5	5	—	—
K_2	5	5	—	—
K_3	4	4	—	—
K_4	4	4	—	—
K_5	4	—	—	—
K_6	4	—	—	—
K_7	3	—	—	—
K_8	3	—	—	—
K_9	3	—	—	—
K_{10}	3	—	—	—
K_{10}	3	—	—	—
TOTAL	49	28	10	4

	E	P	R	K1	K2	K3	K4	K5	K6	K7	K8	K9	K10
	0000												
	0100	00000	0	10011	01110	1001	0111						
	0111	00000	1										
	1101	10010	0	10000	10100	1000	0110	0111	1000	1010	100	101	010
	1101	10011	1										
	1110	10011	1										
	1101	10100	0	01101	01111	1010	1010	1001	0111	1000	100	101	101
HEL	1101	10100	0	01110	01011	1000	1100	1101	1000	0100	100	011	101
	1101	10011	0	10001	01010	0110	1001	1111	1011	0101	010	000	110
	1011	10010	1										
	1010	10010	0	01101	00111	1000	1100	1111	0111	0010	001	010	110
	1001	10001	1										
	1000	01101	1										
	1000	01101	1										
	0010	01110	0	00101	00101	1101	1001	1110	0101	0111	001	011	011
	0000												
	0000												
	0000												
	0111	00000	0	10100	01011	1011	1000						
	0111	00000	0	10001	01011	1011	0110						
P	0101	00000	1										
	0011	00000	0	10011	00111	1010	0110						
	0010	00000	0	10010	00101	1011	0101						
	0000												
	1111												

Figure 8.16 Example of stored code for the word "HELP" in "Speak and Spell" (after Frantz and Wiggins [12], © 1982 IEEE).

Some digital signal processors are also built with Harvard architecture. In the Harvard architecture, the instructions and the data are stored in different areas of the memory and are brought in through different buses. (This architecture is called Harvard architecture as opposed to the von Neuman architecture, where program and data share the same memory.) With this arrangement, program execution can be speeded up even further. Speed is of critical importance in signal processing applications, like speech with real-time requirements.

The programmable DSPs are designed for more general digital signal processing applications, and indeed, they have been used in very diverse areas. However, speech processing has been one of the major motivations for their design, and these DSPs will be examined from this standpoint. Of the different DSPs that have been introduced or announced, the Texas Instruments TMS320 family and the NEC μPD7720 have become the most popular. We are going to look at the TMS32010 as a typical example of a programmable DSP.

Table 8.9 summarizes the features of the TMS32010. Figure 8.17 is a block diagram of its architecture. The device is capable of performing 5 million instructions per second (MIPS) that, coupled

TABLE 8.9 FEATURES OF THE TEXAS INSTRUMENTS TMS32010 DIGITAL SIGNAL PROCESSOR (reprinted by permission of Texas Instruments Incorporated, © 1983).

- 200-ns Instruction Cycle
- 288-Byte On-Chip Data RAM
- ROMless Version—TMS32010
- 3K-Byte On-Chip Program ROM — TMS320M10
- External Memory Expansion to A Total of 8K Bytes at Full Speed
- 16-Bit Instruction/Data Word
- 32-Bit ALU/Accumulator
- 16×16-Bit Multiply in 200 ns
  0 to 15-Bit Barrel Shifter
- Eight Input and Eight Output Channels
- 16-bit Bidirectional Data Bus with 40-Megabits-per-Second Transfer Rate
- Interrupt with Full Context Save
  Signed Two's-Complement Fixed-Point Arithmetic
- NMOS Technology
- Single 5-V Supply

Functional block diagram

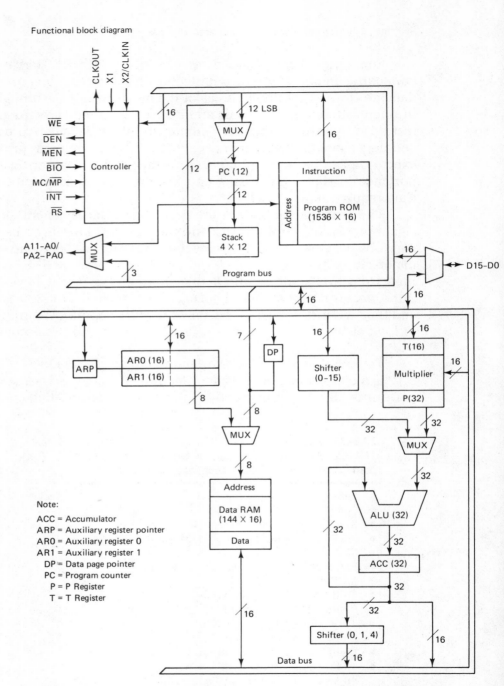

Figure 8.17 Architecture of the Texas Instruments TMS32010 digital signal processor (Reprinted by permission of Texas Instruments Inc., © 1983).

222

with the single-cycle hardware multiplier, makes possible multi-plication-intensive signal processing applications to be implemented in real-time. Such applications are the ones involving FFTs, autocorrelation computations, and filtering.

The TMS32010 is a 16-bit microprocessor, but the accumulator is 32-bits long to accommodate the products of two 16-bit words. This facilitates retention of extended accuracy during the accumulation, and even double-precision arithmetic.

Figure 8.18 is an example of the implementation of an FFT algorithm in TMS32010 assembly language. The TMS32010 has also been used to implement, among other algorithms, a 2,400 bits/s LPC vocoder, a 9,600 bits/s RELP vocoder, a 16 kbit/s subband coder, and a 32 kbit/s ADPCM algorithm.

8.7 BOARD AND SYSTEM LEVEL APPLICATIONS

The hardware examples considered in the previous sections deal primarily with components that can be used in building a system solution to speech coding applications. With the proliferation of speech applications, more and more stand-alone and board-level products are built. Many of these products are for speech recognition and text-to-speech applications, which are beyond the scope of this book. Typically, however, the same configuration supports speech coding in addition to the other speech applications.

It was a happy coincidence that the development of the programmable DSPs occurred at the same time with the increasing popularity of personal computers. The result is that there are many board-level products that have been developed for personal computers.

Texas Instruments markets the TI-SPEECH board for the TI PC (and, more recently, for the IBM PC). The board is based on the TMS32010 for the implementation of the speech algorithms. On that board a 2,400 bits/s LPC vocoder, a 9,600 bits/s RELP vocoder, and a 32 kbit/s ADPCM coder are implemented (in addition to speech recognition and text-to-speech systems). The board has an optional attachment for telephone management. The different coding algorithms can be used very effectively for communication purposes, such as in an answering machine.

The Atlanta Signal Processors Inc. (ASPI) markets a board for the IBM PC which is also based on the TMS32010 signal processor.

```
        IDT 'DFT'

* This program calculates a complex DFT.

* Standard straight DFT algorithm.
* Uses table lookup of coefficients with table size N
*   for sines and cosines.
* Maximum size of DFT is 64 points, complex.
* Keeps a full 32-bit running sum.
* All data begins in RAM and results are output
*   sequentially to port 0.

N  EQU 64            * Size of the transform is N.

X  Equ 0             * Data points are on page
* Rest of the variables are page 1 locations.
ONE     EQU 0        * Contains value 1
K       EQU 1        * Modulo counter, index into sine table
J       EQU 2        * Count of DFT point
HOLDN   EQU 3        * Contains value N
QUARTN  EQU 4        * Contains value N/4
COS     EQU 5        * Current cosine value
SIN     EQU 6        * Current sine value
TABLE   EQU 7        * Contains location of sine table
SUMREH  EQU 8        * Current real DFT summation high
SUMREL  EQU 9        * Current real DFT summation low
SUMIMH  EQU 10       * Current imaginary DFT summation high
SUMIML  EQU 11       * Current imaginary DFT summation high

START   AORG 0
        LDPK 1
        LACK ONE
        SACL ONE
        LT ONE
        MPYK SINE
        PAC
        SACL TABLE       * Save sine table address
        LACK N
        SACL HOLDN       * HOLDN = N
        LACK N/4
        SACL QUARTN      * QUARTN = N/4
        ZAC
        SACL J           * J = 0
JLOOP   LARK AR0, N-2
        LARK AR1, 0
        LARP 1
        LAC* +, 15
        SACH SUMREH
        SACL SUMREL      * Sum real = X(10)
        LAC* +, 15
        SACH SUMIMH
        SACL SUMIML      * Sum imag = Y(0)
        ZAC
        SACL K           * K = 0
ILOOP   LARP 1
        LAC K
        ADD J
        SUB HOLDN
        BGEZ GT2PI       * K = (K + J)mod N
        ADD HOLDN
GT2PI   SACL K           * 0 < = K < 2PI
        ADD TABLE
        TBLR SIN         * Get coefficients
        ADD QUARTN
        TBLR COS

* Main DFT calculations

        ZALH SUMREH      ** Real **
        ADDS SUMREL
        LT COS
        MPY* +
        LTA SIN
        MPY* -
        APAC
        SACH SUMREH      * Sum = sum + cos(k)×x(i) + sin(k)×y(i)
        SACL SUMREL
        ZALH SUMIMH      * Imaginary **
        ADDS SUMIML
        MPY* +
        SPAC
        LT COS
        MPY* +, AR0
        APAC
        SACH SUMIMH      * Sum = sum + cos(k)×y(i) − sin(k)×x(i)
        SACL SUMIML
        BANZ ILOOP       * Repeat for i = 2 to N

* Output DFT results

        OUT  SUMREH,PA0  * Output real part
        OUT  SUMIMH,PA0  * Output imaginary part
        LAC J
        ADD ONE
        SACL J           * J = J + 1
        SUB HOLDN
        BLZ JLOOP        * Repeat for J = 1 to N

* End of program

STOP    B STOP

* Sine and cosine tables (length N).

SINE  EQU $
        DATA 0
        DATA 3211
        DATA 6392
        DATA 9511
        DATA 12539
        DATA 15446
        DATA 18204
        DATA 20787
```

Figure 8.18 Example of FFT in TMS32010 assembly language (after Burrus and Parks [12]. Reprinted by permission of Texas Instruments Inc., © 1985).

224

The board is geared more towards data collection and manipulation, and for algorithm development on the TMS32010 processor. As an example, a 16 kbit/s subband coder has been implemented. Other TMS320-based boards with functionality similar to the one by Texas Instruments are marketed by IBM and Votan.

The speech market sees a continuous stream of new products appearing and it would be very difficult to give an exhaustive account of all of them. Instead, a few examples have been presented to give you a feeling about what has been accomplished, and in what domains and with what tools you could put the speech coding methods presented in this book to use.

8.8 REFERENCES

1. Bristow, G., Ed. *Electronic Speech Synthesis*. London: Granada, 1984.

2. Witten, I. H. *Principles of Computer Speech*. New York: Academic Press, 1982.

3. Morgan, N. *Talking Chips*. New York: McGraw-Hill, 1984.

4. Tremain, T. E. "The Government Standard Linear Predictive Coding Algorithm: LPC-10." *Speech Technology*, Vol. 1, No. 2 (April 1982): 40–49.

5. Documentation of the Government Standard LPC-10 Algorithm.

6. "32 Kbit/s Adaptive Differential Pulse Code Modulation (ADPCM)." *CCITT Recommendation G.721*, October 1984.

7. Reimer, J. B., M. L. McMahan, and M. Arjmand. "32 kbit/s ADPCM with the TMS32010." Texas Instruments Inc., Dallas, Applications Report, 1985 (see Appendix).

8. Holmes, J. N. "The JRSU Channel Vocoder." *IEE Proceed.*, Vol. 127, No. 1 (February 1980): 53–60.

9. Kingsbury, N. G., and W. A. Amos. "A Robust Channel Vocoder for Adverse Environments." *Proc. IEEE 1980 Int. Conf. Acous., Speech, and Signal Proc.* (April 1980): 19–22.

10. Wilson, J. "Marconi: A Look at the Past, Present and Future." *Speech Technology*, Vol. 2, No. 3 (August 1984): 38–42.

11. Lin, K-S., and G. A. Frantz. "Speech Technology in Medicine." In *Applications of Computers in Medicine*, by M. D. Schwartz, Ed. IEEE Engin. in Biol. and Medic. Soc. (1982): 2–16.

12. Frantz, G. A., and R. H. Wiggins. "Design Case History: Speak & Spell Learns to Talk." *IEEE Spectrum* (February 1982): 45–49.

13. Burrus, C. S., and T. W. Parks. *DFT/FFT and Convolution Algorithms*. New York: John Wiley and Sons, 1985.

Appendix I
32-kbit/s ADPCM with the TMS32010

Jay Reimer
Digital Signal Processing - Semiconductor Group
Texas Instruments

Mike McMahan
Corporate Engineering Center
Texas Instruments

Masud Arjmand
Central Research Laboratories
Texas Instruments

INTRODUCTION

Digital voice communication is typically transmitted in a 64-kbit/s PCM bit stream. Voice and data communications demand increasing capacities for signal transmission without significant degradation in the quality of the transmitted signal. One of the recommended solutions for accomplishing this task is that of Adaptative Differential Pulse Code Modulation (ADPCM). This solution has been reviewed by CCITT (International Telegraph and Telephone Consultative Committee), and a specific standard* has been recommended. Two solutions, a full-duplex solution and a half-duplex solution, are discussed in this application report. Both follow the model recommended by CCITT for 32-kbit/s ADPCM, although only the half-duplex solution provides a bit-for-bit compatible data stream as required by the recommendation. At 32 kbit/s, the ADPCM solution provides double the channel capacity of the current 64-kbit/s PCM technique. Each solution has been totally incorporated in the internal memory space of the Texas Instruments TMS32010 microprocessor.

This application report presents a brief review of the basic principles of PCM and ADPCM. Hardware requirements, software logic flow, and key features of the TMS32010 microprocessor for the implementation of ADPCM are also given. Source code is provided for the implementation and creation of an ADPCM transmission channel.

DIGITIZATION

Over the past 20 years, the telecommunications industry has changed from totally analog circuits to networks which integrate both analog and digital circuits. Digital signal encoding has the advantages of greater noise immunity, efficient regeneration, easy and effective encryption, and uniformity in transmitting voice and data signals. Increased bandwidth is required to transmit digital signals while maintaining a given analog signal quality at the receiver.

Voice store and forward systems have been changing from totally analog storage media, such as audio tape, to digitized storage which allows random access of stored data, but with the tradeoff of increased storage media requirements.

Signal quality begins with the digitization of the original analog signal. The process of digitization and coding introduces a distortion associated with the quantization of the digitized signal, as shown in Figure 1. This signal distortion or noise is different from the channel noise normally associated with a transmitted signal. After a signal

*Recommendation G.721, 32 kbits/s Adaptive Differential Pulse Code Modulation'', CCITT, 1984.

has been digitized, the signal is much less susceptible to channel noise since the signal can be regenerated as well as amplified along the way, thus reducing the possibility of being corrupted by the transmission system. The overall quality of digital transmission is then limited by the digitization process in an error-free transmission system.

Figures 2 and 3 show general representations of a digital communication channel. The actual transmission (and storage of a digital waveform) uses an analog channel. The outside points of the communications channel are the transmitter and receiver, as shown in Figure 2. These are commonly combined in a single device known as a combo-CODEC (CODing and DECoding device). The codec supplies, on the coding or transmitting side, the necessary filtering to bandlimit the analog signal and avoid signal alias and A/D conversion. On the decoding or receiving side, the codec performs a D/A conversion and then interpolates or smooths the resultant signal.

Figure 3 shows the digitized signal modulated for transmission in the network and then demodulated at the receiving end to retrieve the transmitted digital signal.

PCM

Digitization and coding of the analog signal at the transmitter can be performed in several ways. The complexity of the chosen method is related to availability of encoder memory and to the resultant delay in the encoding process.

When digital signal transmission is implemented, memory and the resultant delay dictate that a simple scheme, such as Pulse Code Modulation (PCM), be implemented. PCM codes each sampled analog value of the input waveform to a unique or discrete value. The digital quantization introduces distortion into the signal waveform, as shown in Figure 1.

A nonuniform quantization scheme may be used to COMPAND (COMpress and exPAND) the signal in the waveform coding and decoding blocks in the system, generating log-PCM. By using larger quantization steps for large amplitude signals and smaller steps for small amplitude signals, efficient use is made of the data bits for digital transmission while maintaining specific signal-to-quantization noise thresholds. With the two current methods of COMPANDING (A-law and μ-law), the signal quality of a 13-bit digitized signal is maintained while transmitting only 8 bits per sample.

While quantizers remove the irrelevancy in a signal, coders remove the redundancy. In PCM encoding, each sample of the input waveform is independent of all previous samples; no encoder memory is required.

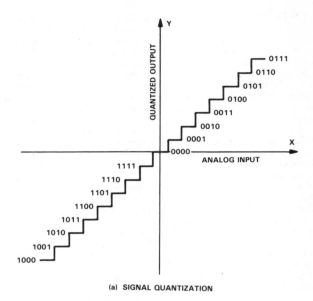

(a) SIGNAL QUANTIZATION

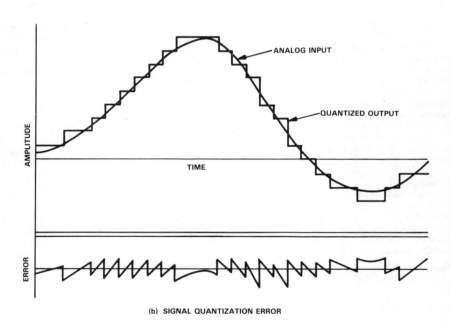

(b) SIGNAL QUANTIZATION ERROR

Figure 1. Quantization Errors in a Digitized Signal

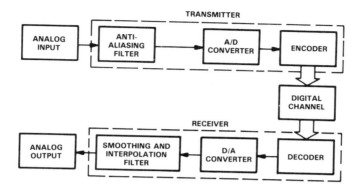

Figure 2. Digital Communication of Waveforms

Figure 3. Digital Channel

ADPCM

Analysis of speech waveforms shows a high sample-to-sample correlation. By taking advantage of this property in speech signals, more efficient coding techniques have been designed to further reduce the transmission bit rate while preserving the overall signal quality.

APCM

Adaptive PCM (APCM) is a method that may be applied to both uniform and nonuniform quantizers. It adapts the stepsize of the coder as the signal changes. This accommodates amplitude variations in a speech signal between one speaker and the next, or even between voiced and unvoiced segments of a continuous signal. The adaptation

may be instantaneous, taking place every few samples. Alternatively, it may occur over a longer period of time, taking advantage of more slowly varying features. This is known as syllabic adaptation.

The basic concept for an adaptive feedback system, APCM, is shown in Figure 4. An input signal, $s(k)$, in the transmitter is quantized and coded to an output, $I(k)$. This output is also processed by stepsize adaptation logic to create a signal, $q(k)$, that adapts the stepsize in the quantizer. Correspondingly, in the receiver, the received signal, $I(k)$, is processed by an inverse quantizer (i.e., decoded), producing the reconstructed signal, $s_r(k)$. Like the transmitter, the quantized signal, $I(k)$, is processed by adaptation logic to create a stepsize control signal, $q(k)$, for the inverse quantizer.

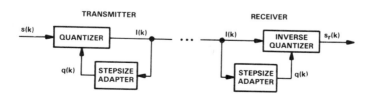

Figure 4. APCM Block Diagram

DPCM

The method of using the sample-to-sample redundancies in the signal is known as differential PCM (DPCM). The overall level of high correlation on a sample-by-sample basis indicates that the difference between adjacent samples produces a waveform with a much lower dynamic range. Correspondingly, an even lower variance can be expected between samples in the difference signal. A signal with a smaller dynamic range may be quantized to a specific signal-to-noise ratio with fewer bits.

A differential PCM system, DPCM, is shown in Figure 5. In Figure 5, the signal difference, $d(k)$, is determined using a signal estimate, $s_e(k)$, rather than the actual previous sample. By using a signal estimate, $s_e(k)$, the transmitter uses the same information available to the receiver. Each successive coding actually compensates for the quantization error in the previous coding. In this way, the reconstructed signal, $s_r(k)$, can be prevented from drifting from the input signal, $s(k)$, as a result of an accumulation of quantization errors. The reconstructed signal, $s_r(k)$, is formed by adding the quantized difference signal, $d_q(k)$, to the previous signal estimate, $s_e(k)$. The sum is the input to predictor logic which determines the next signal estimate. A decoding process is used in both the transmitter and receiver to determine the quantized difference signal, $d_q(k)$, from the transmitted signal, $I(k)$.

ADPCM

ADPCM combines the features of both the APCM and DPCM systems. Figure 6 shows the basic blocks combining adaptation and differencing features in an ADPCM system.

Both quantizer adaptation and signal differencing require the storage (in memory) of one or more samples in both the transmitter and receiver. Furthermore, the transmitter must use some method to ensure that the receiver is operating synchronously. This is accomplished by using only the transmitted signal, $I(k)$, to determine stepsize adaptation in the quantizer and inverse quantizer and to predict the next signal estimate. In this way, the blocks in the receiver can be identical to those in the transmitter. Additionally, the specific adaptation techniques are designed to be convergent and thereby help provide quick recovery following transmission errors.

The ADPCM system, as used in digital telephony, is not an original signal coding system, but is actually a transcoder, converting between log-PCM and ADPCM codes. Currently there are a large number of systems using log-PCM for transmission. The ADPCM system incorporates both an adaptive quantizer and an adaptive predictor. The adaptive quantizer contains speed-control and scale-factor adaptation. A measure of the rate-of-change of the difference signal provides a means of determining the speed control. The scale factor adjustments to the difference signal adapt the fit of the quantization levels to minimize the signal-to-noise ratio. With speed control, the system can take advantage of both the instantaneous and syllabic adaptation rates, thereby adapting better to both speech and data signals. In the adaptive predictor, the prediction filter coefficients are updated by a gradient algorithm. Predictor adaptation improves the performance of the predictor for nonstationary signals (e.g., speech).

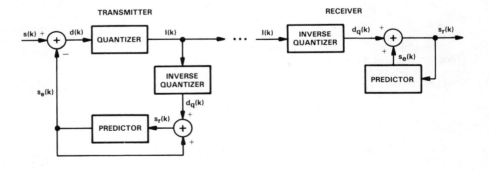

Figure 5. DPCM Block Diagram

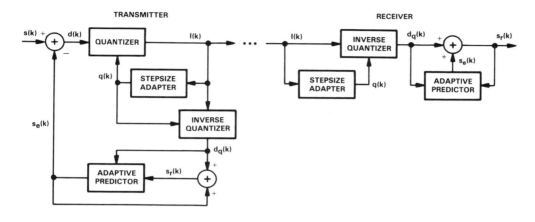

Figure 6. ADPCM Block Diagram

THE ADPCM ALGORITHM

The ADPCM algorithm has a receiver imbedded in the transmitter. This is important since, if the signal feedback used to determine the signal estimate, $s_e(k)$, and consequently the quantized difference signal, $d_q(k)$, is the same as in the decoder, then the compensation for quantization errors can be made with subsequent difference samples. Since the decoder is actually imbedded in the encoder, each of the common blocks for transmitting and receiving is discussed in the following paragraphs.

Figures 7 and 8 show block diagrams of an ADPCM transmitter and receiver as specified by CCITT.

Encoder

The function of the encoder or transmitter, shown in Figure 7, is to receive a 64-kbit/s log-PCM signal and transcode it to a 32-kbit/s ADPCM signal. This is accomplished by converting the log-PCM signal, $s(k)$, to a linear signal, $s_l(k)$, from which an estimate, $s_e(k)$, of the signal is subtracted to obtain a difference signal, $d(k)$. The next step is to adaptively quantize this difference signal, $d(k)$, by first taking the log (base 2), then normalizing by the quantization scale factor, $y(k)$, and finally coding the result, $I(k)$. A more uniform signal-to-noise ratio can be achieved by coding the log of the signal rather than the linear representation. The normalization provides the adaptation to the quantization and is based on past coded samples. Adaptation is controlled bimodally, being comprised of a fast adaptation factor for signals with large amplitude fluctuations (i.e., speech) and a slow adaptation factor for signals which vary more slowly (i.e., data). A speed-control factor, $a_l(k)$, weights the fast and the slow adaptation factors to form a single quantization scale factor, $y(k)$.

The inverse adaptive quantizer uses the same signal, $I(k)$, that has been transmitted to reconstruct a quantized version of the difference, $d_q(k)$, and the same adaptive quantization characteristics as the adaptive quantizer section.

The quantized difference signal, $d_q(k)$, is input to an adaptive predictor which uses this input to compute a signal estimate, $s_e(k)$. The signal estimate, $s_e(k)$, is combined with the difference signal, $d_q(k)$, to determine a reconstructed signal, $s_r(k)$, which is the output in the decoder. This output is then subtracted from the next input sample to complete the feedback loop.

The adaptive predictor makes use of both an all-pole filter and an all-zero filter. The all-pole filter is a second-order filter with constrained adaptive coefficient values designed to match the slowly varying aspects of the speech signal. Since an all-pole predictor is particularly sensitive to errors, the predictor makes use of a sixth-order all-zero filter to offer signal stability even with transmission errors.

Decoder

The function of the decoder or receiver, shown in Figure 8, is to receive a 32-kbit/s ADPCM signal and transcode it to a 64-kbit/s log-PCM signal. To accomplish this, the decoder utilizes many of the elements used by the encoder. The received data, $I(k)$, is processed by an inverse adaptive quantizer, identical to the one in the corresponding encoder, to determine a quantized difference signal, $d_q(k)$. By filtering the difference signal, $d_q(k)$, through the adaptive predictor together with the previously reconstructed signal, $s_r(k)$, a signal estimate, $s_e(k)$, is obtained. The signal estimate, $s_e(k)$, is added to the difference signal, $d_q(k)$, to compute the reconstructed signal, $s_r(k)$. The reconstructed signal, $s_r(k)$, is converted from a linear-PCM to a log-PCM signal, $s_p(k)$, which is then output following a synchronous

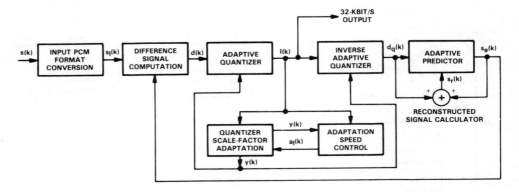

**Figure 7. ADPCM Encoder Block Diagram
(Diagram taken from CCITT Recommendation G.721)**

coding adjustment. The coding adjustment limits the errors in tandem codings of a signal.

Note that the algorithm design achieves a convergence of the states of the encoder and decoder in spite of transmission errors. This convergence is a part of each of the adaptation computations and is demonstrated equationally in the following sections. The convergence is brought about by the inclusion of $(1-2^{-N})$ terms which provide a finiteness to the memory of the adaptation parameters.

Adaptive Quantization

Adaptive quantization, a multistage process, is used to determine the quantization scale factor and the speed control that controls the rate at which the scale factor is adapted. Quantization is actually a four-bit quantization (a sign bit plus three-bit magnitude), since a four-bit signal is the transmitted output of the ADPCM transcoder. The adaptive quantizer block can be noted in Figure 7.

The difference signal, $d(k)$, an input to the quantization process, is calculated by subtracting the signal estimate, $s_e(k)$, from the linear-PCM signal, $s_l(k)$.

$$d(k) = s_l(k) - s_e(k) \qquad (1)$$

This difference signal is normalized by taking the log (base 2) and subtracting from it the quantizer scale factor, $y(k)$.

$$|I(k)| - \log_2 |d(k)| - y(k) \qquad (2)$$

Table 1 is used to provide the magnitude of the quantization result, $|I(k)|$, from this normalized input. The

sign bit of the ADPCM output value, $I(k)$, is the sign of the difference signal, $d(k)$.

The quantizer scale factor, $y(k)$, is comprised of two parts, and therefore bimodal in nature. The two parts, $y_l(k)$ and $y_u(k)$, are weighted by the speed-control factor, $a_l(k)$. For speech signals, $a_l(k)$ will tend toward a value of one; for voiceband data, $a_l(k)$ will tend toward zero. Refer to both Figures 7 and 8 for the inclusion of the quantizer scale factor and speed-control factor adaptation blocks.

$$y(k) = a_l(k)y_u(k-1) + [1 - a_l(k)] \, y_l(k-1) \qquad (3)$$

where $0 \le a_l(k) \le 1$

One of the factors, $y_u(k)$, is considered to be unlocked, since it can adapt quickly to rapidly changing signals (e.g., speech) and has a relatively short-term memory. This factor, $y_u(k)$, is recursively determined from the quantizer factor, $y(k)$, and the discrete function, $W(I)$.

$$y_u(k) = [1 - 2^{-5}] \, y(k) + 2^{-5}W[I(k)] \qquad (4)$$

where $1.06 \le y_u(k) \le 10.00$

The factor, $W(I)$, found in Table 2, is a function of I which causes $y_u(k)$ to adapt by larger steps for larger values of I. This gives $y_u(k)$ the freedom to track a signal almost instantaneously. Since $y(k)$ is in the logarithmic domain, $W(I)$ is effectively a multiplier of the scale factor.

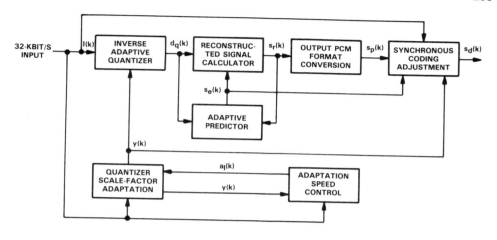

Figure 8. ADPCM Decoder Block Diagram
(Diagram taken from CCITT Recommendation G.721)

Table 1. I/O Characteristics of the Normalized Quantizer

Normalized Quantizer Input Range $\log_2\lvert d(k)\rvert - y(k)$	$\lvert I(k)\rvert$	Normalized Quantizer Output $\log_2\lvert d_q(k)\rvert - y(k)$
[3.16, $+\infty$)	7	3.34
[2.78, 3 16)	6	2.95
[2.42, 2.78)	5	2.59
[2.04, 2.42)	4	2.23
[1.58, 2.04)	3	1.81
[0.96, 1.58)	2	1.29
[-0.05, 0.96)	1	0.53
($-\infty$, -0.05)	0	-1.05

The other factor, $y_l(k)$, adapts more slowly and tracks signals which change slowly (e.g., voiceband data). This factor includes a lowpass filtering of the unlocked factor, $y_u(k)$. By including $y_u(k)$ in the manner shown, $y_l(k)$ is implicitly limited to the same range of values as the explicit limit placed on $y_u(k)$. Furthermore, the unity limit of $a_l(k)$ provides the same limit implicitly for $y(k)$ as for $y_l(k)$ and $y_u(k)$.

$$y_l(k) = [1 - 2^{-6}] y_l(k-1) + 2^{-6}y_u(k) \qquad (5)$$

A speed-control factor, $a_l(k)$, adjusts the relative weighting of these two scale factors by making use of the short- and long-term averages, $d_{ms}(k)$ and $d_{ml}(k)$, respectively, of the coded output to determine how rapidly the signal is changing. The combined scale factor, $y(k)$, cannot be larger than either the unlocked, $y_u(k)$, or locked $y_l(k)$, terms. Therefore, $a_l(k)$ is limited to one even if the predicted speed control, $a_p(k)$, is larger than one.

$$a_l(k) = \begin{cases} 1 & \text{,if } a_p(k-1) > 1 \\ a_p(k-1) & \text{,if } a_p(k-1) \leq 1 \end{cases} \qquad (6)$$

Note that $a_p(k)$ is implicitly limited to a maximum value of 2, while the speed-control factor used to mix the two scale factors is capped at a value of 1. In determining $a_p(k)$, an additional term of 1/8 is added each time if the difference in the short- and long-term averages becomes too large (i.e., $\lvert d_{ms}(k) - d_{ml}(k)\rvert \geq 2^{-3}d_{ml}(k)$) or if there is an idle channel (i.e., $y(k) < 3$). Where neither of these conditions exist, a uniform, slowly varying signal can be assumed, such as occurs in data transmission.

Table 2. Scale-Factor Multipliers

$\lvert I\rvert$	7	6	5	4	3	2	1	0
W(I)	69.25	21.25	11.50	6.12	3.12	1.69	0.25	-0.75

$$a_p(k) = \begin{cases} [1 - 2^{-4}] a_p(k-1) + 2^{-3}, \text{ if} \\ \quad |d_{ms}(k) - d_{ml}(k)| \geq 2^{-3}d_{ml}(k) \\ [1 - 2^{-4}] a_p(k-1) + 2^{-3}, \text{ if } y(k) < 3 \\ \\ [1 - 2^{-4}] a_p(k-1), \text{ otherwise} \end{cases} \quad (7)$$

The short-, $d_{ms}(k)$, and long-term, $d_{ml}(k)$, averages of the transmitted ADPCM signal, $I(k)$, are actually determined by averaging a weighted function, $F(I)$, of the transmitted I, shown in Table 3.

$$d_{ms}(k) = [1 - 2^{-5}] d_{ms}(k-1) + 2^{-5}F [I(k)] \quad (8)$$

$$d_{ml}(k) = [1 - 2^{-7}] d_{ml}(k-1) + 2^{-7}F [I(k)] \quad (9)$$

The scale-factor and speed-control adaptations are a part of both the encoder and decoder logic. The adaptive quantization block has been specifically included in Figure 7, showing the encoder. For the decoder, the adaptive quantizer is included as part of the synchronization block to aid in the reduction of errors in tandem codings.

Table 3. Rate-of-Change Weighting Function

|I|	7	6	5	4	3	2	1	0
F(I)	7	3	1	1	1	0	0	0

Inverse Adaptive Quantization

Inverse adaptive quantization is a process in which the four-bit ADPCM signal, $I(k)$, is used to determine the normalized log of the difference signal from Table 1. The result is actually a quantized version of the difference signal, $d_q(k)$, determined by adding the scale factor, $y(k)$, to the value specified by Table 1 and calculating, the inverse log (base 2) of this sum.

$$d_q(k) = \log_2{}^{-1} [\{\log_2 |d_q(k)| - y(k)\} + y(k)] \quad (10)$$

For both the encoder and decoder, this quantized difference signal is the input to the reconstruction signal calculator and the adaptive predictor, as shown in Figures 7 and 8.

Adaptive Prediction

The adaptive predictive filter is a two-pole, six-zero filter used to determine the signal estimate. The combination of both poles and zeroes allows the filter to model more effectively any general input signal. The sixth-order all-zero section helps to stabilize the filter and prevent it from drifting into oscillation. For both the poles and the zeroes, the coefficients, $a_i(k)$ and $b_i(k)$, respectively, are adapted. This adaptation is based upon a gradient algorithm to further adjust the filter model to the input signal. Figures 9 and 10 show the sixth-order and second-order filters, respectively.

The signal estimate, $s_e(k)$, represents the sum of the all-pole filter and the all-zero filter. Since the sum of the all-zero filter is used to aid the determination of the pole coefficients, it is also extracted as a separate sum, $s_{ez}(k)$. The reconstructed signal, the output in the receiver, is the sum determined by the quantized difference signal $d_q(k)$, and the signal estimate, $s_e(k)$.

$$s_e(k) = \sum_{i=1}^{2} a_i(k-1)s_r(k-i) + s_{ez}(k) \quad (11)$$

$$s_{ez}(k) = \sum_{i=1}^{6} b_i(k-1)d_q(k-i) \quad (12)$$

$$s_r(k-i) = s_e(k-i) + d_q(k-i) \quad (13)$$

The adaptation of the pole coefficients, $a_i(k)$, is shown in the equations below. The gradient function is determined from a signal, $p(k)$, that is equivalent to the reconstructed signal minus the contribution of the pole filter output. Stability of the filter is further provided by explicitly limiting the coefficients.

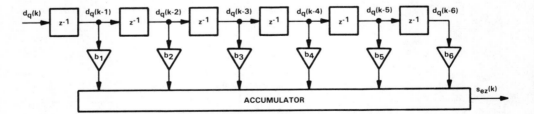

Figure 9. Sixth-Order All-Zero (FIR) Filter

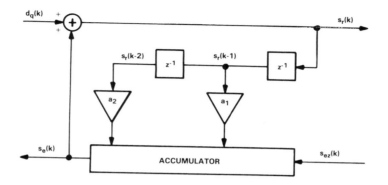

Figure 10. Second-Order IIR Filter

$$a_1(k) = [1 - 2^{-8}]\, a_1(k-1)$$
$$+\, 3 \cdot 2^{-8} \text{sgn}\, [p(k)]\, \text{sgn}[p(k-1)] \qquad (14)$$

where $|a_1(k)| \leq 1 - 2^{-4} - a_2(k)$

$$a_2(k) = [1 - 2^{-7}]\, a_2(k-1)$$
$$+\, 2^{-7}\{\text{sgn}\, [p(k)]\, \text{sgn}\, [p(k-2)]$$
$$-\, f[a_1(k-1)]\, \text{sgn}\, [p(k)]\, \text{sgn}\, [p(k-1)]\} \qquad (15)$$

where $|a_2(k)| \leq 0.75$

$$p(k) = d_q(k) + s_{ez}(k) \qquad (16)$$

$$f(a_1) = \begin{cases} 4a_1 & , \text{if}\, |a_1| \leq 1/2 \\ \\ 2\text{sgn}(a_1), & \text{if}\, |a_1| > 1/2 \end{cases} \qquad (17)$$

where $\text{sgn}(0) = +1$

For the coefficients, $b_i(k)$, of the sixth-order all-zero filter, the adaptation procedure is similar, but the limit is implicit in the equations to a maximum of ± 2. The gradient function, in this case, is determined by the current difference signal, $d_q(k)$, and corresponding difference signal, $d_q(k-i)$, at the specific filter tap.

$$b_i(k) = [1 - 2^{-8}]\, b_i(k-1)$$
$$+\, 2^{-7}\text{sgn}\, [d_q(k)]\, \text{sgn}\, [d_q(k-i)] \qquad (18)$$

where $i = 1, 2, \ldots 6$ and $-2 \leq b_i(k) \leq +2$

Signal Conversion

Signal conversion consists of the conversion from an 8-bit log-PCM representation of a signal to a 13-bit linear PCM representation (note Figure 7), or the reverse (note Figure 8). Signal conversions of this type are described in the application report on COMPANDING ROUTINES FOR THE TMS32010. In the encoder, the log-PCM signal, $s(k)$, is expanded to create the linear-PCM value, $s_l(k)$. The decoder, on the other hand, compresses the reconstructed signal, $s_r(k)$, to create the log-PCM signal, $s_p(k)$.

Reconstructed Signal Synchronization

To avoid a cumulative distortion in synchronous tandem codings, an adjustment to the reconstructed signal is specified. The adjustment block, shown in Figure 8, estimates the quantization of the encoder by determining a difference signal and executing the adaptive quantization logic. The quantization result is an estimate of the received value of $I(k)$.

The difference signal, $d_x(k)$, is determined by subtracting the signal estimate, $s_e(k)$, from the linear-PCM signal, $s_{lx}(k)$, which is itself determined by expanding the log-PCM signal, $s_p(k)$.

$$d_x(k) = s_{lx}(k) - s_e(k) \qquad (19)$$

The adaptive quantization process produces the estimate of the ADPCM code value, $I_d(k)$. If the estimate implies a difference signal that is lower than the received interval boundary, the log-PCM code is changed to the next most positive value. An estimate implying a difference signal larger than the received interval boundary requires the log-PCM code to be changed to the next most negative value; otherwise, the log-PCM value is left unchanged. The adjusted log-PCM value is denoted as $s_d(k)$ in the following equation to differentiate it from the input value, $s_p(k)$.

$$s_d(k) = \begin{cases} s_p^+(k), \ d_x(k) < \text{lower interval boundary} \\ s_p^-(k), \ d_x(k) \geq \text{upper interval boundary} \\ s_p(k), \text{ otherwise} \end{cases} \quad (20)$$

where

$s_d(k)$ = output PCM of the decoder

$s_p^+(k)$ = next more positive PCM level (if $s_p(k)$ is the most positive level, then $s_p^+(k) = s_p(k)$)

$s_p^-(k)$ = next more negative PCM level (if $s_p(k)$ is the most negative level, then $s_p^-(k) = s_p(k)$)

FULL-DUPLEX IMPLEMENTATION OF ADPCM ON A TMS32010

The specific implementation of ADPCM presented here involves the use of a single TMS320M10 to accomplish a full-duplex transcoder. The TMS320M10 is a masked ROM, microcomputer version of the TMS32010, which requires no external program memories. A full-duplex transcoder provides transmission in both directions simultaneously. Such a transcoder is depicted in Figure 11. A complete system diagram of a full-duplex communications channel is shown in Figure 12. In comparison to current systems that modulate a 64-kbit/s A-law or μ-law PCM signal on a carrier for transmission, the described system transcodes the 64-kbit/s code to a 32-kbit/s code. This 32-kbit/s code, which requires correspondingly less bandwidth, is modulated on the carrier for transmission.

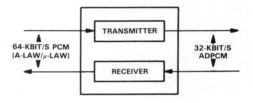

Figure 11. Full-Duplex ADPCM Transcoder

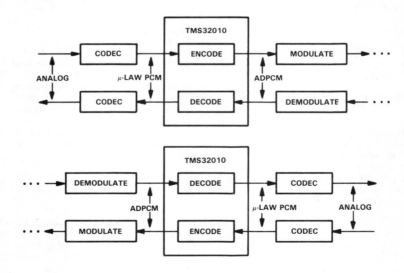

Figure 12. Full-Duplex Telecommunications Channel

Hardware Logic and I/O

The hardware required to implement the ADPCM system consists of an addition to an existing circuit. As shown in Figure 13, the TMS32010 addresses the external I/O blocks through its port addressing structure. The lower three address lines, A2-A0, form a port address that can be decoded by port decode logic to provide specific enable lines (e.g., WRTEN1 and RDEN1) to the various peripheral blocks. The TMS32010 reads and writes the 64-kbit/s data through the codec interface eight bits at a time. The sampling frequency is 8 kHz. For this full-duplex implementation, one sample is written and one sample is read every 125 μs.

Figure 13 also shows the serial interface to the codec that provides the μ-law companded PCM data, although this is not part of the transcoding system itself. The log-PCM signal may already be available (e.g., in existing digital telecom networks) and, as such, may be interfaced to the TMS32010 either directly as parallel data or serially through conversion logic. Parallel codecs are also becoming available to reduce the hardware logic and interface required for those systems which do not already include a codec. The TMS32010 is available at crystal and clock input rates of 20.5 MHz which may be divided down to provide the codec timing and further reduce the logic requirement.

At the other end of the transcoder function, the TMS32010 reads and writes the 32-kbit/s ADPCM data through the ADPCM interface four bits at a time for each 125-μs period. This interface provides four-bit parallel data which may be serialized, if required, for transmission or storage.

Software Logic and Flow

Tables 4 and 5 list the various blocks in the algorithm, directly relating them to Figures 7 and 8 by the signal names given in the description and function. The blocks are listed in the order in which they are executed. Also listed is processor demand or loading which consists of the amount of program memory used to implement the given function and the number of instruction cycles executed in worst case. There are more blocks in the table than are shown in the figures (e.g., the algorithm uses the adaptive predictor at one point to produce the signal estimate, and later returns to update or adapt the predictor coefficients). Each block has been implemented using the equations given in previous sections concerning the ADPCM algorithm. For convenience, the equations implemented in each block are listed in the description section for the block. A more detailed description of the TMS32010 implementation is given in the next section.

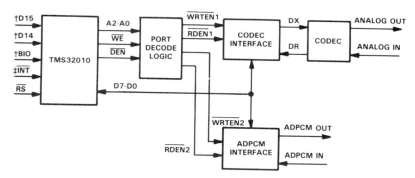

† Half-duplex, CCITT bit-compatible, version only
‡ Full-duplex version only

Figure 13. System Interface of a TMS32010 ADPCM Transcoder

Table 4. Full-Duplex Transmitter

Order	Function	Description	CPU Clocks	Program Memory (Words)
1.	INPUT PCM	Read an 8 bit μ-law PCM sample $[s(k)]$ and linearize it to a 12-bit sample $[s_l(k)]$.	7	0004
2.	COMPUTE SIGNAL ESTIMATE	Calculate the signal estimate $[s_e(k)]$ from the previous data samples $[d_q(k)]$ and reconstructed samples $[s_r(k)]$ through the predictor filter. (12),(11)	30	001E
3.	COMPUTE ADAPTIVE QUANTIZER	Calculate speed control $[a_l(k)]$ and quantizer scale factor $[y(k)]$ from past quantizer output $[I(k)]$. (6),(3)	33	0021
4.	COMPUTE DIFFERENCE SIGNAL	Calculate the difference signal $[d(k)]$ from the current sample $[s_l(k)]$ and signal estimate $[s_e(k)]$. (1)	3	0003
5.	COMPUTE QUANTIZED OUTPUT	Calculate the log of the difference signal $[d(k)]$ and adaptively quantize the result to yield the ADPCM output $[I(K)]$. (2)	46	00AD
6.	OUTPUT ADPCM	Write the ADPCM output $[I(k)]$.	2	0001
7.	COMPUTE RECON- STRUCTED SIGNAL	Calculate the inverse of the adaptively quantized signal $[d_q(k)]$ and the reconstructed signal difference $[s_r(k)]$. (10),(13)	43	0027
8.	COMPUTE SCALE FACTOR	Calculate the updates for the scale-factor adaptation. (4),(5)	46	002F
9.	COMPUTE SPEED CONTROL	Calculate the update for the speed-control adaptation. (8),(9),(7)	30	001B
10.	COMPUTE PREDICTOR ADAPTATION	Calculate the updates for the adaptive predictor filter coefficients. (18),(16),(17),(14),(15)	102	006B

Table 5. Full-Duplex Receiver

Order	Function	Description	CPU Clocks	Program Memory (Words)
1.	INPUT ADPCM	Read the ADPCM input [I(k)].	2	0001
2.	COMPUTE SIGNAL ESTIMATE	Calculate the signal estimate [$s_e(k)$] from the previous data samples [$d_q(k)$] and reconstructed samples [$s_r(k)$] through the predictor filter. (12),(11)	30	001E
3.	COMPUTE ADAPTIVE QUANTIZER	Calculate speed control [$a_l(k)$] and quantizer scale factor [y(k)] from the past quantizer output [I(k)]. (6),(3)	33	0021
4.	COMPUTE QUANTIZED DIFFERENCE	Calculate the inverse of the adaptively quantized signal [$d_q(k)$]. (10)	47	002F
5.	COMPUTE SCALE FACTOR	Calculate the updates for the scale-factor adaptation. (4),(5)	48	002F
6.	COMPUTE SPEED CONTROL	Calculate the update for the speed-control adaptation. (8),(9),(7)	29	001B
7.	COMPUTE RECON- STRUCTED SIGNAL	Calculate the reconstructed signal [$s_r(k)$]. (13)	3	0003
8.	COMPUTE PREDICTOR ADAPTATION	Calculate the updates for the adaptive predictor filter coefficients. (18),(16),(17),(14),(15)	90	006B
9.	COMPUTE LOG-PCM	Convert the reconstructed linear-PCM signal [$s_r(k)$] to a μ-law PCM signal [$s_p(k)$].	39	0074
10.	OUTPUT PCM	Write the μ-law output [s_p)k)].	2	0001
11.	WAIT	Spin until the next interrupt.	—	0006

Implementation and Advantages of TMS32010 Architecture

This implementation is only concerned with μ-law PCM, although A-law PCM may also be used. Additional information on log-PCM companding is found in an application report, COMPANDING ROUTINES FOR THE TMS32010. The implementation is simplified here so that the expansion is a simple table lookup which saves 21 instruction cycles over the algorithmic approach.

The processing of the signal through the predictor filter is similar to the processing discussed in the application report, IMPLEMENTATION OF FIR/IIR FILTERS WITH THE TMS32010. The filter used in this ADPCM algorithm is a combination of a second-order IIR filter and a sixth-order

all-zero or FIR filter. The filters are shown in Figures 9 and 10, respectively, with the system interaction shown in Figure 14.

Several manipulations of data format occur in adapting the predictor coefficients. In updating the coefficients of the all-zero filter (the B_i's), the coefficients that are normally Q14 numbers are loaded with a shift allowing the calculations to be done in a Q29 representation. This greatly simplifies the subtraction of the leakage term and the prediction gain. The leakage term, which occurs here in the predictor coefficient adaptation and also in the speed-control and scale-factor adaptation, controls the rate of change of the parameter away from zero and towards the absolute maximum limits of the particular parameter. The prediction gain also uses

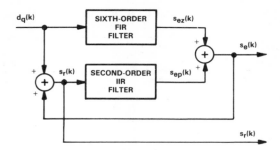

Figure 14. Predictor Filter

an approach whereby the signs are actually stored as a signed Q11 value. In this way, the product is a Q22 value of the correct sign and can be added to the B value, equivalent to a Q29 value times 2^{-7}. As with the filter process itself, the signs of the Dq values are propagated through each filter tap delay with the LTD instruction. An example for one of the B_i values is shown in Figure 15.

A similar process takes place in adapting the prediction coefficients (A_i's) in the second-order filter, although the fixed-point representation of the coefficients is Q26. The remaining requirement is to limit-check the A_i values.

The adaptive quantization section requires that the log (base 2) of the difference signal be taken, the result normalized, and the normalized value quantized. Taking the log (base 2) of a number is accomplished by using the approximation

$$\log_2(1 + x) = x \tag{21}$$

```
*;*****************************************************************
*;
*;   COMPUTE COEFFICIENTS OF THE 6TH-ORDER PREDICTOR
*;
*;   Bi(k) = [1 - 2**-8] * Bi(k-1)
*;           + 2**-7 * SGN[DQ(k)] * SGN[DQ(k-i)]
*;
*;         FOR  i = 1 ... 6
*;         AND Bi IS IMPLICITLY LIMITED TO +/- 2
*;
*;         NOTATION:    Bn   -- 16b TC (Q14)
*;                      SDQn -- +2048 IF DQn POSITIVE (Q11)
*;                              -2048 IF DQn NEGATIVE (Q11)
*;
*;*****************************************************************
*;
GETB6   LT    SDQ6         * (Q11)
        LAC   B6,15        * (Q29)
        SUB   B6,7         * B6 * 2**-8  (Q29)
        MPY   SDQ          * SGN(SDQ)*SGN(SDQ6)*2**-7 (Q29)
        LTD   SDQ5         * (Q11)
        SACH  B6,1         * (Q14)
        .
        .
        .
```

Figure 15. Predictor Coefficient Adaptation Code

The characteristic of the result is the bit position of the most significant one digit in the absolute value. The result can be represented as a Q7 value. Finding the most significant digit is most efficiently done by a binary search technique. This technique is discussed in the application report, FLOATING-POINT ARITHMETIC WITH THE TMS32010. Since the exponent is part of the number instead of being stored in a separate register, one of the auxiliary registers is loaded with the exponent value. The auxiliary register stores it in memory and adds it to the mantissa in the accumulator. A short example of this is shown in the excerpted code in Figure 16 where the signal has an assumed exponent value of 9.

Normalization of this log value is simply a subtraction of a scale factor which may be as large in fixed magnitude as the largest logarithmic value represented in Q7 notation. The result of the subtraction may be a negative value. Since the normalized result is to be quantized in a nonuniform manner and one of the quantization levels could contain both positive and negative values, the normalized result is scaled by adding a fixed value of 2048. Nonuniform quantization can be performed by a binary-type search technique. The normalization and quantization are included in the program shown in Figure 16.

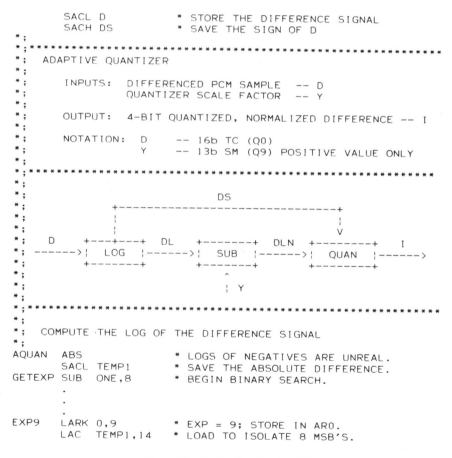

Figure 16. Adaptive Quantization Code

```
              SACH  TEMP1        * SAVE MANTISSA.
              LAC   TEMP1        * RELOAD FOR MANTISSA RECOMBINATION.
              B     GETMAN
               .
               .
               .
GETMAN  AND   M127         * MASK TO RETAIN ONLY SEVEN BITS.
        SAR   0,TEMP1      * MOVE EXPONENT TO MEMORY FROM AR0.
        ADD   TEMP1,7      * ADD EXPONENT TO MANTISSA FOR LOG VALUE.
*;
*;  SCALE BY SUBTRACTION
*;
SUBTB   ADD   ONE,11       * ADD AN OFFSET OF 2048.
        SUB   TEMP3        * TEMP3 = Y(K) >> 2

*;
*;  4-BIT QUANTIZER
*;
*;  QUANTIZATION TABLE FOR 32KB OUTPUT (OFFSET: 2048)
*;
ITAB1   EQU   2041
ITAB2   EQU   2171
ITAB3   EQU   2250
ITAB4   EQU   2309
ITAB5   EQU   2358
ITAB6   EQU   2404
ITAB7   EQU   2453
*;
QUAN    SUB   K2309        * ITAB4
        BGEZ  CI4TO7
CI0TO3  ADD   K138         * ITAB2          I = 0-3
        BGEZ  CI2TO3
CI0TO1  ADD   K130         * ITAB1          I = 0-1
        BGEZ  IEQ1
IEQ0    LACK  0
        B     GETIM
IEQ1    LACK  1
        B     GETIM
CI2TO3  SUB   K79          * ITAB3          I = 2-3
        BGEZ  IEQ3
IEQ2    LACK  2
        B     GETIM
IEQ3    LACK  3
        B     GETIM
CI4TO7  SUB   K95          * ITAB6          I = 4-7
        BGEZ  CI6TO7
CI5TO6  ADD   K46          * ITAB5          I = 5-6
        BGEZ  IEQ5
IEQ4    LACK  4
        B     GETIM
IEQ5    LACK  5
        B     GETIM
CI6TO7  SUB   K49          * ITAB6          I = 6-7
        BGEZ  IEQ7
```

Figure 16. Adaptive Quantization Code (Continued)

```
IEQ6    LACK 6
        B    GETIM
IEQ7    LACK 7
GETIM   SACL IM      * ACCUM = ¦I¦
        XOR  DS      * ADD SIGN BIT AND FLIP IF NECESSARY.
        AND  M15     * MASK FINAL FOUR-BIT VALUE.
        SACL I       * SAVE ADPCM OUTPUT VALUE.
        .
        .
```

Figure 16. Adaptive Quantization Code (Concluded)

Determining the inverse of the 4-bit quantized ADPCM value involves another technique. The code to complete this task is much shorter in program memory requirement and somewhat faster in execution time. The same type of approximation is involved in determining the antilog as used in taking the log,

$$\log_2{}^{-1}(x) = 1 + x \qquad (22)$$

After separating the exponent from the mantissa in the log representation, the quantized difference signal may be recovered by using the exponent to select a scaling factor. The scaling factor or multiplier is used to shift the mantissa to the proper representation, either right or left. Some of the multipliers may be stored as negative values rather than positive values, using the sign of the result to determine whether the answer is obtained from the high half of the accumulator (effectively a right shift) or from the low half of the accumulator (a left shift). The program for this process is shown in Figure 17.

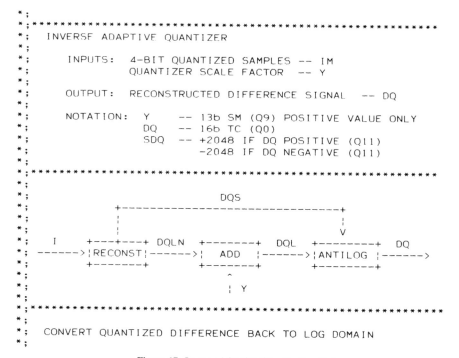

Figure 17. Inverse Adaptive Quantization Code

```
IAQUAN LAC   IM
       ADD   INQTAB      * RECONSTRUCTION TABLE
       TBLR  TEMP1       * READ NORMALIZED VALUE.
*;
*;  ADD NORMALIZING SCALE FACTOR BACK IN
*;
ADDA   LAC   TEMP1
       ADD   TEMP3       * Y >> 2
       AND   M2047
       SACL  TEMP2
*;
*;   CONVERT THE LOG VALUE TO THE LINEAR DOMAIN
*;
*;
ALOG   LAC   TEMP2,9     * EXTRACT EXPONENT.
       SACH  TEMP1       * SAVE EXPONENT VALUE.
       LACK  127
       AND   TEMP2       * MASK FOR LOG MANTISSA ONLY.
       ADD   ONE,7       * 1+x
       SACL  TEMP2       * EXTRACT MANTISSA.
       LT    TEMP2       * PREPARE TO SHIFT.
       LAC   TEMP1
       ADD   SHIFT       * LOOK UP MULTIPLIER.
       TBLR  TEMP3
       MPY   TEMP3       * MULTIPLY MANTISSA BY SHIFT FACTOR.
       PAC
       BLZ   LEFTSF      * NEGATIVE VALUES CORRESPOND TO LEFT SHIFT.
       SACH  DQ,1        * RIGHT SHIFT; SAVE MAGNITUDE OF DQ.
       B     ADDSGN
LEFTSF ABS               * LEFT SHIFT; RESTORE MAGNITUDE.
       SACL  DQ          * SAVE MAGNITUDE OF DQ.
ADDSGN LAC   ONE,11      * ASSUME POSITIVE AND SAVE THE SIGN.
       SACL  SDQ         *   (SIGN IS Q11; REMEMBER FILTER.)
       LAC   I           * CHECK SIGN OF SAMPLE.
       SUB   ONE,3
       BLZ   QSFA        * FINISHED FOR POSITIVE VALUES (I<8).
       ZAC
       SUB   DQ          * COMPUTE TWO'S COMPLEMENT OF THE MAGNITUDE.
       SACL  DQ          * SAVE NEGATIVE DQ VALUE.
       LAC   MINUS,11    * SIGN IS Q11; REMEMBER FILTER.
       SACL  SDQ         * SAVE SIGN.
       .
       .
       .

*;
*; INVERSE QUANTIZING TABLE
*;
IQTAB  BSS   0
       DATA  65401
       DATA  68
       DATA  165
       DATA  232
       DATA  285
       DATA  332
       DATA  377
       DATA  428
```

Figure 17. Inverse Adaptive Quantization Code (Continued)

```
*;
*; SHIFT MULTIPLIER TABLE
*;
SHFT    BSS   0
        DATA  256
        DATA  512
        DATA  1024
        DATA  2048
        DATA  4096
        DATA  8192
        DATA  16384
        DATA  -1
        DATA  -2
        DATA  -4
        DATA  -8
        DATA  -16
        DATA  -32
        DATA  -64
        DATA  -128
```

Figure 17. Inverse Adaptive Quantization Code (Concluded)

The adaptation of the speed-control and the scale-factor parameters, used to adapt the stepsize in the adaptive quantizer and inverse adaptive quantizer, requires multiple uses of the technique of adjusting the fixed-point representation. The Q point is adjusted for convenience of the table constants which are part of the adaptation process and for saving the output value from the accumulator. Some limit-checking must also take place in calculating the unlocked-scale factor and the speed-control parameter.

In the calculation of the locked-scale factor and its inclusion in the mixing process for determining the overall scale factor used for stepsize quantization, the parameter is maintained with a greater resolution (19 bits of value plus its sign) than can be stored in a single memory. Calculations involving this parameter must then become two stage, both in terms of accumulations and in determining products. The code involving this parameter is listed in Figures 18 and 19.

```
*;
*;****************************************************************
*;
*;   QUANTIZER SCALE FACTOR ADAPTATION
*;
*;      INPUT:   I : 32KB CODED SAMPLES
*;
*;      OUTPUT:  YU,YL : NEXT SAMPLE SCALE FACTOR
*;
*;      NOTATION:   Y    -- 13b SM (Q9) POSITIVE VALUE ONLY
*;                  YU   -- 13b SM (Q9) POSITIVE VALUE ONLY
*;                  YL   -- 19b SM (Q15) POSITIVE VALUE ONLY
*;
*;****************************************************************
*;
          .
          .
          .
*;
*;   UPDATE SLOW ADAPTATION SCALE FACTOR -- CONSTANT = 1/64
*;
*;   YL(k) = (1-2**-6)*YL(k-1) + 2**-6 * YU(k)
*;
FILTE  LAC   YLH,6      * SHIFT YL LEFT BY 6.
       SACL  TEMP1      * TEMP1 = YLH * 2**6
       LAC   YLL,6
       SACL  TEMP2
       SACH  TEMP3      * TEMP3 | TEMP2 = YLL * 2**6
       LAC   TEMP3      * SUPPRESS SIGN EXTENSION.
       AND   M63
       SACL  TEMP3
       ZALH  TEMP1
       ADDH  TEMP3
       ADDS  TEMP2      * ACCUM = YL * 2**6
       SUBH  YLH
       SUBS  YLL        * ACCUM = YL * 2**6 - YL
       ADD   YU,6       * ACCUM = YL * 2**6 - YL + YU
       SACL  TEMP1
       SACH  TEMP2      * RESULT = YL (SHIFTED LEFT BY 6)
       LAC   TEMP1,10   * SHIFT RESULT RIGHT 6 --> q15
       SACH  TEMP1
       LAC   TEMP1
       AND   M1023      * MASK SIGN EXTENSION.
       ADD   TEMP2,10
       SACL  YLL        * SAVE YLL.
       SACH  YLH
       LACK  7          * MASK UPPER 13 BITS.
       AND   YLH
       SACL  YLH        * SAVE YLH.
          .
          .
```

Figure 18. Quantizer Scale-Factor Adaptation: Locked-Factor Calculation

```
   .
   .
   .
*;
*;  FORM LINEAR COMBINATION OF FAST AND SLOW SCALE FACTORS
*;
*;  Y(k) = (1-AL(k))*YL(k-1) + AL(k)*YU(k-1)
*;
MIX     LAC   YLL,10      * SHIFT YL RIGHT BY 6.
        SACH  TEMP3       * (IE SCALE YL TO MATCH YU SINCE YL
        LAC   TEMP3       *  CONTAINS 6 MORE LSB'S)
        AND   M1023
        ADD   YLH,10
        SACL  TEMP3       * LOW HALF
        LAC   YU
        SUB   TEMP3       * YU-(YLL>>6)
        SACL  TEMP3
        ZALH  YLH
        ADDS  YLL
        LT    AL          * AL IS IN 1.Q6
        MPY   TEMP3
        APAC              * YL + AL*(YU-(YLL>>6))
        SACL  TEMP3
        SACH  TEMP2       * TEMP2 : TEMP3 = Y * 2**6
        LAC   TEMP3,10    * SHIFT RIGHT BY 6.
        SACH  TEMP3
        LAC   TEMP3
        AND   M1023       * MASK SIGN EXTENSION.
        ADD   TEMP2,10
        AND   M8191
        SACL  Y           * SAVE Y.
        LAC   Y,14
        SACH  TEMP3       * SAVE Y >> 2 .
   .
   .
   .
```

Figure 19. Quantizer Scale-Factor Adaptation: Mixing

CCITT IMPLEMENTATION OF ADPCM ON A TMS32010

The implementation of ADPCM that produces a bit-for-bit compatible solution with the CCITT test vectors uses a single TMS320M10 to accomplish a half-duplex transcoder. This solution can provide capability as either a transmitter or a receiver using either A-law or μ-law companding.

Hardware Logic and I/O

The hardware system for this transcoder implementation differs from Figure 13 in that data pins D15 and D14 are used to determine the mode of operation. Table 6 shows the operating mode for the various combined states of the data pin inputs.

Additionally, as has been noted in Figure 13, the interrupt or sample timing is an input to the INT pin in

Table 6. Operating Mode Selection

D15*	D14*	Operating Mode
L	L	μ-law transmitter
L	H	μ-law receiver
H	L	A-law transmitter
H	H	A-law receiver

*H = High logic level
 L = Low logic level

the full-duplex implementation; here it is an input to the BIO pin. Each 125-μs period, the TMS32010 reads a 64-kbit/s sample from the codec and writes a 32-kbit/s sample to the ADPCM interface, or it reads the 4-bit ADPCM sample and writes an 8-bit PCM sample to the codec.

For real-time execution, the TMS32010 requires the use of a 25-MHz clock input.

Software Logic and Flow

Tables 7 and 8 list the various blocks in the algorithm, directly relating them to Figures 7 and 8 by the signal names given in the description and function. No differentiation is made between the transmitter or receiver using A-law or μ-law. The blocks are listed in the order in which they are executed. Also listed is processor demand or loading which consists of the amount of program memory used to implement the given function and the number of instruction cycles executed in worst case. There are more blocks in the tables than are shown in the figures (e.g., the algorithm uses the adaptive predictor at one point to produce the signal estimate, and later returns to update or adapt the predictor coefficients). Each block has been implemented using the equations given in previous sections concerning the ADPCM algorithm. For convenience, the equations implemented in each block are listed in the description section for the block. Additional details of the TMS32010 implementation are given in the next section, especially as they differ from the full-duplex implementation. The appendix contains a complete listing of the code.

Table 7. CCITT Transmitter

Order	Function	Description	CPU Clocks	Program Memory (Words)
1.	INPUT PCM	Read an 8 bit log-PCM sample [s(k)] and linearize it to a 12-bit sample [$s_l(k)$].	25 μ-law 24 A-law	0024 μ-law 0031 A-law
2.	COMPUTE SIGNAL ESTIMATE	Calculate the signal estimate [$s_e(k)$] from the previous data samples [$d_q(k)$] and reconstructed samples [$s_r(k)$] through the predictor filter. (12), (11)	396	0167
3.	COMPUTE ADAPTIVE QUANTIZER	Calculate speed control [$a_l(k)$] and quantizer scale factor [y(k)] from past quantizer output [I(k)]. (6), (3)	30	001E
4.	COMPUTE DIFFERENCE SIGNAL	Calculate the difference signal [d(k)] from the current sample [$s_l(k)$] and signal estimate [$s_e(k)$]. (1)	3	0003
5.	COMPUTE QUANTIZED OUTPUT	Calculate the log of the difference signal [d(k)] and adaptively quantize the result to yield the ADPCM output [I(k)]. (2)	42	00AD
6.	OUTPUT ADPCM	Write the ADPCM output [I(k)].	6	0005
7.	COMPUTE RECON- STRUCTED SIGNAL	Calculate the inverse of the adaptively quantized signal [$d_q(k)$] and the reconstructed signal difference [$s_r(k)$]. (10), (13)	66	00B0
8.	COMPUTE SCALE FACTOR	Calculate the updates for the scale-factor adaptation. (4), (5)	33	0022
9.	COMPUTE SPEED CONTROL	Calculate the update for the speed-control adaptation. (8), (9), (7)	30	001C
10.	COMPUTE PREDICTOR ADAPTATION	Calculate the updates for the adaptive predictor filter coefficients. (18), (16), (17), (14), (15)	111	0074
11.	WAIT	Spin until the next sample is available.	2 +	0004

Table 8. CCITT Receiver

Order	Function	Description	CPU Clocks	Program Memory (Words)
1.	INPUT ADPCM	Read the ADPCM input [I(k)].	10	0009
2.	COMPUTE SIGNAL ESTIMATE	Calculate the signal estimate [$s_e(k)$] from the previous data samples [$d_q(k)$] and reconstructed samples [$s_r(k)$] through the predictor filter. (12), (11)	396	0167
3.	COMPUTE ADAPTIVE QUANTIZER	Calculate speed control [$a_l(k)$] and quantizer scale factor [y(k)] from past quantizer output [I(k)]. (6), (3)	30	001E
4.	COMPUTE QUANTIZED DIFFERENCE AND RECON-STRUCTED SIGNAL	Calculate the inverse of the adaptively quantized signal [$d_q(k)$] and the reconstructed signal [$s_r(k)$]. (10), (13)	66	00B0
5.	COMPUTE SCALE FACTOR	Calculate the updates for the scale-factor adaptation. (4), (5)	33	0022
6.	COMPUTE SPEED CONTROL	Calculate the update for the speed-control adaptation. (8), (9), (7)	30	001C
7.	COMPUTE PREDICTOR ADAPTATION	Calculate the updates for the adaptive predictor filter coefficients. (18), (16), (17), (14), (15)	111	0074
8.	COMPUTE LOG-PCM	Convert the reconstructed linear-PCM signal [$s_r(k)$] to a log-PCM signal [$s_p(k)$].	35 μ-law 33 A-law	0074 μ-law 0072 A-law
9.	SYNCHRON-OUS CODING ADJUSTMENT	Calculate an ADPCM signal from the output [$s_p(k)$] and adjust to create [$s_d(k)$] if it differs from [I(k)].	63	00DA
10.	OUTPUT PCM	Write the log-PCM output [$s_d(k)$].	4	0003
11.	WAIT	Spin until the next interrupt.	2 +	0004

Implementation and Advantages of TMS32010 Architecture

Many of the same features are used in the bit-compatible implementation as were discussed in the full-duplex implementation. Some changes are imperative, since performance to the recommended specification requires executing certain calculations in a floating-point representation. These changes or additions require further modifications in order to limit the required amount of program memory to the internal memory space of the TMS32010.

One of the first observed requirements is that the processor must be capable of doing either A-law or μ-law companding and function as either a transmitter or a receiver.

The burden of determining the mode of operation is simplified by selecting one of the four modes from information available at the time of reset, and then executing from one of the four control loops until the next reset. Each loop, therefore, tests the $\overline{BIO}$ pin to determine when the next input sample is ready, rather than depending on the hardware interrupt.

The requirement of selecting either A-law of μ-law companding also means that a table lookup approach is beyond the program memory capacity. The conversion must be done algorithmically to reduce the amount of memory. Figures 20 and 21 illustrate μ-law companding as it is implemented in this algorithm.

```
XMTMU   IN      SCRACH,ADC
EXPNDU  LAC     SCRACH,8    ; SEEE MMMM 0000 0000
        XOR     KFF00       ; INVERT FROM TRANSMISSION FORMAT
        SACL    TEMP1       ; SAVE VALUE FOR PCM SIGN
        AND     M32767      ; 0EFE MMMM 0000 0000
        SACH    TEMP2,4     ; SAVE EXPONENT VALUE
        AND     M4095       ; 0000 MMMM 0000 0000
        ADD     BIAS,7      ; 0001 MMMM 1000 0000
        SACL    SCRACH
        LAC     TEMP1
        SACH    TEMP1       ; SIGN = FFFF OR 0000
        LACK    SBASE
        ADD     TEMP2,1     ; CALCULATE PCM SHIFT ADDRESS
        CALA
        SUB     BIAS,12     ; 0000000X XXXXXXXX XXXX0000 00000000
        SACH    SAMPLE,4
        LAC     SAMPLE      ; 000XXXXX XXXXXXXX
        XOR     TEMP1       ; POS - DO NOTHING : NEG - 1's COMP
        SUB     TEMP1       ; POS - DO NOTHING : NEG - 2's COMP
        SACL    SAMPLE
         .
         .
         .
*;
SBASE   LAC     SCRACH,5    ; 00000000 0000001M MMM10000 00000000
        RET
        LAC     SCRACH,6    ; 00000000 000001MM MM100000 00000000
        RET
        LAC     SCRACH,7    ; 00000000 00001MMM M1000000 00000000
        RET
        LAC     SCRACH,8    ; 00000000 0001MMMM 10000000 00000000
        RET
        LAC     SCRACH,9    ; 00000000 001MMMM1 00000000 00000000
        RET
        LAC     SCRACH,10   ; 00000000 01MMMM10 00000000 00000000
        RET
        LAC     SCRACH,11   ; 00000000 1MMMM100 00000000 00000000
        RET
        LAC     SCRACH,12   ; 00000001 MMMM1000 00000000 00000000
        RET
```

Figure 20. μ-Law Expansion Code

```
          LAC      SR                  ; GET RECONSTRUCTED SIGNAL
*;
*; COMPRESS--CONVERT TO PCM
*;
CMPRSU    SACH     TEMP4               ; SAVE SIGN OF SR
          ABS
          ADD      BIAS                ; ADD BIAS
          SACL     SCRACH              ; SAVE BIASED PCM VALUE
          SUB      ONE,9               ; EXP = 7 - 4 OR 3 - 0
          BGEZ     SCL427
SCL023    ADD      THREE,7             ; EXP = 3 - 2 OR 1 - 0
          BGEZ     SCL223
SCL021    ADD      ONE,6               ; EXP = 1 OR 0
          BGEZ     SCALE1
SCALE0    LAC      M15,1               ; EXP = 0
          AND      SCRACH              ; MASK FOR MANTISSA
          SACL     SCRACH
          ADD      BIAS
          SACL     SAMPLE              ; BIASED QUANTIZED VALUE
          LAC      SCRACH,15
          LARK     0,0
          B        FINI
SCALE1    LAC      M15,2               ; EXP = 1
          AND      SCRACH              ; MASK FOR MANTISSA
          SACL     SCRACH
          ADD      BIAS,1
          SACL     SAMPLE              ; BIASED QUANTIZED VALUE
          LAC      SCRACH,14
          LARK     0,1
          B        FINI
           .
           .
           .
FINI      SACH     SCRACH              ; SAVE NORMALIZED MANTISSA
          LAC      SCRACH
          SAR      0,TEMP1
          ADD      TEMP1,4             ; ADD EXPONENT
CLNUP     ADD      TEMP4,7
          AND      M255
          SACL     SCRACH              ; 2's COMPLEMENT OF MULAW-PCM
          LAC      SAMPLE              ; REMOVE BIAS FROM QUANTIZED VALUE
          SUB      BIAS
          XOR      TEMP4
          SUB      TEMP4
          SACL     SAMPLE              ; 2's COMPLEMENT OF QUANTIZED SAMPLE
*;
          CALL     AQUAN
*;
          CALL     SYNC
*;
          XOR      M255                ; FLIP BITS FOR TRANSMISSION
          SACL     SCRACH
          OUT      SCRACH,DAC
```

Figure 21. μ-**Law Compression Code**

The predictor filter implementation is also modified from what has been previously presented. In the CCITT recommendation, the processing of the signal through the predictor filter is performed in a floating-point format. This requirement leads to several modifications. First, all input signals to the filter, $d_q(k)$ and $s_r(k)$, must be converted to a floating-point notation. The conversion to this notation is accomplished by a binary search of the original fixed-point word. As previously mentioned, this technique is explained in some detail in the application report, FLOATING-POINT ARITHMETIC WITH THE TMS32010. Second, the filter coefficients, $a_i(k)$ and $b_i(k)$, must also be floated for each sample so that a floating-point multiply can be executed for each filter tap.

Accumulation of the filter taps is carried out in fixed-point notation. Fixing a floating-point number is equivalent to the scaling presented for taking the anti-log of a number. Some of the floating-point results must be left-shifted, while others need to be right-shifted. The shift is accomplished by use of a scaling factor or multiplier, selected by the exponent sum of the floating-point multiply. Positive multipliers are used to indicate what is effectively a right shift with the result being stored from the high half of the accumulator. Negative multipliers indicate that the result is in the low half of the accumulator and is used for values which have been left shifted.

The process of a single filter tap, not including the code to float the signal and the coefficient, is shown in Figure 22.

```
*;************************************************************
*;
*;    COMPUTE SEZ -- PARTIAL SIGNAL ESTIMATE
*;
*;    SEZ(k) = B1(k-1)*DQ(k-1) + ... + B6(k-1)*DQ(k-6)
*;
*;         MULTIPLIES ARE DONE IN FLOATING POINT
*;           DQ's ARE STORED IN FLOATING-POINT NOTATION
*;           B's ARE FLOATED EACH PASS
*;
*;         NOTATION: DQnEXP    -- 4 bits + OFFSET
*;                   DQnMAN*8  -- 9 bits
*;                   Bn        -- 16 b TC ; q14
*;                   SEZ       -- 16 b TC ; q0
*;
*;************************************************************
*;
SIGDIF   LAC      B6,14    ; COMPUTE B6*DQ5.
         CALL     FLOAT    ; RET/W MANTISSA IN TEMP1; EXP IN ACC.
         ADD      DQ5EXP
         SACL     SUM1
         LAR      0,SUM1   ; EXP OF PRODUCT.
         LT       DQ5MAN   ; DQnMAN SCALED BY 2**3.
         LAC      THREE,7  ; PRODUCT FUDGE FACTOR (48*8).
         MPY      TEMP1
         LTA      *,0      ; B6MAN*(DQ5MAN*8)+(48*8)
         AND      KFF80    ; SAVE ONLY 8 MSB'S.
         SACL     TEMP1
         MPY      TEMP1    ; APPLY SHIFT FACTOR.
         PAC
         BLZ      RS1      ; EXP >= 26
         SACH     SUM1,1   ; EXP <  26
CHK1     ZALS     B6       ; CHECK SIGN OF PRODUCT.
         XOR      SDQ6
         AND      K32768
         BZ       POS1
NEG1     ZAC               ; NEGATE IF NECESSARY.
         SUB      SUM1
```

Figure 22. Predictor Filter Execution

```
          SACL     SUM1
POS1      LAC      B5,14       ; COMPUTE B5*DQ4.
          .
          .
          .
RS1       ABS                  ; MAKE POSITIVE BEFORE MASK.
          AND      M32767      ; KEEP LOWER 15 BITS.
          SACL     SUM1        ; SAVE RESULT.
          B        CHK1
```

Figure 22. Predictor Filter Execution (Concluded)

SUMMARY

The TMS32010 provides an efficient solution to transcoding a 64-kbit/s PCM signal to a 32-kbit/s bit stream. Transcoding, as described in this application report, is an effective way to maintain the signal quality provided by 7-bit PCM while reducing the data rate.

The basic ADPCM algorithm has been implemented in two slightly different ways. One solution provides CCITT bit-for-bit compatibility. Using this algorithm, a half-duplex transcoder is created that can transcode either A-law or μ-law signals as either a transmitter or a receiver. No external program memory is required for this implementation, although it does require the use of a 25-MHz TMS32010 microprocessor. The second described solution is particularly attractive since it uses a single, 20.5-MHz TMS32010 microprocessor that requires no external program memory to perform a real-time full-duplex (non-CCITT) channel transcoding.

In selecting one of these two solutions, the primary consideration is the network interfacing requirement. For systems that only have analog interfaces to other parts of the network, the full-duplex solution will provide the best choice. On the other hand, a network that may include a digital interface to other ADPCM transcoders will probably require the CCITT bit-compatible solution. Both solutions provide high-quality signal transcoding.

A complete assembled code listing is provided in the appendix of this report and is also available in 1600-BPI VAX/VMS tape format. The software may be purchased by ordering the TMS32010 Software Exchange Library, TMDC3240212-18, from Texas Instruments. For further information, please contact your nearest TI sales representative.

REFERENCES

"Recommendation G.721, 32 kbit/s Adaptive Differential Pulse Code Modulation," *CCITT* (1984).

N.S. Jayant (ed.), *Waveform Quantization and Coding,* IEEE Press (1976).

N.S. Jayant and Peter Noll, *Digital Coding of Waveforms,* Prentice-Hall (1984).

L.R. Rabiner and R.W. Schafer, *Digital Processing of Speech Signals,* Prentice-Hall (1978).

J.C. Bellamy, *Digital Telephony,* John Wiley & Sons (1982).

Bernhard E. Keiser, *Digital Telephony: Speech Digitization,* George Washington University (1981).

Companding Routines for the TMS32010, Texas Instruments Incorporated (1984).

Floating-Point Arithmetic with the TMS32010, Texas Instruments Incorporated (1984).

Implementation of FIR/IIR Filters with the TMS32010, Texas Instruments Incorporated (1984).

TMS32010 User's Guide, Texas Instruments Incorporated (1983).

Appendix II

ADPCM Assembly Language Programs

```
CCITT        32010 FAMILY MACRO ASSEMBLER    PC2.1 84.107    16:36:03  03-20-85
                                                                 PAGE 0001

 0001                     COPY    INPUT.ASM
A0001                     IDT     'CCITT'
A0002                     OPTION  XREF
A0003            *;
A0004            *;*************************************************************
A0005            *;*************************************************************
A0006            *; This is the source module for a half-duplex CCITT
A0007            *; compatible 32-kbps ADPCM speech system. The transmitter
A0008            *; assumes that log-PCM data will be available at each
A0009            *; interrupt (every 125 microseconds) in the lower 8 bits of
A0010            *; the data bus via I/O port 1 and it supplies ADPCM data on
A0011            *; the lower 4 bits of the bus via port 2. The receiver does
A0012            *; the inverse.  An interrupt in this case is determined by
A0013            *; polling the BIO line, with a low signal level signifying
A0014            *; the presence of a new data sample.
A0015            *;
A0016            *; The 'R' reset function in the CCITT spec is implemented
A0017            *; with a hardware reset. At the time of reset, it is
A0018            *; assumed that the operating mode has been established and
A0019            *; input via the upper two bits of the data bus.  The bit
A0020            *; condition is read from port 0 so as not to disrupt any
A0021            *; pending data sample on either of the other two ports.
A0022            *; Since it is anticipated that the mode pins will be
A0023            *; selected and maintained in a manner similar to a hardwire
A0024            *; selection, the actual port from which the mode is read
A0025            *; is arbitrary.
A0026            *;
A0027            *;*************************************************************
A0028            *;
A0029            *; System I/O channel assignments
A0030            *;
A0031      0001  ADC     EQU     1        ; codec input
A0032      0001  DAC     EQU     1        ; codec output
A0033      0002  CCITT   EQU     2        ; adpcm output/input
A0034      0000  CTL     EQU     0        ; control input to select mode
A0035            *;                       ; 0000 = mulaw transmitter
A0036            *;                       ; 4000 = mulaw receiver
A0037            *;                       ; 8000 = alaw transmitter
A0038            *;                       ; C000 = alaw receiver
A0039            *;
A0040            *;*************************************************************
A0041 0000               AORG    0
A0042            *;
A0043 0000 F900          B       RESET    ; power-up reset
     0001 0542
A0044            *;
A0045            *;*************************************************************
A0046            *; INTERRUPT HANDLING ROUTINE -- SYSTEM HANDLES CODEC
A0047            *; SAMPLES ON A SAMPLE BY SAMPLE BASIS.
A0048            *;*************************************************************
A0049            *;
A0050 0002 F900  INTRPT B        INTRPT
     0003 0002
A0051            *;
```

```
A0053                    *;
A0054                    *;   MU-LAW TRANSMITTER
A0055                    *;
A0056 0004 411B  XMTMU  IN      SCRACH,ADC   ; input mu-law PCM
A0057                    *;
A0058                    *;*****************************************************
A0059                    *;  MU-LAW TO LINEAR PCM EXPANSION
A0060                    *;
A0061                    *;     INPUT:  MU-LAW PCM SAMPLE  -- S  (SCRACH)
A0062                    *;
A0063                    *;     OUTPUT: LINEAR PCM SAMPLE  -- SL (SAMPLE)
A0064                    *;
A0065                    *;     NOTATION:  S  -- 8b SM (Q4)
A0066                    *;                SL -- 14b TC (Q0)
A0067                    *;
A0068                    *;*****************************************************
A0069                    *;
A0070                    *;                     S   +--------+  SL
A0071                    *;                 ------->| EXPAND |------->
A0072                    *;                         +--------+
A0073                    *;
A0074                    *;*****************************************************
A0075                    *;
A0076 0005 281B  EXPNDU LAC     SCRACH,8     ; seee mmmm 0000 0000
A0077 0006 7875         XOR     KFF00        ; SEEE MMMM 0000 0000
A0078 0007 5021         SACL    TEMP1        ; save value for PCM sign
A0079 0008 7974         AND     M32767       ; 0EEE MMMM 0000 0000
A0080 0009 5C22         SACH    TEMP2,4      ; save exponent value
A0081 000A 7972         AND     M4095        ; 0000 MMMM 0000 0000
A0082 000B 074D         ADD     BIAS,7       ; 0001 MMMM 1000 0000
A0083 000C 501B         SACL    SCRACH
A0084 000D 2021         LAC     TEMP1
A0085 000E 5821         SACH    TEMP1        ; sign = FFFF or 0000
A0086 000F 7E24         LACK    SBASE
A0087 0010 0122         ADD     TEMP2,1      ; calculate PCM shift address
A0088 0011 7F8C         CALA
A0089 0012 1C4D         SUB     BIAS,12 ; 0000000X XXXXXXXX XXXX0000 00000000
A0090 0013 5C26         SACH    SAMPLE,4
A0091 0014 2026         LAC     SAMPLE       ; 000X XXXX XXXX XXXX
A0092 0015 7821         XOR     TEMP1        ; pos - no change : neg - 1's compl
A0093 0016 1021         SUB     TEMP1        ; pos - no change : neg - 2's compl
A0094 0017 5026         SACL    SAMPLE
A0095                    *;
A0096                    *; Now convert PCM value in SAMPLE to ADPCM value in I
A0097                    *;
A0098 0018 F800  GETI   CALL    SIGDIF
      0019 01B3
A0099 001A F800         CALL    AQUAN
      001B 02AA
A0100 001C 5001         SACL    I
A0101 001D 4A01         OUT     I,CCITT      ; output ADPCM
A0102 001E F800         CALL    PRDICT
      001F 0355
A0103 0020 F600  MULAWX BIOZ    XMTMU        ; wait for next sample
      0021 0004
A0104 0022 F900         B       MULAWX
      0023 0020
```

```
CCITT          32010 FAMILY MACRO ASSEMBLER    PC2.1 84.107      16:36:03  03-20-85
                                                                       PAGE 0003

A0105                    *;
A0106 0024 251B   SBASE  LAC    SCRACH,5  ;  00000000 0000001M MMM10000 00000000
A0107 0025 7F8D          RET
A0108 0026 261B          LAC    SCRACH,6  ;  00000000 000001MM MM100000 00000000
A0109 0027 7F8D          RET
A0110 0028 271B          LAC    SCRACH,7  ;  00000000 00001MMM M1000000 00000000
A0111 0029 7F8D          RET
A0112 002A 281B          LAC    SCRACH,8  ;  00000000 0001MMMM 10000000 00000000
A0113 002B 7F8D          RET
A0114 002C 291B          LAC    SCRACH,9  ;  00000000 001MMMM1 00000000 00000000
A0115 002D 7F8D          RET
A0116 002E 2A1B          LAC    SCRACH,10 ;  00000000 01MMMM10 00000000 00000000
A0117 002F 7F8D          RET
A0118 0030 2B1B          LAC    SCRACH,11 ;  00000000 1MMMM100 00000000 00000000
A0119 0031 7F8D          RET
A0120 0032 2C1B          LAC    SCRACH,12 ;  00000001 MMMM1000 00000000 00000000
A0121 0033 7F8D          RET
```

Appendix II

```
CCITT        32010 FAMILY MACRO ASSEMBLER    PC2.1 84.107    16:36:03  03-20-85
                                                                PAGE 0004
A0123                   *;
A0124                   *;   A-LAW TRANSMITTER
A0125                   *;
A0126 0034 411B  XMTA   IN      SCRACH,ADC  ; input A-law PCM
A0127                   *;
A0128                   *;*****************************************************
A0129                   *; A-LAW TO LINEAR PCM EXPANSION
A0130                   *;
A0131                   *;      INPUT:  A-LAW PCM SAMPLE  -- S  (SCRACH)
A0132                   *;
A0133                   *;      OUTPUT: LINEAR PCM SAMPLE  -- SL (SAMPLE)
A0134                   *;
A0135                   *;      NOTATION:  S  -- 8b SM (Q4)
A0136                   *;                 SL -- 14b TC (Q0)
A0137                   *;
A0138                   *;*****************************************************
A0139                   *;
A0140                   *;               S    +--------+   SL
A0141                   *;               ------->¦ EXPAND ¦------->
A0142                   *;                    +--------+
A0143                   *;
A0144                   *;*****************************************************
A0145                   *;
A0146 0035 281B  EXPNDA LAC     SCRACH,8   ; sEEE MMMM 0000 0000
A0147 0036 7848         XOR     K32768     ; SEEE MMMM 0000 0000
A0148 0037 5021         SACL    TEMP1      ; save value for PCM sign
A0149 0038 7974         AND     M32767     ; 0EEE MMMM 0000 0000
A0150 0039 5C22         SACH    TEMP2,4    ; save exponent value
A0151 003A 7972         AND     M4095      ; 0000 MMMM 0000 0000
A0152 003B 501B         SACL    SCRACH
A0153 003C 2021         LAC     TEMP1
A0154 003D 5821         SACH    TEMP1      ; sign = FFFF or 0000
A0155 003E 7E52         LACK    SBASEA
A0156 003F 0222         ADD     TEMP2,2    ; calculate PCM shift address
A0157 0040 7F8C         CALA
A0158 0041 5C26         SACH    SAMPLE,4
A0159 0042 2026         LAC     SAMPLE     ; 000X XXXX XXXX XXXX
A0160 0043 7821         XOR     TEMP1      ; pos - no change : neg - 1's compl
A0161 0044 1021         SUB     TEMP1      ; pos - no change : neg - 2's compl
A0162 0045 5026         SACL    SAMPLE
A0163                   *
A0164                   *;
A0165                   *; Now convert PCM value in SAMPLE to ADPCM value in I
A0166                   *;
A0167 0046 F800         CALL    SIGDIF
      0047 01B3
A0168 0048 F800         CALL    AQUAN
      0049 02AA
A0169 004A 5001         SACL    I
A0170 004B 4A01         OUT     I,CCITT    ; output ADPCM
A0171 004C F800         CALL    PRDICT
      004D 0355
A0172 004E F600  ALAWX  BIOZ    XMTA       ; wait for next sample
      004F 0034
A0173 0050 F900         B       ALAWX
      0051 004E
A0174                   *;
```

```
A0175 0052 261B  SBASEA LAC    SCRACH,6   ; 00000000 000000MM MM000000 00000000
A0176 0053 0D4C         ADD    ONE,13     ; 00000000 000000MM MM100000 00000000
A0177 0054 7F8D         RET
A0178 0055 7F80         NOP
A0179 0056 261B         LAC    SCRACH,6   ; 00000000 000001MM MM100000 00000000
A0180 0057 0671         ADD    BIASA,6    ; 00000000 000001MM MM100000 00000000
A0181 0058 7F8D         RET
A0182 0059 7F80         NOP
A0183 005A 271B         LAC    SCRACH,7   ; 00000000 00000MMM M0000000 00000000
A0184 005B 0771         ADD    BIASA,7    ; 00000000 00001MMM M1000000 00000000
A0185 005C 7F8D         RET
A0186 005D 7F80         NOP
A0187 005E 281B         LAC    SCRACH,8   ; 00000000 0000MMMM 00000000 00000000
A0188 005F 0871         ADD    BIASA,8    ; 00000000 0001MMMM 10000000 00000000
A0189 0060 7F8D         RET
A0190 0061 7F80         NOP
A0191 0062 291B         LAC    SCRACH,9   ; 00000000 000MMMM0 00000000 00000000
A0192 0063 0971         ADD    BIASA,9    ; 00000000 001MMMM1 00000000 00000000
A0193 0064 7F8D         RET
A0194 0065 7F80         NOP
A0195 0066 2A1B         LAC    SCRACH,10  ; 00000000 00MMMM00 00000000 00000000
A0196 0067 0A71         ADD    BIASA,10   ; 00000000 01MMMM10 00000000 00000000
A0197 0068 7F8D         RET
A0198 0069 7F80         NOP
A0199 006A 2B1B         LAC    SCRACH,11  ; 00000000 0MMMM000 00000000 00000000
A0200 006B 0B71         ADD    BIASA,11   ; 00000000 1MMMM100 00000000 00000000
A0201 006C 7F8D         RET
A0202 006D 7F80         NOP
A0203 006E 2C1B         LAC    SCRACH,12  ; 00000000 MMMM0000 00000000 00000000
A0204 006F 0C71         ADD    BIASA,12   ; 00000001 MMMM1000 00000000 00000000
A0205 0070 7F8D         RET
```

Appendix II

```
CCITT        32010 FAMILY MACRO ASSEMBLER    PC2.1 84.107      16:36:03  03-20-85
                                                                PAGE 0006

A0207                    *;
A0208                    *;   MU-LAW RECEIVER
A0209                    *;
A0210  0071 4201  RCVMU  IN     I,CCITT      ; input ADPCM
A0211                    *;
A0212  0072 2001         LAC    I            ; determine magnitude of ADPCM
A0213  0073 5002         SACL   IM
A0214  0074 134C         SUB    ONE,3
A0215  0075 FA00         BLZ    DO32KU
       0076 007A
A0216  0077 2002         LAC    IM
A0217  0078 786D         XOR    M15
A0218  0079 5002         SACL   IM
A0219                    *;
A0220                    *; compute pcm output
A0221                    *;
A0222  007A F800  DO32KU CALL   SIGDIF
       007B 01B3
A0223  007C F800         CALL   PRDICT
       007D 0355
A0224                    *;
A0225                    *;************************************************************
A0226                    *; LINEAR TO U-LAW PCM COMPRESSION/U-LAW TO LINEAR EXPANSION
A0227                    *;
A0228                    *;    INPUT:  LINEAR PCM SAMPLE  -- SR
A0229                    *;
A0230                    *;    OUTPUT: A-LAW PCM SAMPLE    -- SP  (SCRACH)
A0231                    *;            LINEAR PCM SAMPLE   -- SLX (SAMPLE)
A0232                    *;
A0233                    *;    NOTATION:  SR  -- 16b TC (Q0)
A0234                    *;               SP  -- 8b SM (Q4)
A0235                    *;               SLX -- 14b TC (Q0)
A0236                    *;
A0237                    *;************************************************************
A0238                    *;
A0239                    *;      SR    +----------+        SP    +--------+  SLX
A0240                    *;   ------>¦ COMPRESS ¦-----*------>¦ EXPAND ¦------->
A0241                    *;            +----------+        ¦      +--------+
A0242                    *;                                ¦                 SP
A0243                    *;                                +------------------------>
A0244                    *;
A0245                    *;************************************************************
A0246                    *;
A0247  007E 2013         LAC    SR           ; get reconstructed signal
A0248                    *;
A0249                    *; compress--convert to pcm
A0250                    *;
A0251  007F 5824  CMPRSU SACH   TEMP4        ; save sign of SR
A0252  0080 7F88         ABS
A0253  0081 004D         ADD    BIAS         ; add bias
A0254  0082 501B         SACL   SCRACH       ; save biased PCM value
A0255  0083 194C         SUB    ONE,9        ; exp = 7 - 4 or 3 - 0
A0256  0084 FD00         BGEZ   SCL427
       0085 00B3
A0257  0086 077D  SCL023 ADD    THREE,7      ; exp = 3 - 2 or 1 - 0
A0258  0087 FD00         BGEZ   SCL223
       0088 009E
```

```
A0259  0089 064C   SCL021 ADD      ONE,6        ; exp = 1 or 0
A0260  008A FD00          BGEZ     SCALE1
       008B 0095
A0261  008C 216D   SCALE0 LAC      M15,1        ; exp = 0
A0262  008D 791B          AND      SCRACH       ; mask for mantissa
A0263  008E 501B          SACL     SCRACH
A0264  008F 004D          ADD      BIAS
A0265  0090 5026          SACL     SAMPLE       ; biased quantized value
A0266  0091 2F1B          LAC      SCRACH,15
A0267  0092 7000          LARK     0,0
A0268  0093 F900          B        FINI
       0094 00E6
A0269  0095 226D   SCALE1 LAC      M15,2        ; exp = 1
A0270  0096 791B          AND      SCRACH       ; mask for mantissa
A0271  0097 501B          SACL     SCRACH
A0272  0098 014D          ADD      BIAS,1
A0273  0099 5026          SACL     SAMPLE       ; biased quantized value
A0274  009A 2E1B          LAC      SCRACH,14
A0275  009B 7001          LARK     0,1
A0276  009C F900          B        FINI
       009D 00E6
A0277  009E 174C   SCL223 SUB      ONE,7        ; exp = 3 or 2
A0278  009F FD00          BGEZ     SCALE3
       00A0 00AA
A0279  00A1 236D   SCALE2 LAC      M15,3        ; exp = 2
A0280  00A2 791B          AND      SCRACH       ; mask for mantissa
A0281  00A3 501B          SACL     SCRACH
A0282  00A4 024D          ADD      BIAS,2
A0283  00A5 5026          SACL     SAMPLE       ; biased quantized value
A0284  00A6 2D1B          LAC      SCRACH,13
A0285  00A7 7002          LARK     0,2
A0286  00A8 F900          B        FINI
       00A9 00E6
A0287  00AA 246D   SCALE3 LAC      M15,4        ; exp = 3
A0288  00AB 791B          AND      SCRACH       ; mask for mantissa
A0289  00AC 501B          SACL     SCRACH
A0290  00AD 034D          ADD      BIAS,3
A0291  00AE 5026          SACL     SAMPLE       ; biased quantized value
A0292  00AF 2C1B          LAC      SCRACH,12
A0293  00B0 7003          LARK     0,3
A0294  00B1 F900          B        FINI
       00B2 00E6
A0295  00B3 197D   SCL427 SUB      THREE,9      ; exp = 7 - 6 or 5 - 4
A0296  00B4 FD00          BGEZ     SCL627
       00B5 00CB
A0297  00B6 0A4C   SCL425 ADD      ONE,10       ; exp = 5 or 4
A0298  00B7 FD00          BGEZ     SCALE5
       00B8 00C2
A0299  00B9 256D   SCALE4 LAC      M15,5        ; exp = 4
A0300  00BA 791B          AND      SCRACH       ; mask for mantissa
A0301  00BB 501B          SACL     SCRACH
A0302  00BC 044D          ADD      BIAS,4
A0303  00BD 5026          SACL     SAMPLE       ; biased quantized value
A0304  00BE 2B1B          LAC      SCRACH,11
A0305  00BF 7004          LARK     0,4
A0306  00C0 F900          B        FINI
       00C1 00E6
```

```
A0307 00C2 266D  SCALE5 LAC    M15,6       ; exp = 5
A0308 00C3 791B         AND    SCRACH      ; mask for mantissa
A0309 00C4 501B         SACL   SCRACH
A0310 00C5 054D         ADD    BIAS,5
A0311 00C6 5026         SACL   SAMPLE      ; biased quantized value
A0312 00C7 2A1B         LAC    SCRACH,10
A0313 00C8 7005         LARK   0,5
A0314 00C9 F900         B      FINI
      00CA 00E6
A0315 00CB 1B4C  SCL627 SUB    ONE,11      ; exp = 7 or 6
A0316 00CC FD00         BGEZ   SCALE7
      00CD 00D7
A0317 00CE 276D  SCALE6 LAC    M15,7       ; exp = 6
A0318 00CF 791B         AND    SCRACH      ; mask for mantissa
A0319 00D0 501B         SACL   SCRACH
A0320 00D1 064D         ADD    BIAS,6
A0321 00D2 5026         SACL   SAMPLE      ; biased quantized value
A0322 00D3 291B         LAC    SCRACH,9
A0323 00D4 7006         LARK   0,6
A0324 00D5 F900         B      FINI
      00D6 00E6
A0325 00D7 1C4C  SCALE7 SUB    ONE,12      ; exp = 7
A0326 00D8 FA00         BLZ    NORMAL      ; mag > 8191 ?
      00D9 00DF
A0327 00DA 2767  SATCH  LAC    K63,7
A0328 00DB 5026         SACL   SAMPLE      ; save max biased quantized value
A0329 00DC 7E7F         LACK   127         ; set maximum mulaw magnitude
A0330 00DD F900         B      CLNUP
      00DE 00EA
A0331 00DF 286D  NORMAL LAC    M15,8
A0332 00E0 791B         AND    SCRACH      ; mask for mantissa
A0333 00E1 501B         SACL   SCRACH
A0334 00E2 074D         ADD    BIAS,7
A0335 00E3 5026         SACL   SAMPLE      ; biased quantized value
A0336 00E4 281B         LAC    SCRACH,8
A0337 00E5 7007         LARK   0,7
A0338 00E6 581B  FINI   SACH   SCRACH      ; save normalized mantissa
A0339 00E7 201B         LAC    SCRACH
A0340 00E8 3021         SAR    0,TEMP1
A0341 00E9 0421         ADD    TEMP1,4     ; add exponent
A0342 00EA 0724  CLNUP  ADD    TEMP4,7
A0343 00EB 7947         AND    M255
A0344 00EC 501B         SACL   SCRACH      ; signed magnitude of mulaw-PCM
A0345 00ED 2026         LAC    SAMPLE      ; remove bias from quantized value
A0346 00EE 104D         SUB    BIAS
A0347 00EF 7824         XOR    TEMP4
A0348 00F0 1024         SUB    TEMP4
A0349 00F1 5026         SACL   SAMPLE      ; 2's complement of quantized sample
A0350           *;
A0351 00F2 F800         CALL   AQUAN
      00F3 02AA
A0352           *;
A0353 00F4 F800         CALL   SYNC
      00F5 0188
A0354           *;
A0355 00F6 7847         XOR    M255        ; flip bits for transmission
A0356 00F7 501B         SACL   SCRACH
```

```
A0357  00F8 491B           OUT    SCRACH,DAC  ; output mu-law PCM
A0358  00F9 F600  MULAWR BIOZ     RCVMU       ; wait for next sample
       00FA 0071
A0359  00FB F900         B        MULAWR
       00FC 00F9
```

```
A0361                   *;
A0362                   *;   A-LAW RECEIVER
A0363                   *;
A0364 00FD 4201   RCVA  IN      I,CCITT      ; input ADPCM
A0365                   *;
A0366 00FE 2001         LAC     I            ; determine magnitude of ADPCM
A0367 00FF 5002         SACL    IM
A0368 0100 134C         SUB     ONE,3
A0369 0101 FA00         BLZ     DO32KA
      0102 0106
A0370 0103 2002         LAC     IM
A0371 0104 786D         XOR     M15
A0372 0105 5002         SACL    IM
A0373                   *;
A0374                   *; compute pcm output
A0375                   *;
A0376 0106 F800  DO32KA CALL    SIGDIF
      0107 01B3
A0377 0108 F800         CALL    PRDICT
      0109 0355
A0378                   *;
A0379                   *;******************************************************
A0380                   *; LINEAR TO A-LAW PCM COMPRESSION/A-LAW TO LINEAR EXPANSION
A0381                   *;
A0382                   *;    INPUT:  LINEAR PCM SAMPLE  -- SR
A0383                   *;
A0384                   *;    OUTPUT: A-LAW PCM SAMPLE   -- SP  (SCRACH)
A0385                   *;            LINEAR PCM SAMPLE  -- SLX (SAMPLE)
A0386                   *;
A0387                   *;    NOTATION:  SR  -- 16b TC (Q0)
A0388                   *;               SP  -- 8b SM (Q4)
A0389                   *;               SLX -- 14b TC (Q0)
A0390                   *;
A0391                   *;******************************************************
A0392                   *;
A0393                   *;    SR  +---------+            SP  +--------+  SLX
A0394                   *; ----->| COMPRESS |-----*----->| EXPAND |------->
A0395                   *;       +---------+      |      +--------+
A0396                   *;                        |      +--------+
A0397                   *;                        |                  SP
A0398                   *;                        +--------------------->
A0399                   *;******************************************************
A0400                   *;
A0401 010A 2013         LAC     SR           ; get reconstructed signal
A0402                   *;
A0403                   *; compress--convert to pcm
A0404                   *;
A0405 010B 5824  CMPRSA SACH    TEMP4        ; save sign of SR
A0406 010C 7F88         ABS
A0407 010D 0024         ADD     TEMP4        ; add 1 for negative vals
A0408 010E 501B         SACL    SCRACH       ; save PCM value
A0409 010F 194C         SUB     ONE,9        ; exp = 7 - 4 or 3 - 0
A0410 0110 FD00         BGEZ    SCL4T7
      0111 013F
A0411 0112 077D  SCL0T3 ADD     THREE,7      ; exp = 3 - 2 or 1 - 0
A0412 0113 FD00         BGEZ    SCL2T3
      0114 012A
```

```
A0413 0115 064C  SCLOT1 ADD     ONE,6        ; exp = 1 or 0
A0414 0116 FD00         BGEZ    SCAL1A
      0117 0121
A0415 0118 226D  SCAL0A LAC     M15,2        ; exp = 0
A0416 0119 791B         AND     SCRACH       ; mask for mantissa
A0417 011A 501B         SACL    SCRACH
A0418 011B 014C         ADD     ONE,1
A0419 011C 5026         SACL    SAMPLE       ; quantized value
A0420 011D 2E1B         LAC     SCRACH,14
A0421 011E 7000         LARK    0,0
A0422 011F F900         B       FINISH
      0120 0172
A0423 0121 226D  SCAL1A LAC     M15,2        ; exp = 1
A0424 0122 791B         AND     SCRACH       ; mask for mantissa
A0425 0123 501B         SACL    SCRACH
A0426 0124 014D         ADD     BIAS,1
A0427 0125 5026         SACL    SAMPLE       ; quantized value
A0428 0126 2E1B         LAC     SCRACH,14
A0429 0127 7001         LARK    0,1
A0430 0128 F900         B       FINISH
      0129 0172
A0431 012A 174C  SCL2T3 SUB     ONE,7        ; exp = 3 or 2
A0432 012B FD00         BGEZ    SCAL3A
      012C 0136
A0433 012D 236D  SCAL2A LAC     M15,3        ; exp = 2
A0434 012E 791B         AND     SCRACH       ; mask for mantissa
A0435 012F 501B         SACL    SCRACH
A0436 0130 024D         ADD     BIAS,2
A0437 0131 5026         SACL    SAMPLE       ; quantized value
A0438 0132 2D1B         LAC     SCRACH,13
A0439 0133 7002         LARK    0,2
A0440 0134 F900         B       FINISH
      0135 0172
A0441 0136 246D  SCAL3A LAC     M15,4        ; exp = 3
A0442 0137 791B         AND     SCRACH       ; mask for mantissa
A0443 0138 501B         SACL    SCRACH
A0444 0139 034D         ADD     BIAS,3
A0445 013A 5026         SACL    SAMPLE       ; quantized value
A0446 013B 2C1B         LAC     SCRACH,12
A0447 013C 7003         LARK    0,3
A0448 013D F900         B       FINISH
      013E 0172
A0449 013F 197D  SCL4T7 SUB     THREE,9      ; exp = 7 - 6 or 5 - 4
A0450 0140 FD00         BGEZ    SCL6T7
      0141 0157
A0451 0142 0A4C  SCL4T5 ADD     ONE,10       ; exp = 5 or 4
A0452 0143 FD00         BGEZ    SCAL5A
      0144 014E
A0453 0145 256D  SCAL4A LAC     M15,5        ; exp = 4
A0454 0146 791B         AND     SCRACH       ; mask for mantissa
A0455 0147 501B         SACL    SCRACH
A0456 0148 044D         ADD     BIAS,4
A0457 0149 5026         SACL    SAMPLE       ; quantized value
A0458 014A 2B1B         LAC     SCRACH,11
A0459 014B 7004         LARK    0,4
A0460 014C F900         B       FINISH
      014D 0172
```

```
A0461 014E 266D  SCAL5A LAC      M15,6          ; exp = 5
A0462 014F 791B         AND      SCRACH         ; mask for mantissa
A0463 0150 501B         SACL     SCRACH
A0464 0151 054D         ADD      BIAS,5
A0465 0152 5026         SACL     SAMPLE         ; quantized value
A0466 0153 2A1B         LAC      SCRACH,10
A0467 0154 7005         LARK     0,5
A0468 0155 F900         B        FINISH
      0156 0172
A0469 0157 1B4C  SCL6T7 SUB      ONE,11         ; exp = 7 or 6
A0470 0158 FD00         BGEZ     SCAL7A
      0159 0163
A0471 015A 276D  SCAL6A LAC      M15,7          ; exp = 6
A0472 015B 791B         AND      SCRACH         ; mask for mantissa
A0473 015C 501B         SACL     SCRACH
A0474 015D 064D         ADD      BIAS,6
A0475 015E 5026         SACL     SAMPLE         ; quantized value
A0476 015F 291B         LAC      SCRACH,9
A0477 0160 7006         LARK     0,6
A0478 0161 F900         B        FINISH
      0162 0172
A0479 0163 1C4C  SCAL7A SUB      ONE,12         ; exp = 7
A0480 0164 FA00         BLZ      NORMLA         ; mag > 8191 ?
      0165 016B
A0481 0166 2767  SATCHA LAC      K63,7
A0482 0167 5026         SACL     SAMPLE         ; save maximum quantized value
A0483 0168 7E7F         LACK     127            ; save maximum alaw magnitude
A0484 0169 F900         B        CLNUPA
      016A 0176
A0485 016B 286D  NORMLA LAC      M15,8
A0486 016C 791B         AND      SCRACH         ; mask for mantissa
A0487 016D 501B         SACL     SCRACH
A0488 016E 074D         ADD      BIAS,7
A0489 016F 5026         SACL     SAMPLE         ; quanitzed value
A0490 0170 281B         LAC      SCRACH,8
A0491 0171 7007         LARK     0,7
A0492 0172 581B  FINISH SACH     SCRACH         ; save normalized mantissa
A0493 0173 201B         LAC      SCRACH
A0494 0174 3021         SAR      0,TEMP1
A0495 0175 0421         ADD      TEMP1,4        ; add exponent
A0496 0176 0724  CLNUPA ADD      TEMP4,7
A0497 0177 7947         AND      M255
A0498 0178 501B         SACL     SCRACH         ; signed magnitude of alaw-PCM
A0499 0179 2026         LAC      SAMPLE
A0500 017A 7824         XOR      TEMP4
A0501 017B 1024         SUB      TEMP4
A0502 017C 5026         SACL     SAMPLE         ; 2's complement of quantized sample
A0503            *;
A0504 017D F800         CALL     AQUAN
      017E 02AA
A0505            *;
A0506 017F F800         CALL     SYNC
      0180 0188
A0507            *;
A0508 0181 787F         XOR      M0080          ; flip bits for transmission
A0509 0182 501B         SACL     SCRACH
A0510 0183 491B         OUT      SCRACH,DAC     ; output A-law PCM
```

```
A0511 0184 F600   ALAWR   BIOZ      RCVA           ; wait for next sample
      0185 00FD
A0512 0186 F900           B         ALAWR
      0187 0184
```

Appendix II

CCITT   32010 FAMILY MACRO ASSEMBLER   PC2.1 84.107   16:36:03 03-20-85
                                                             PAGE 0014

A0514   *;
A0515   *;***
A0516   *; SYNCHRONOUS CODING ADJUSTMENT
A0517   *;
A0518   *;   INPUT: LOG PCM SAMPLE   -- SP (SCRACH)
A0519   *;   RECEIVED ADPCM   -- I
A0520   *;   REGENERATED ADPCM   -- ID (TEMP1)
A0521   *;
A0522   *;   OUTPUT: ADJUSTED LOG PCM   -- SD (SCRACH)
A0523   *;
A0524   *;   NOTATION: I   -- 4b SM (Q0)
A0525   *;   ID -- 4b SM (Q0)
A0526   *;   SP -- 8b SM (Q4)
A0527   *;   SD -- 8b SM (Q4)
A0528   *;
A0529   *;***
A0530   *;
A0531   *;   I   +------+
A0532   *;   ------>| |
A0533   *;   ID | | SD
A0534   *;   ------>| SYNC |------->
A0535   *;   SP | |
A0536   *;   ------>| |
A0537   *;   +------+
A0538   *;
A0539   *;***
A0540   *;
A0541 0188 7838 SYNC   XOR   EIGHT
A0542 0189 5021   SACL   TEMP1   ; flip the polarity bit in ID
A0543 018A 234C   LAC   ONE,3
A0544 018B 7801   XOR   I   ; flip the polarity bit in I
A0545 018C 1021   SUB   TEMP1   ; IM - ID
A0546 018D FA00   BLZ   IDGTIM   ; ID > IM ... -
      018E 01A0
A0547 018F FF00   BZ   IDEQIM   ; ID = IM
      0190 01B1
A0548 0191 201B IDLTIM LAC   SCRACH   ; ID < IM ... +
A0549 0192 106F   SUB   M127
A0550 0193 FC00   BGZ   SUBONE
      0194 019B
A0551 0195 FF00   BZ   MAXPOS
      0196 0199
A0552 0197 074C   ADD   ONE,7   ; SD = SP + 1 : 0 <= SP < 127
A0553 0198 7F8D   RET
A0554 0199 7E7F MAXPOS LACK   127   ; SD = 127   : SP = 127
A0555 019A 7F8D   RET
A0556 019B 104C SUBONE SUB   ONE
A0557 019C FF00   BZ   ANOMLE   ; SD = 0   : SP = 128
      019D 019F
A0558 019E 006F   ADD   M127   ; SD = SP + 1 : 255 >= SP > 128
A0559 019F 7F8D ANOMLE RET
A0560 01A0 201B IDGTIM LAC   SCRACH
A0561 01A1 174C   SUB   ONE,7
A0562 01A2 FD00   BGEZ   ADDONE
      01A3 01A8
A0563 01A4 006F   ADD   M127   ; SD = SP - 1 : 0 < SP <= 127
A0564 01A5 FA00   BLZ   ANOMLY
```
```

```
CCITT          32010 FAMILY MACRO ASSEMBLER     PC2.1 84.107     16:36:03  03-20-85
                                                                        PAGE 0015

        01A6 01AF
A0565 01A7 7F8D              RET
A0566 01A8 106F    ADDONE SUB    M127
A0567 01A9 FD00           BGEZ   MAXNEG
        01AA 01AD
A0568 01AB 084C           ADD    ONE,8        ; SD = SP - 1 : 255 > SP >= 128
A0569 01AC 7F8D           RET
A0570 01AD 7EFF    MAXNEG LACK   255          ; SD = 255    : SP = 255
A0571 01AE 7F8D           RET
A0572 01AF 7E80    ANOMLY LACK   128          ; SD = 128    : SP = 0
A0573 01B0 7F8D           RET
A0574 01B1 201B    IDEQIM LAC    SCRACH       ; SD = SP
A0575 01B2 7F8D           RET
```

```
CCITT        32010 FAMILY MACRO ASSEMBLER     PC2.1 84.107      16:36:03  03-20-85
                                                                 PAGE 0016

  0002                          COPY    SIGDIF.ASM
B0001                *;
B0002                *;****************************************************************
B0003                *; SIGDIF
B0004                *;
B0005                *; Implements the following modules (per CCITT spec):
B0006                *;
B0007                *;      DELAY D -- delay of DQ and SR derivatives
B0008                *;      FMULT   -- Bn * DQn, An * SRn
B0009                *;      DELAY A -- (implicit in use of last frames data)
B0010                *;      ACCUM   -- Accumulate partial products for SEZ, SE
B0011                *;
B0012                *;      LIMA    -- compute AL(k)
B0013                *;      MIX     -- compute Y(k)
B0014                *;
B0015                *;****************************************************************
B0016                *;
B0017                *; compute SEZ-- partial signal estimate
B0018                *;
B0019                *;   SEZ(k) = B1(k-1)*DQ(k-1) + ... + B6(k-1)*DQ(k-6)
B0020                *;
B0021                *;      Multiplies are done in floating pt
B0022                *;       DQ's are stored in f.p. notation
B0023                *;       B's are floated each pass
B0024                *;
B0025                *;****************************************************************
B0026                *; FLOATING POINT MULTIPLY (FMULT)
B0027                *;
B0028                *;      INPUT:   QUANTIZED DIFFERENCE   -- DQn (DQnEXP/DQnMAN)
B0029                *;               PREDICTOR COEFFICIENTS -- Bn
B0030                *;
B0031                *;      OUTPUT: FILTER TAP OUTPUTS      -- WBn (SUMn)
B0032                *;
B0033                *;      NOTATION: DQnEXP    -- 4b + offset
B0034                *;                DQnMAN*8  -- 9b magnitude
B0035                *;                Bn        -- 16b TC (Q14)
B0036                *;                SUMn      -- 16b TC (Q1)
B0037                *;
B0038                *;****************************************************************
B0039                *;
B0040                *;      -1       -1       -1       -1       -1       -1
B0041                *; DQ   z        z        z        z        z        z
B0042                *; o--->---o--->---o--->---o--->---o--->---o--->---o
B0043                *;         :       :       :       :       :       :
B0044                *;         :       :       :       :       :       :
B0045                *;       vB1(k)  vB2(k)  vB3(k)  vB4(k)  vB5(k)  vB6(k)
B0046                *;         :       :       :       :       :       :
B0047                *;         :       :       :       :       :       :
B0048                *;       o--->---o--->---o--->---o--->---o--->---o--->---o
B0049                *;       WB1     WB2     WB3     WB4     WB5     WB6     SEZ
B0050                *;
B0051                *;****************************************************************
B0052                *;
B0053 01B3 2E0F  SIGDIF LAC     B6,14    ; compute B6*DQ5
B0054 01B4 F800         CALL    FLOAT    ; ret/w mantissa in TEMP1; exp in ac
      01B5 04DE
B0055 01B6 001A         ADD     DQ5EXP
```

```
B0056 01B7 5022          SACL    SUM1
B0057 01B8 3822          LAR     0,SUM1  ; exp of product offset by table add
B0058 01B9 6A60          LT      DQ5MAN  ; scaled up by 2**3
B0059 01BA 277D          LAC     THREE,7 ; multiply fudge factor
B0060 01BB 6D21          MPY     TEMP1
B0061 01BC 6C80          LTA     *,0     ; mult mant, add 48, fetch shift fac
B0062 01BD 796E          AND     KFF80
B0063 01BE 5021          SACL    TEMP1
B0064 01BF 6D21          MPY     TEMP1   ; apply shift factor = f(exp)
B0065 01C0 7F8E          PAC
B0066 01C1 FA00          BLZ     RS1     ; exp >= 26
      01C2 04B6
B0067 01C3 5922          SACH    SUM1,1  ; exp < 26
B0068 01C4 660F  CHK1    ZALS    B6      ; check sign of product
B0069 01C5 785A          XOR     SDQ6
B0070 01C6 7948          AND     K32768
B0071 01C7 FF00          BZ      POS1
      01C8 01CC
B0072 01C9 7F89  NEG1    ZAC             ; negate if necessary
B0073 01CA 1022          SUB     SUM1
B0074 01CB 5022          SACL    SUM1
B0075 01CC 2E0E  POS1    LAC     B5,14   ; compute B5*DQ4
B0076 01CD F800          CALL    FLOAT   ; ret/w mantissa in TEMP1; exp in ac
      01CE 04DE
B0077 01CF 0019          ADD     DQ4EXP
B0078 01D0 6919          DMOV    DQ4EXP
B0079 01D1 5023          SACL    SUM2
B0080 01D2 3823          LAR     0,SUM2  ; exp of product offset by table add
B0081 01D3 6B5F          LTD     DQ4MAN  ; scaled up by 2**3
B0082 01D4 277D          LAC     THREE,7 ; multiply fudge factor
B0083 01D5 6D21          MPY     TEMP1
B0084 01D6 6C80          LTA     *,0     ; mult mant, add 48, fetch shift fac
B0085 01D7 796E          AND     KFF80
B0086 01D8 5021          SACL    TEMP1
B0087 01D9 6D21          MPY     TEMP1   ; apply shift factor = f(exp)
B0088 01DA 7F8E          PAC
B0089 01DB FA00          BLZ     RS2     ; exp >= 26
      01DC 04BB
B0090 01DD 5923          SACH    SUM2,1  ; exp < 26
B0091 01DE 660E  CHK2    ZALS    B5      ; check sign of product
B0092 01DF 7859          XOR     SDQ5
B0093 01E0 7948          AND     K32768
B0094 01E1 FF00          BZ      POS2
      01E2 01E6
B0095 01E3 7F89  NEG2    ZAC             ; negate if necessary
B0096 01E4 1023          SUB     SUM2
B0097 01E5 5023          SACL    SUM2
B0098 01E6 2E0D  POS2    LAC     B4,14   ; compute B4*DQ3
B0099 01E7 F800          CALL    FLOAT   ; ret/w mantissa in TEMP1; exp in ac
      01E8 04DE
B0100 01E9 0018          ADD     DQ3EXP
B0101 01EA 6918          DMOV    DQ3EXP
B0102 01EB 5025          SACL    SUM3
B0103 01EC 3825          LAR     0,SUM3  ; exp of product offset by table add
B0104 01ED 6B5E          LTD     DQ3MAN  ; scaled up by 2**3
B0105 01EE 277D          LAC     THREE,7 ; multiply fudge factor
B0106 01EF 6D21          MPY     TEMP1
```

```
B0107 01F0 6C80        LTA      *,0        ; mult mant, add 48, fetch shift fac
B0108 01F1 796E        AND      KFF80
B0109 01F2 5021        SACL     TEMP1
B0110 01F3 6D21        MPY      TEMP1      ; apply shift factor = f(exp)
B0111 01F4 7F8E        PAC
B0112 01F5 FA00        BLZ      RS3        ; exp >= 26
      01F6 04C0
B0113 01F7 5925        SACH     SUM3,1     ; exp < 26
B0114 01F8 660D  CHK3  ZALS     B4         ; check sign of product
B0115 01F9 7858        XOR      SDQ4
B0116 01FA 7948        AND      K32768
B0117 01FB FF00        BZ       POS3
      01FC 0200
B0118 01FD 7F89  NEG3  ZAC                 ; negate if necessary
B0119 01FE 1025        SUB      SUM3
B0120 01FF 5025        SACL     SUM3
B0121 0200 2E0C  POS3  LAC      B3,14      ; compute B3*DQ2
B0122 0201 F800        CALL     FLOAT      ; ret/w mantissa in TEMP1; exp in ac
      0202 04DE
B0123 0203 0017        ADD      DQ2EXP
B0124 0204 6917        DMOV     DQ2EXP
B0125 0205 501E        SACL     SUM4
B0126 0206 381E        LAR      0,SUM4     ; exp of product offset by table add
B0127 0207 6B5D        LTD      DQ2MAN     ; scaled up by 2**3
B0128 0208 277D        LAC      THREE,7    ; multiply fudge factor
B0129 0209 6D21        MPY      TEMP1
B0130 020A 6C80        LTA      *,0        ; mult mant, add 48, fetch shift fac
B0131 020B 796E        AND      KFF80
B0132 020C 5021        SACL     TEMP1
B0133 020D 6D21        MPY      TEMP1      ; apply shift factor = f(exp)
B0134 020E 7F8E        PAC
B0135 020F FA00        BLZ      RS4        ; exp >= 26
      0210 04C5
B0136 0211 591E        SACH     SUM4,1     ; exp < 26
B0137 0212 660C  CHK4  ZALS     B3         ; check sign of product
B0138 0213 7857        XOR      SDQ3
B0139 0214 7948        AND      K32768
B0140 0215 FF00        BZ       POS4
      0216 021A
B0141 0217 7F89  NEG4  ZAC                 ; negate if necessary
B0142 0218 101E        SUB      SUM4
B0143 0219 501E        SACL     SUM4
B0144 021A 2E0B  POS4  LAC      B2,14      ; compute B2*DQ1
B0145 021B F800        CALL     FLOAT      ; ret/w mantissa in TEMP1; exp in ac
      021C 04DE
B0146 021D 0016        ADD      DQ1EXP
B0147 021E 6916        DMOV     DQ1EXP
B0148 021F 501F        SACL     SUM5
B0149 0220 381F        LAR      0,SUM5     ; exp of product offset by table add
B0150 0221 6B5C        LTD      DQ1MAN     ; scaled up by 2**3
B0151 0222 277D        LAC      THREE,7    ; multiply fudge factor
B0152 0223 6D21        MPY      TEMP1
B0153 0224 6C80        LTA      *,0        ; mult mant, add 48, fetch shift fac
B0154 0225 796E        AND      KFF80
B0155 0226 5021        SACL     TEMP1
B0156 0227 6D21        MPY      TEMP1      ; apply shift factor = f(exp)
B0157 0228 7F8E        PAC
```

```
B0158 0229 FA00           BLZ     RS5       ; exp >= 26
      022A 04CA
B0159 022B 591F           SACH    SUM5,1    ; exp < 26
B0160 022C 660B    CHK5   ZALS    B2        ; check sign of product
B0161 022D 7856           XOR     SDQ2
B0162 022E 7948           AND     K32768
B0163 022F FF00           BZ      POS5
      0230 0234
B0164 0231 7F89    NEG5   ZAC               ; negate if necessary
B0165 0232 101F           SUB     SUM5
B0166 0233 501F           SACL    SUM5
B0167 0234 2E0A    POS5   LAC     B1,14     ; compute B1*DQ
B0168 0235 F800           CALL    FLOAT     ; ret/w mantissa in TEMP1; exp in accum
      0236 04DE
B0169 0237 0015           ADD     DQEXP
B0170 0238 6915           DMOV    DQEXP
B0171 0239 5020           SACL    SUM6
B0172 023A 3820           LAR     0,SUM6    ; exp of product offset by table addr
B0173 023B 6B5B           LTD     DQMAN     ; scaled up by 2**3
B0174 023C 277D           LAC     THREE,7   ; multiply fudge factor
B0175 023D 6D21           MPY     TEMP1
B0176 023E 6C80           LTA     *,0       ; mult mant, add 48, fetch shift factor
B0177 023F 796E           AND     KFF80
B0178 0240 5021           SACL    TEMP1
B0179 0241 6D21           MPY     TEMP1     ; apply shift factor = f(exp)
B0180 0242 7F8E           PAC
B0181 0243 FA00           BLZ     RS6       ; exp >= 26
      0244 04CF
B0182 0245 5920           SACH    SUM6,1    ; exp < 26
B0183 0246 660A    CHK6   ZALS    B1        ; check sign of product
B0184 0247 7855           XOR     SDQ1
B0185 0248 7948           AND     K32768
B0186 0249 FF00           BZ      POS6
      024A 024E
B0187 024B 7F89    NEG6   ZAC               ; negate if necessary
B0188 024C 1020           SUB     SUM6
B0189 024D 5020           SACL    SUM6
B0190      024E    POS6   EQU     $
B0191              *;
B0192              *;*************************************************************
B0193              *;
B0194              *; compute SE -- signal estimate
B0195              *;
B0196              *;   SE = A1(k-1)*SR(k-1) + A2(k-1)*SR(k-1) + SEZ(k)
B0197              *;
B0198              *;      Multiplies are dONE in floating pt
B0199              *;       SR's are stored in f.p. notation
B0200              *;       A's are floated each pass
B0201              *;
B0202              *;*************************************************************
B0203              *; FLOATING POINT MULTIPLY (FMULT)
B0204              *;
B0205              *;   INPUT:  RECONSTRUCTED SIGNAL   -- SRn (SRnEXP/SRnMAN)
B0206              *;           PREDICTOR COEFFICIENTS -- An
B0207              *;
B0208              *;   OUTPUT: FILTER TAP OUTPUTS     -- WAn (SUMn+6)
B0209              *;
```

```
B0210            *;      NOTATION: SRnEXP   -- 4b + offset
B0211            *;                SRnMAN*8 -- 9b magnitude
B0212            *;                An       -- 16b TC (Q14)
B0213            *;                SUMn+6   -- 16b TC (Q1)
B0214            *;
B0215            *;*************************************************************
B0216            *;
B0217            *;                    -1           -1
B0218            *;            SR   z            z
B0219            *;            o--->---o--->---o
B0220            *;                    :           :
B0221            *;                    :           :
B0222            *;                  vA1(k)     vA2(k)
B0223            *;                    :           :
B0224            *;                    :           :
B0225            *;            o---<---o---<---o---<---o
B0226            *;            SE    WA1      WA2     SEZ
B0227            *;
B0228            *;*************************************************************
B0229            *;
B0230 024E 2E12  GETSE LAC    A2,14     ; compute A2*SR1
B0231 024F F800        CALL   FLOAT     ; ret/w mantissa in TEMP1; exp in accum
      0250 04DE
B0232 0251 001D        ADD    SR1EXP
B0233 0252 5027        SACL   SUM7
B0234 0253 3827        LAR    0,SUM7    ; exp of product offset by table addr
B0235 0254 6A53        LT     SR1MAN    ; scaled up by 2**3
B0236 0255 277D        LAC    THREE,7   ; multiply fudge factor
B0237 0256 6D21        MPY    TEMP1
B0238 0257 6C80        LTA    *,0       ; mult mant, add 48, fetch shift factor
B0239 0258 796E        AND    KFF80
B0240 0259 5021        SACL   TEMP1
B0241 025A 6D21        MPY    TEMP1     ; apply shift factor = f(exp)
B0242 025B 7F8E        PAC
B0243 025C FA00        BLZ    RS11      ; exp >= 26
      025D 04D4
B0244 025E 5927        SACH   SUM7,1    ; exp < 26
B0245 025F 6612  CHK11 ZALS   A2        ; check sign of product
B0246 0260 7814        XOR    SR1
B0247 0261 7948        AND    K32768
B0248 0262 FF00        BZ     POS11
      0263 0267
B0249 0264 7F89  NEG11 ZAC              ; negate if necessary
B0250 0265 1027        SUB    SUM7
B0251 0266 5027        SACL   SUM7
B0252 0267 2E11  POS11 LAC    A1,14     ; compute A1*SR
B0253 0268 F800        CALL   FLOAT     ; ret/w mantissa in TEMP1; exp in accum
      0269 04DE
B0254 026A 001C        ADD    SREXP
B0255 026B 691C        DMOV   SREXP
B0256 026C 5028        SACL   SUM8
B0257 026D 3828        LAR    0,SUM8    ; exp of product offset by table addr
B0258 026E 6852        LTD    SRMAN     ; scaled up by 2**3
B0259 026F 277D        LAC    THREE,7   ; multiply fudge factor
B0260 0270 6D21        MPY    TEMP1
B0261 0271 6C80        LTA    *,0       ; mult mant, add 48, fetch shift factor
B0262 0272 796E        AND    KFF80
```

```
B0263 0273 5021          SACL    TEMP1
B0264 0274 6D21          MPY     TEMP1    ; apply shift factor = f(exp)
B0265 0275 7F8E          PAC
B0266 0276 FA00          BLZ     RS21     ; exp >= 26
      0277 04D9
B0267 0278 5928          SACH    SUM8,1   ; exp < 26
B0268 0279 6913   CHK21  DMOV    SR
B0269 027A 6613          ZALS    SR       ; check sign of product
B0270 027B 7811          XOR     A1
B0271 027C 7948          AND     K32768
B0272 027D FF00          BZ      POS21
      027E 0282
B0273 027F 7F89   NEG21  ZAC              ; negate if necessary
B0274 0280 1028          SUB     SUM8
B0275 0281 5028          SACL    SUM8
B0276      0282   POS21  EQU     $
B0277            *;
B0278            *;***************************************************************
B0279            *; ACCUMULATE FILTER TAP OUTPUTS (ACCUM)
B0280            *;
B0281            *;    INPUT:  FILTER TAP OUTPUTS -- WAn & WBn (SUMm)
B0282            *;
B0283            *;    OUTPUT: PARTIAL SUM OF ZEROES FILTER -- SEZ
B0284            *;            SIGNAL ESTIMATE              -- SE
B0285            *;
B0286            *;    NOTATION: SUMm -- 16b TC (Q1)
B0287            *;              SEZ  -- 15b TC (Q0) [sign extended]
B0288            *;              SE   -- 15b TC (Q0) [sign extended]
B0289            *;
B0290            *;***************************************************************
B0291            *;
B0292 0282 2F20          LAC     SUM6,15 ; accumulate products
B0293 0283 0F1F          ADD     SUM5,15
B0294 0284 0F1E          ADD     SUM4,15
B0295 0285 0F25          ADD     SUM3,15
B0296 0286 0F23          ADD     SUM2,15
B0297 0287 0F22          ADD     SUM1,15
B0298 0288 5904          SACH    SEZ,1
B0299 0289 0F27          ADD     SUM7,15
B0300 028A 0F28          ADD     SUM8,15
B0301 028B 5903          SACH    SE,1
B0302 028C 2F03          LAC     SE,15
B0303 028D 5803          SACH    SE
B0304            *;
B0305            *;***************************************************************
B0306            *; limit speed control parameter: AL <= 1.0
B0307            *;
B0308            *;    AL = 1        if APP >  1
B0309            *;    AL = APP      if APP <= 1
B0310            *;
B0311            *;    INPUT:  UNLIMITED SPEED CONTROL -- AP (APP)
B0312            *;
B0313            *;    OUTPUT: LIMITED SPEED CONTROL -- AL
B0314            *;
B0315            *;    NOTATION:  APP -- unsigned 10b (Q8)
B0316            *;               AL  -- unsigned  7b (Q6)
B0317            *;
```

```
B0318                  *;*********************************************************
B0319                  *;
B0320 028E 2C4C  LIMA    LAC     ONE,12
B0321 028F 5006          SACL    AL
B0322 0290 2005          LAC     APP                 ; check if APP >=1
B0323 0291 184C          SUB     ONE,8
B0324 0292 FD00          BGEZ    MIX                 ;APP >= 1
      0293 0297
B0325 0294 2405          LAC     APP,4
B0326 0295 7970          AND     MFFC0
B0327 0296 5006          SACL    AL                  ;APP < 1
B0328                  *;
B0329                  *;*********************************************************
B0330                  *; MIX
B0331                  *; form linear combination of fast and slow scale factors
B0332                  *;
B0333                  *;      Y(k) = (1-AL(k))*YL(k-1) + AL(k)*YU(k-1)
B0334                  *;
B0335                  *;      INPUT:  SLOW QUANTIZER SCALE FACTOR -- YL (YLL/YLH)
B0336                  *;              FAST QUANTIZER SCALE FACTOR -- YU
B0337                  *;              LIMITED SPEED CONTROL       -- AL
B0338                  *;
B0339                  *;      OUTPUT: QUANTIZER SCALE FACTOR          -- Y
B0340                  *;              RESCALED QUANTIZER SCALE FACTOR -- YOVER4
B0341                  *;
B0342                  *;      NOTATION: YL    -- 19b unsigned (Q15)
B0343                  *;                      stored as:
B0344                  *;                        low 15b -- YLL
B0345                  *;                        hi   4b -- YLH
B0346                  *;                YU    -- 13b unsigned (Q9)
B0347                  *;                AL    -- 7b unsigned  (Q6)
B0348                  *;                Y     -- 13b unsigned (Q9)
B0349                  *;                YOVER4 -- 11b unsigned (Q7)
B0350                  *;
B0351                  *;*********************************************************
B0352                  *;
B0353 0297 2A4A  MIX     LAC     YLL,10              ; shift yl right by 6
B0354 0298 5823          SACH    TEMP3
B0355 0299 2949          LAC     YLH,9
B0356 029A 0023          ADD     TEMP3
B0357 029B 5023          SACL    TEMP3               ; YL>>6
B0358 029C 204E          LAC     YU
B0359 029D 1023          SUB     TEMP3               ; YU-(YL>>6)
B0360 029E 5021          SACL    TEMP1
B0361 029F 6A06          LT      AL
B0362 02A0 6D21          MPY     TEMP1
B0363 02A1 7F8E          PAC                         ; AL*(YU-(YL>>6))
B0364 02A2 FD00          BGEZ    NONNEG              ; negative truncation
      02A3 02A5
B0365 02A4 0072          ADD     M4095
B0366 02A5 0C23  NONNEG  ADD     TEMP3,12
B0367 02A6 5C09          SACH    Y,4
B0368 02A7 2E09          LAC     Y,14                ; compute and save y>>2
B0369 02A8 5829          SACH    YOVER4
B0370 02A9 7F8D          RET                         ; ret from SIGDIF
```

```
CCITT        32010 FAMILY MACRO ASSEMBLER    PC2.1 84.107    16:36:03  03-20-85
                                                                 PAGE 0023

  0003                          COPY     AQUAN.ASM
C0001               *;
C0002               *;*******************************************************
C0003               *; DIFFERENCE SIGNAL COMPUTATION
C0004               *;
C0005               *;      INPUT:  LINEAR PCM SAMPLE -- SL (SAMPLE)
C0006               *;              SIGNAL ESTIMATE    -- SE
C0007               *;
C0008               *;      OUTPUT: DIFFERENCE SIGNAL -- D (accumulator)
C0009               *;
C0010               *;      NOTATION:  SL -- 14b TC (Q0) [sign extended]
C0011               *;                 SE -- 15b TC (Q0) [sign extended]
C0012               *;                 D  -- 16b TC (Q0)
C0013               *;
C0014               *;*******************************************************
C0015               *;
C0016               *;                     SL  +-------+
C0017               *;                ------->¦       ¦   D
C0018               *;                     SE ¦ SUBTA ¦------->
C0019               *;                ------->¦       ¦
C0020               *;                        +-------+
C0021               *;
C0022               *;*******************************************************
C0023               *;
C0024 02AA 2026     AQUAN  LAC     SAMPLE          ; compute difference sig
C0025 02AB 1003            SUB     SE
C0026               *;
C0027               *;*******************************************************
C0028               *;  ADAPTIVE QUANTIZER
C0029               *;
C0030               *; Implements the following modules (per CCITT spec):
C0031               *;
C0032               *;      LOG     -- computes log of difference signal
C0033               *;      SUBTB   -- scales log by subtracting Y
C0034               *;      QUAN    -- computes 4b output
C0035               *;
C0036               *;*******************************************************
C0037               *;
C0038               *;      INPUT:  DIFFERENCED PCM SAMPLE -- D (accumulator)
C0039               *;              QUANTIZER SCALE FACTOR -- Y (YOVER4)
C0040               *;
C0041               *;      OUTPUT: ADPCM OUTPUT SAMPLE    -- I
C0042               *;
C0043               *;      NOTATION:  D     -- 16b TC (Q0)
C0044               *;                 YOVER4 -- 11b SM (Q7) POSITIVE VALUE ONLY
C0045               *;                 I     -- 4b SM (Q0)
C0046               *;
C0047               *;*******************************************************
C0048               *;
C0049               *;                          DS
C0050               *;            +----------------------------+
C0051               *;            ¦                            ¦
C0052               *;            ¦                            V
C0053               *;  D  +---+---+  DL  +-------+  DLN +--------+   I
C0054               *;  ----->¦ LOG ¦----->¦ SUBTB ¦----->¦  QUAN  ¦----->
C0055               *;        +-------+     +-------+      +--------+
C0056               *;                         ^
```

```
C0057              *;                                  ; Y
C0058              *;
C0059              *;************************************************************
C0060              *;
C0061              *; first get log of difference signal -- express
C0062              *; as unsigned 11b number (4b exp/7b mantissa)
C0063              *;
C0064              *; First order log approximation: log2 (1+x) = x.
C0065              *;
C0066 02AC 5824            SACH     TEMP4    ; -1 if neg; 0 if positive (DS)
C0067 02AD 7F88            ABS
C0068 02AE 5021            SACL     TEMP1
C0069 02AF 184C  GETEXP    SUB      ONE,8    ; binary search to get exponent
C0070 02B0 FD00            BGEZ     C8TO14
      02B1 02E7
C0071 02B2 046D  C0TO7     ADD      M15,4    ; TEMP1-16       exp = 0-7
C0072 02B3 FD00            BGEZ     C4TO7
      02B4 02CE
C0073 02B5 027D  C0TO3     ADD      THREE,2  ; TEMP1-4        exp = 0-3
C0074 02B6 FD00            BGEZ     C2TO3
      02B7 02C3
C0075 02B8 014C  C0TO1     ADD      ONE,1    ; TEMP1-2        exp = 0-1
C0076 02B9 FD00            BGEZ     EXP1
      02BA 02BF
C0077 02BB 7000  EXP0      LARK     0,0      ; exp = 0
C0078 02BC 2721            LAC      TEMP1,7
C0079 02BD F900            B        GETMAN   ; save exponent and get mantissa
      02BE 0321
C0080 02BF 7001  EXP1      LARK     0,1      ; exp = 1
C0081 02C0 2621            LAC      TEMP1,6
C0082 02C1 F900            B        GETMAN
      02C2 0321
C0083 02C3 124C  C2TO3     SUB      ONE,2    ; TEMP1-8        exp = 2-3
C0084 02C4 FD00            BGEZ     EXP3
      02C5 02CA
C0085 02C6 7002  EXP2      LARK     0,2      ; exp = 2
C0086 02C7 2521            LAC      TEMP1,5
C0087 02C8 F900            B        GETMAN
      02C9 0321
C0088 02CA 7003  EXP3      LARK     0,3      ; exp = 3
C0089 02CB 2421            LAC      TEMP1,4
C0090 02CC F900            B        GETMAN
      02CD 0321
C0091 02CE 147D  C4TO7     SUB      THREE,4  ; TEMP1-64       exp = 4-7
C0092 02CF FD00            BGEZ     C6TO7
      02D0 02DC
C0093 02D1 054C  C4TO5     ADD      ONE,5    ; TEMP1-32       exp = 4-5
C0094 02D2 FD00            BGEZ     EXP5
      02D3 02D8
C0095 02D4 7004  EXP4      LARK     0,4      ; exp = 4
C0096 02D5 2321            LAC      TEMP1,3
C0097 02D6 F900            B        GETMAN
      02D7 0321
C0098 02D8 7005  EXP5      LARK     0,5      ; exp = 5
C0099 02D9 2221            LAC      TEMP1,2
C0100 02DA F900            B        GETMAN
      02DB 0321
```

```
C0101 02DC 164C  C6TO7   SUB     ONE,6     ; TEMP1-128       exp = 6-7
C0102 02DD FD00          BGEZ    EXP7
      02DE 02E3
C0103 02DF 7006  EXP6    LARK    0,6       ; exp = 6
C0104 02E0 2121          LAC     TEMP1,1
C0105 02E1 F900          B       GETMAN
      02E2 0321
C0106 02E3 7007  EXP7    LARK    0,7       ; exp = 7
C0107 02E4 2021          LAC     TEMP1
C0108 02E5 F900          B       GETMAN
      02E6 0321
C0109 02E7 186D  C8TO14  SUB     M15,8     ; TEMP1-4096      exp = 8-14
C0110 02E8 FD00          BGEZ    CCTOE
      02E9 030B
C0111 02EA 0A7D  C8TO11  ADD     THREE,10  ;TEMP1-1024       exp = 8-11
C0112 02EB FD00          BGEZ    CATOB
      02EC 02FC
C0113 02ED 094C  C8TO9   ADD     ONE,9     ; TEMP1-512       exp = 8-9
C0114 02EE FD00          BGEZ    EXP9
      02EF 02F6
C0115 02F0 7008  EXP8    LARK    0,8       ; exp = 8
C0116 02F1 2F21          LAC     TEMP1,15
C0117 02F2 5821          SACH    TEMP1
C0118 02F3 2021          LAC     TEMP1
C0119 02F4 F900          B       GETMAN
      02F5 0321
C0120 02F6 7009  EXP9    LARK    0,9       ; exp = 9
C0121 02F7 2E21          LAC     TEMP1,14
C0122 02F8 5821          SACH    TEMP1
C0123 02F9 2021          LAC     TEMP1
C0124 02FA F900          B       GETMAN
      02FB 0321
C0125 02FC 1A4C  CATOB   SUB     ONE,10    ; TEMP1-2048      exp = 10-11
C0126 02FD FD00          BGEZ    EXP11
      02FE 0305
C0127 02FF 700A  EXP10   LARK    0,10      ; exp = 10
C0128 0300 2D21          LAC     TEMP1,13
C0129 0301 5821          SACH    TEMP1
C0130 0302 2021          LAC     TEMP1
C0131 0303 F900          B       GETMAN
      0304 0321
C0132 0305 700B  EXP11   LARK    0,11      ; exp = 11
C0133 0306 2C21          LAC     TEMP1,12
C0134 0307 5821          SACH    TEMP1
C0135 0308 2021          LAC     TEMP1
C0136 0309 F900          B       GETMAN
      030A 0321
C0137 030B 1C7D  CCTOE   SUB     THREE,12  ; TEMP1-16384     exp = 12-14
C0138 030C FD00          BGEZ    EXP14
      030D 031D
C0139 030E 0D4C  CCTOD   ADD     ONE,13    ; TEMP1-8192      exp = 13-14
C0140 030F FD00          BGEZ    EXP13
      0310 0317
C0141 0311 700C  EXP12   LARK    0,12      ; exp = 12
C0142 0312 2B21          LAC     TEMP1,11
C0143 0313 5821          SACH    TEMP1
C0144 0314 2021          LAC     TEMP1
```

```
CCITT        32010 FAMILY MACRO ASSEMBLER    PC2.1 84.107    16:36:03  03-20-85
                                                                       PAGE 0026

C0145 0315 F900          B       GETMAN
      0316 0321
C0146 0317 700D   EXP13   LARK    0,13      ; exp = 13
C0147 0318 2A21          LAC     TEMP1,10
C0148 0319 5821          SACH    TEMP1
C0149 031A 2021          LAC     TEMP1
C0150 031B F900          B       GETMAN
      031C 0321
C0151 031D 700E   EXP14   LARK    0,14      ; exp = 14
C0152 031E 2921          LAC     TEMP1,9
C0153 031F 5821          SACH    TEMP1
C0154 0320 2021          LAC     TEMP1
C0155 0321 796F   GETMAN  AND     M127
C0156 0322 3021          SAR     0,TEMP1
C0157 0323 0721          ADD     TEMP1,7   ; DL  4e...7m (sign=SGN(D))
C0158            *;
C0159            *;---------------------------------------------------
C0160            *;
C0161            *; scale LOG D by subtraction (Y>>2 is in YOVER4)
C0162            *;
C0163            *;---------------------------------------------------
C0164            *;
C0165 0324 0B4C   SUBTB   ADD     ONE,11    ; offset by 2K
C0166 0325 1029          SUB     YOVER4
C0167            *;
C0168            *;---------------------------------------------------
C0169            *; 16 LEVEL quantizer
C0170            *;
C0171            *; Table values defined in CCITT spec p67
C0172            *; Implemented table is offset by 2048
C0173            *;---------------------------------------------------
C0174            *;
C0175      07F9   ITAB1   EQU     2041      ; bottom of level 1
C0176      087B   ITAB2   EQU     2171      ; bottom of level 2
C0177      08CA   ITAB3   EQU     2250      ; bottom of level 3
C0178      0905   ITAB4   EQU     2309      ; bottom of level 4
C0179      0936   ITAB5   EQU     2358      ; bottom of level 5
C0180      0964   ITAB6   EQU     2404      ; bottom of level 6
C0181      0995   ITAB7   EQU     2453      ; bottom of level 7
C0182            *;
C0183 0326 107C   QUAN    SUB     K2309     ; TEMP2-2309
C0184 0327 FD00          BGEZ    CI4TO7
      0328 033E
C0185 0329 007B   CI0TO3  ADD     K138      ; TEMP2-2171    I = 0-3
C0186 032A FD00          BGEZ    CI2TO3
      032B 0335
C0187 032C 007A   CI0TO1  ADD     K130      ; TEMP2-2041    I = 0-1
C0188 032D FD00          BGEZ    IEQ1
      032E 0332
C0189 032F 7E00   IEQ0    LACK    0
C0190 0330 F900          B       GETIM
      0331 0351
C0191 0332 7E01   IEQ1    LACK    1
C0192 0333 F900          B       GETIM
      0334 0351
C0193 0335 1078   CI2TO3  SUB     K79       ; TEMP2-2250    I = 2-3
C0194 0336 FD00          BGEZ    IEQ3
```

```
        0337 033B
C0195 0338 7E02   IEQ2    LACK    2
C0196 0339 F900           B       GETIM
      033A 0351
C0197 033B 7E03   IEQ3    LACK    3
C0198 033C F900           B       GETIM
      033D 0351
C0199 033E 1079   CI4TO7  SUB     K95     ; TEMP2-2404     I = 4-7
C0200 033F FD00           BGEZ    CI6TO7
      0340 034A
C0201 0341 0064   CI5TO6  ADD     K46     ; TEMP2-2358     I = 5-6
C0202 0342 FD00           BGEZ    IEQ5
      0343 0347
C0203 0344 7E04   IEQ4    LACK    4
C0204 0345 F900           B       GETIM
      0346 0351
C0205 0347 7E05   IEQ5    LACK    5
C0206 0348 F900           B       GETIM
      0349 0351
C0207 034A 1065   CI6TO7  SUB     K49     ; TEMP2-2453     I = 6-7
C0208 034B FD00           BGEZ    IEQ7
      034C 0350
C0209 034D 7E06   IEQ6    LACK    6
C0210 034E F900           B       GETIM
      034F 0351
C0211 0350 7E07   IEQ7    LACK    7
C0212 0351 5002   GETIM   SACL    IM      ; accumulator = |I|
C0213 0352 7824           XOR     TEMP4   ; add sign bit and flip if necessary
C0214 0353 796D           AND     M15     ; mask for final four-bit value
C0215 0354 7F8D   QDONE   RET             ; return from AQUAN
```

```
CCITT        32010 FAMILY MACRO ASSEMBLER    PC2.1 84.107    16:36:03  03-20-85
                                                                       PAGE 0028

    0004                    COPY    PRDICT.ASM
    D0001           *;
    D0002           *;***************************************************************
    D0003           *; ADAPTATION/PREDICTION
    D0004           *;
    D0005           *;   Implements the following modules per CCITT spec:
    D0006           *;
    D0007           *;     Inverse Adaptive Quantizer
    D0008           *;       RECONST              -- reconstructs D from I
    D0009           *;       ADDA                 -- adds back scale factor
    D0010           *;       ANTILOG              -- log to lin conversion to get DQ
    D0011           *;       FLOAT A              -- float DQ
    D0012           *;     Scale Factor Adaptation
    D0013           *;       FUNCTW               -- map I to log scale factor
    D0014           *;       FILTD                -- update fast scale factor
    D0015           *;       LIMB                 -- limit scale factor
    D0016           *;       FILTE                -- update slow scale factor
    D0017           *;     Adaptation Speed Control
    D0018           *;       FUNCTF               -- map I to F function
    D0019           *;       FILTA                -- update short term ave of F
    D0020           *;       FILTB                -- update long term ave of F
    D0021           *;       SUBTC                -- determ speed control update
    D0022           *;                               technique
    D0023           *;       FILTC                -- update speed control
    D0024           *;     Adaptive Predictor
    D0025           *;       ADDB                 -- compute reconstructed signal
    D0026           *;       FLOAT A              -- float SR
    D0027           *;       ADDC                 -- compute sign of PK
    D0028           *;       UPA2                 -- update A2 coeff of 2nd order pred
    D0029           *;       LIMC                 -- limit A2
    D0030           *;       UPA1                 -- update A1 coeff of 2nd order pred
    D0031           *;       LIMD                 -- limit A1
    D0032           *;       UPB                  -- update coeffs of 6th order pred
    D0033           *;       XOR                  -- compute sign of DQ*DQn
    D0034           *;
    D0035           *;     NOTE: DELAY A/B/C implicit in timing of MIX/LIMA
    D0036           *;           and computation of SEZ/SE
    D0037           *;
    D0038           *;***************************************************************
    D0039           *;
    D0040           *; First convert quantized difference back to log domain.
    D0041           *; This is done by table look-up.  Also use ADPCM magnitude
    D0042           *; to look-up the scale-factor multipliers WI and rate-of-
    D0043           *; change weighting function FI.
    D0044           *;
    D0045 0355 2002 PRDICT LAC     IM
    D0046 0356 006A         ADD     INQTAB   ; reconst table
    D0047 0357 6721         TBLR    TEMP1    ; DQLN
    D0048 0358 034C         ADD     ONE,3    ; WI table address and offset
    D0049 0359 6769         TBLR    WI       ; lookup WI
    D0050 035A 034C         ADD     ONE,3    ; FI table address and offset
    D0051 035B 6768         TBLR    FI       ; lookup FI
    D0052           *;
    D0053           *;***************************************************************
    D0054           *; INVERSE ADAPTIVE QUANTIZER
    D0055           *;
    D0056           *;     INPUT:  ADPCM INPUT SAMPLE    -- I (IM->TEMP1)
```

```
CCITT        32010 FAMILY MACRO ASSEMBLER    PC2.1 84.107      16:36:03  03-20-85
                                                                       PAGE 0029
D0057              *;              QUANTIZER SCALE FACTOR -- Y (YOVER4)
D0058              *;
D0059              *;      OUTPUT: QUANTIZED DIFFERENCE SIGNAL -- DQ
D0060              *;
D0061              *;      NOTATION:  I      -- 4b SM (Q0)
D0062              *;                 IM     -- 3b magnitude (Q0)
D0063              *;                 DQLN(TEMP1) -- 12b TC (Q7) [sign extended]
D0064              *;                 YOVER4 -- 11b SM (Q7) POSITIVE VALUE ONLY
D0065              *;                 DQ     -- 15b TC (Q0) [sign extended]
D0066              *;                 DQMAN*8-- 9b magnitude
D0067              *;                 DQEXP  -- 4b magnitude
D0068              *;
D0069              *;****************************************************************
D0070              *;
D0071              *;                                     DQS
D0072              *;             +-----------------------------+
D0073              *;             |                             |
D0074              *;             |                             V
D0075              *;   I   +---+---+ DQLN  +-------+  DQL  +--------+  DQ
D0076              *; ----->|RECONST|------>| ADDA  |------>|ANTILOG |------>
D0077              *;       +-------+       +-------+       +--------+
D0078              *;                           ^
D0079              *;                           | Y
D0080              *;
D0081              *;****************************************************************
D0082              *;
D0083              *; add back scale factor
D0084              *;
D0085 035C 2521  ADDA    LAC     TEMP1,5
D0086 035D 0529          ADD     YOVER4,5
D0087              *;
D0088              *; now covert to linear domain
D0089              *;
D0090 035E 0C4C  ALOG    ADD     ONE,12          ; inc exponent for floated value
D0091 035F 5C15          SACH    DQEXP,4         ; save exponent + sign ext
D0092 0360 7972          AND     M4095           ; isolate mantissa * 2**5
D0093 0361 0C4C          ADD     ONE,12          ; Alog x = 1 + x
D0094 0362 505B          SACL    DQMAN           ; DQMAN = 0001 XXXX XXX0 0000
D0095 0363 2015          LAC     DQEXP
D0096 0364 0066          ADD     SHIFT           ; add table ptr
D0097 0365 6723          TBLR    TEMP3           ; get multiplier
D0098 0366 6A23          LT      TEMP3
D0099 0367 044C          ADD     ONE,4           ; offset to mask table
D0100 0368 6723          TBLR    TEMP3           ; mask for dqman
D0101 0369 6D5B          MPY     DQMAN           ; adjust mantissa
D0102 036A 7F8E          PAC
D0103 036B 5C10          SACH    DQ,4
D0104 036C 2B4C  ADDSGN  LAC     ONE,11          ; +2048 represents +sign
D0105 036D 5054          SACL    SDQ
D0106 036E 2001          LAC     I               ; check sign
D0107 036F 134C          SUB     ONE,3
D0108 0370 FA00          BLZ     FLTDQ
      0371 0377
D0109 0372 7F89          ZAC                     ; I carried negative sign
D0110 0373 1010          SUB     DQ
D0111 0374 5010          SACL    DQ
D0112 0375 2B4B          LAC     MINUS,11        ; -2048 represents -sign
```

```
CCITT        32010 FAMILY MACRO ASSEMBLER    PC2.1 84.107      16:36:03  03-20-85
                                                                      PAGE 0030
D0113 0376 5054          SACL    SDQ
D0114                *;
D0115                *;***********************************************************
D0116                *; FLOAT DQ -- convert 2's comp number to floating
D0117                *;
D0118                *;     INPUT:  DQ
D0119                *;
D0120                *;     OUTPUT: 4b exponent in DQEXP (saved from log value)
D0121                *;             6b mantissa*8 in DQMAN (adjusted from log)
D0122                *;             sign preserved in DQ
D0123                *;
D0124                *;***********************************************************
D0125                *;
D0126 0377 255B  FLTDQ  LAC     DQMAN,5 ; 00000000 0000001X XXXXXX00 00000000
D0127 0378 5C5B         SACH    DQMAN,4 ; DQMAN = 0000 0000 001X XXXX
D0128 0379 235B         LAC     DQMAN,3 ; DQMAN * 2**3
D0129 037A 7923         AND     TEMP3
D0130 037B 505B         SACL    DQMAN
D0131                *;
D0132                *;***********************************************************
D0133                *; QUANTIZER SCALE FACTOR ADAPTATION
D0134                *;
D0135                *;     INPUT:  ADPCM SAMPLE  -- I
D0136                *;
D0137                *;     OUTPUT: FAST QUANTIZER SCALE FACTOR -- YU
D0138                *;             SLOW QUANTIZER SCALE FACTOR -- YL (YLL/YLH)
D0139                *;
D0140                *;     NOTATION: I  -- 4b SM (Q0)
D0141                *;               YU -- 13b unsigned (Q9)
D0142                *;               YL -- 19b unsigned (Q15)
D0143                *;                  stored as:
D0144                *;                     low 15b -- YLL
D0145                *;                     hi   4b -- YLH
D0146                *;
D0147                *;***********************************************************
D0148                *;
D0149                *; WI  +-------+YUT +------+YUP +--------+         YU
D0150                *; --->| FILTD |--->| LIMB |-+->| DELAYB |---------------->
D0151                *;     +-------+    +------+ | +--------+
D0152                *;         ^                 |
D0153                *;         | Y               |   +-------+YLP +--------+ YL
D0154                *;         |                 +->| FILTE |--->| DELAYC |-+->
D0155                *;         |                    +-------+    +--------+ |
D0156                *;         |                        ^                   |
D0157                *;         |                        +-------------------+
D0158                *;
D0159                *;***********************************************************
D0160                *; Update fast adaptation scale factor
D0161                *;
D0162                *;   YU(k) = (1-2**-5)*Y(k) + (2**-5)*W(I(k))
D0163                *;
D0164                *;     INPUT:  QUANTIZER SCALE FACTOR  -- Y
D0165                *;             SCALE FACTOR MULTIPLIER -- WI
D0166                *;
D0167                *;     OUTPUT: FAST QUANTIZER SCALE FACTOR -- YU
D0168                *;
D0169                *;     NOTATION:  WI -- 12b TC (Q4) [sign extended]
```

```
D0170                    *;                        Y  -- 13b unsigned (Q9)
D0171                    *;                        YU -- 13b unsigned (Q9)
D0172                    *;
D0173                    *;*************************************************************
D0174                    *;
D0175 037C 2C09   FILTD  LAC      Y,12             ; Y        (Q21)
D0176 037D 1709          SUB      Y,7              ; Y/32     (Q21)
D0177 037E 0C69          ADD      WI,12            ; WI/32    (Q21)
D0178 037F 5C4E          SACH     YU,4             ; YU       (Q9)
D0179                    *;
D0180                    *; limit quant scale factor 1.06 <= YU <= 10.0
D0181                    *;
D0182 0380 1C6B   LIMB   SUB      K544,12          ; check lo threshold
D0183 0381 FD00          BGEZ     CHKHI
      0382 0386
D0184 0383 206B          LAC      K544
D0185 0384 F900          B        STRLIM           ; go store limited value
      0385 038A
D0186 0386 1C61   CHKHI  SUB      K4576,12         ; check hi threshold
D0187 0387 FB00          BLEZ     FILTE            ; within limits--continue
      0388 038B
D0188 0389 206C          LAC      K5120
D0189 038A 504E   STRLIM SACL     YU
D0190                    *;
D0191                    *;*************************************************************
D0192                    *; Update slow adaptation scale factor
D0193                    *;
D0194                    *;    YL(k) = (1-2**-6)*YL(k-1) + 2**-6 * YU(k)
D0195                    *;
D0196                    *;    INPUT:  SLOW QUANTIZER SCALE FACTOR -- YL (YLL/YLH)
D0197                    *;            FAST QUANTIZER SCALE FACTOR -- YU
D0198                    *;
D0199                    *;    OUTPUT: SLOW QUANTIZER SCALE FACTOR -- YL (YLL/YLH)
D0200                    *;
D0201                    *;    NOTATION:  YU -- 13b unsigned (Q9)
D0202                    *;               YL -- 19b unsigned (Q15)
D0203                    *;                  stored as:
D0204                    *;                      low 15b -- YLL
D0205                    *;                      hi   4b -- YLH
D0206                    *;
D0207                    *;*************************************************************
D0208                    *;
D0209 038B 2649   FILTE  LAC      YLH,6            ; shift yl left by 6
D0210 038C 5021          SACL     TEMP1
D0211 038D 2F21          LAC      TEMP1,15         ; YL       (Q21)
D0212 038E 064A          ADD      YLL,6
D0213 038F 1F49          SUB      YLH,15           ; YL/64    (Q21)
D0214 0390 104A          SUB      YLL
D0215 0391 064E          ADD      YU,6             ; YU/64    (Q21)
D0216 0392 5921          SACH     TEMP1,1
D0217 0393 7974          AND      M32767
D0218 0394 5022          SACL     TEMP2            ; result = yl (shifted left by 6)
D0219 0395 2A22          LAC      TEMP2,10         ; shift result right 6 --> 4.Q15
D0220 0396 5822          SACH     TEMP2
D0221 0397 2921          LAC      TEMP1,9          ; YL       (Q15)
D0222 0398 0022          ADD      TEMP2
D0223 0399 5949          SACH     YLH,1
```

```
D0224 039A 7974             AND      M32767
D0225 039B 504A             SACL     YLL
D0226              *;
D0227              *;*************************************************************
D0228              *; ADAPTATION SPEED CONTROL
D0229              *;
D0230              *;    INPUT:  ADPCM SAMPLE   -- I
D0231              *;
D0232              *;    OUTPUT: UNLIMITED SPEED CONTROL -- AP (APP)
D0233              *;
D0234              *;    NOTATION: I   -- 4b SM (Q0)
D0235              *;              APP -- 10b unsigned (Q8)
D0236              *;
D0237              *;*************************************************************
D0238              *;
D0239              *;                          ¦ Y
D0240              *;                          V
D0241              *; FI  +-------+DMSP+-------+ AX +-------+APP +--------+ AP
D0242              *; -+->¦ FILTA ¦-+->¦ SUBTC ¦--->¦ FILTC ¦--->¦ DELAYA ¦-+->
D0243              *;  ¦  +-------+ ¦ ¦ +-------+    +-------+    +--------+ ¦
D0244              *;  ¦           V ¦             ^                        ¦
D0245              *;  ¦ DMS¦ +-------+ ¦            +--------------------+
D0246              *;  ¦    +-¦ DELAYA ¦ ¦
D0247              *;  ¦      +--------+ ¦
D0248              *;  ¦                 ¦
D0249              *;  ¦ +-------+ DMLP ¦
D0250              *;  +->¦ FILTB ¦--+------+
D0251              *;     +-------+ ¦
D0252              *;       ^       V
D0253              *; DML¦ +--------+
D0254              *;    +-¦ DELAYA ¦
D0255              *;      +--------+
D0256              *;
D0257              *;*************************************************************
D0258              *; update short term average of FI
D0259              *;
D0260              *;    DMS(k) = (1-2**-5)*DMS(k-1) + 2**-5 * FI(k)
D0261              *;
D0262              *;    INPUT:  SHORT TERM AVERAGE     -- DMS
D0263              *;            RATE-OF-CHANGE FUNCTION -- FI
D0264              *;
D0265              *;    OUTPUT: SHORT TERM AVERAGE -- DMS
D0266              *;
D0267              *;    NOTATION:  DMS -- 12b unsigned (Q9)
D0268              *;               FI  -- 7b unsigned (Q4)
D0269              *;
D0270              *;*************************************************************
D0271              *;
D0272 039C 2F68  FILTA LAC   FI,15          ; FI/32   (Q24)
D0273 039D 0F07        ADD   DMS,15         ; DMS     (Q24)
D0274 039E 1A07        SUB   DMS,10         ; DMS/32  (Q24)
D0275 039F 5907        SACH  DMS,1
D0276              *;
D0277              *;*************************************************************
D0278              *; update long term average of FI
D0279              *;
D0280              *;    DML(k) = (1-2**-7)*DML(k-1) + 2**-7 * FI(k)
```

```
CCITT        32010 FAMILY MACRO ASSEMBLER    PC2.1 84.107      16:36:03  03-20-85
                                                                 PAGE 0033

D0281                   *;
D0282                   *;      INPUT:  LONG TERM AVERAGE          -- DML
D0283                   *;              RATE-OF-CHANGE FUNCTION -- FI
D0284                   *;
D0285                   *;      OUTPUT: LONG TERM AVERAGE -- DML
D0286                   *;
D0287                   *;      NOTATION:  DML -- 14b unsigned (Q11)
D0288                   *;                 FI  -- 7b unsigned (Q4)
D0289                   *;
D0290                   *;****************************************************************
D0291                   *;
D0292 03A0 2F68  FILTB  LAC      FI,15              ; FI/128     (Q26)
D0293 03A1 0F08         ADD      DML,15             ; DML        (Q26)
D0294 03A2 1808         SUB      DML,8              ; DML/128    (Q26)
D0295 03A3 5908         SACH     DML,1
D0296                   *;
D0297                   *;------------------------------------------------------------
D0298                   *; Compute mag of diff of short and long term functions of
D0299                   *; quantizer output sequence and perform threshold
D0300                   *; comparison to compute speed control parameter--low-pass
D0301                   *; result.
D0302                   *;
D0303                   *;   APP(k) = (1-2**-4)*APP(k-1) + 2**-3 , if Y < 3 or
D0304                   *;                                if |DMS-DML| > 2**-3 * DML
D0305                   *;   else
D0306                   *;
D0307                   *;   APP(k) = (1-2**-4)*APP(k-1)
D0308                   *;
D0309                   *;      INPUT:  SHORT TERM AVERAGE         -- DMS
D0310                   *;              LONG TERM AVERAGE          -- DML
D0311                   *;              UNLIMITED SPEED CONTROL -- APP
D0312                   *;              QUANTIZER SCALE FACTOR  -- Y
D0313                   *;
D0314                   *;      OUTPUT: UNLIMITED SPEED CONTROL -- APP
D0315                   *;
D0316                   *;      NOTATION:  APP -- 10b unsigned (Q8)
D0317                   *;                 Y   -- 13b unsigned (Q9)
D0318                   *;                 DMS -- 12b unsigned (Q9)
D0319                   *;                 DML -- 14b unsigned (Q11)
D0320                   *;
D0321                   *;****************************************************************
D0322                   *;
D0323 03A4 6505  FILTC  ZALH     APP                ; APP            (Q24)
D0324 03A5 1C05         SUB      APP,12             ; APP/16         (Q24)
D0325 03A6 5805         SACH     APP                ; (1-2**-4)*APP  (Q8)
D0326 03A7 2009         LAC      Y
D0327 03A8 197D         SUB      THREE,9            ; 3       (Q9)
D0328 03A9 FA00         BLZ      ADD18
      03AA 03B3
D0329 03AB 2D08         LAC      DML,13             ; DML/8    (Q27)
D0330 03AC 5823         SACH     TEMP3              ; DML/8    (Q11)
D0331 03AD 2207         LAC      DMS,2              ; DMS      (Q11)
D0332 03AE 1008         SUB      DML                ; DMS-DML
D0333 03AF 7F88         ABS
D0334 03B0 1023         SUB      TEMP3              ; |DMS-DML|-DML/8
D0335 03B1 FA00         BLZ      APRED
      03B2 03B6
```

```
D0336 03B3 2005  ADD18  LAC    APP                ; APP      (Q8)
D0337 03B4 054C         ADD    ONE,5
D0338 03B5 5005         SACL   APP                ; + 1/8    (Q8)
D0339            *;
D0340            *;******************************************************
D0341            *; ADAPTIVE PREDICTOR
D0342            *;
D0343            *;******************************************************
D0344            *;
D0345      03B6  APRED  EQU    $
D0346            *;
D0347            *;******************************************************
D0348            *; compute coeff of 6th order predictor
D0349            *;
D0350            *; Bi(k) = (1-2**-8)*Bi(k-1) + 2**-7*SGN[DQ(k)]*SGN[DQ(k-i)]
D0351            *;      for i = 1...6
D0352            *;      and Bi is implicitly limited to +/- 2
D0353            *;
D0354            *;    NOTATION:      Bn   -- 16b TC (Q14)
D0355            *;                   SDQn -- +2048 if sign positive
D0356            *;                        -2048 if sign negative
D0357            *;
D0358            *;******************************************************
D0359            *;
D0360 03B6 6A5A  GETB6  LT     SDQ6
D0361 03B7 280F         LAC    B6,8     ; B6 * 2**-8 TRUNCATED
D0362 03B8 5821         SACH   TEMP1
D0363 03B9 2F0F         LAC    B6,15    ; Q29
D0364 03BA 1F21         SUB    TEMP1,15
D0365 03BB 6D54         MPY    SDQ      ; SGN(SDQ)*SGN(SDQ6) * 2**-7  (Q29)
D0366 03BC 6B59         LTD    SDQ5
D0367 03BD 590F         SACH   B6,1     ; Q14
D0368 03BE 280E  GETB5  LAC    B5,8     ; B5 * 2**-8 TRUNCATED
D0369 03BF 5821         SACH   TEMP1
D0370 03C0 2F0E         LAC    B5,15    ; Q29
D0371 03C1 1F21         SUB    TEMP1,15
D0372 03C2 6D54         MPY    SDQ
D0373 03C3 6B58         LTD    SDQ4
D0374 03C4 590E         SACH   B5,1     ; Q14
D0375 03C5 280D  GETB4  LAC    B4,8     ; B4 * 2**-8 TRUNCATED
D0376 03C6 5821         SACH   TEMP1
D0377 03C7 2F0D         LAC    B4,15    ; Q29
D0378 03C8 1F21         SUB    TEMP1,15
D0379 03C9 6D54         MPY    SDQ
D0380 03CA 6B57         LTD    SDQ3
D0381 03CB 590D         SACH   B4,1     ; Q14
D0382 03CC 280C  GETB3  LAC    B3,8     ; B3 * 2**-8 TRUNCATED
D0383 03CD 5821         SACH   TEMP1
D0384 03CE 2F0C         LAC    B3,15    ; Q29
D0385 03CF 1F21         SUB    TEMP1,15
D0386 03D0 6D54         MPY    SDQ
D0387 03D1 6B56         LTD    SDQ2
D0388 03D2 590C         SACH   B3,1     ; Q14
D0389 03D3 280B  GETB2  LAC    B2,8     ; B2 * 2**-8 TRUNCATED
D0390 03D4 5821         SACH   TEMP1
D0391 03D5 2F0B         LAC    B2,15    ; Q29
D0392 03D6 1F21         SUB    TEMP1,15
```

290

```
D0393 03D7 6D54          MPY     SDQ
D0394 03D8 6B55          LTD     SDQ1
D0395 03D9 590B          SACH    B2,1     ; Q14
D0396 03DA 280A  GETB1   LAC     B1,8     ; B1 * 2**-8 TRUNCATED
D0397 03DB 5821          SACH    TEMP1
D0398 03DC 2F0A          LAC     B1,15    ; Q29
D0399 03DD 1F21          SUB     TEMP1,15
D0400 03DE 6D54          MPY     SDQ
D0401 03DF 6B54          LTD     SDQ
D0402 03E0 590/          SACH    B1,1     ; Q14
D0403            *;
D0404            *;********************************************************
D0405            *; To update coefficients of 2nd order predictor,
D0406            *; First get sign of sum of SEZ and DQ
D0407            *;
D0408            *;    NOTATION: if SEZ+DQ >= 0 then PK0 = 512
D0409            *;              else                PK0 = -512
D0410            *;
D0411            *;********************************************************
D0412            *;
D0413 03E1 6950  ADDC    DMOV    PK1                ; PK1==>PK2
D0414 03E2 694F          DMOV    PK0                ; PK0==>PK1
D0415 03E3 2004          LAC     SEZ
D0416 03E4 0110          ADD     DQ,1
D0417 03E5 5821          SACH    TEMP1    ; FFFF or 0000
D0418 03E6 2A21          LAC     TEMP1,10 ; FC00 or 0000
D0419 03E7 094C          ADD     ONE,9    ; FE00 or 0200 ; -512 or +512
D0420 03E8 504F          SACL    PK0
D0421 03E9 6A4F  SUMGT0  LT      PK0
D0422            *;
D0423            *;********************************************************
D0424            *;  now calculate 1/2 * f[A1(k-1)]
D0425            *;
D0426            *;    = 2*A1        if |A1| <= 1/2
D0427            *;    = SGN(A1)     if |A1| >  1/2
D0428            *;
D0429            *;********************************************************
D0430            *;
D0431 03EA 2111  GETF    LAC     A1,1               ; 2*A1
D0432 03EB 5023          SACL    TEMP3
D0433 03EC FA00          BLZ     GETF2
      03ED 03F4
D0434 03EE 1E4C  GETF1   SUB     ONE,14             ; is |A1| < 1/2
D0435 03EF FA00          BLZ     GETA1
      03F0 03FA
D0436 03F1 2062          LAC     K16382             ; approx 1
D0437 03F2 F900          B       DONEF
      03F3 03F9
D0438 03F4 7F88  GETF2   ABS
D0439 03F5 1E4C          SUB     ONE,14             ; is |A1| < 1/2
D0440 03F6 FA00          BLZ     GETA1
      03F7 03FA
D0441 03F8 2063          LAC     M16382             ; approx -1
D0442 03F9 5023  DONEF   SACL    TEMP3
D0443            *;
D0444            *;********************************************************
D0445            *; Compute A1 coeff of 2nd order predictor
```

```
CCITT        32010 FAMILY MACRO ASSEMBLER    PC2.1 84.107    16:36:03  03-20-85
                                                                  PAGE 0036

D0446               *;
D0447               *;   A1(k) = (1-2**-8)*A1(k-1)
D0448               *;                    + (3*2**-8)*SGN[p(k)]*SGN[p(k-1)]
D0449               *;
D0450               *;   NOTATION:  A1  -- 16b TC (Q14)
D0451               *;              PKn -- +512 if SGN[p(k)] =  1
D0452               *;                     -512 if SGN[p(k)] = -1
D0453               *;
D0454               *;***********************************************************
D0455               *;
D0456 03FA 2811  GETA1 LAC    A1,8              ; A1*2**-8 TRUNCATED
D0457 03FB 5822        SACH   TEMP2
D0458 03FC 2C11        LAC    A1,12             ; Q26
D0459 03FD 1C22        SUB    TEMP2,12
D0460 03FE 6D50        MPY    PK1               ; SGN[p(k-1)]*SGN[p(k)]
D0461 03FF 7F8F        APAC
D0462 0400 7F8F        APAC
D0463 0401 7F8F        APAC                     ; +3*SGN[p(k-1)]*SGN[p(k)]
D0464 0402 5C11        SACH   A1,4              ; store as Q14
D0465 0403 7F8E        PAC                      ; save sign
D0466               *;
D0467               *;***********************************************************
D0468               *; Compute A2 coeff of 2nd order predictor
D0469               *;
D0470               *;   A2(k) = (1-2**-7)*A2(k-1)
D0471               *;            + (2**-7)*{SGN[p(k)]*SGN[(p(k-2)]
D0472               *;                    - f[A1(k-1)]*SGN[p(k)]*SGN[p(k-1)]}
D0473               *;
D0474               *;   NOTATION:  A2         -- 16b TC (Q14)
D0475               *;              F(),TEMP3  -- 16b TC (Q14)
D0476               *;              PKn.       -- +512 if SGN[p(k)] =  1
D0477               *;                            -512 if SGN[p(k)] = -1
D0478               *;
D0479               *;***********************************************************
D0480               *;
D0481 0404 FD00  GETA2 BGEZ   SUBF              ; if sign + --> subtract F
     0405 0409
D0482 0406 7F89        ZAC                      ;  else negate F and subtract
D0483 0407 1023        SUB    TEMP3
D0484 0408 5023        SACL   TEMP3
D0485               *;
D0486 0409 2912  SUBF  LAC    A2,9              ; A2*2**-7 TRUNCATED
D0487 040A 581E        SACH   SUM4
D0488 040B 6D51        MPY    PK2               ; SGN[p(k-2)]*SGN[p(k)]
D0489 040C 7F8E        PAC
D0490 040D 7F8F        APAC                     ; 2*2**-8*above   (Q26)
D0491 040E 1623        SUB    TEMP3,6           ; 2*TEMP3*2**-7   (Q26)
D0492 040F 5C23        SACH   TEMP3,4           ; Q14
D0493 0410 2012        LAC    A2
D0494 0411 101E        SUB    SUM4              ; leak factor
D0495 0412 0023        ADD    TEMP3
D0496 0413 5012        SACL   A2                ; Q14
D0497               *
D0498 0414 5821        SACH   TEMP1             ; save sign to make +/- .75
D0499               *;
D0500               *; limit A2 to +/- .75 and prevent overflow
D0501               *;
```

```
D0502 0415 7F88  LIMC   ABS
D0503 0416 1C7D         SUB    THREE,12      ; |value| must be < .75
D0504 0417 FB00         BLEZ   LIMD
      0418 041D
D0505 0419 2C7D         LAC    THREE,12      ; .75  (Q14)
D0506 041A 7821         XOR    TEMP1         ; 1's complement if negative
D0507 041B 1021         SUB    TEMP1         ; 2's complement if negative
D0508 041C 5012  DONEC  SACL   A2            ; Q14
D0509             *;
D0510             *; limit A1(k) to +/- [1-2**-4 - A2(k)]
D0511             *;
D0512 041D 2A6D  LIMD   LAC    M15,10        ; 1-2**-4        (Q14)
D0513 041E 1012         SUB    A2
D0514 041F 5021         SACL   TEMP1         ; 1-2**-4-A2P  (Q14)
D0515 0420 2011         LAC    A1
D0516 0421 5824  .      SACH   TEMP4         ; save sign to make +/- LIMIT
D0517 0422 7F88         ABS
D0518 0423 1021         SUB    TEMP1
D0519 0424 FB00         BLEZ   FLTSR         ; A1 <= LIMIT
      0425 042A
D0520 0426 2021  A1LIM  LAC    TEMP1         ; ABS value of LIMIT
D0521 0427 7824         XOR    TEMP4         ; 1's complement if negative
D0522 0428 1024         SUB    TEMP4         ; 2's complement if negative
D0523 0429 5011         SACL   A1            ; Q14
D0524             *;
D0525             *;**************************************************************
D0526             *; COMPUTE RECONSTRUCTED SIGNAL
D0527             *;
D0528             *;    INPUT:   QUANTIZED DIFFERENCE SIGNAL -- DQ
D0529             *;             SIGNAL ESTIMATE             -- SE
D0530             *;
D0531             *;    OUTPUT: RECONSTRUCTED SIGNAL -- SR
D0532             *;
D0533             *;    NOTATION:  DQ -- 15b TC (Q0) [sign extended]
D0534             *;               SE -- 15b TC (Q0) [sign extended]
D0535             *;               SR -- 16b TC (Q0)
D0536             *;
D0537             *;**************************************************************
D0538             *; FLOAT SR -- convert 2's comp number to floating
D0539             *;
D0540             *;    INPUT:  accumulator
D0541             *;
D0542             *;    OUTPUT: --4b exponent left in SREXP
D0543             *;            --6b mantissa*8 left in SRMAN
D0544             *;            --sign preserved in SR
D0545             *;
D0546             *;**************************************************************
D0547             *;
D0548 042A 2010  FLTSR  LAC    DQ            ; compute reconstructed signal
D0549 042B 0003         ADD    SE
D0550 042C 5013         SACL   SR
D0551 042D 7F88         ABS                  ; convert to floating point notation
D0552 042E 5052         SACL   SRMAN
D0553 042F 174C         SUB    ONE,7         ; binary search to get exponent
D0554 0430 FD00         BGEZ   D8TOF
      0431 0469
D0555 0432 036D  D0TO7  ADD    M15,3         ; TEMP1-8 -- exp = 0-7
```

```
D0556 0433 FD00          BGEZ    D4TO7
      0434 044A
D0557 0435 017D  D0TO3   ADD     THREE,1 ; TEMP1-2 -- exp = 0-3
D0558 0436 FD00          BGEZ    D2TO3
      0437 043D
D0559 0438 2052  D0TO1   LAC     SRMAN    ; exp = 0-1
D0560 0439 501C  EXX01   SACL    SREXP
D0561 043A 284C          LAC     ONE,8
D0562 043B 5052          SACL    SRMAN
D0563 043C 7F8D          RET
D0564 043D 114C  D2TO3   SUB     ONE,1    ; TEMP1-4 -- exp = 2-3
D0565 043E FD00          BGEZ    EXX3
      043F 0445
D0566 0440 2752  EXX2    LAC     SRMAN,7 ; exp=2
D0567 0441 5052          SACL    SRMAN
D0568 0442 7E02          LACK    2
D0569 0443 501C          SACL    SREXP
D0570 0444 7F8D          RET
D0571 0445 2652  EXX3    LAC     SRMAN,6 ; exp=3
D0572 0446 5052          SACL    SRMAN
D0573 0447 7E03          LACK    3
D0574 0448 501C          SACL    SREXP
D0575 0449 7F8D          RET
D0576 044A 137D  D4TO7   SUB     THREE,3 -- TEMP1-32 -- exp = 4-7
D0577 044B FD00          BGEZ    D6TO7
      044C 045A
D0578 044D 044C  D4TO5   ADD     ONE,4    ; TEMP1-16 -- exp = 4-5
D0579 044E FD00          BGEZ    EXX5
      044F 0455
D0580 0450 2552  EXX4    LAC     SRMAN,5 ; exp=4
D0581 0451 5052          SACL    SRMAN
D0582 0452 7E04          LACK    4
D0583 0453 501C          SACL    SREXP
D0584 0454 7F8D          RET
D0585 0455 2452  EXX5    LAC     SRMAN,4 ; exp=5
D0586 0456 5052          SACL    SRMAN
D0587 0457 7E05          LACK    5
D0588 0458 501C          SACL    SREXP
D0589 0459 7F8D          RET
D0590 045A 154C  D6TO7   SUB     ONE,5    ; TEMP1-64 -- exp = 6-7
D0591 045B FD00          BGEZ    EXX7
      045C 0462
D0592 045D 2352  EXX6    LAC     SRMAN,3 ; exp=6
D0593 045E 5052          SACL    SRMAN
D0594 045F 7E06          LACK    6
D0595 0460 501C          SACL    SREXP
D0596 0461 7F8D          RET
D0597 0462 2F52  EXX7    LAC     SRMAN,15
D0598 0463 5852          SACH    SRMAN
D0599 0464 2352          LAC     SRMAN,3
D0600 0465 5052          SACL    SRMAN
D0601 0466 7E07          LACK    7
D0602 0467 501C          SACL    SREXP
D0603 0468 7F8D          RET
D0604 0469 1177  D8TOF   SUB     K960,1  ; TEMP1-2048 -- exp = 8-15
D0605 046A FD00          BGEZ    DCTOF
      046B 0491
```

```
D0606 046C 097D  D8TOB  ADD   THREE,9 ; TEMP1-512 -- exp = 8-11
D0607 046D FD00         BGEZ  DATOB
      046E 0480
D0608 046F 084C  D8TO9  ADD   ONE,8   ; TEMP1-256 -- exp = 8-9
D0609 0470 FD00         BGEZ  EXX9
      0471 0479
D0610 0472 2E52  EXX8   LAC   SRMAN,14 ; exp=8
D0611 0473 5852         SACH  SRMAN
D0612 0474 2352         LAC   SRMAN,3
D0613 0475 5052         SACL  SRMAN
D0614 0476 7E08         LACK  8
D0615 0477 501C         SACL  SREXP
D0616 0478 7F8D         RET
D0617 0479 2D52  EXX9   LAC   SRMAN,13 ; exp=9
D0618 047A 5852         SACH  SRMAN
D0619 047B 2352         LAC   SRMAN,3
D0620 047C 5052         SACL  SRMAN
D0621 047D 7E09         LACK  9
D0622 047E 501C         SACL  SREXP
D0623 047F 7F8D         RET
D0624 0480 194C  DATOB  SUB   ONE,9    ; TEMP1-1024 -- exp=10-11
D0625 0481 FD00         BGEZ  EXX11
      0482 048A
D0626 0483 2C52  EXX10  LAC   SRMAN,12 ; exp=10
D0627 0484 5852         SACH  SRMAN
D0628 0485 2352         LAC   SRMAN,3
D0629 0486 5052         SACL  SRMAN
D0630 0487 7E0A         LACK  10
D0631 0488 501C         SACL  SREXP
D0632 0489 7F8D         RET
D0633 048A 2B52  EXX11  LAC   SRMAN,11 ; exp=11
D0634 048B 5852         SACH  SRMAN
D0635 048C 2352         LAC   SRMAN,3
D0636 048D 5052         SACL  SRMAN
D0637 048E 7E0B         LACK  11
D0638 048F 501C         SACL  SREXP
D0639 0490 7F8D         RET
D0640 0491 1B7D  DCTOF  SUB   THREE,11 ; TEMP1-8192 -- exp=12-15
D0641 0492 FD00         BGEZ  DETOF
      0493 04A5
D0642 0494 0C4C  DCTOD  ADD   ONE,12   ; TEMP1-4096 -- exp=12-13
D0643 0495 FD00         BGEZ  EXX13
      0496 049E
D0644 0497 2A52  EXX12  LAC   SRMAN,10 ; exp=12
D0645 0498 5852         SACH  SRMAN
D0646 0499 2352         LAC   SRMAN,3
D0647 049A 5052         SACL  SRMAN
D0648 049B 7E0C         LACK  12
D0649 049C 501C         SACL  SREXP
D0650 049D 7F8D         RET
D0651 049E 2952  EXX13  LAC   SRMAN,9  ; exp=13
D0652 049F 5852         SACH  SRMAN
D0653 04A0 2352         LAC   SRMAN,3
D0654 04A1 5052         SACL  SRMAN
D0655 04A2 7E0D         LACK  13
D0656 04A3 501C         SACL  SREXP
D0657 04A4 7F8D         RET
```

```
CCITT         32010 FAMILY MACRO ASSEMBLER    PC2.1 84.107    16:36:03  03-20-85
                                                                PAGE 0040

D0658 04A5 1D4C  DETOF  SUB    ONE,13   ; TEMP1-16384 -- exp=14-15
D0659 04A6 FD00         BGEZ   EXX15
      04A7 04AF
D0660 04A8 2852  EXX14  LAC    SRMAN,8  ; exp=14
D0661 04A9 5852         SACH   SRMAN
D0662 04AA 2352         LAC    SRMAN,3
D0663 04AB 5052         SACL   SRMAN
D0664 04AC 7E0E         LACK   14
D0665 04AD 501C         SACL   SREXP
D0666 04AE 7F8D         RET
D0667 04AF 2752  EXX15  LAC    SRMAN,7  ; exp=15
D0668 04B0 5852         SACH   SRMAN
D0669 04B1 2352         LAC    SRMAN,3
D0670 04B2 5052         SACL   SRMAN
D0671 04B3 7E0F         LACK   15
D0672 04B4 501C         SACL   SREXP
D0673 04B5 7F8D         RET
```

```
CCITT        32010 FAMILY MACRO ASSEMBLER    PC2.1 84.107    16:36:03  03-20-85
                                                             PAGE 0041

 0005                       COPY    UTILITY.ASM
E0001              *;
E0002              *;  code to do left shifts for SEZ/SE calculations
E0003              *;
E0004 04B6 7F88  RS1    ABS                    ; make positive before mask
E0005 04B7 7974         AND     M32767         ; keep lower 15 bits
E0006 04B8 5022         SACL    SUM1           ; save result
E0007 04B9 F900         B       CHK1           ; return
      04BA 01C4
E0008 04BB 7F88  RS2    ABS
E0009 04BC 7974         AND     M32767
E0010 04BD 5023         SACL    SUM2
E0011 04BE F900         B       CHK2
      04BF 01DE
E0012 04C0 7F88  RS3    ABS
E0013 04C1 7974         AND     M32767
E0014 04C2 5025         SACL    SUM3
E0015 04C3 F900         B       CHK3
      04C4 01F8
E0016 04C5 7F88  RS4    ABS
E0017 04C6 7974         AND     M32767
E0018 04C7 501E         SACL    SUM4
E0019 04C8 F900         B       CHK4
      04C9 0212
E0020 04CA 7F88  RS5    ABS
E0021 04CB 7974         AND     M32767
E0022 04CC 501F         SACL    SUM5
E0023 04CD F900         B       CHK5
      04CE 022C
E0024 04CF 7F88  RS6    ABS
E0025 04D0 7974         AND     M32767
E0026 04D1 5020         SACL    SUM6
E0027 04D2 F900         B       CHK6
      04D3 0246
E0028 04D4 7F88  RS11   ABS
E0029 04D5 7974         AND     M32767
E0030 04D6 5027         SACL    SUM7
E0031 04D7 F900         B       CHK11
      04D8 025F
E0032 04D9 7F88  RS21   ABS
E0033 04DA 7974         AND     M32767
E0034 04DB 5028         SACL    SUM8
E0035 04DC F900         B       CHK21
      04DD 0279
```

```
E0037                 *;
E0038                 *;--------------------------------------------------------------
E0039                 *; FLOAT SUBROUTINE--convert 2's comp number to floating
E0040                 *;             INPUT: accumulator
E0041                 *;             OUTPUT:
E0042                 *;                      --4b exponent left in accum
E0043                 *;                      --6b mantissa left in TEMP1
E0044                 *;                      --sign preserved in original number
E0045                 *;
E0046                 *;--------------------------------------------------------------
E0047      002A  FLTSFT EQU     42        ; address of shift multipliers
E0048                 *;
E0049                 *;
E0050 04DE 5821  FLOAT SACH    TEMP1
E0051 04DF 2021        LAC     TEMP1
E0052 04E0 7F88        ABS
E0053 04E1 5021        SACL    TEMP1
E0054 04E2 164C        SUB     ONE,6     ; binary search to get expONEnt
E0055 04E3 FD00        BGEZ    E7TOD
      04E4 0511
E0056 04E5 0076  E0TO7 ADD     K56       ; TEMP1-8 -- exp = 0-6
E0057 04E6 FD00        BGEZ    E4TO6
      04E7 0501
E0058 04E8 017D  E0TO3 ADD     THREE,1   ; TEMP1-2 -- exp = 0-3
E0059 04E9 FD00        BGEZ    E2TO3
      04EA 04F6
E0060 04EB 2021  E0TO1 LAC     TEMP1     ; exp = 0-1
E0061 04EC FE00        BNZ     E1
      04ED 04F2
E0062 04EE 254C  E0    LAC     ONE,5     ; exp=0
E0063 04EF 5021        SACL    TEMP1
E0064 04F0 7E2A        LACK    FLTSFT+0
E0065 04F1 7F8D        RET
E0066 04F2 2521  E1    LAC     TEMP1,5   ; exp=1
E0067 04F3 5021        SACL    TEMP1
E0068 04F4 7E2B        LACK    FLTSFT+1
E0069 04F5 7F8D        RET
E0070 04F6 114C  E2TO3 SUB     ONE,1     ; TEMP1-4 -- exp = 2-3
E0071 04F7 FD00        BGEZ    E3
      04F8 04FD
E0072 04F9 2421  E2    LAC     TEMP1,4   ; exp=2
E0073 04FA 5021        SACL    TEMP1
E0074 04FB 7E2C        LACK    FLTSFT+2
E0075 04FC 7F8D        RET
E0076 04FD 2321  E3    LAC     TEMP1,3   ; exp=3
E0077 04FE 5021        SACL    TEMP1
E0078 04FF 7E2D        LACK    FLTSFT+3
E0079 0500 7F8D        RET
E0080 0501 134C  E4TO6 SUB     ONE,3     ; TEMP1-16 -- exp = 4-6
E0081 0502 FD00        BGEZ    E5TO6
      0503 0508
E0082 0504 2221  E4    LAC     TEMP1,2   ; exp=4
E0083 0505 5021        SACL    TEMP1
E0084 0506 7E2E        LACK    FLTSFT+4
E0085 0507 7F8D        RET
E0086 0508 144C  E5TO6 SUB     ONE,4     ; TEMP1-32 -- exp = 5-6
E0087 0509 FD00        BGEZ    E6
```

```
           050A 050F
E0088 050B 2121  E5     LAC     TEMP1,1 ; exp=5
E0089 050C 5021         SACL    TEMP1
E0090 050D 7E2F         LACK    FLTSFT+5
E0091 050E 7F8D         RET
E0092 050F 7E30  E6     LACK    FLTSFT+6        ; exp=6
E0093 0510 7F8D         RET
E0094 0511 1077  E7TOD  SUB     K960     ; TEMP1-1024 -- exp = 7-13
E0095 0512 FD00         BGEZ    EBTOD
           0513 052D
E0096 0514 087D  E7TOA  ADD     THREE,8 ; TEMP1-256  -- exp = 7-10
E0097 0515 FD00         BGEZ    E9TOA
           0516 0522
E0098 0517 074C  E7TO8  ADD     ONE,7   ; TEMP1-128  -- exp = 7-8
E0099 0518 FD00         BGEZ    E8
           0519 051E
E0100 051A 2F21  E7     LAC     TEMP1,15 ; exp=7
E0101 051B 5821         SACH    TEMP1
E0102 051C 7E31         LACK    FLTSFT+7
E0103 051D 7F8D         RET
E0104 051E 2E21  E8     LAC     TEMP1,14 ; exp=8
E0105 051F 5821         SACH    TEMP1
E0106 0520 7E32         LACK    FLTSFT+8
E0107 0521 7F8D         RET
E0108 0522 184C  E9TOA  SUB     ONE,8   ; TEMP1-512  -- exp = 9-10
E0109 0523 FD00         BGEZ    E10
           0524 0529
E0110 0525 2D21  E9     LAC     TEMP1,13 ; exp=9
E0111 0526 5821         SACH    TEMP1
E0112 0527 7E33         LACK    FLTSFT+9
E0113 0528 7F8D         RET
E0114 0529 2C21  E10    LAC     TEMP1,12 ; exp=10
E0115 052A 5821         SACH    TEMP1
E0116 052B 7E34         LACK    FLTSFT+10
E0117 052C 7F8D         RET
E0118 052D 1A7D  EBTOD  SUB     THREE,10          ; TEMP1-4096 -- exp=11-13
E0119 052E FD00         BGEZ    EDTOE
           052F 053B
E0120 0530 0B4C  EBTOC  ADD     ONE,11  ; TEMP1-2048 -- exp=11-12
E0121 0531 FD00         BGEZ    E12
           0532 0537
E0122 0533 2B21  E11    LAC     TEMP1,11 ; exp=11
E0123 0534 5821         SACH    TEMP1
E0124 0535 7E35         LACK    FLTSFT+11
E0125 0536 7F8D         RET
E0126 0537 2A21  E12    LAC     TEMP1,10 ; exp=12
E0127 0538 5821         SACH    TEMP1
E0128 0539 7E36         LACK    FLTSFT+12
E0129 053A 7F8D         RET
E0130 053B 1C4C  EDTOE  SUB     ONE,12  ; TEMP1-8192 -- exp=0
E0131 053C FD00         BGEZ    E0
           053D 04EE
E0132 053E 2921  E13    LAC     TEMP1,9  ; exp=13
E0133 053F 5821         SACH    TEMP1
E0134 0540 7E37         LACK    FLTSFT+13
E0135 0541 7F8D         RET
```

```
CCITT           32010 FAMILY MACRO ASSEMBLER    PC2.1 84.107     16:36:03  03-20-85
                                                                  PAGE 0044

  0006                          COPY    INIT.ASM
 F0001              *;**********************************************************
 F0002              *; SYSTEM INITIALIZATION
 F0003              *;**********************************************************
 F0004      004A    NOCONS EQU     74
 F0005      0036    PTCONS EQU     54
 F0006              *;
 F0007 0542 7F81    RESET  DINT                        ; Disable interrupts
 F0008 0543 6E00           LDPK    0                    ; Initialize data page
 F0009              *;
 F0010 0544 7035    SETPAC LARK    0,53
 F0011 0545 6880           LARP    0
 F0012 0546 7F89           ZAC                          ; Zero iram
 F0013 0547 5080    ZRAMA  SACL    *,0,0
 F0014 0548 F400           BANZ    ZRAMA.
      0549 0547
 F0015              *;
 F0016 054A 7E01           LACK    1
 F0017 054B 504C           SACL    ONE
 F0018 054C 6A4C           LT      ONE
 F0019 054D 859B           MPYK    CONS
 F0020 054E 7F8E           PAC                          ; ROM ADDR
 F0021 054F 7136           LARK    1,PTCONS             ; RAM ADDR
 F0022 0550 7049           LARK    0,NOCONS-1
 F0023 0551 6881    NXCONS LARP    1
 F0024 0552 67A0           TBLR    *+,0
 F0025 0553 004C           ADD     ONE
 F0026 0554 F400           BANZ    NXCONS
      0555 0551
 F0027              *;
 F0028 0556 4021           IN      TEMP1,CTL
 F0029 0557 2021           LAC     TEMP1
 F0030 0558 FA00           BLZ     ALAW
      0559 055E
 F0031 055A FF00    MULAW  BZ      MULAWX
      055B 0020
 F0032 055C F900           B       MULAWR
      055D 00F9
 F0033 055E 7974    ALAW   AND     M32767
 F0034 055F FF00           BZ      ALAWX
      0560 004E
 F0035 0561 F900           B       ALAWR
      0562 0184
 F0036              *;
```

```
CCITT          32010 FAMILY MACRO ASSEMBLER    PC2.1 84.107    16:36:03  03-20-85
                                                                 PAGE 0045

   0007                         COPY    ROMRAM.ASM
  G0001                   *;
  G0002                   *;*************************************************************
  G0003                   *;    ROM
  G0004                   *;*************************************************************
  G0005  0563      ROMLOC BSS      0
  G0006                   *; SHIFT MULT TABLE
  G0007  0563      SHFT   BSS      0
  G0008  0563 0000        DATA     0         ; log dq to flt dq exponent adjustment
  G0009  0564 0001        DATA     1
  G0010  0565 0002        DATA     2
  G0011  0566 0004        DATA     4
  G0012  0567 0008        DATA     8
  G0013  0568 0010        DATA     16
  G0014  0569 0020        DATA     32
  G0015  056A 0040        DATA     64
  G0016  056B 0080        DATA     128
  G0017  056C 0100        DATA     256
  G0018  056D 0200        DATA     512
  G0019  056E 0400        DATA     1024
  G0020  056F 0800        DATA     2048
  G0021  0570 1000        DATA     4096
  G0022  0571 2000        DATA     8192
  G0023  0572 4000        DATA     16384
  G0024                   *; DQMAN MASK TABLE
  G0025  0573 FE00        DATA     65024
  G0026  0574 FF00        DATA     65280
  G0027  0575 FF80        DATA     65408
  G0028  0576 FFC0        DATA     65472
  G0029  0577 FFE0        DATA     65504
  G0030  0578 FFF0        DATA     65520
  G0031  0579 FFF8        DATA     65528
  G0032  057A FFF8        DATA     65528
  G0033  057B FFF8        DATA     65528
  G0034  057C FFF8        DATA     65528
  G0035  057D FFF8        DATA     65528
  G0036  057E FFF8        DATA     65528
  G0037  057F FFF8        DATA     65528
  G0038  0580 FFF8        DATA     65528
  G0039  0581 FFF8        DATA     65528
  G0040  0582 FFF8        DATA     65528
  G0041                   *; INVERSE QUANTIZING TABLE
  G0042  0583      IQTAB  BSS      0
  G0043  0583 FF79        DATA     65401
  G0044  0584 0044        DATA     68
  G0045  0585 00A5        DATA     165
  G0046  0586 00E8        DATA     232
  G0047  0587 011D        DATA     285
  G0048  0588 014C        DATA     332
  G0049  0589 0179        DATA     377
  G0050  058A 01AC        DATA     428
  G0051                   *; WI TABLE
  G0052  058B      WTABLE BSS      0
  G0053  058B FFF4        DATA     65524
  G0054  058C 0004        DATA     4
  G0055  058D 001B        DATA     27
  G0056  058E 0032        DATA     50
```

```
G0057 058F 0062          DATA    98
G0058 0590 00B8          DATA    184
G0059 0591 0154          DATA    340
G0060 0592 0454          DATA    1108
G0061              *; FI TABLE
G0062 0593        FITABL BSS     0
G0063 0593               BSS     0
G0064 0593 0000          DATA    0
G0065 0594 0000          DATA    0
G0066 0595 0000          DATA    0
G0067 0596 0010          DATA    16
G0068 0597 0010          DATA    16
G0069 0598 0010          DATA    16
G0070 0599 0030          DATA    48
G0071 059A 0070          DATA    112
G0072              *;
G0073              *; misc constants to be initialized
G0074              *;
G0075 059B        CONS   BSS     0
G0076 059B 0002          DATA    2     ; 12th entry of shift table (1st 11 all 0)
G0077 059C 0004          DATA    4
G0078 059D 0008          DATA    8
G0079 059E 0010          DATA    16
G0080 059F 0020          DATA    32
G0081 05A0 0040          DATA    64
G0082 05A1 0080          DATA    128
G0083 05A2 0100          DATA    256
G0084 05A3 0200          DATA    512
G0085 05A4 0400          DATA    1024
G0086 05A5 0800          DATA    2048
G0087 05A6 1000          DATA    4096
G0088 05A7 2000          DATA    8192
G0089 05A8 4000          DATA    16384
G0090 05A9 FFFF          DATA    -1
G0091 05AA FFFE          DATA    -2
G0092 05AB FFFC          DATA    -4
G0093 05AC 00FF          DATA    255      ;M255
G0094 05AD 8000          DATA    32768    ;K32768
G0095 05AE 0001          DATA    1        ;YLH
G0096 05AF 0800          DATA    2048     ;YLL
G0097 05B0 FFFF          DATA    -1
G0098 05B1 0001          DATA    1
G0099 05B2 0021          DATA    33       ; BIAS
G0100 05B3 0220          DATA    544      ;YU
G0101 05B4 0200          DATA    512      ;PK0
G0102 05B5 0200          DATA    512      ;PK1
G0103 05B6 0200          DATA    512      ;PK2
G0104 05B7 0100          DATA    256      ;SRMAN
G0105 05B8 0100          DATA    256      ;SRIMAN
G0106 05B9 0800          DATA    2048     ;SDQ
G0107 05BA 0800          DATA    2048     ;SDQ1
G0108 05BB 0800          DATA    2048     ;SDQ2
G0109 05BC 0800          DATA    2048     ;SDQ3
G0110 05BD 0800          DATA    2048     ;SDQ4
G0111 05BE 0800          DATA    2048     ;SDQ5
G0112 05BF 0800          DATA    2048     ;SDQ6
G0113 05C0 0100          DATA    256      ;DQMAN
```

```
CCITT        32010 FAMILY MACRO ASSEMBLER    PC2.1 84.107      16:36:03  03-20-85
                                                                   PAGE 0047

G0114 05C1 0100        DATA    256       ;DQ1MAN
G0115 05C2 0100        DATA    256       ;DQ2MAN
G0116 05C3 0100        DATA    256       ;DQ3MAN
G0117 05C4 0100        DATA    256       ;DQ4MAN
G0118 05C5 0100        DATA    256       ;DQ5MAN
G0119 05C6 11E0        DATA    4576      ;K4576
G0120 05C7 3FFE        DATA    16382     ;K16382
G0121 05C8 C002        DATA    -16382    ;M16382
G0122 05C9 002E        DATA    46        ;K46
G0123 05CA 0031        DATA    49        ;K49
G0124 05CB 0563        DATA    SHFT      ;SHIFT
G0125 05CC 003F        DATA    63        ;K63
G0126 05CD 0000        DATA    0         ;FI
G0127 05CE 0000        DATA    0         ;WI
G0128 05CF 0583        DATA    IQTAB     ;INQTAB
G0129 05D0 0220        DATA    544       ;K544
G0130 05D1 1400        DATA    5120      ;K5120
G0131 05D2 000F        DATA    15        ;M15
G0132 05D3 FF80        DATA    -128      ;KFF80
G0133 05D4 007F        DATA    127       ;K127
G0134 05D5 FFC0        DATA    -64       ;MFFC0
G0135 05D6 1080        DATA    4224      ; BIAS*2**7
G0136 05D7 0FFF        DATA    4095      ;M4095
G0137 05D8 0000        DATA    0         ;spare
G0138 05D9 7FFF        DATA    32767     ;M32767
G0139 05DA FF00        DATA    -256      ;KFF00
G0140 05DB 0038        DATA    56        ;K56
G0141 05DC 03C0        DATA    960       ;K960
G0142 05DD 004F        DATA    79        ;K79
G0143 05DE 005F        DATA    95        ;K95
G0144 05DF 0082        DATA    130       ;K130
G0145 05E0 008A        DATA    138       ;K138
G0146 05E1 0905        DATA    2309      ;K2309
G0147 05E2 0003        DATA    3         ;THREE
G0148 05E3 0000        DATA    0         ;spare
G0149 05E4 0080        DATA    128       ;M0080
```

Appendix II

```
CCITT        32010 FAMILY MACRO ASSEMBLER   PC2.1 84.107    16:36:03  03-20-85
                                                                      PAGE 0048
G0151              *;**************************************************************
G0152              *;        RAM
G0153              *;**************************************************************
G0154 05E5         RAMLOC BSS     0
G0155 0000                DORG    0
G0156              *;
G0157              *;  RAM Location # 000
G0158 0000 0000           DATA    0        ; spare
G0159              *;
G0160              *;  RAM Location # 001
G0161 0001 0000    I      DATA    0        ; 32Kb output
G0162              *;
G0163              *;  RAM Location # 002
G0164 0002 0000    IM     DATA    0        ; 8-level version of I
G0165              *;
G0166              *;  RAM Location # 003
G0167 0003 0000    SE     DATA    0        ; signal estimate
G0168              *;
G0169              *;  RAM Location # 004
G0170 0004 0000    SEZ    DATA    0        ; partial signal estimate
G0171              *;
G0172              *;  RAM Location # 005
G0173 0005 0000    APP    DATA    0        ; unlimited speed control parm
G0174              *;
G0175              *;  RAM Location # 006
G0176 0006 0000    AL     DATA    0        ; limited speed control parm
G0177              *;
G0178              *;  RAM Location # 007
G0179 0007 0000    DMS    DATA    0        ; short term average of F
G0180              *;
G0181              *;  RAM Location # 008
G0182 0008 0000    DML    DATA    0        ; long term average of F
G0183              *;
G0184              *;  RAM Location # 009
G0185 0009 0000    Y      DATA    0        ; quantizer scale factor
G0186              *;
G0187              *;  RAM Location # 010
G0188 000A 0000    B1     DATA    0        ; 6th order predictor coefficient
G0189              *;
G0190              *;  RAM Location # 011
G0191 000B 0000    B2     DATA    0        ; 6th order predictor coefficient
G0192              *;
G0193              *;  RAM Location # 012
G0194 000C 0000    B3     DATA    0        ; 6th order predictor coefficient
G0195              *;
G0196              *;  RAM Location # 013
G0197 000D 0000    B4     DATA    0        ; 6th order predictor coefficient
G0198              *;
G0199              *;  RAM Location # 014
G0200 000E 0000    B5     DATA    0        ; 6th order predictor coefficient
G0201              *;
G0202              *;  RAM Location # 015
G0203 000F 0000    B6     DATA    0        ; 6th order predictor coefficient
G0204              *;
G0205              *;  RAM Location # 016
G0206 0010 0000    DQ     DATA    0        ; quantized diff signal
G0207              *;
```

```
CCITT        32010 FAMILY MACRO ASSEMBLER    PC2.1 84.107    16:36:03  03-20-85
                                                                  PAGE 0049

G0208               *;   RAM Location # 017
G0209 0011 0000  A1      DATA    0         ; coefficients of 2nd order predictor
G0210               *;
G0211               *;   RAM Location # 018
G0212 0012 0000  A2      DATA    0         ; coefficients of 2nd order predictor
G0213               *;
G0214               *;   RAM Location # 019
G0215 0013 0000  SR      DATA    0         ; reconstructed signal frame k
G0216               *;
G0217               *;   RAM Location # 020
G0218 0014 0000  SR1     DATA    0         ; reconstructed signal frame k
G0219               *;
G0220               *;   RAM Location # 021
G0221 0015 0000  DQEXP   DATA    0         ; exponent of DQ
G0222               *;
G0223               *;   RAM Location # 022
G0224 0016 0000  DQ1EXP  DATA    0         ; exponent of DQ1
G0225               *;
G0226               *;   RAM Location # 023
G0227 0017 0000  DQ2EXP  DATA    0         ; exp of DQ2
G0228               *;
G0229               *;   RAM Location # 024
G0230 0018 0000  DQ3EXP  DATA    0         ; exp of DQ3
G0231               *;
G0232               *;   RAM Location # 025
G0233 0019 0000  DQ4EXP  DATA    0         ; exp of DQ4
G0234               *;
G0235               *;   RAM Location # 026
G0236 001A 0000  DQ5EXP  DATA    0         ; exp of DQ5
G0237               *;
G0238               *;   RAM Location # 027
G0239 001B 0000  SCRACH  DATA    0         ; scrach variable
G0240               *;
G0241               *;   RAM Location # 028
G0242 001C 0000  SREXP   DATA    0         ; exp of SR
G0243               *;
G0244               *;   RAM Location # 029
G0245 001D 0000  SR1EXP  DATA    0         ; exp of SR1
G0246               *;
G0247               *;   RAM Location # 030
G0248 001E 0000  SUM4    DATA    0         ; temp
G0249               *;
G0250               *;   RAM Location # 031
G0251 001F 0000  SUM5    DATA    0         ; temp
G0252               *;
G0253               *;   RAM Location # 032
G0254 0020 0000  SUM6    DATA    0         ; temp
G0255               *;
G0256               *;   RAM Location # 033
G0257 0021 0000  TEMP1   DATA    0         ; temp
G0258               *;
G0259               *;   RAM Location # 034
G0260 0022       SUM1    BSS     0         ; temp
G0261 0022 0000  TEMP2   DATA    0         ; temp
G0262               *;
G0263               *;   RAM Location # 035
G0264 0023       SUM2    BSS     0         ; temp
```

```
G0265 0023 0000    TEMP3  DATA     0        ; temp
G0266                      *;
G0267                      *;  RAM Location # 036
G0268 0024 0000    TEMP4  DATA     0        ; temp
G0269                      *;
G0270                      *;  RAM Location # 037
G0271 0025 0000    SUM3   DATA     0        ; temp
G0272                      *;
G0273                      *;  RAM Location # 038
G0274 0026 0000    SAMPLE DATA     0        ; Linear sample
G0275                      *;
G0276                      *;  RAM Location # 039
G0277 0027 0000    SUM7   DATA     0        ; temp storage of SR1*A1 tap
G0278                      *;
G0279                      *;  RAM Location # 040
G0280 0028 0000    SUM8   DATA     0        ; temp storage of SR2*A2 tap
G0281                      *;
G0282                      *;  RAM Location # 041
G0283 0029 0000    YOVER4 DATA     0        ; Y>>2
G0284                      *;
G0285                      *;  RAM Location # 042
G0286 002A 0000           DATA     0        ; first location of shift table
G0287                      *;
G0288                      *;  RAM Location # 043
G0289 002B 0000           DATA     0
G0290                      *;
G0291                      *;  RAM Location # 044
G0292 002C 0000           DATA     0
G0293                      *;
G0294                      *;  RAM Location # 045
G0295 002D 0000           DATA     0
G0296                      *;
G0297                      *;  RAM Location # 046
G0298 002E 0000           DATA     0
G0299                      *;
G0300                      *;  RAM Location # 047
G0301 002F 0000           DATA     0
G0302                      *;
G0303                      *;  RAM Location # 048
G0304 0030 0000           DATA     0
G0305                      *;
G0306                      *;  RAM Location # 049
G0307 0031 0000           DATA     0
G0308                      *;
G0309                      *;  RAM Location # 050
G0310 0032 0000           DATA     0
G0311                      *;
G0312                      *;  RAM Location # 051
G0313 0033 0000           DATA     0
G0314                      *;
G0315                      *;  RAM Location # 052
G0316 0034 0000           DATA     0
G0317                      *;
G0318                      *;  RAM Location # 053
G0319 0035 0000           DATA     0
G0320                      *;
G0321                      *;  RAM Location # 054
```

```
G0322 0036 0000           DATA    0
G0323                 *;
G0324                 *;  RAM Location # 055
G0325 0037 0000           DATA    0
G0326                 *;
G0327                 *;  RAM Location # 056
G0328 0038 0000  EIGHT DATA    0
G0329                 *;
G0330                 *;  RAM Location # 057
G0331 0039 0000           DATA    0
G0332                 *;
G0333                 *;  RAM Location # 058
G0334 003A 0000           DATA    0
G0335                 *;
G0336                 *;  RAM Location # 059
G0337 003B 0000           DATA    0
G0338                 *;
G0339                 *;  RAM Location # 060
G0340 003C 0000           DATA    0
G0341                 *;
G0342                 *;  RAM Location # 061
G0343 003D 0000           DATA    0
G0344                 *;
G0345                 *;  RAM Location # 062
G0346 003E 0000           DATA    0
G0347                 *;
G0348                 *;  RAM Location # 063
G0349 003F 0000           DATA    0
G0350                 *;
G0351                 *;  RAM Location # 064
G0352 0040 0000           DATA    0
G0353                 *;
G0354                 *;  RAM Location # 065
G0355 0041 0000           DATA    0
G0356                 *;
G0357                 *;  RAM Location # 066
G0358 0042 0000           DATA    0
G0359                 *;
G0360                 *;  RAM Location # 067
G0361 0043 0000           DATA    0
G0362                 *;
G0363                 *;  RAM Location # 068
G0364 0044 0000           DATA    0
G0365                 *;
G0366                 *;  RAM Location # 069
G0367 0045 0000           DATA    0
G0368                 *;
G0369                 *;  RAM Location # 070
G0370 0046 0000           DATA    0        ; last loc of table (42-70)
G0371                 *;
G0372                 *;  RAM Location # 071
G0373 0047 0000  M255  DATA    0
G0374                 *;
G0375                 *;  RAM Location # 072
G0376 0048 0000  K32768 DATA    0          ; sign bit
G0377                 *;
G0378                 *;  RAM Location # 073
```

```
G0379 0049 0000   YLH    DATA    0       ; fast quant scale factor (hi word)
G0380                     *;
G0381                     *;   RAM Location # 074
G0382 004A 0000   YLL    DATA    0       ; slow quant scale factor (lo word)
G0383                     *;
G0384                     *;   RAM Location # 075
G0385 004B 0000   MINUS  DATA    0       ; -1
G0386                     *;
G0387                     *;   RAM Location # 076
G0388 004C 0000   ONE    DATA    0       ; 1
G0389                     *;
G0390                     *;   RAM Location # 077
G0391 004D 0000   BIAS   DATA    0       ; constant for mulaw conversions
G0392                     *;
G0393                     *;   RAM Location # 078
G0394 004E 0000   YU     DATA    0       ; fast quant scale factor
G0395                     *;
G0396                     *;   RAM Location # 079
G0397 004F 0000   PK0    DATA    0       ; sign of p(k)
G0398                     *;
G0399                     *;   RAM Location # 080
G0400 0050 0000   PK1    DATA    0       ; sign of p(k-1)
G0401                     *;
G0402                     *;   RAM Location # 081
G0403 0051 0000   PK2    DATA    0       ; sign of p(k-2)
G0404                     *;
G0405                     *;   RAM Location # 082
G0406 0052 0000   SRMAN  DATA    0       ; mantissa of SR
G0407                     *;
G0408                     *;   RAM Location # 083
G0409 0053 0000   SR1MAN DATA    0       ; mantissa of SR1
G0410                     *;
G0411                     *;   RAM Location # 084
G0412 0054 0000   SDQ    DATA    0       ; sign DQ(k)
G0413                     *;
G0414                     *;   RAM Location # 085
G0415 0055 0000   SDQ1   DATA    0       ; sign DQ(k-1)
G0416                     *;
G0417                     *;   RAM Location # 086
G0418 0056 0000   SDQ2   DATA    0       ; sign DQ(k-2)
G0419                     *;
G0420                     *;   RAM Location # 087
G0421 0057 0000   SDQ3   DATA    0       ; sign DQ(k-3)
G0422                     *;
G0423                     *;   RAM Location # 088
G0424 0058 0000   SDQ4   DATA    0       ; sign DQ(k-4)
G0425                     *;
G0426                     *;   RAM Location # 089
G0427 0059 0000   SDQ5   DATA    0       ; sign DQ(k-5)
G0428                     *;
G0429                     *;   RAM Location # 090
G0430 005A 0000   SDQ6   DATA    0       ; sign DQ(k-6)
G0431                     *;
G0432                     *;   RAM Location # 091
G0433 005B 0000   DQMAN  DATA    0       ; mantissa of DQ
G0434                     *;
G0435                     *;   RAM Location # 092
```

```
CCITT        32010 FAMILY MACRO ASSEMBLER    PC2.1 84.107     16:36:03  03-20-85
                                                                  PAGE 0053

G0436 005C 0000   DQ1MAN DATA     0        ; mantissa of DQ1
G0437                    *;
G0438                    *;   RAM Location # 093
G0439 005D 0000   DQ2MAN DATA     0        ; mantissa of DQ2
G0440                    *;
G0441                    *;   RAM Location # 094
G0442 005E 0000   DQ3MAN DATA     0        ; mantissa of DQ3
G0443                    *;
G0444                    *;   RAM Location # 095
G0445 005F 0000   DQ4MAN DATA     0        ; mantissa of DQ4
G0446                    *;
G0447                    *;   RAM Location # 096
G0448 0060 0000   DQ5MAN DATA     0        ; mantissa of DQ5
G0449                    *;
G0450                    *;   RAM Location # 097
G0451 0061 0000   K4576  DATA     0        ; 4576
G0452                    *;
G0453                    *;   RAM Location # 098
G0454 0062 0000   K16382 DATA     0        ; +16382
G0455                    *;
G0456                    *;   RAM Location # 099
G0457 0063 0000   M16382 DATA     0        ; -16382
G0458                    *;
G0459                    *;   RAM Location # 100
G0460 0064 0000   K46    DATA     0        ; 46
G0461                    *;
G0462                    *;   RAM Location # 101
G0463 0065 0000   K49    DATA     0        ; 49
G0464                    *;
G0465                    *;   RAM Location # 102
G0466 0066 0000   SHIFT  DATA     0        ; SHIFT table address
G0467                    *;
G0468                    *;   RAM Location # 103
G0469 0067 0000   K63    DATA     ^        ; 63
G0470                    *;
G0471                    *;   RAM Location # 104
G0472 0068 UU00   FI     DATA     0        ; FI value
G0473                    *;
G0474                    *;   RAM Location # 105
G0475 0069 0000   WI     DATA     0        ; WI value
G0476                    *;
G0477                    *;   RAM Location # 106
G0478 006A 0000   INQTAB DATA     0        ; Inverse quan table address
G0479                    *;
G0480                    *;   RAM Location # 107
G0481 006B 0000   K544   DATA     0        ; 544
G0482                    *;
G0483                    *;   RAM Location # 108
G0484 006C 0000   K5120  DATA     0        ; 5120
G0485                    *;
G0486                    *;   RAM Location # 109
G0487 006D 0000   M15    DATA     0        ; 15
G0488                    *;
G0489                    *;   RAM Location # 110
G0490 006E 0000   KFF80  DATA     0        ; >FF80
G0491                    *;
G0492                    *;   RAM Location # 111
```

```
G0493 006F 0000  M127   DATA    0      ; 127
G0494                   *;
G0495                   *;   RAM Location # 112
G0496 0070 0000  MFFC0  DATA    0      ; -64
G0497                   *;
G0498                   *;   RAM Location # 113
G0499 0071 0000  BIASA  DATA    0      ; 33*128
G0500                   *;
G0501                   *;   RAM Location # 114
G0502 0072 0000  M4095  DATA    0      ; 4095
G0503                   *;
G0504                   *;   RAM Location # 115
G0505 0073 0000         DATA    0      ; spare
G0506                   *;
G0507                   *;   RAM Location # 116
G0508 0074 0000  M32767 DATA    0      ; 32767
G0509                   *;
G0510                   *;   RAM Location # 117
G0511 0075 0000  KFF00  DATA    0      ; >FF00
G0512                   *;
G0513                   *;   RAM Location # 118
G0514 0076 0000  K56    DATA    0      ; 56
G0515                   *;
G0516                   *;   RAM Location # 119
G0517 0077 0000  K960   DATA    0      ; 960
G0518                   *;
G0519                   *;   RAM Location # 120
G0520 0078 0000  K79    DATA    0      ; constants used for quantizing table
G0521                   *;
G0522                   *;   RAM Location # 121
G0523 0079 0000  K95    DATA    0      ; constants used for quantizing table
G0524                   *;
G0525                   *;   RAM Location # 122
G0526 007A 0000  K130   DATA    0      ; constants used for quantizing table
G0527                   *;
G0528                   *;   RAM Location # 123
G0529 007B 0000  K138   DATA    0      ; constants used for quantizing table
G0530                   *;
G0531                   *;   RAM Location # 124
G0532 007C 0000  K2309  DATA    0      ; constants used for quantizing table
G0533                   *;
G0534                   *;   RAM Location # 125
G0535 007D 0000  THREE  DATA    0      ; 3
G0536                   *;
G0537                   *;   RAM Location # 126
G0538 007E 0000         DATA    0      ; spare
G0539                   *;
G0540                   *;   RAM Location # 127
G0541 007F 0000  M0080  DATA    0      ; alaw mask
G0542                   *;
NO ERRORS, NO WARNINGS
```

```
CCITT        32010 FAMILY MACRO ASSEMBLER    PC2.1 84.107    16:36:03  03-20-85
LABEL       VALUE   DEFN    REFERENCES                              PAGE 0055

A1          0011    G0209   B0252 B0270 D0431 D0456 D0458 D0464 D0515 D0523
A1LIM       0426    D0520
A2          0012    G0212   B0230 B0245 D0486 D0493 D0496 D0508 D0513
ADC         0001    A0031   A0056 A0126
ADD18       03B3    D0336   D0328
ADDA        035C    D0085
ADDC        03E1    D0413
ADDONE      01A8    A0566   A0562
ADDSGN      036C    D0104
AL          0006    G0176   B0321 B0327 B0361
ALAW        055E    F0033
ALAWR       0184    A0511   A0512 F0035
ALAWX       004E    A0172   A0173 F0034
ALOG        035E    D0090
ANOMLE      019F    A0559   A0557
ANOMLY      01AF    A0572   A0564
APP         0005    G0173   B0322 D0323 D0324 D0325 D0336 D0338
APRED       03B6    D0345   D0335
AQUAN       02AA    C0024   A0099 A0168 A0351 A0504
B1          000A    G0188   B0167 B0183 D0396 D0398 D0402
B2          000B    G0191   B0144 B0160 D0389 D0391 D0395
B3          000C    G0194   B0121 B0137 D0382 D0384 D0388
B4          000D    G0197   B0098 B0114 D0375 D0377 D0381
B5          000E    G0200   B0075 B0091 D0368 D0370 D0374
B6          000F    G0203   B0053 B0068 D0361 D0363 D0367
BIAS        004D    G0391   A0082 A0089 A0253 A0264 A0272 A0282 A0290 A0302 A0310
                            A0320 A0334 A0346 A0426 A0436 A0444 A0456 A0464 A0474
                            A0488
BIASA       0071    G0499   A0180 A0184 A0188 A0192 A0196 A0200 A0204
C0TO1       02B8    C0075
C0TO3       02B5    C0073
C0TO7       02B2    C0071
C2TO3       02C3    C0083   C0074
C4TO5       02D1    C0093
C4TO7       02CE    C0091   C0072
C6TO7       02DC    C0101   C0092
C8TO11      02EA    C0111
C8TO14      02E7    C0109   C0070
C8TO9       02ED    C0113
CATOB       02FC    C0125   C0112
CCITT       0002    A0033   A0101 A0170 A0210 A0364
CCTOD       030E    C0139
CCTOE       030B    C0137   C0110
CHK1        01C4    B0068   E0007
CHK11       025F    B0245   E0031
CHK2        01DE    B0091   E0011
CHK21       0279    B0268   E0035
CHK3        01F8    B0114   E0015
CHK4        0212    B0137   E0019
CHK5        022C    B0160   E0023
CHK6        0246    B0183   E0027
CHKHI       0386    D0186   D0183
C10TO1      032C    C0187
C10TO3      0329    C0185
C12TO3      0335    C0193   C0186
C14TO7      033E    C0199   C0184
C15TO6      0341    C0201
```

```
CCITT        32010 FAMILY MACRO ASSEMBLER    PC2.1 84.107      16:36:03  03-20-85
LABEL        VALUE    DEFN   REFERENCES                              PAGE 0056

C16TO7       034A     C0207   C0200
CLNUP        00EA     A0342   A0330
CLNUPA       0176     A0496   A0484
CMPRSA       010B     A0405
CMPRSU       007F     A0251
CONS         059B     G0075   F0019
CTL          0000     A0034   F0028
D0TO1        0438     D0559
D0TO3        0435     D0557
D0TO7        0432     D0555
D2TO3        043D     D0564   D0558
D4TO5        044D     D0578
D4TO7        044A     D0576   D0556
D6TO7        045A     D0590   D0577
D8TO9        046F     D0608
D8TOB        046C     D0606
D8TOF        0469     D0604   D0554
DAC          0001     A0032   A0357 A0510
DATOB        0480     D0624   D0607
DCTOD        0494     D0642
DCTOF        0491     D0640   D0605
DETOF        04A5     D0658   D0641
DML          0008     G0182   D0293 D0294 D0295 D0329 D0332
DMS          0007     G0179   D0273 D0274 D0275 D0331
DO32KA       0106     A0376   A0369
DO32KU       007A     A0222   A0215
DONEC        041C     D0508
DONEF        03F9     D0442   D0437
DQ           0010     G0206   D0103 D0110 D0111 D0416 D0548
DQ1EXP       0016     G0224   B0146 B0147
DQ1MAN       005C     G0436   B0150
DQ2EXP       0017     G0227   B0123 B0124
DQ2MAN       005D     G0439   B0127
DQ3EXP       0018     G0230   B0100 B0101
DQ3MAN       005E     G0442   B0104
DQ4EXP       0019     G0233   B0077 B0078
DQ4MAN       005F     G0445   B0081
DQ5EXP       001A     G0236   B0055
DQ5MAN       0060     G0448   B0058
DQEXP        0015     G0221   B0169 B0170 D0091 D0095
DQMAN        005B     G0433   B0173 D0094 D0101 D0126 D0127 D0128 D0130
E0           04EE     E0062   E0131
E0TO1        04EB     E0060
E0TO3        04E8     E0058
E0TO7        04E5     E0056
E1           04F2     E0066   E0061
E10          0529     E0114   E0109
E11          0533     E0122
E12          0537     E0126   E0121
E13          053E     E0132
E2           04F9     E0072
E2TO3        04F6     E0070   E0059
E3           04FD     E0076   E0071
E4           0504     E0082
E4TO6        0501     E0080   E0057
E5           050B     E0088
E5TO6        0508     E0086   E0081
```

```
CCITT        32010 FAMILY MACRO ASSEMBLER    PC2.1 84.107    16:36:03  03-20-85
LABEL      VALUE    DEFN    REFERENCES                                PAGE 0057

E6         050F     E0092   E0087
E7         051A     E0100
E7TO8      0517     E0098
E7TOA      0514     E0096
E7TOD      0511     E0094   E0055
E8         051E     E0104   E0099
E9         0525     E0110
E9TOA      0522     E0108   E0097
EBTOC      0530     E0120
EBTOD      052D     E0118   E0095
EDTOE      053B     E0130   E0119
EIGHT      0038     G0328   A0541
EXP0       02BB     C0077
EXP1       02BF     C0080   C0076
EXP10      02FF     C0127
EXP11      0305     C0132   C0126
EXP12      0311     C0141
EXP13      0317     C0146   C0140
EXP14      031D     C0151   C0138
EXP2       02C6     C0085
EXP3       02CA     C0088   C0084
EXP4       02D4     C0095
EXP5       02D8     C0098   C0094
EXP6       02DF     C0103
EXP7       02E3     C0106   C0102
EXP8       02F0     C0115
EXP9       02F6     C0120   C0114
EXPNDA     0035     A0146
EXPNDU     0005     A0076
EXX01      0439     D0560
EXX10      0483     D0626
EXX11      048A     D0633   D0625
EXX12      0497     D0644
EXX13      049E     D0651   D0643
EXX14      04A8     D0660
EXX15      04AF     D0667   D0659
EXX2       0440     D0566
EXX3       0445     D0571   D0565
EXX4       0450     D0580
EXX5       0455     D0585   D0579
EXX6       045D     D0592
EXX7       0462     D0597   D0591
EXX8       0472     D0610
EXX9       0479     D0617   D0609
FI         0068     G0472   D0051 D0272 D0292
FILTA      039C     D0272
FILTB      03A0     D0292
FILTC      03A4     D0323
FILTD      037C     D0175
FILTE      038B     D0209   D0187
FINI       00E6     A0338   A0268 A0276 A0286 A0294 A0306 A0314 A0324
FINISH     0172     A0492   A0422 A0430 A0440 A0448 A0460 A0468 A0478
FITABL     0593     G0062
FLOAT      04DE     E0050   B0054 B0076 B0099 B0122 B0145 B0168 B0231 B0253
FLTDQ      0377     D0126   D0108
FLTSFT     002A     E0047   E0064 E0068 E0074 E0078 E0084 E0090 E0092 E0102 E0106
                            E0112 E0116 E0124 E0128 E0134
```

```
CCITT          32010 FAMILY MACRO ASSEMBLER     PC2.1 84.107    16:36:03  03-20-85
LABEL     VALUE    DEFN    REFERENCES                                    PAGE 0058

FLTSR     042A     D0548   D0519
GETA1     03FA     D0456   D0435 D0440
GETA2     0404     D0481
GETB1     03DA     D0396
GETB2     03D3     D0389
GETB3     03CC     D0382
GETB4     03C5     D0375
GETB5     03BE     D0368
GETB6     03B6     D0360
GETEXP    02AF     C0069
GETF      03EA     D0431
GETF1     03EE     D0434
GETF2     03F4     D0438   D0433
GETI      0018     A0098
GETIM     0351     C0212   C0190 C0192 C0196 C0198 C0204 C0206 C0210
GETMAN    0321     C0155   C0079 C0082 C0087 C0090 C0097 C0100 C0105 C0108 C0119
                           C0124 C0131 C0136 C0145 C0150
GETSE     024E     B0230
I         0001     G0161   A0100 A0101 A0169 A0170 A0210 A0212 A0364 A0366 A0544
                           D0106
IDEQIM    01B1     A0574   A0547
IDGTIM    01A0     A0560   A0546
IDLTIM    0191     A0548
IEQ0      032F     C0189
IEQ1      0332     C0191   C0188
IEQ2      0338     C0195
IEQ3      033B     C0197   C0194
IEQ4      0344     C0203
IEQ5      0347     C0205   C0202
IEQ6      034D     C0209
IEQ7      0350     C0211   C0208
IM        0002     G0164   A0213 A0216 A0218 A0367 A0370 A0372 C0212 D0045
INQTAB    006A     G0478   D0046
INTRPT    0002     A0050   A0050
IQTAB     0583     G0042   G0128
ITAB1     07F9     C0175
ITAB2     087B     C0176
ITAB3     08CA     C0177
ITAB4     0905     C0178
ITAB5     0936     C0179
ITAB6     0964     C0180
ITAB7     0995     C0181
K130      007A     G0526   C0187
K138      007B     G0529   C0185
K16382    0062     G0454   D0436
K2309     007C     G0532   C0183
K32768    0048     G0376   A0147 B0070 B0093 B0116 B0139 B0162 B0185 B0247 B0271
K4576     0061     G0451   D0186
K46       0064     G0460   C0201
K49       0065     G0463   C0207
K5120     006C     G0484   D0188
K544      006B     G0481   D0182 D0184
K56       0076     G0514   E0056
K63       0067     G0469   A0327 A0481
K79       0078     G0520   C0193
K95       0079     G0523   C0199
K960      0077     G0517   D0604 E0094
```

```
CCITT        32010 FAMILY MACRO ASSEMBLER     PC2.1 84.107      16:36:03  03-20-85
LABEL     VALUE    DEFN    REFERENCES                                PAGE 0059
KFF00     0075     G0511   A0077
KFF80     006E     G0490   B0062 B0085 B0108 B0131 B0154 B0177 B0239 B0262
LIMA      028E     B0320
LIMB      0380     D0182
LIMC      0415     D0502
LIMD      041D     D0512   D0504
M0080     007F     G0541   A0508
M127      006F     G0493   A0549 A0558 A0563 A0566 C0155
M15       006D     G0487   A0217 A0261 A0269 A0279 A0287 A0299 A0307 A0317 A0331
                           A0371 A0415 A0423 A0433 A0441 A0453 A0461 A0471 A0485
                           C0071 C0109 C0214 D0512 D0555
M16382    0063     G0457   D0441
M255      0047     G0373   A0343 A0355 A0497
M32767    0074     G0508   A0079 A0149 D0217 D0224 E0005 E0009 E0013 E0017 E0021
                           E0025 E0029 E0033 F0033
M4095     0072     G0502   A0081 A0151 B0365 D0092
MAXNEG    01AD     A0570   A0567
MAXPOS    0199     A0554   A0551
MFFC0     0070     G0496   B0326
MINUS     004B     G0385   D0112
MIX       0297     B0353   B0324
MULAW     055A     F0031
MULAWR    00F9     A0358   A0359 F0032
MULAWX    0020     A0103   A0104 F0031
NEG1      01C9     B0072
NEG11     0264     B0249
NEG2      01E3     B0095
NEG21     027F     B0273
NEG3      01FD     B0118
NEG4      0217     B0141
NEG5      0231     B0164
NEG6      024B     B0187
NOCONS    004A     F0004   F0022
NONNEG    02A5     B0366   B0364
NORMAL    00DF     A0331   A0326
NORMLA    016B     A0485   A0480
NXCONS    0551     F0023   F0026
ONE       004C     G0388   A0176 A0214 A0255 A0259 A0277 A0297 A0315 A0325 A0368
                           A0409 A0413 A0418 A0431 A0451 A0469 A0479 A0543 A0552
                           A0556 A0561 A0568 B0320 B0323 C0069 C0075 C0083 C0093
                           C0101 C0113 C0125 C0139 C0165 D0048 D0050 D0090 D0093
                           D0099 D0104 D0107 D0337 D0419 D0434 D0439 D0553 D0561
                           D0564 D0578 D0590 D0608 D0624 D0642 D0658 E0054 E0062
                           E0070 E0080 E0086 E0098 E0108 E0120 E0130 F0017 F0018
                           F0025
PK0       004F     G0397   D0414 D0420 D0421
PK1       0050     G0400   D0413 D0460
PK2       0051     G0403   D0488
POS1      01CC     B0075   B0071
POS11     0267     B0252   B0248
POS2      01E6     B0098   B0094
POS21     0282     B0276   B0272
POS3      0200     B0121   B0117
POS4      021A     B0144   B0140
POS5      0234     B0167   B0163
POS6      024E     B0190   B0186
PRDICT    0355     D0045   A0102 A0171 A0223 A0377
```

Appendix II

315

```
PTCONS     0036    F0005    F0021
QDONE      0354    C0215
QUAN       0326    C0183
RAMLOC     05E5    G0154
RCVA       00FD    A0364    A0511
RCVMU      0071    A0210    A0358
RESET      0542    F0007    A0043
ROMLOC     0563    G0005
RS1        04B6    E0004    B0066
RS11       04D4    E0028    B0243
RS2        04BB    E0008    B0089
RS21       04D9    E0032    B0266
RS3        04C0    E0012    B0112
RS4        04C5    E0016    B0135
RS5        04CA    E0020    B0158
RS6        04CF    E0024    B0181
SAMPLE     0026    G0274    A0090 A0091 A0094 A0158 A0159 A0162 A0265 A0273 A0283
                            A0291 A0303 A0311 A0321 A0328 A0335 A0345 A0349 A0419
                            A0427 A0437 A0445 A0457 A0465 A0475 A0482 A0489 A0499
                            A0502 C0024
SATCH      00DA    A0327
SATCHA     0166    A0481
SBASE      0024    A0106    A0086
SBASEA     0052    A0175    A0155
SCAL0A     0118    A0415
SCAL1A     0121    A0423    A0414
SCAL2A     012D    A0433
SCAL3A     0136    A0441    A0432
SCAL4A     0145    A0453
SCAL5A     014E    A0461    A0452
SCAL6A     015A    A0471
SCAL7A     0163    A0479    A0470
SCALE0     008C    A0261
SCALE1     0095    A0269    A0260
SCALE2     00A1    A0279
SCALE3     00AA    A0287    A0278
SCALE4     00B9    A0299
SCALE5     00C2    A0307    A0298
SCALE6     00CE    A0317
SCALE7     00D7    A0325    A0316
SCL021     0089    A0259
SCL023     0086    A0257
SCL0T1     0115    A0413
SCL0T3     0112    A0411
SCL223     009E    A0277    A0258
SCL2T3     012A    A0431    A0412
SCL425     00B6    A0297
SCL427     00B3    A0295    A0256
SCL4T5     0142    A0451
SCL4T7     013F    A0449    A0410
SCL627     00CB    A0315    A0296
SCL6T7     0157    A0469    A0450
```

```
CCITT        32010 FAMILY MACRO ASSEMBLER    PC2.1 84.107    16:36:03  03-20-85
LABEL   VALUE    DEFN    REFERENCES                                    PAGE 0061

SCRACH  001B    G0239   A0056 A0076 A0083 A0106 A0108 A0110 A0112 A0114 A0116
                        A0118 A0120 A0126 A0146 A0152 A0175 A0179 A0183 A0187
                        A0191 A0195 A0199 A0203 A0254 A0262 A0263 A0266 A0270
                        A0271 A0274 A0280 A0281 A0284 A0288 A0289 A0292 A0300
                        A0301 A0304 A0308 A0309 A0312 A0318 A0319 A0322 A0332
                        A0333 A0336 A0338 A0339 A0344 A0356 A0357 A0408 A0416
                        A0417 A0420 A0424 A0425 A0428 A0434 A0435 A0438 A0442
                        A0443 A0446 A0454 A0455 A0458 A0462 A0463 A0466 A0472
                        A0473 A0476 A0486 A0487 A0490 A0492 A0493 A0498 A0509
                        A0510 A0548 A0560 A0574
SDQ     0054    G0412   D0105 D0113 D0365 D0372 D0379 D0386 D0393 D0400 D0401
SDQ1    0055    G0415   B0184 D0394
SDQ2    0056    G0418   B0161 D0387
SDQ3    0057    G0421   B0138 D0380
SDQ4    0058    G0424   B0115 D0373
SDQ5    0059    G0427   B0092 D0366
SDQ6    005A    G0430   B0069 D0360
SE      0003    G0167   B0301 B0302 B0303 C0025 D0549
SETPAC  0544    F0010
SEZ     0004    G0170   B0298 D0415
SHFT    0563    G0007   G0124
SHIFT   0066    G0466   D0096
SIGDIF  01B3    B0053   A0098 A0167 A0222 A0376
SR      0013    G0215   A0247 A0401 B0268 B0269 D0550
SR1     0014    G0218   B0246
SR1EXP  001D    G0245   B0232
SR1MAN  0053    G0409   B0235
SREXP   001C    G0242   B0254 B0255 D0560 D0569 D0574 D0583 D0588 D0595 D0602
                        D0615 D0622 D0631 D0638 D0649 D0656 D0665 D0672
SRMAN   0052    G0406   B0258 D0552 D0559 D0562 D0566 D0567 D0571 D0572 D0580
                        D0581 D0585 D0586 D0592 D0593 D0597 D0598 D0599 D0600
                        D0610 D0611 D0612 D0613 D0617 D0618 D0619 D0620 D0626
                        D0627 D0628 D0629 D0633 D0634 D0635 D0636 D0644 D0645
                        D0646 D0647 D0651 D0652 D0653 D0654 D0660 D0661 D0662
                        D0663 D0667 D0668 D0669 D0670
STRLIM  038A    D0189   D0185
SUBF    0409    D0486   D0481
SUBONE  019B    A0556   A0550
SUBTB   0324    C0165
SUM1    0022    G0260   B0056 B0057 B0067 B0073 B0074 B0297 E0006
SUM2    0023    G0264   B0079 B0080 B0090 B0096 B0097 B0296 E0010
SUM3    0025    G0271   B0102 B0103 B0113 B0119 B0120 B0295 E0014
SUM4    001E    G0248   B0125 B0126 B0136 B0142 B0143 B0294 D0487 D0494 E0018
SUM5    001F    G0251   B0148 B0149 B0159 B0165 B0166 B0293 E0022
SUM6    0020    G0254   B0171 B0172 B0182 B0188 B0189 B0292 E0026
SUM7    0027    G0277   B0233 B0234 B0244 B0250 B0251 B0299 E0030
SUM8    0028    G0280   B0256 B0257 B0267 B0274 B0275 B0300 E0034
SUMGT0  03E9    D0421
SYNC    0188    A0541   A0353 A0506
```

```
TEMP1      0021    G0257    A0093 A0148 A0153 A0154 A0160 A0161 A0340 A0341 A0494
                            A0495 A0542 A0545 B0060 B0063 B0064 B0083 B0086 B0087
                            B0106 B0109 B0110 B0129 B0132 B0133 B0152 B0155 B0156
                            B0175 B0178 B0179 B0237 B0240 B0241 B0260 B0263 B0264
                            B0360 B0362 C0068 C0078 C0081 C0086 C0089 C0096 C0099
                            C0104 C0107 C0116 C0117 C0118 C0121 C0122 C0123 C0128
                            C0129 C0130 C0133 C0134 C0135 C0142 C0143 C0144 C0147
                            C0148 C0149 C0152 C0153 C0154 C0156 C0157 D0047 D0085
                            D0210 D0211 D0216 D0221 D0362 D0364 D0369 D0371 D0376
                            D0378 D0383 D0385 D0390 D0392 D0397 D0399 D0417 D0418
                            D0498 D0506 D0507 D0514 D0518 D0520 E0050 E0051 E0053
                            E0060 E0063 E0066 E0067 E0072 E0073 E0076 E0077 E0082
                            E0083 E0088 E0089 E0100 E0101 E0104 E0105 E0110 E0111
                            E0114 E0115 E0122 E0123 E0126 E0127 E0132 E0133 F0028
                            F0029
TEMP2      0022    G0261    A0080 A0087 A0150 A0156 D0218 D0219 D0220 D0222 D0457
                            D0459
TEMP3      0023    G0265    B0354 B0356 B0357 B0359 B0366 D0097 D0098 D0100 D0129
                            D0330 D0334 D0432 D0442 D0483 D0484 D0491 D0492 D0495
TEMP4      0024    G0268    A0251 A0342 A0347 A0348 A0405 A0407 A0496 A0500 A0501
                            C0066 C0213 D0516 D0521 D0522
THREE      007D    G0535    A0257 A0295 A0411 A0449 B0059 B0082 B0105 B0128 B0151
                            B0174 B0236 B0259 C0073 C0091 C0111 C0137 D0327 D0503
                            D0505 D0557 D0576 D0606 D0640 E0058 E0096 E0118
WI         0069    G0475    D0049 D0177
WTABLE     058B    G0052
XMTA       0034    A0126    A0172
XMTMU      0004    A0056    A0103
Y          0009    G0185    B0367 B0368 D0175 D0176 D0326
YLH        0049    G0379    B0355 D0209 D0213 D0223
YLL        004A    G0382    B0353 D0212 D0214 D0225
YOVER4     0029    G0283    B0369 C0166 D0086
YU         004E    G0394    B0358 D0178 D0189 D0215
ZRAMA      0547    F0013    F0014
```

Index

Intelligibility, 114, 186–191
Interpolation, 64, 70, 72, 132
Inverse sine transform, 132
  transformation, 76
Itakura distance, 108, 142, 184–185

JRSU channel vocoder, 210–212

Karhunen-Loeve transform (KLT), 78

Lag, 163
Lattice filter (see Log-area ratios)
LeRoux-Gueguen, 125
Levels of quantization, 28
Levinson's method (see Durbin's method)
Likelihood ratio (see Itakura distance)
Linear delta modulation, 43–45
Linear predictive coding (LPC), 38, 88,
    104, 113–149, 182, 184, 203, 223
Line spectrum pairs, 114, 143–144
Logarithmic quantization, 19, 23–26
Log-area ratios, 131, 186
Log-likelihood distance, 108, 142, 184
Log-spectral distance, 130, 182–184
LPC (see Linear predictive coding)
LPC parameters, 114, 117–137
LSP (see Line spectrum pairs)

Masking of noise, 81
Max quantization, 19, 27–28
Maximum entropy quantization, 19, 28
Mean opinion score, 196–197
Median smoothing, 172, 210
Midriser quantizer, 20, 32
Midtread quantizer, 20
μ-law quantization, 23, 207, 212
Modified rhyme test, 191
MOS (see Mean opinion score)
Motorola, 214
Mozer coding, 19, 48–50
Multipulse excitation, 114, 134–136
Multirate system, 139

Narrowband spectrogram, 67
NEC, 221

Noise shaping, 43
Nonparametric representation, 60
Nonuniform quantization, 26–30
Normalization of signal, 33
NSA LPC standard, 133, 168, 199,
    203–207
Nyquist rate, 8

Objective measures (see Distance mea-
    sures)
Oversampling, 44

Paired comparisons, 196
Parallel formant synthesizer (see Formant
    synthesis)
  processing pitch tracker, 153
Partial correlation coefficients (PARCOR),
    123
PCM (see Pulse code modulation)
Personal computers, 223
Phase modulation, 98
Phase vocoder, 88, 97–102
Phonemes, 108, 201
Phonetic vocoder, 88, 108
Pitch
  doubling, 51, 161
  frequency, 151
  period, 115, 132, 151
  predictor, 41
  -synchronous analysis, 205
  tracking, 151–176 (see also Gold-
    Rabiner, homomorphic,
    autocorrelation, AMDF, SIFT pitch
    trackers)
Poles of LPC filter, 129, 139
Post-processing of pitch, 152, 171–174

Quadrature mirror filer (QMF), 72
Quality of speech, 4, 177
  test, 191–197, 198
Quantization, 9, 18, 19–30

Rectangular window, 61
Reflection coefficients, 114, 123, 126